Couple Treatment

Couple Treatment

Assessment and Intervention

by

Judith C. Nelsen, D.S.W.

JASON ARONSON INC.
Northvale, New Jersey
London

This book was set in 11 pt. Galliard.

10 9 8 7 6 5 4 3 2 1

Library of Congress Cataloging-in-Publication Data

Nelsen, Judith C.
Couple treatment : assessment and intervention / by Judith C. Nelsen.
p. cm.
Includes bibliographical references and index.
ISBN 0-7657-0166-9 (alk. paper)
1. Marital psychotherapy. 2. Psychoanalysis. I. Title.
[DNLM: 1. Couples Therapy—methods. WM 430.5.M3 N424i 1998]
RC488.5.N443 1998
616.89'156—dc21
DNLM/DLC
for Library of Congress 98-12033

Printed in the United States of America on acid-free paper. Jason Aronson offers books and cassettes. For information and catalog write to Jason Aronson Inc., 230 Livingston Street, Northvale, NJ 07647-1726. Or visit our website: http://www.aronson.com

In memory of
my beloved husband, Marvin,
and to his children

Contents

Introduction

Most people live in couple relationships, whether heterosexual or same-sex, for a good part of their adult lives. Mates may be bound together by love, need, loyalty, children, or myriad other possible ties. With their great promise of need fulfillment and potential for need frustration, such relationships tend to have significant impact on life satisfaction. When couples are distressed, many seek professional help or are referred to it by others.

This book has been written to assist psychiatrists, psychologists, social workers, nurses, pastoral counselors, and other clinicians to whom couples turn for help. Most of these professionals have received graduate-level training in work with individuals and families, but not necessarily in couple treatment. For many years, couple work was seen as a minor variant of family treatment, requiring brief attention in training programs. Only recently has the need to learn a separate and complex body of knowledge and skills been recognized.

Much of the existing literature on couple practice is focused on couples coping with special problems such as battering, substance abuse, or one mate's incest history. Books and articles geared toward more general couple treatment have often been based on single theoretical approaches. There are many on behavioral, cognitive-behavioral, and object relations approaches, for example. While research studies support the usefulness of conjoint treatment for distressed couples, no one theoretical approach has been shown to best meet the needs of all (Bray and Jouriles 1995). A further limitation of the couple practice literature is that sociocultural influences on couples and their treatment, especially the influences of ethnicity and poverty, have received scant attention.

This book's approach to couple treatment integrates several major theories of couple functioning and practice, relevant research findings, and additional knowledge from my own and others' clinical experience. Detailed guidelines for assessment and the use of interventions in beginning, middle, and ending phases of couple treatment are presented. Sociocultural influences on couples are seen as important in assessment and their treatment implications spelled out. Consideration is given to deciding when couple work is and is not appropriate and to the treatment of couples dealing with special circumstances, such as affairs or narcissistic vulnerability. The book is geared to help clinicians seeing couples in a variety of service settings or in private practice.

Chapter 1 explains the theory and research base of my integrative approach to couple treatment and its primary value assumptions. Relevant concepts from systems theory, information and communication theories, behavioral and cognitive-behavioral theories, ego psychology and object relations theories are reviewed, and related research findings given. The book's value position is that knowledge from multiple theories as well as other sources, including sociocultural information, is needed to help many couples. Heterosexual and same-sex couple relationships are seen as of equal worth and case examples of both are used throughout. An additional value is that couples' own goals and intervention preferences, while often influenced by clinicians' input, must be honored insofar as possible even in the rare instance when couple treatment is involuntary.

Chapter 2 offers a detailed framework for assessing the environmental, individual, and couple system influences that must be considered in every case. Chapter 3 reviews factors necessary to evaluate in order to decide when couple treatment may be indicated and, in some instances, whether individual sessions should be offered before or soon after couples are seen. Such individual evaluation is warranted when there is any risk of violence and often when mates are abusing substances, showing psychiatric symptoms or sexual dysfunction, having undisclosed affairs, or struggling to decide whether they want to try to save the couple relationship. In Chapter 4, initial telephone contacts and couple interviews are considered, including modifications needed to take into account the mates' genders, sexual orientations, sociocultural characteristics, and possible resistance to being seen.

Chapters 5, 6, and 7 explain intervention strategies and related issues, including maintenance of a constructive therapeutic alliance, in ongoing treatment with most couples. They offer guidelines for help with communication, problem solving, insight, and intimacy, and for considering couple diversity in all such work. In regard to diversity, Chapter 5 includes discussion of work with couples living in poverty and Chapter 7 considers implications of gender, sexual orientation, ethnicity, religion, and social class for all three participants in couple treatment.

Two chapters then review work in a number of special situations clinicians commonly encounter. Chapter 8 is devoted entirely to the practice complexities of dealing with narcissistically vulnerable couples, so called because they show extreme sensitivity to hurt and blame as well as an intensity of emotion most other pairs do not. Often one or both such partners exhibit at least some characteristics of borderline or narcissistic personality disorder. Chapter 9 offers guidelines for couple work when an affair has been revealed, a couple is separated and possibly heading for a breakup, or one mate is showing mild to moderate symptoms of anxiety or depression.

A brief final chapter, Chapter 10, discusses termination when couple treatment has and has not been completed successfully.

CHAPTER

1

Conceptual Foundations

Couple treatment takes place in a variety of settings, from private practice to mental health and social service agencies. The need is widespread. Research suggests that at any given time 20 percent of marital partners are likely to report being distressed (Sayers et al. 1993). Couples may seek professional help to improve their communication, their coping with specific problems, or their feelings of intimacy. Sometimes others push them to get treatment. No matter what their reasons, a couple is likely to approach the experience with a mixture of hopes and fears. By seeing a clinician, they expose perhaps the most significant relationship of their lives to the possibility of change.

This book intends to help clinicians in most settings practice effectively with couples. Its value position is that the two members of a couple entering treatment deserve respect for their strengths and empathy for their pain no matter how messy their lives have become. Further, couples generally have the right to determine what they want to get out of treatment and what they are willing to do to get it. Also recognized is that couples are diverse. Their characteristics, problems, strengths, dynamics, and environments differ. No two have the same treatment needs and preferences. The position taken here is that clinicians need multiple theories and treatment approaches as well as knowledge of relevant biological and sociocultural influences on human functioning to help the couples they see. The book presents an approach to couple practice based on integrating key knowledge from theoretical, research, and clinical literatures, and from my own extensive experience treating couples.

This chapter begins by explaining several assumptions on which the book is based. It then examines three major theoretical approaches useful in understanding and treating couples: systems/communication, behavioral/cognitive-behavioral, and ego psychological/object relations. Research findings relevant to each approach are reviewed. After noting the additional importance of understanding biological and sociocultural influences on couples, a brief overview of the book's integrative approach is given.

While the present chapter is largely theoretical, later ones offer step-by-step guidance on how to assess and intervene with most couples based on their diverse needs and preferences. The book does not cover divorce counseling, counseling undertaken only to enhance couples' parenting skills, or couple work adjunct to one partner's specialized treatment for battering, substance abuse, or serious mental or physical illness. Even in these cases, however, clinicians may find much of its content useful.

BASIC ASSUMPTIONS

All treatment approaches are based on underlying assumptions as well as theory, research, and clinical experience. The assumptions implicit in this work are spelled out below.

Who Constitutes a Couple?

In the narrowest sense, only people married to each other may be considered couples. But some legally married people do not live together and may not have seen each other for years. Another difficulty with considering marriage to be synonymous with couplehood is that some very committed couples cannot legally marry. They may be of the same gender or unable to obtain divorces from earlier partners. Commitment to each other is also not a good sole criterion. Couples who are married but unsure whether they want to stay together are not totally committed to the relationship. Some unmarried couples, whether living together or not, seek conjoint treatment to determine whether they can achieve a good enough relationship to be able to commit to it.

The assumption here is that two people may legitimately define themselves as a couple whether they are married or unmarried, living together or not, heterosexual or same-sex. Their conjoint treatment can be considered couple treatment if they are meeting, want to meet, or want to determine if they can meet their primary intimacy needs—for affection, companionship, emotional support, and probably sex—with each other. Since the two people seen as a couple may be unmarried or of the same gender, the neutral terms *partners* or *mates* are used to connote them throughout the book.

How Should Couples' Difficulties Be Understood?

People undoubtedly enter into couple relationships for a variety of reasons. Everyone has physical needs, such as for food, shelter, and sexual expression, that a mate may help them meet. Complex emotional needs for intimacy and validation compel couplehood. There can be pressures from others to settle down. To some degree, mate selection is a semirational process of potential partners weighing who will best meet their needs. Largely, however, it is based on irrational feelings of love and "chemistry." Some theorists speculate that people select mates whose characteristics seem to promise resolution of childhood conflicts by meeting previously unmet needs, such as needs for validation, without arousing related fears, such as fears of being rejected if one asks for too much. In any case, expected need-meeting is a large part of a couple's implicit bargain with each other. Those who marry or live together also take on the task of dividing up responsibilities for carrying on their mutual life. They must in some way work out everything from who will take out the garbage, cook, and bring in money for living expenses to what to do with their free time and perhaps, eventually, how to rear their children. Amazingly, some meet each other's needs and work out how to live together with little or only moderate difficulty. Many do not, and these couples' anxiety, frustration, disappointment, or anger may sooner or later motivate them to seek treatment.

One problem of couple practice models based on a single theory is that these often posit only one set of reasons for why couples are having difficulties. They may also overlook strengths. This book takes the position that a wide combination of factors most often influences couples' functioning. First, their environments can be a source of various stresses, can present good or poor opportunities for partners to meet personal needs, and may or may not provide needed resources. Each partner's age, gender, race, intelligence, health, and sexual orientation will significantly affect both. Both mates participate in the relationship according to their unique personality dynamics, partly based on childhood experiences that taught each how to handle key needs and feelings, relate to an intimate partner, and avoid dangers in close relationships. Each partner also brings to the couple relationship vast stores of general and specific information gleaned from parental families, school, friends, prior intimate relationships, others of the same ethnicity and social class, the media, and all other life experiences. This information and related cognitions shape more of partners' behavior than clinicians sometimes realize. For example, each will function based on his or her knowledge of how to communicate and beliefs about what gender roles in a relationship should be. Inaccurate cognitions may lead to inaccurate assumptions, such as that people who love each other never disagree.

In response to these myriad influences, a couple relationship develops its own dynamics and patterns. The ways partners eventually communicate, meet needs, or otherwise interact tend to be self-perpetuating. When their patterned interaction leaves important needs unmet or does not allow adequate coping with whatever life situations they face, couple distress results.

Theories to be elaborated below illuminate how any of these factors may influence couple functioning at a given time. The major point to be made here is that no one explanation or theory adequately helps clinicians understand all couples' problems. An environmental stress or health problem may be a couple's primary difficulty or a negative influence among others. Ethnic differences between partners may bring joy as well as arguments about how to relate to extended families. Unresolved childhood conflicts or distorted cognitions can leave partners struggling to deal with unrealistic needs or fears. But it is just as likely that a couple's inadequate knowledge about how to communicate or solve problems constructively is contributing to their distress. Couple interaction patterns, whatever their source, can perpetuate dysfunction and make positive change difficult. Clinicians' understanding of negative influences on couples must always be balanced by an awareness of their strengths.

Who Determines the Goals of Couple Treatment?

Couples usually approach treatment with potential goals in mind. Many say they want to communicate better or feel closer. Some want to prevent recurrent negatives like frequent arguing or verbal abuse. Some identify specific problems they want to resolve, such as how to handle their children, in-laws, money, or sex. As a reaction to a major negative event, such as an affair, a couple's initial goal may be to decide if their relationship can be repaired. Sometimes each partner envisions different goals. Assumed here is that couples' preferred goals should normally be the ultimate goals of treatment. That is, the partners rather than the clinician should determine what final outcomes they and the clinician will attempt. If a couple's goals are not ethical or feasible to achieve, or the two partners' goals are incompatible, a clinician must say so and discuss alternatives.

Clinicians often suggest additional changes they believe will be needed to reach a couple's goals. For example, a clinician might suggest that a couple who wants to stop frequent arguing learn better communication and problem-solving strategies as means toward this end. Having assessed another couple's interaction, a clinician might propose both better communication and insight into the partners' fears of intimacy as changes needed to help the couple reach their ultimate goal of feeling closer. A clinician working with a couple in which one partner has had an affair might suggest that both need to deal with their feelings and understand why the affair happened before they can determine whether the relationship can be saved. The point is that the clinician, based on careful assessment of a couple's functioning and situation, offers an expert opinion about which changes will be necessary to get the partners where they want to go. In the approach espoused here, clinicians explain the basis for any such recommendations. A couple is then free to ask questions, make suggestions, and decide whether they are willing to proceed.

While the above may seem commonsensical, it is far from what happens in some couple practice. Too often, like the small boy with the hammer who decides that everything needs nailing, clinicians have pushed partners to remedy what the clinician's practice model assumes is wrong with all troubled couples. Sometimes with little attention to the particular couple's needs or goals, partners have been asked to follow directives, exchange desired behaviors in a quid pro quo, examine and correct their cognitions, work on mutual intrapsychic issues, or improve relationships with their families of origin. While some couples have been highly satisfied with the treatment they received, probably when it did fit their specific needs, others have dropped out or persevered with minimal improvement. I recently treated a couple still distressed after a year of prior conjoint work spent entirely on discussing their dreams. They turned out to be helped instead by recognizing that they were fighting because the wife's tendency to handle anxiety by wanting to process everything in detail and the husband's tendency to handle it by joking were making each feel disconnected and frightened. Meanwhile, they were dealing with some problems in their extended families that were understandably making both very anxious.

Across numerous research studies, only about 50 percent of distressed couples consider themselves happy with their relationship at the end of treatment (Alexander et al. 1995). When research compares different treatment models using random assignment of couples to each, findings are usually that the models studied are equally effective (Shadish et al. 1995). Baucom and Epstein (1990) note that such findings do not mean that each model meets the needs of all couples equally well. Some couples are probably helped more by one and some by another, canceling out any apparent differences.

What Should Influence How Couple Treatment Is Conducted?

The issue here again is the weighing of various inputs into what should happen in treatment to help couples achieve their goals. Couples themselves may have unrealistic expectations of what will go on. For example, they may think the clinician will say which partner is right or tell them what to do in their lives together. Some think the clinician will figure out the one "real reason" for their troubles. However, couples can also have valid and realistic wishes about what will happen. Certainly, they will hope to feel accepted and reasonably comfortable with a clinician. To achieve their goals, they may expect clinicians to tell them what they are doing wrong, give them new information, teach them skills, and help them understand each other better or gain insights that will move them past blocks to change. In the course of treatment, couples may respond well to some interventions and poorly to others. Clinicians must monitor these reactions and modify what they do accordingly. They should also ask which treatment activities partners are and are not finding helpful, and should be accountable for their work by evaluating carefully whether couples are making progress toward their goals.

Various other influences bear on which interventions clinicians use. Besides their preferred couple treatment models, clinicians' genders, ethnic backgrounds, and prior life experiences will influence their comfort with possible intervention choices. Their experiences with how other couples have responded to given interventions will be weighed. Supervision or consultation may be a legitimate and significant influence. Finally, and often neglected as a source of information about how couple treatment should be conducted, is research. Research suggests that work to help most couples improve their relationships is best done through conjoint sessions or a combination of individual and conjoint, rather than solely individual sessions with one or both partners (Gurman et al. 1986). Existing studies demonstrate the usefulness of some treatment models or intervention strategies to help couples with certain characteristics or problems achieve specific goals (Alexander et al. 1995). When a clinician is working with similar couples toward the same or similar goals, use of research-validated intervention strategies should be strongly considered. These studies are reported below and relied on in later chapters whenever feasible.

Let us now examine three major theoretical approaches to understanding and treating couples. These form the foundation for the integrative approach to couple practice used throughout this book.

SYSTEMS AND COMMUNICATION THEORIES

Systems theory and closely related ideas from ecological theory provide a conceptual framework for understanding relationships between individual human beings and their human and nonhuman environments. They also facilitate important understanding of interactive dynamics within couples, families, and small groups. Information and communication theories clarify further how systems interact and influence each other. These theories are not sufficient in themselves for understanding couples and planning how to treat them. But they suggest a framework or metatheory into which other theories of couple functioning and treatment can be integrated.

Systems and Ecological Theories

Systems theory had its beginnings in the physical sciences and was originally concerned with the dynamics of matter and energy (von Bertalanffy 1968). In the social and behavioral sciences, systems theory has been used to explain how small social systems, such as families or peer groups, maintain their equilibrium and interact with each other, the physical world, and the larger contexts of community and society (Buckley 1967). Developmental systems theory sees individual behavior as an outcome of reciprocal biological, psychological, and contextual transactions (Ford and Lerner 1992). Ecological theories, developed in the biological sciences, focus on the balance between living systems and their environments that is necessary to maintain functioning and growth (Bronfenbrenner 1979).

A system may be defined as "a set of units or elements standing in some consistent relationship or interactional stance with each other" (Steinglass 1978, p. 305). Systems are characterized by wholeness; that is, they are more than the sum of their parts. Within any social system, it can be observed that members relate to each other in patterned interactions over time. In fact, all participants contribute to and are constrained by their mutual interaction patterns. According to the concept of homeostasis, adaptive mechanisms within systems tend to maintain these patterns by counteracting any impetus toward change beyond a certain range. Finally, systems have boundaries. The nature of the relationship between or among system members defines them as an entity, setting a boundary that excludes others in some fundamental way (Steinglass 1978).

One can easily see that a couple constitutes a system. The couple relationship is something more than the two partners as individuals. Their mutual interaction tends to become patterned in ways both may find hard to modify. They consider themselves a couple, as discussed earlier, and are usually so considered by others. The concepts of boundaries, patterns, and homeostasis are especially important in understanding and treating couples because they are intrinsically related to the possibility of change.

All living systems are influenced by their environments through an exchange of energy or information across boundaries (Buckley 1967). In this sense, they are undergoing constant change. Different systems may interact hierarchically or horizontally. Hierarchically, one "can view any level of a system as a system in itself" (Breunlin et al. 1992). A couple system may be part of and influenced by a nuclear family system, a family system may be part of and influenced by a community, and so on. One may even conceptualize each couple partner as an individual system. Both partners influence the couple system by bringing their own biological and psychological needs and capacities to bear.

Horizontally, a couple interacts with other social systems such as mutual friends, extended families, or the like, and each partner may interact with a job system, separate friendship systems, and so on. Both also interact with their physical environments. The interaction of other social systems with a couple are affected by these other systems' own patterns and boundaries. For example, if a mother-in-law has become unhappy in her own marriage, she may withdraw from her husband and intrude more in her offspring's couple relationship. The father-in-law's response may then influence whether she continues to intrude or is drawn back into greater interaction with him.

While living systems constantly adapt to input from members and the environment, this input usually does not cause what theorists call second-order change (Watzlawick et al. 1974), or change in a system's patterns, due to the system's tendency toward homeostasis. A couple relationship may be disturbed by the weeklong visit of a friend but quickly readjust after the friend leaves. However, homeostasis does not always prevent change in system patterns. Human systems can show morphogenesis, or pattern change, in response to changing needs or circumstances (Buckley 1967). Morphogenesis may be gradual, and may or may not result from conscious awareness of the desirability of change. Sometimes new information, such as one partner learning the other has had an affair, leads to rapid and possibly dysfunctional pattern change. The permeability of a system's boundaries affects its response to input. Too permeable a boundary may result in too rapid change, perhaps even disintegration of a system. Too rigid a boundary prevents the system from receiving enough information to respond when change is needed. A given system's boundaries may also be more or less open depending on the source or timing of potential input.

Ecological theory, which can build on and elaborate systems theory, looks at human adaptation as influenced by the goodness of fit between people and their human and nonhuman environments

(Bronfenbrenner 1979, Lerner et al. 1985). Interactions between people's needs and capacities and those of their environment at a given time are viewed as representing a better or worse fit. The totality of environmental influences, in interaction with people who are in turn impacting their environments, must be considered. For example, when a woman's self-esteem is at a low ebb due to an exacerbation of a chronic health problem, her husband's job promotion may make her feel worse. An environmental circumstance that usually would be experienced as positive has become a stress; it does not fit the woman's needs well at the moment. The husband's pleasure at the promotion may make him less sensitive than usual to the woman's need for support, and make her less willing to dampen his pleasure by sharing her upset feelings. However, if the woman has supportive friends, she may be able to talk about her feelings with them and eventually share these with her mate.

Later chapters incorporate systems and ecological concepts in suggesting how children, extended families, peers, work environments, economic circumstances, and the like have major impact on partners' and couples' functioning. Ecological theory's emphasis on looking at the fit between people and their environments, and at capacities or resources within people and environments as well as stresses and needs, is especially useful in this book's integrative approach to couple treatment. In the case example just given, the woman's not having access to supportive friends might have tipped the couple's balance in a more negative direction. If it did, treatment might help.

Once a couple begins treatment, they and the clinician form a new social system. The couple's goal is usually second-order change, or some change in their interaction patterns, even if it is just to be able to communicate more effectively. Clinicians may try to stimulate and harness the couple's natural capacity for morphogenesis (Breunlin et al. 1992). In the helping process, the fit between the clinician's capacities and the couple's needs, the couple's openness to influence, and interaction patterns formed in the treatment system will be matters of concern.

A final systems concept relevant to couple practice is that of equifinality. Equifinality holds that the same end state within a system may be reached by many different pathways (Breunlin et al. 1992). The case described above can again serve as an example. If the couple had sought help for marital upset following the husband's promotion, a clinician might try a number of different interventions directed toward any of several goals. He or she might try to increase the woman's self-esteem by validating her strengths in coping with her health problem or referring the couple to a support group. Another likely goal would be to enhance the partners' communication, perhaps by suggesting mutual expression and understanding of each other's feelings. A third goal might be that the husband convey more consistent support, perhaps after examining his concerns about his wife's health condition or related issues of his own that may have been getting in the way. Even one of these changes might be enough to ameliorate the couple's distress.

Information and Communication Theories

To understand more about how people within and between systems influence each other, one may turn to theories about information and communication. "*Information* . . . can be defined as that which does logical work on the organism's orientation (whether correctly or not, and whether by adding to, replacing, or confirming the functional linkages of the orienting system)" (MacKay as quoted in Buckley 1967, p. 49, italics in original). For human beings, information consists of all data taken in. It includes people's perceptions of what they taste, touch, smell, see, and hear from others and the nonhuman environment as well as their own bodily sensations, emotions, cognitions, and knowledge stored in memory (Anderson 1991a,b). People perceive and respond to myriad bits of information every second, with only a small part of this information processing conducted at a conscious level. Much information is rejected or quickly forgotten. Some is stored for a longer time but still may or may not be acted upon (Bateson 1972). Heavy users of alcohol may know that their intake jeopardizes their health but manage to ignore this fact and keep on drinking.

Couple partners receive ongoing information from each other as well as from all other aspects of their environment and from within themselves. Some information may be misperceived or misinterpreted, as a review of cognitive-behavioral theory will soon elaborate. The interpretation of others' nonverbal behavior is often inaccurate (Watzlawick et al. 1967). Some information may be accurately received but then forgotten or ignored although it may be important to the mate. A woman frequently asks her male partner to give more time to sexual foreplay, but he claims accurately that he "forgets." Often partners reject or ignore information from their mates when they think that acting on it might conflict with their own interests or the content arouses anxiety, even if they do not make such decisions consciously. In the example just given, the information the woman is conveying may conflict with the man's belief that more foreplay will diminish his pleasure, or the idea may arouse his fears of greater intimacy.

Couples in treatment receive information not only from clinicians' words but also from their nonverbal behaviors, appearance, office furniture, and so on. For example, sitting behind a large desk may convey that the clinician wants to maintain distance and an authority position. Clinicians need to be aware of the myriad kinds of information they are conveying to couples. Their major tasks are usually to help partners seek, receive, and use new information they may need to achieve their treatment goals, as well as to access fuller information from within themselves.

Our discussion has now slipped imperceptibly into the realm of communication theory. Human beings, alone or in social systems, are heavily influenced by information. In turn, they influence others by conveying information to them. When information conveyed by one person has been received by another, communication has occurred (Watzlawick et al. 1967).

One issue in studying human communication is to determine how people can exchange information effectively to achieve the outcomes desired. Couple partners may or may not communicate effectively to solve problems, meet needs, and cope with realities of their lives together. There is a definite skill in being able to convey information that is clear, direct, relevant, and in such form as to facilitate acceptance by the mate. A great deal of research has been done on effective and ineffective couple communication. Since understanding such communication and teaching couples to communicate effectively are major foci in behavioral and cognitive-behavioral couple practice, the relevant concepts and research findings are reviewed in the next section of this chapter.

Theory about human communication also conceptualizes ways in which communication influences and sustains interaction patterns within small social systems. Much of this theory as applied to couples and families was developed at the Palo Alto Mental Research Institute in the 1960s (Watzlawick et al. 1967) and has since been built upon by others. The Palo Alto Group conceived that all human communication not only conveys information content, but also proposes a particular relationship between speaker and listener. If a wife says, "Take out the garbage," she is not just conveying that she wants her husband to take the garbage out. By giving him an order, she also proposes at the moment a relationship in which she is more powerful or one-up. Similar content but a more symmetrical or co-equal relationship might be proposed by saying, "One of us needs to take out the garbage." In either instance, if the husband replies, "I'll take it out right now," he is accepting both the content information conveyed and his wife's definition of their power positions in the relationship at the time. Of course, within their patterned interaction, the wife's reminding her husband may be a homeostatic mechanism if he is the one who usually takes the garbage out. If she has to remind him almost every time, it has become part of their pattern that he will not usually act until the reminder happens.

A healthy couple relationship presumably incorporates each partner taking one-up, one-down, and symmetrical relationship stances at various times (Watzlawick et al. 1967). Sometimes one partner appropriately gives a directive. Offering support to someone who seems to need it is also a one-up stance because it is the more powerful position just then. Problematic is either partner being one-up or one-down almost all the time, or both frequently wanting to be either one-up or one-down at the same time. Indirectly supporting these theoretical notions, research has found couples who enact a hierarchical power structure to show more negative behaviors, such as complaints or hostile comments toward each other, than couples in egalitarian relationships (Gray-Little et al. 1996). However, couples who seem not to have developed any clear decision-making strategies apparently show the most such behaviors.

Communication theorists closely examine couples' dysfunctional interaction patterns that tend to become more and more extreme over time, such as increased arguing or one partner pursuing more and the other distancing more. They suggest that these patterns are often the result of escalations in which each partner's behavior brings out an opposite or balancing response from the mate, stimulating a more extreme counterresponse, and so on, as both believe they are acting in the way the other's behavior requires (Shoham et al. 1995, Watzlawick et al. 1967). Clinicians, no matter what their theory base, usually seek to change such dysfunctional patterns when couples seek help. However, two current treatment models based on communication theory concentrate almost exclusively on bringing about such change. One, brief problem-focused therapy, was developed by Fisch, Weakland, Watzlawick and others at the Palo Alto Mental Research Institute, and the other, brief solution-focused therapy, by de Shazer and his associates in Milwaukee (Shoham et al. 1995).

In these models, couples present their complaints and clinicians assess the interaction patterns believed to be causing them (Shoham et al. 1995). Clinicians using the brief problem-focused model see such patterns as representing both partners' escalating attempts to "solve" the problem of their mates' more and more extreme behavior. They intervene by giving specific directives to each mate to carry out some alternative response that, in effect, amounts to doing "less of the same." Reframing the meaning of partners' repetitious behaviors in ways they do not expect and paradoxical injunctions to "go slow" are used to help couples be less resistant to change. In de Shazer's solution-focused model, clinicians help couples look at what they are doing when their problematic interaction patterns are *not* happening or what they would be doing in the future if these were not happening, to help them apply their own new or underutilized solutions to bring about change. Partners' efforts to solve their own problems are thereby reframed as competent. Both these communication-theory–based approaches claim high success rates but have not been studied in controlled clinical trials.

Examining couples' dysfunctional interaction patterns, reframing their meaning, and helping partners to do "less of the same" are intervention strategies used in this book's integrative approach to couple treatment. Helping couples develop their own solutions to problems is also emphasized, but more in a manner used by behaviorists than by these communication models.

BEHAVIORAL AND COGNITIVE-BEHAVIORAL THEORIES

Behavioral and cognitive-behavioral theories of couple functioning and treatment did not develop based on systems or communication theories. They have, however, focused compatibly on the influence of people's learning and environments on their behavior. Since couple partners are each other's most intimate environment, behaviorists have closely examined partner–partner interactions and developed techniques to make these more relationship-enhancing. Cognitive behaviorists have paid additional attention to cognitions and affects in their work. Both models typically incorporate research findings about couple interaction and the effects of various interventions on it.

Behavioral Couple Approaches

Behaviorists espouse the idea that partners enter into a couple relationship expecting to experience many benefits or reinforcers without too great a cost to themselves (Christensen et al. 1995). In successful relationships, partners probably do reward each other at a cost acceptable to each. Those less successful may find that, over time, benefits received dwindle or become more routine. Further, when a couple encounters incompatibilities but has inadequate communication or problem-solving skills to reconcile them, the partner who prevails will benefit while the other is deprived or harmed. If either engages in coercive behavior such as bullying or withdrawing and the other gives in, coercion has been reinforced as a coping technique. But the coerced partner may eventually rebel, withdraw, or coerce in return. Partners' dissatisfaction and increased unwillingness to reward each other are likely to follow.

Research verifies that partners in distressed relationships experience higher rates of negative or unpleasant behaviors from each other in their daily interaction and lower rates of pleasant ones than those in nondistressed relationships do (Gray-Little et al. 1996). Both partners in distressed relationships think they would be happier if they received more positive behaviors from each other (Weiss and Heyman 1990). In general, wives and husbands in any couple have been found to produce numbers of positive and negative behaviors that are similar to those of their mate. However, partners in distressed relationships are more likely to reciprocate immediately in kind, especially when negative behaviors have occurred. Also interesting is that a reduction in a couple's negative behaviors does not necessarily lead to a significant increase in positive ones (Bornstein and Bornstein 1993). The opposite is also true. Clearly, both types of behavior must be addressed in treatment.

Earlier behavioral couple treatment placed heavy emphasis on behavioral exchanges to try to decrease negatives and increase benefits each partner received (O'Leary and Turkewitz 1978). Couples complaining about their relationship might be asked to specify which behaviors each wanted the other to change. The two might then be encouraged to bargain or negotiate to arrive at a quid pro quo contract, in which each would agree to engage in specific behaviors the other wanted if the other would reciprocate. Or, in a good faith contract, a partner who did something the other requested might earn a reward, not necessarily directly from the other. For example, a man who did the dinner dishes might earn the right to watch TV uninterrupted for an hour thereafter. Deficits in couples' communication and problem-solving skills were often addressed primarily to assist successful negotiation of such contracts (Bornstein and Bornstein 1993). As behavioral couple treatment has changed over time, quid pro quo or good faith contracts have come to be viewed as just one of many tools couples can be taught to use during more extensive work on communication and problem solving.

The first step in current behavioral couple treatment, after conducting a thorough assessment, may be simply to help both partners increase their positive behaviors toward each other (Bornstein and Bornstein 1993, Christensen et al. 1995). The hope is mainly to renew their positive feelings about the relationship and enhance their motivation for further work. These behavioral contracts are typically devised *not* to be based on a quid pro quo in order to de-emphasize a competitive or bargaining atmosphere. For example, in Stuart's "caring days" (Christensen et al. 1995), partners are encouraged to list positive things their mates could do that would demonstrate caring. Then, each is asked to commit to do some of these regularly for the other and monitor what is done. As another strategy, partners may identify and perform positive behaviors they think would make their mates feel better about the relationship. Or partners may be taught to "research" which of their own positive behaviors will increase their mates' relationship satisfaction. In all instances, planned positive behaviors are to be of minimal cost to givers at this stage of treatment, and recipients may need to be taught to offer appreciation for them (Christensen et al. 1995, Sayers et al. 1993).

Behavioral clinicians next pay a great deal of attention to teaching couples communication and problem-solving skills. These are considered more important than any specific problems the couples may solve during the course of treatment (Christensen et al. 1995). Research has confirmed a number of specific communication or problem-solving difficulties to be associated with couple distress (Baucom and Epstein 1990). Compared with other couples, those who are distressed offer fewer statements disclosing emotions, wishes, and needs. They more frequently send unclear messages. Distressed partners less often acknowledge what the other says. They give more negative verbal and nonverbal responses, fewer positive ones such as support or encouragement, and more uncensored messages of all kinds. When couples attempt problem-solving discussions, those who are distressed are more likely to make negative comments, such as criticisms or put-downs, in direct response to their partners' efforts while nondistressed couples are more likely to make positive ones. The latter also are more likely to engage in other constructive problem-solving behaviors and eventually reach solutions. Distressed couples tend to show communication sequences in which complaints are followed by complaints or defensive remarks, withdrawal is followed by hostility (Sayers et al. 1993), or demands are followed by withdrawal (Christensen and Shenk 1991). Studies that have attempted to trace longer sequences affirm that the communication of both distressed and nondistressed couples can negatively escalate. But those who are not distressed are able to back away from the escalation sooner (Weiss and Heyman 1990).

Some behavioral clinicians teach partners specific communication skills, such as expressive and listening skills, before they begin work on problem solving (Sayers et al. 1993). Others concentrate on helping couples learn problem-solving strategies and address needed communication skills, such as sticking to one topic and presenting ideas positively, while doing so (Bornstein and Bornstein 1993, Christensen et al. 1995). Usually the problem-solving stages taught are to define problems, express thoughts and feelings about them, generate solutions, reach agreements, carry these out, and evaluate results. Often, agreements are written down as contracts and the couple is asked to formally monitor the results at home. Clinicians may offer direct instruction, model, coach, role-play, suggest the couple practice new communication or problem-solving techniques in the session, and give homework to try these at home. In all instances, they give feedback on the partners' efforts.

Research has found standard behavioral couple treatment, based primarily on communication/problem-solving skills training and some form of behavioral exchanges, effective in decreasing couples' presenting complaints and negative communication when compared to waiting list or placebo conditions (Baucom and Epstein 1990). It has been less successful in increasing positive communication and leading to changes in couples' perceived sense of closeness. Moreover, while up to 72 percent of couples have shown improvement by the end of behavioral treatment, relapse rates run as high as 30 percent over the two years following it. Severely distressed couples are among those least likely to benefit from standard behavioral treatment (Alexander et al. 1995, Jacobson 1992). Weiss and Heyman (1990) point out that most behavioral practitioners use a flexible clinical approach, tailoring their interventions to specific couples' needs, rather than following an invariant protocol as in a research study. They may also pay some attention to partners' cognitions and emotions. Therefore, existing research may underestimate the effectiveness of behavioral couple treatment. One outcome study that compared couples treated with a prescribed behavioral protocol to those treated with a more clinically flexible behavioral approach found no differences in improvement at the end of treatment, but the couples treated flexibly maintained their gains much better at six-month follow-up (Jacobson et al. 1989).

Standard behavioral theories and treatment techniques have contributed greatly to clinicians' understanding of and work with couples. This book's integrative approach draws heavily on behavioral clinicians' considerable knowledge about teaching problem-solving and communication skills. Still, by the mid-1980s, it had become clear that "standard behavioral techniques are not always effective" in helping couples improve their relationships (Jacobson and Holtzworth-Munroe 1986, p. 30).

Jacobson (1992) and later Christensen and Jacobson (Christensen et al. 1995) have tried to address the problem of limited effectiveness while affirming the value of standard behavioral couple treatment. In their integrative behavioral couple therapy model, they suggest that a functional analysis of each couple's unique interaction should lead to behavioral clinicians' uncovering and addressing underlying themes in the problems couples say they want to solve. For example, an underlying theme in a wife's complaints that her husband does not tell her their income or that he leaves household chores for her to do might be his unwillingness to share equal power with her. Helping the pair problem solve in regard to each complaint without addressing the underlying theme would be in error. While claiming that the integrative behavioral couple model does not aim to alter cognitions, its founders suggest that treatment can be facilitated when clinicians help partners become less blaming and more accepting of each other. Means to do so include identifying problematic patterns in which both partners participate, pointing out that both are well intentioned and suffering, and, when needed, helping one partner to give up unrealistic expectations of the other and do more self-care.

Cognitive-Behavioral Couple Approaches

In a further expansion of the standard behavioral model, cognitive-behavioral clinicians routinely attend not only to couple partners' behaviors but to their cognitions and often their emotions as well. Cognitive-behavioral theories have much affinity with information and communication theories. By addressing both cognitions and emotions, they also provide a bridge to ego psychology and object relations theories.

In cognitive-behavioral theory, cognitions seen as playing a significant role in couple interaction are the partners' "*perceptions* (about *what* events occur), *attributions* (about *why* events occur), *expectancies* (predictions of what *will* occur), *assumptions* (about the nature of the world and correlations between events), and *beliefs* or *standards* (about what 'should' be)" (Baucom and Epstein 1990, p. 47, italics in original).

Whereas the validity of the first four cognitive types can be evaluated against reality, beliefs or standards may be judged only as to whether they are reasonable or fair (Baucom and Epstein 1990). Partners inevitably hold beliefs or standards about how intimate relationships should be conducted. Some believe they should never be mad at each other. Some think relationships should be egalitarian, mates should put each other before extended families, or sexual experiences should take place several times per week. When partners' standards are unrealistic, problems are clearly likely. Or their reasonable but different standards may be problematic if the two do not know how to negotiate compromise or if each views his or her standard as "right."

Relationship problems can also occur when mates hold false attributions or assumptions about what each other's behaviors mean, especially since such thinking is usually automatic (Baucom and Epstein 1990). For example, one partner may believe without any doubt that the other is angry based on a dour facial expression, and further, that the anger connotes disapproval of something the original partner did. Partners then respond with behavior or emotions based on their inaccurate thoughts. As another difficulty, they may develop expectancies of what their mates will do based on past experiences. These can lead to selective attention, that is, noticing or perceiving behaviors that fit expectancies and failing to perceive those that do not. Expected negative behaviors are often the ones to be noticed while unexpected positive ones are ignored. Finally, partners will hold assumptions about each other's characteristics that are thought to occur together. For example, a man may assume that loving wives are caretakers without needs of their own. When his wife shows a need for friends or her extended family, he may attribute her behavior to not loving him. Partners' dysfunctional assumptions about which characteristics go together may be based on inaccurate interpretations of prior life events or learned from others in their parental families, communities, or society.

Considerable research supports cognitive behaviorists' interest in distressed couples' cognitions, including their beliefs and standards. Studies show that such couples are more likely than those who are not distressed to disagree in their perceptions of what actually happened between them (Baucom et al. 1995). They more often misunderstand each other's messages as positive or negative when independent observers rate these as neutral (Baucom and Epstein 1990). In one study, partners who tended to see each other's neutral behaviors as being negative were also less likely to reciprocate when their mates behaved positively (Bradbury and Fincham, cited in Weiss and Heyman 1990). As Jacobson and Holtzworth-Munroe (1986) note, distressed couples are more likely to "attribute their partners' negative behavior to factors that maximize its negative impact and at the same time undermine the impact of positive behavior through causal attributions that deny the partner credit for it" (p. 31). Specifically, they may believe the negative behavior is meant to hurt them or may attribute it to their partners' having long-term, relatively immutable character flaws (Sayers et al. 1993). Not surprisingly, couples with negative expectancies about their relationship in general perceive more negatives in their specific interactions (Baucom et al. 1995). Finally, a number of studies have found correlations between couples' unrealistic standards for intimate relationships and relationship distress (Baucom and Epstein 1990).

Yet cognitive behaviorists also see affect states as important. Besides impacting partners' sense of well-being, affect states can influence their cognitions or behaviors, or the affects, cognitions, or behaviors of their mates (Baucom and Epstein 1990). An already angry partner will be more likely to interpret the mate's behaviors in the worst possible light and respond accordingly. Someone who perceives his or her partner to be sad may be annoyed or rush to offer a hug. Research has confirmed the importance of understanding couples' affect states. Studies have found a significant correlation between mates' self-reports of negative affects and relationship distress up to three years later (Weiss and Heyman 1990). Longitudinal research suggests that relationship distress often contributes to the development of depression in one partner, while a partner's depression also contributes to relationship distress. In one study, husbands' lack of response to wives' affective behavior was predictive of later relationship distress. Affects have been found related to moment-to-moment relationship satisfaction in both partners. Couples may also misinterpret each other's affect expression. Several studies have found that husbands are more likely to interpret their wives' lack of positive affect as hostility, whereas wives are more likely to interpret their husbands' lack of negative affect as meaning something positive.

Cognitive behaviorists believe that cognitions, affects, and behaviors and the interplay among them must be assessed to understand a couple's functioning. A number of formal and informal assessment instruments as well as clinical interviews may be used (Baucom and Epstein 1990, Baucom et al. 1995, Sayers et al. 1993). Treatment may address any of the three areas, always tailored to couples' unique needs. Interventions to change behavior can include standard behavioral exchanges, contracts, and the teaching of problem-solving and communication skills.

To counteract partners' selective attention to negative events, they may be asked to keep a written record of at least one of each other's positive behaviors, no matter how inconsequential, each day (Sayers et al. 1993). To modify partners' inaccurate perceptions, attributions, expectancies, or assumptions, clinicians may first suggest that these can occur, using examples from a couple's own interaction (Baucom and Epstein 1990). Mates can be taught to identify their own automatic thoughts, examine their underlying beliefs, and test their validity. One partner's possibly inaccurate cognitions in regard to the other can often be tested by the simple expedient of asking the other whether they are correct. Baucom and colleagues (1995) note that clinicians must devote careful attention to the process and content of partners' interactions to teach them the necessary self-observational skills. These authors also suggest that clinicians help couples identify the circularity of repetitive dysfunctional interactions, such as mutual arguing, that each is causally attributing to the other. If negative expectancies are preventing needed behavioral changes, partners may be asked to test out whether the feared consequences will occur if they make the change (Sayers et al. 1993). For example, one partner who believes the other will make light of a deeply felt wish if it is expressed can be asked to express the wish and see. Finally, partners can be helped to evaluate the reasonableness of their beliefs or standards (Baucom and Epstein 1990). If the two are struggling with different standards, a clinician can ask whether each can live with his or her own standard or can help the two negotiate a compromise.

Partners may also be helped to recognize their own emotions and determine the behavioral interactions and cognitions that stimulate these (Baucom and Epstein 1990). Training to help both partners express emotions constructively and listen to each other empathically is crucial. Negative emotions stemming from distorted cognitions or dysfunctional couple interaction in the present may be acknowledged and future prevention worked on by changing the problematic cognitions or behaviors. Negative emotions stemming from the past, such as anger over a past affair, may need to be ventilated and their ramifications discussed. Jealousy, depression, or anxiety beyond what is understandable in response to couple problems may require further treatment modifications.

Research has found cognitive-behavioral couple treatment to demonstrate equal but not greater effectiveness than standard behavioral treatment alone in improving couples' relationship satisfaction (Alexander et al. 1995, Baucom et al. 1995). However, adding cognitive interventions to a standard behavioral package has led to changes in partners' cognitions, especially their unrealistic relationship standards. Those espousing use of the cognitive-behavioral model have offered a number of explanations for these unexpectedly weak results, among them the fact that all the research studies have required clinicians to carry out interventions in a prescribed manner and sequence regardless of couples' needs. Also, none included interventions focused on couples' affects, although in recent cognitive-behavioral treatment such work has been fairly standard. Interestingly, one earlier study (Baucom 1985, cited in Baucom and Epstein 1990) did show that emotional expressiveness training combined with traditional behavioral couple treatment led to couples' reporting increased closeness and intimacy as well as increases in general relationship satisfaction.

Cognitive-behavioral theories can enrich clinicians' understanding of how partners' cognitions and emotions influence them and how their greater awareness of what they are thinking and feeling can help them change. Such understanding is especially useful in work on couple communication and problem solving, as will be shown in later chapters of this book. However, to help many couples, clinicians need greater depth in understanding emotional influences on partners and their interaction. Such understanding can come from ego psychological and object relations theories.

EGO PSYCHOLOGICAL AND OBJECT RELATIONS THEORIES

Building on earlier psychoanalytic theories, ego psychological and object relations theories primarily address the impact of people's childhood experiences on their later coping and interpersonal functioning. Ego psychology posits certain innate drives, affects, or needs, and explores how people learn in childhood to deal with these needs as well as with their environments (Blanck and Blanck 1994). It suggests that learned fears about the dangers of need or affect expression can lead to the development of complex intrapsychic defense mechanisms. An important notion is that conflicts between needs and fears of expressing them can be unconscious, leaving people unaware of what they are defending against. Object relations theories, while incorporating much from ego psychology, focus more on the impact of people's primary relationships than on their basic needs or drives (Scharff 1995). The infant's need to be in a caretaking relationship is seen as paramount, with defense mechanisms being developed primarily to protect against loss. Both theories can be useful to illuminate the impact of early family-of-origin experiences on couple partners. Related approaches to couple treatment focus extensively on helping couples gain insight into their intrapsychic and relationship dynamics to promote growth and change. Object relations theories especially help clinicians understand and intervene with partners' unconscious collusion in maintaining interactions that, however dysfunctional, in some way permit need-meeting while defending against deep-seated relationship fears.

Theories of Intrapsychic Functioning

Ego psychological and object relations theories hold that everyone must struggle with how to meet needs for dependency or affiliation, self-esteem, sexuality, aggression or assertiveness, and stimulation (Blanck and Blanck 1994, Scharff and Scharff 1991, White 1963). Starting in childhood, cognitive capacities called autonomous ego functions, such as thinking and reality testing, develop to assist in coping with these needs as well as with other aspects of the self and reality. Children inevitably learn that others will not always meet their needs and that some expressions of needs or affects will meet with negative responses. They must then cope with anxiety about the possibility of encountering these negative outcomes or the recriminations of their own superegos, which eventually incorporate others' messages about what is right or wrong. Such anxiety may cause them to repress conflicts between needs and fears into the unconscious. They may develop defense mechanisms that bind their anxiety by preventing conscious awareness and direct release of the needs or affects in question but that perhaps allow some disguised expression (A. Freud 1966). For example, someone criticized as a child for expressions of sexuality may later be sexually inhibited but show inordinate interest in the sexual behavior of his or her teenaged offspring.

Some adults are aware of many of their own needs and feelings and make conscious decisions about how to deal with them. Most have some awareness, but cope with needs and feelings in ways modeled, allowed, or rewarded in childhood without thinking a great deal about the matter. However, unconscious fears of others' negative responses or of their own shame or guilt can cause people to defend dysfunctionally against direct expression of some needs or feelings.

The unconscious human mind is wonderfully inventive. The person defending against direct expression of anger may sublimate it into overly aggressive intellectual efforts, direct it back toward the self, or become resistant to being influenced, among a number of other possibilities. Expression of one affect can even defend against awareness and expression of another. For example, for someone fearful of being dominated or rejected, excessive anger can defend against experiencing affiliative needs. Most people hope to have basic needs met in their adult relationships, but harbor at least some unconscious fears of how others will respond to them.

Object relations theorists focus especially on what happens to people's core needs for connection and self-esteem in human relationships. They suggest that young children need a caretaker's soothing presence to deal with distress and a caretaker's mirroring of aspects of themselves to develop a positive sense of identity or self-esteem (Scharff and Scharff 1991, Siegel 1992). Because children's affiliative and self-esteem needs cannot always be reliably met, they inevitably encounter some experiences of anxiety and loss. However, with healthy caretaking, children learn that their needs will usually be met and, gradually, that they can take on more responsibility for dealing with their own anxieties and being proactive in seeking diverse ways to meet their needs (Siegel 1992). They may then continue to develop healthy capacities for connection and self-esteem.

Poorer parenting can lead to a variety of problems. Children whose needs for an empathic affectional connection are not adequately met will experience more intense anxiety and rage (Siegel 1992). Such reactions are especially likely in response to abuse, perceived rejection, or threats of abandonment. Children in these instances may see themselves as worthless or destructive for having failed to evoke a more caring response. To defend against further danger, they may repress into the unconscious those aspects of themselves, such as neediness or anger, that they believe have caused negative responses from others. They will also continue to be overly reliant on others for soothing and validation.

Object relations theorists explicate the key defense mechanisms of splitting and projection (Scharff 1995, Siegel 1992). In splitting, people unknowingly hold "good" and "bad" aspects of the self or others separate and see self or others as all good or all bad. Splitting serves to protect individuals' relationships with "good" others who are meeting some of their needs by allowing them to divert elsewhere, toward "bad" others, any frustration or anger that might otherwise threaten to tap into overwhelming childhood rage and destroy these need-meeting relationships. As long as "good" self-feelings can be maintained, splitting within the self similarly prevents overwhelming and rageful "bad" self-feelings, derived from caretaking figures' negative reactions to the self in childhood, from being experienced. When made aware of any imperfections, however, the individual may be flooded by bad self-feelings and feel "all bad." In projection, a more common and less inherently pathological defense mechanism, anger, neediness, or other disowned parts of the self may be projected onto, or seen as emanating from, someone else. This mechanism is further discussed below.

Ego psychologists and object relations theorists agree that people almost always carry forward from childhood experiences some unmet needs and fears about the dangers of trying to meet these in close relationships. They may cope with their needs and fears in more or less healthy ways. Because people are influenced by their innate strengths and characteristics as well as by the caretaking they receive and a variety of other life experiences, they vary immensely in the intensity of their needs and ways of handling needs and feelings in relationships.

Couple Functioning and Treatment

Childhood experiences and learned ways of coping with needs and fears are presumably a major influence on how each partner functions in a couple relationship. The concept of intimacy encompasses the two mates' likely hopes and expectations that they will meet sexual needs, significant affiliative needs, and many needs for self-esteem and stimulation with each other. Yet issues from childhood that are not fully resolved probably significantly influence mate selection. People may choose each other based on their relationship seeming to promise that old conflicts will be reworked and old hurts redressed without old fears being realized (Atwood 1993, Kovacs 1994). Sometimes these hopes are fulfilled (Wallerstein 1994), and partners achieve the level of intimacy they desire. However, as Siegel (1992) points out, entering an intimate relationship evokes both childhood desires and disappointments long repressed. People whose needs for affection or self-esteem were not met adequately may expect the partner to provide these at an unrealistic level. At the same time, they may harbor unconscious fears that if they let themselves be vulnerable, their partners will eventually abandon them, hurt them, abuse them, expect them to become the caretaker, or extract some other heavy price.

Because both unmet needs and unconscious fears are aroused, partners who have been hurt or deprived in childhood may not be able to ask directly to have their needs met. They are likely to expect the same response a parent made and, in covertly conveying this expectation, may elicit it. For example, a partner who desperately wants love but expects criticism may become extra alert to criticism from the mate, perceive it when it is not there, and attack or cower in response—thereby evoking criticism. The mate, perhaps also having experienced criticism in childhood, may identify with the parent who gave it and assume the aggressor role. "Thus, the struggles that originate in the family of childhood are perpetuated in the dynamics of the . . . [partner relationship]" (Siegel 1992, p. 5).

The concept of transference between partners captures the idea that, for each, needs and fears originating from early caretaking experiences can become transferred onto the mate (Blanck and Blanck 1994). Moreover, because the needs and fears and their origins are at least partly unconscious, partners may not be able to realize, without a clinician's help, how their mates actually differ from their parents (Atwood 1993, Scharff and Scharff 1991). For example, a man who learned in childhood that his mother would expect overwhelming closeness if he let himself depend on her may be unable to be close to his wife. The fact that she does not have such expectations does not enable him to act differently because he does not move close enough to test the fears impelling his behavior. The wife may have had a father who spent very little time at home. Wanting more attention from him, she may have surmised that her father retreated from her and her mother when they asked for too much. Based on her transference fear that a man will withdraw if she asks for too much, she may stifle her need and accept lack of closeness with her husband.

The relationship between these two partners may still be reasonably satisfying if they can get enough of their needs for closeness met elsewhere, perhaps from their children, peers, extended families, or a close-knit community. However, an early balance based on mutual transference may begin not to work after awhile or under different circumstances. If the wife becomes isolated while staying home with their children, she may need and hope for more attention from her husband. Her new expectations may trigger his unconscious fears of being trapped or overwhelmed and instead of giving more, he may withdraw and give less. As he does so, her fear and hurt may cause her to pursue him more. The more she pursues, the more he may withdraw and vice versa. A more and more exaggerated cycle leading to more and more distress will have begun. Further, the negative transference expectations of each will have been confirmed. While the theoretical approaches reviewed earlier see such interaction patterns as destructive, only ego psychological and object relations theories posit partners' intrapsychic needs and fears as perpetuating them.

Couples may also become involved in unconscious collusion in which each projects unacceptable needs, fears, or parts of the self onto the other. The other may then "carry" these, or the projections may be "tossed" between mates with neither accepting them (Atwood 1993). Continuing the above case example, the husband, unconsciously fearful that his own affiliative needs make him vulnerable to becoming dangerously dependent on his wife, may project these needs onto her and see her as weak and dependent. Whether he berates her, ignores her, or claims she needs psychiatric help, he has succeeded in seeing the problematic need as hers, not his. If the wife resists and attempts instead to see her husband as the inadequate one, these mutual projection processes will very likely lead to a distressed relationship. If the husband's actions induce her to accept the projection that she is dependent and needy, projection has turned into projective identification. She may then become more overtly dependent or depressed. Some authors see projection and projective identification as synonymous, whereas others see partners' collusion as differentiating the latter. According to Scharff and Scharff (1991):

> Projective identification is the process through which a person projects a disclaimed part of the self onto the other, and the other person unconsciously takes it in and feels like that projected part through introjective identification, and then behaves in such a way as to confirm it or, in more mature states, to modify it. [p. 8]

In projective identification, there is boundary confusion between partners. "What is projected is simultaneously identified with [in the other] and is experienced as part of the self" (Meissner, quoted in

Scharff and Scharff 1991, p. 49). Projective identification can also be unhealthy when one partner's carrying projected parts of the other prevents both from integrating all aspects of themselves (Scharff and Scharff 1991). The use of splitting, projection, and projective identification are especially common in partners who show features of borderline or narcissistic personality disorders, leading to the type of couple interaction called narcissistically vulnerable, to be discussed in Chapter 8.

Object relations theorists believe that intimate relationships represent partners' attempts to resolve childhood issues and grow, even though in many relationships the balance achieved between meeting needs and defending against fears ends up preventing growth (Scharff and Scharff 1991). In the latter instance, distress with the status quo or a wish to feel more fulfilled may impel couples into treatment, where the impetus toward growth can be rediscovered and nurtured. No distinct school of couple treatment has emerged from ego psychology, which has always had more of an individual focus. Object relations theorists have begun to establish a rich couple treatment literature, however.

The object relations approach requires clinicians to establish a "holding environment" in the treatment, that is, a place where partners can experience a safe and nurturing ambiance similar to what good parenting provides (Scharff and Scharff 1991, Siegel 1992). Empathic understanding of partners' feelings and needs is an important component. So may be setting limits on destructive behavior. In a secure atmosphere, partners may be able to reveal more about their hopes, needs, painful feelings or fears, and childhood experiences. Both individual and couple dynamics must be understood and addressed, with the clinician's own reactions or countertransference a valuable clue as to what might be going on (Siegel 1997). Siegel (1992) suggests that clinicians help partners begin to learn how to meet needs together in more realistic ways before promoting insight into underlying issues from childhood. Some couples may prefer, or only be capable of, stabilizing their relationships in treatment. Others, whose motivation and ego strengths are greater, may proceed into self-awareness of previously unconscious material to achieve greater individual growth and couple intimacy. In such insight-oriented work, clinicians may observe and comment on couple interactions, use dream and fantasy material, and probe affects to reach beneath surface feelings

(Scharff and Scharff 1991, Siegel 1992). They may also interpret possible underlying reasons for partners' difficulties in revealing parts of themselves, defenses, or conflicts. Eventually, partners' significant early experiences with caretakers may be uncovered and sequelae in the couple's relationship resolved.

Clinicians using ego psychological or object relations theories sometimes combine insight work with a variety of other treatment strategies, from a focus on communication to use of genograms and bringing partners' parents into the conjoint sessions (Nichols 1988). Research on insight-oriented couple treatment may therefore cover use of a wide variety of techniques. In general, approaches designated as insight-oriented have been found effective relative to no-treatment control groups, but no more so than other forms of couple treatment (Alexander et al. 1995, Bakely 1996). The exception is one long-term study in which couples receiving insight-oriented treatment experienced significantly fewer divorces and less deterioration in marital satisfaction at four-year follow-up than did those who had received behavioral couple treatment. However, the behavioral treatment given was the traditional behavioral exchange and communication/problem-solving skills package alone, while the insight treatment included communication training along with insight-oriented interventions in which clinicians interpreted "underlying intrapersonal and interpersonal dynamics . . . and addressed developmental issues, collusive interactions, incongruent expectations, and maladaptive relationship rules" (Snyder et al. 1991, p. 139). Behavioral practitioners have complained that the behavioral approaches used in this study were not as clinically sensitive as in actual current behavioral practice. Finally, several studies have confirmed the effectiveness of the emotionally focused model of couple treatment with mildly to moderately distressed couples (Alexander et al. 1995, Bakely 1996). Emotionally focused couple treatment is based on attachment theory, which is closely related to object relations theory (Johnson and Greenberg 1995). It encourages partners' insight into and resolution of strong emotions, often with origins in the past, that are stirred up in their relationship.

Ego psychological and object relations theories contribute a great deal to this book's integrative approach to couple treatment. First, they clarify how partners' needs, fears, and childhood experiences can influence their interactions. An understanding of interventions needed to establish a treatment environment facilitative of partners' growth, especially in cases where early nurturing was inadequate, is also a major contribution. Finally, object relations approaches highlight ways in which clinical intervention can promote partners' awareness of hitherto unconscious aspects of themselves to allow resolution, growth, and change.

AN INTEGRATIVE APPROACH TO COUPLE TREATMENT

The major theories so far reviewed can serve as a conceptual foundation for an integrative approach to couple treatment, as will be elaborated below. Research findings on these models' treatment strategies also provide inferential support for such an approach. There is no question that the behavioral interventions of teaching better communication and problem-solving skills are of use to many couples. Attention to partners' cognitions and affects has been found to enrich such work. Several studies have validated interventions used to help couples deal with emotions or achieve insight into the emotional influence of their pasts. Yet the insight-oriented model found in one study to be effective up to four years after couple treatment ended also incorporated some use of behavioral techniques, including communication training. It bears many similarities to the practice method presented in this book.

The book's integrative approach relies on two additional areas of knowledge crucial in assessing couples' functioning and planning effective treatment. One is an understanding of the partners' physical selves. Human beings are affected by their physical characteristics, especially age, gender, sexual orientation, and health, as well as by their psychological functioning and environments. Also significant are sociocultural influences. A considerable literature exists on race and ethnicity as they may affect couple and family functioning. Less has been written about the effects of social class, religion, and socioeconomic status. Also, "Virtually no research has specifically examined the effectiveness of marital therapy for couples from various ethnic groups or varying socioeconomic backgrounds" (Alexander et al. 1995, p. 615). Gurman and Jacobson (1995) and Alexander and colleagues (1995) are among those calling for increased attention to such influences in couple treatment. Clinicians and researchers have especially tended to disregard poverty as an influence on couples. Yet one out of every seven people in America lives below the poverty line (Mantsios 1995), with a substantial number of them presumably in couple relationships.

Let us now briefly provide an overview of the integrative approach to couple treatment to be explicated throughout this book. There are four major components of any couple treatment, overlapping in actual practice. These are assessment, goals, clinician–partner relationships, and interventions.

Assessment is a circular process of receiving information about partners, couples, and their environments, evaluating what is learned to decide where to seek more information or take other action, and again receiving information based on actions taken. Assessment is heavily emphasized in early interviews but takes place throughout treatment, in part to make sure the interventions used are helping couples toward their treatment goals. To organize and understand what they learn in assessment, clinicians using this book's integrative approach may first consider the impact of each partner's and the couple's current environments, using systems and ecological theories. Environmental systems are the context in which partners and couples function. The concept of "fit" is useful in evaluating environmental stresses and resources as balanced against partners' needs and coping capacities. Ego psychology suggests that everyone has needs for affiliation, assertiveness or the discharge of anger, self-esteem, sexuality, and stimulation, and that everyone must cope at one time or another with anxiety. Clinicians can assess partners' environments partly by considering where and how these allow them to meet such needs and cope with such feelings. Stress from the environment tends to be cumulative. Dealing with a number of stresses at the same time obviously taxes partners' coping capacities more than dealing with a few. Partners who encounter many stresses and few need-meeting opportunities or supports in their environments usually have more trouble functioning constructively and look less emotionally healthy than they really are.

In looking at partners as individuals, clinicians may assess the influence of gender, sexual orientation, age, intelligence, appearance, and health on each. Sociocultural factors constitute both an environmental and an individual influence. Partners' current socioeconomic circumstances and others' reactions to their race, ethnicity, social class, and religion will certainly affect them. So will other people of their ethnicity and social class with whom they interact and religious activities in which they participate. However, internalized learning from past experiences influenced by partners' sociocultural backgrounds also combines with all other internalized earlier life experiences to affect the partners' functioning.

When clinicians evaluate partners' personality functioning, several of the theoretical approaches reviewed earlier apply. Each partner may or may not have trouble with autonomous ego functioning. Sometimes partners are not coping as well as they might because they lack needed information—from how to deal with anger to how to manage a budget. Clinicians may use behavioral and cognitive-behavioral theories to assess whether partners have adequate problem-solving and communication skills and whether they hold dysfunctional perceptions, attributions, expectancies, assumptions, or standards, especially in regard to each other. Ego psychological and object relations theories can assist in considering the intricacies of partners' coping with needs and feelings as influenced by their childhood experiences. Important to assess in some cases will be defense mechanisms they may be using to deal with emotions and fears.

Finally, assessment must consider the couple as a system influenced not only by its members and environment but by its history, interaction patterns, and potential for allowing intimacy. Systems theory alerts clinicians to look for homeostatic mechanisms that may tend to prevent change in couple system patterns, or second-order change. Communication theory clarifies ways in which couples' interaction patterns can become more extreme and problematic. Behavioral theories suggest examining whether partners are receiving too few rewards or whether their ways of communicating and problem solving are leading to unnecessary conflict. Ego psychological and object relations theories facilitate understanding partners' attempts to meet intimacy needs and possible reasons for dysfunctional patterns in the dynamic interplay between the two partners' needs, fears, coping, and defenses.

In this book's integrative approach to couple treatment, assessment eventuates in a set of hypotheses about what factors seem to be causing or maintaining a couple's problems and what strengths or resources may be brought to bear in solving them. While ultimate *goals* of treatment will be to ameliorate problems couples identify, clinicians may suggest working to change any of the factors they believe may be contributing to these. Such clinician-generated goals might include change in any aspects of a couple's environment, partners' individual functioning, or the couple system, depending on hypotheses developed in the particular case. Couples must agree to these clinician-generated goals before work on them can begin. Such a safeguard tends to preclude, among other things, the imposition of clinicians' culturally insensitive values.

Clinicians must also seek to facilitate positive *relationships* with both partners to help couples engage in treatment and continue to participate constructively. While all couple treatment models endorse such clinician–partner relationships, only ego psychological and object relations theorists emphasize their curative value for some partners. The book's integrative approach endorses clinicians' use of acceptance, empathy, humor, structure, and selected self-disclosure as *interventions* to enhance their relationships with partners. Clinicians must also remain aware of how their own and partners' genders, sexual orientations, ethnicities, and other sociocultural characteristics influence their mutual relationships, and must be open to discussing these with partners. When needed or desirable for partners' growth, clinicians may encourage insight into transference aspects of clinician–partner relationships. They must always be aware of their own countertransference reactions and may sometimes share these with partners. Especially during insight work and in the treatment of narcissistically vulnerable couples, clinician–partner relationships may serve a curative function as well.

Other interventions serve to gather information needed for assessment. Clinicians ask questions, observe couples' functioning in sessions, and may seek information from other professionals who have interacted with partners. Borrowing primarily from behavioral and cognitive-behavioral models, clinicians may also ask partners to fill out questionnaires or self-monitor selected cognitions, affects, or behaviors at home. Once couples have become engaged in treatment and agreed on changes needed, many interventions mainly offer new information in areas where partners may not know what to do differently or how to do it. When couples need help with communication and problem-solving skills, useful interventions suggested by behavioral and cognitive-behavioral models include teaching, modeling, coaching, directing the partners in practicing, and offering feedback. Underlying cognitions or feelings may be explored. Homework tasks may be given to facilitate transfer of new learning to couples' daily lives. Some couples may need information clinicians can provide on how to deal with crises, such as an affair, or with a partner's psychiatric symptoms. In some situations, clinicians may offer needed information about how partners can cope with an environmental problem, such as the threat of being evicted, or how they can make use of outside resources such as legal assistance.

When couples' goals require change in their coping with needs and feelings, including the need for intimacy, the first interventions used may again be educational ones. For example, a clinician might explain the benefits of expressing angry feelings rather than bottling them up, and might coach partners on how to express them constructively. However, further work will often be needed. It may include the object relations interventions of interpreting underlying fears or conflicts or uncovering these, perhaps by analyzing dreams or other forms of expression, to help partners gain insights into the continuing influence of their childhood experiences. Clinicians may also probe partners' learned expectations and valuations of self and the mate based on gender, sexual orientation, or sociocultural characteristics to try to help them resolve any problems related to these.

Interventions to help couples change dysfunctional patterns in their interaction are needed in almost every case. One of the most important is clinicians' reframing of what happens in such interactions, so as to reduce partners' blaming each other and to help both take responsibility for change. Such reframing, a concept largely derived from communication theory, is now endorsed by most models of couple treatment. When reframing and educational interventions are not enough, clinicians may use object relations interventions to explore or interpret individual or relationship dynamics possibly underlying partners' difficulties in changing. These may include partners' transference reactions to each other, splitting, or projective identification.

Environmental interventions on behalf of couples are not emphasized in any of the treatment approaches reviewed earlier. Yet couples are often affected by stressful environments or may not be making use of available resources there. If clinicians using this book's integrative approach cannot help couples figure out how to cope better with their environments, they may sometimes intervene directly with these. As one example, a clinician may call another professional treating a partner not just to share information, but to affect the other clinical work. Or a clinician might intervene with the child welfare system to help a couple falsely accused of child abuse.

Finally, when resistance to change occurs at any stage of couple treatment, a clinician using the book's integrative approach assumes it may spring from his or her own activities or from an individual partner, the couple system, or environmental influences, and considers intervening in regard to any of these.

The integrative approach to couple treatment just outlined is elaborated in subsequent chapters. Chapter 2 considers a general framework for assessment, while Chapter 3 covers indications and possible contraindications for couple treatment. Chapter 4 suggests how to conduct initial telephone contacts and interviews. Chapters 5 through 9 deal with ongoing treatment of couples with varied needs, while a brief final chapter, Chapter 10, discusses termination.

CHAPTER

2

A Framework for Assessment

It may seem odd to present a framework for assessment before discussing first contacts with one partner or a couple. Yet clinicians must assess partners and couples to make decisions about how to proceed from the first moment they learn of a potential case. Should they agree to see a couple together at all? If both partners do come in for an initial interview, should further couple work be recommended? How should ongoing couple treatment be conducted? All such decisions, to be discussed in later chapters, rest on a clinician's ability to assess couples' functioning and circumstances.

This chapter reviews areas to consider in assessing why couples are functioning as they are. It considers influences of the couple's environment; each partner as an individual; and the couple's history, developmental stage, and current system dynamics. Concepts from the theories introduced in Chapter 1 are used throughout. Clinicians can use this integrative framework as a guide to conceptualizing why couples are having problems and where change may be needed. Key ideas to keep in mind in what follows are that (1) environmental influences may be stressful or a potential resource for couples; (2) partners as individuals can meet key needs and deal with important feelings both with each other and with others in their environments; (3) gender, sexual orientation, race, ethnicity, and social class are important influences on everyone; (4) couple dynamics, while influenced by partners as individuals and the environment, also take on a life of their own; and (5) clinicians must always assess partners' strengths. Several case examples are given to make these points clearer. Assessment of circumstances that may contraindicate couple treatment or require major modifications in it, such as severe psychopathology, substance abuse, or battering, are considered in Chapter 3. In undertaking assessment of couples, clinicians must always try to be aware of how their own genders, ethnicities, and other aspects of self may contribute to blind spots or biases.

The sequence of material in this chapter is not intended to reflect the order in which clinicians should gather assessment data. When and how to seek information for assessment and how to make treatment decisions based on it are discussed subsequently. Also, while assessments of environmental influences, partners as individuals, and the couple system have been separated for discussion purposes below, these areas are always to some degree evaluated simultaneously.

ENVIRONMENTAL INFLUENCES

As clinicians begin to think about why couples are having problems and what strengths or resources may be brought to bear in solving them, they may first assess how factors external to the couple may be an influence. These factors can be easily overlooked; in fact, couples often overlook them. Partners may describe ups and downs in their relationship with no awareness of how closely these reflect changes in external stressors and need-meeting possibilities in their environment. A case in point is that of Tina and John.

> Tina and John, aged 32 and 34, sought treatment primarily because of difficulties talking to each other. Tina felt John was withdrawing from her while John felt Tina was making unreasonable demands and constantly nagging him. The ethnic origin of both was German American several generations removed. The couple had moved to this city, where John had grown up and gone to college, a year and a half before. They had been married six years and both saw themselves as happier for the first four years. Shortly after they moved, John got a management job in a bank and began taking evening classes toward an advanced degree. He still had family and friends in the area. Tina had been pursuing a career earlier but decided to take a secretarial job because she thought

the reduced stress might help her get pregnant. But "no luck yet." Tina had made a few friends whom she saw primarily at work.

Assessment of Tina and John's environment reveals a significant imbalance in their need-meeting opportunities. John had moved to a city where he had friends and family readily available to meet his affiliative needs, and job and school experiences to meet his needs for stimulation and self-esteem. At the same time, his long hours with work and school were stressful and made him less available to Tina. Meanwhile Tina had few ways to meet these basic needs in her environment and was looking to John to meet more of them than before. She was also probably feeling stress and low self-esteem because of a possible physical problem, infertility. No wonder a dysfunctional interaction pattern, her pursuing and John withdrawing, had begun to occur. Their ethnic background might also be influencing them to place a great deal of value on hard work and starting a family (Winawer and Wetzel 1996). This couple showed many strengths, including four years of marriage that had gone well. A serious assessment error, without further evidence, would be to see Tina as excessively needy or John as having major intimacy fears.

Sometimes an environmental influence is simply that, an influence pushing partners in certain directions in their daily functioning. Sometimes it is a stress, a resource, or both at the same time. The mother-in-law who bosses a working-class couple around may also allow them to make ends meet by babysitting while they work. People or activities in partners' environments that meet or could meet their needs for affiliation, assertion, self-esteem, or stimulation are especially important to recognize. Eventually, clinicians must evaluate the totality of influences from partners' environments and their fit with the partners' needs and ways of coping. A number of these possible external influences are reviewed below.

Children and Extended Families

A couple with *children* constitutes a family system, with all the intricate dynamics this designation implies. Family treatment models based mainly on systems theory, such as the structural model (Fishman 1993), can be useful in understanding couples' interactions with their children. Clearly, children enter directly into their parents' stress, need-meeting, and coping balances. Infants and young children create a great deal of stress simply because they require almost continuous attention, entail considerable expense, and cause intermittent worry along with the stimulation and joy they bring. Perfectly normal couples may describe their lives as chaotic if they have children under age 4, and research has shown marital happiness to decrease for many at this time (Anderson et al. 1995, Crohan 1996). Sometimes partners' own painful childhood experiences or struggles to cope with difficult needs or feelings are evoked by seeing their young children's primitive nurturing needs and uninhibited affect expression. As children grow, most couples experience disagreements about how to deal with them. Feelings such as jealousy, anger, guilt, and frustration inevitably arise from time to time. Teenagers can cause greater stress as they struggle to deal with sexuality, independence, identity, and peers who may be a positive or negative influence. These struggles can evoke realistic fears for the adolescents' well-being or activate a parent's struggles with similar issues that have not been fully resolved (Kovacs 1994). Grown children continue their relationships with their parents and influence them in a variety of ways. When children of any age have significant health or behavioral problems, the parents' difficulties increase.

As a positive influence, children almost always meet some of their parents' needs for stimulation, affiliation, and self-esteem. They may at times serve as an outlet for parents' displaced anger at each other. Within limits, these benefits are normal. A family's ethnicity must always be taken into account in evaluating whether or not the boundary around a couple is too permeable, with more of either or both partners' needs being met through their children than is appropriate. If parents in couple treatment start to feel closer to each other, some overinvolved children happily turn outside the family to meet more of their needs. However, such children may instead uphold family interaction patterns that compel everyone to maintain homeostasis in dysfunctional ways. As they do so, the couple may be pulled back into the old patterns as well. For example, if children whose parents are becoming closer fear abandonment or are behind in learning how to deal with peers, they may act up to reinvolve a parent. One or both parents' guilt or anxiety may then cause them again to move closer to the children and away from the couple relationship or to withdraw from both.

For couples dealing with stepchildren, family system dynamics are even more complex (Visher and Visher 1996). For one thing, the children's loyalties may be partly or fully with another natural parent. Children often resent the stepparent and try to impede the couple's relationship. Both couple partners may be uncertain what the stepparent's role should be, or they may not agree. Even in the best of situations, stepparents and stepchildren become immediate family when they are not necessarily comfortable with being so close. Stepsiblings may get into conflicts that pull on the parents' loyalties and guilt. Finally, both partners' relationships with any ex-spouses are likely to be fraught with difficult feelings. The financial burdens and struggles over child support and other expenses of the children will probably represent more stress.

Couples' relationships with both partners' *extended families*, or the lack thereof, are an important influence in many cases. Again the potential for extended family members to be involved in meeting partners' needs, providing resources, and creating stress is considerable. It is appropriate for both partners to meet some affiliative needs with their own parents, siblings, or other relatives, and to derive stimulation and self-esteem from these relationships. Members of one partner's extended family may also meet some of these needs for the other partner. It is not unusual to hear, "Oh, I really enjoy his family. They make me feel welcome," or, "They're the family my own parents could never be." As long as both partners are comfortable with their relationships with members of both extended families, these are most likely a positive influence on the couple. While extensive need-meeting with extended family members may contribute to less closeness between partners, clinicians need not see this balance as a problem if the couple does not. Ethnicity and social class, to be discussed below, have an impact on how much couples believe extended family members should be involved with them. Clinicians should not impose their own biases on this decision.

Besides meeting some of the partners' personal needs, extended family members often provide couples with additional resources. They may give financial help or let the couple know they would help out if needed. They may provide caretaking services, from regular babysitting to physical help in emergencies. A parent, sibling, or other relative may be a resource for emotional support or advice needed at particular times.

Also, and often at the same time as they are a help, extended family members can add to a couple's stress. Anger, guilt, anxiety, lower self-esteem, or difficulties in coping may result. Research has shown parental intrusiveness to contribute to instability in early marriages (Timmer and Veroff 1996, Veroff et al. 1995). The question of how to relate to extended families may be a major source of disagreement between partners, especially if differences in their social class or ethnic backgrounds have led to different beliefs about what their relationships with extended families should be (Ho 1990). Sometimes relatives are so intrusive that a couple seeks treatment mainly to figure out how to deal with them, as will be seen in the Ron and Lynn case below. Parental families may be cool or even openly rejecting, especially when the couple relationship is interracial, interethnic, or same-sex. In the latter instance, extended families may not even know the partners are a couple. When extended families create stress but also are meeting a partner's important needs or providing resources, the couple's conflicts about what to do are heightened. Finally, it is highly likely that painful aspects of the partners' childhood histories with their parental families will make them extra sensitive to similar issues arising in adulthood. For example, if a wife's mother favored her younger sister in childhood, the wife may be "irrationally" jealous of her husband's later close relationship with either her mother or her sister. For partners whose parental families still behave dysfunctionally, old painful wounds are reopened again and again.

Extended family members have their own needs and issues with couple partners, as well as stresses and resources in their own lives. All these make their potential interactions with a couple far from static and predictable. There are several periods in a couple's relationship during which the couple's needs and those of the extended family members are most likely to be in conflict. One is when the partners first make a commitment to each other. They may be struggling to take a major emotional step toward each other, to "become a couple," at the same time that parents or siblings are having trouble letting them go. Same-sex couples are especially likely not to receive family validation for separating even if their relationship is not condemned (Ellis and Murphy 1994). For any couple, the birth and early years of children can provoke extended family troubles. While a couple struggles to adjust to being parents, they may need their own parents' financial or caretaking help but not too much of their advice or intrusion into child-rearing. Much later, elderly parents may need caretaking from the partners or their siblings, causing a variety of stresses (Anderson et al. 1995).

Some partners deal with their problems with extended family members by limiting contact or even totally cutting off from them. While such rigid boundaries or "emotional cutoffs" (Papero 1995) may not be ideal, they can be a practical solution if the partners agree on them. Partners from ethnic groups that highly value ties to extended families and community are likely to suffer most with such arrangements.

Other Involvements and Finances

Partners' *jobs or other productive activities* can be a resource in meeting many of their needs as well as serving important financial and caretaking functions for the family. First, such activities almost always affect self-esteem. Partners who believe they are doing something important and doing it well, whether work, school, homemaking, child-care, volunteer activities, or a combination, have come a long way toward feeling good about themselves. The perception that one is appreciated for these activities also helps a lot. Sometimes work or other productive activities are a negative or mixed influence on self-esteem. A partner may think that what he or she does is not important or may not feel competent at it. Or a partner can feel competent in an important role but feel less self-esteem because others do not seem to notice. In the Tina and John case, both partners may have felt Tina's job and homemaking activities were not especially important, contributing to her lowered self-esteem. The poorest self-esteem usually ensues when a partner is engaged in few, if any, productive activities, perhaps because of being unemployed and with little that he or she considers worthwhile to do (Rubin 1994).

People also benefit when work or other productive activities meet many of their needs for stimulation. When they do not—for example, when a partner is bored with child-care or has a boring job—a great deal of dissatisfaction can result. Blue-collar jobs are frequently boring and repetitive (Rubin 1992). Often overlooked is that some of the partners' affiliative and assertiveness needs may be met in the workplace, at school, or wherever productive activities involve repeated interactions with others. The coffee breaks or bantering a partner shares with co-workers, schoolmates, or other parents in a play group may be a source of both support and stimulation. Partners may have chances to be assertive with others, such as children or co-workers, on the job or while engaged in other productive activities.

Of course, various stresses can accrue from such activities as well. Stress arises when there is pressure from too much to do and too little time to do it, when others with whom one must interact are problematic, or the like. A partner's isolation, lack of self-esteem, or lack of stimulation in a job or other productive activities can create stress by placing more pressure for such needs to be met in the couple relationship, as with Tina and John. Partners' differences of opinion about what each should be doing in regard to work, school, or other productive activities may create tension between them.

The *couple's or family's financial situation* is a closely related influence. Most couples depend on work as an income source. For some this is supplemented or replaced by public welfare, unemployment, or disability checks; by family money; or by income from investments or pensions. Whoever brings in more of the couple's money, more often the man in a heterosexual relationship, may feel entitled to a greater say in how it is to be used (Rampage 1995). Couples' disagreements about money can reflect a variety of issues, from honest differences about priorities to struggles over who has greater power. Use of money can be a way one or both partners meet emotional needs. For example, partners who felt deprived as children may want to spend money on material things as a way of nurturing themselves and feeling more self-esteem. A partner who feels unappreciated may spend money to self-nurture but also to deal with anger toward the mate, especially if the latter earns more of their money or wants to see it spent differently. Such ways of coping with underlying feelings may or may not be conscious.

Regardless of its source, the amount of money available to a couple significantly affects their lifestyle and sense of well-being or distress. People's financial condition, of course, always depends on money available compared with their necessary and discretionary spending. Research consistently verifies that economic hardship contributes to couples' emotional distress (Conger et al. 1990, Elder et al. 1995, Veroff et al. 1993, 1995). Stresses may come from the need for partners to commute long distances or work different shifts to avoid paying for child-care, with no time alone together (Rubin 1994). A sense of barely surviving at a subsistence level, constantly anxious about money and perhaps accruing debts in order to get by or to have any luxuries, wears both partners down. Poverty may even interfere with the partners being able to make a clear commitment to their relationship, as either may fear not being able to survive financially if they stay together. To the degree that poverty or inadequate income means couples must live in dangerous neighborhoods, endure crowded or rundown housing, use unreliable transportation, experience inadequate medical care, or the like, the stresses they endure can be enormous (Mantsios 1995). Financial stresses are more painful and discouraging if they are perceived as likely to be long-lasting rather than a temporary prelude to better times (Veroff et al. 1995).

Often underestimated as an influence on couples are their *peer relationships, religious and recreational activities, and pets*. On the positive side, it is usual and desirable that partners meet some of their needs for self-esteem, affiliation, and stimulation through these means. Friends may be a source of companionship and support over many years. Partners may be involved with religious services or other religious activities that meet a variety of needs, including spiritual ones. Recreational activities such as sports or movies provide welcome stimulation, an opportunity for companionship, and often self-esteem. Especially when a couple has no children, pets can enter strategically into their need-meeting balance.

However, any of these influences can become problematic as well. Partners unable to meet needs in these ways due to lack of opportunities or too rigid a boundary around their relationship may want too much from their mates, as Tina seemed to. At the opposite extreme, either or both partners may dilute time and emotional investment in their relationship by throwing themselves into peer relationships, religion, recreation, or involvement with pets. Friends or pets may openly prefer one partner, perhaps causing the other jealousy or feelings of being left out. Couples can disagree about how much time and with whom each should engage in friendships or other outside activities. Partners whose ethnic or social class backgrounds differ may especially disagree because these factors influence such beliefs. For example, a working-class man may expect to spend most of his recreational time with male friends or together with both his wife and children (Rubin 1992). His middle-class wife may expect to spend more time alone with him.

The stresses from peer relationships, religious activities, recreation, or pets can also be more direct. A friend may say something hurtful, demand more time than a partner can realistically give, or directly interfere in the couple relationship (Veroff et al. 1995). Peers may encourage a partner to abuse substances. Couples' disagreements about their own or their children's participation in religious activities can cause great stress, sometimes partly because of extended family pressures (McGoldrick and Giordano 1996). Failure at sports or recreational activities, especially if a large part of a partner's self-esteem is tied to these, can be a major blow. Pets' chronic health or behavioral problems can be very stressful. For example, pets that resist being housebroken or misbehave in other ways can cause almost as many arguments as misbehaving children do.

Finally, as another environmental influence, some partners are receiving more than routine medical care at a given time because of health problems. Or one or both may be in psychotherapeutic individual, group, or family treatment, or in a self-help group such as Alcoholics Anonymous, while they are in couple treatment. Such *other treatment or self-help experiences* will influence both partners in a variety of ways. They may benefit a great deal. Partners not participating may be relieved that their mates are receiving help and be generally supportive of the process. However, any treatment or self-help experience takes time, money, and some amount of emotional energy. Dealing with medical caregivers, procedures, scheduling, payment, and all related matters can be a significant source of stress (Rolland 1994). Partners participating in other psychotherapeutic treatment or a self-help group usually experience it as a support and stimulation, as well as intermittently stressful. Nonparticipating partners sometimes disagree about whether such help is needed and about the benefits received there, or are jealous of their mates' positive relationships with their clinicians or other group members. In some cases, such experiences encourage one partner to push for changes the mate does not want, or a partner may bring back insights unfavorable to the mate, as in, "My therapist says you're selfish and narcissistic." Sometimes negative transference not being handled by another clinician is acted out with the mate. For example, a woman whose male clinician has not been dealing with her negative feelings toward him may displace unwarranted anger toward her husband. Occasionally other treatment or a self-help group is not very helpful or is even destructive to partners involved in it.

The Physical Environment and Larger Social Contexts

The *physical surroundings* in which a couple lives are always an influence on them. Circumstances such as their housing being cramped or otherwise unpleasant, their neighborhood unsafe, or their home being broken into can cause immense stress. Not having enough bathrooms for family members' ready use is a lesser but still notable strain. All couples are influenced by whether their environment is urban, suburban, exurban, small town, or rural, and by their region of the country. Natural disasters, weather, seasons, and physical isolation from others are a major influence in some cases.

Larger social contexts include people and institutions with whom a couple interacts more peripherally than with those identified above. Examples are people from the neighborhood and community, and service people, such as children's teachers. While no one person in these larger contexts is likely to meet the partners' personal needs, such individuals' smiles, nods of hello, or friendly conversation can make a small contribution. The totality of the larger social context may also feel comfortable or affirming to partners who feel valued or at least accepted in their neighborhood, community, and society. With adequate services from schools, police, garbage collectors, and the like, partners may rarely think about these matters. But some partners experience stress from their larger social context on an intermittent or regular basis. At the very least, unreasonable neighbors or unresponsive institutions can be a problem. People may also feel uncomfortable in neighborhoods or communities where they feel they do not fit in. Language or cultural differences between a couple and their neighbors can be a source of stress.

Stereotyping, prejudice, discrimination, or oppression that partners encounter from neighbors, a community, or others is even more stressful. Stereotypes are inherently a denial of the unique self. Many people also encounter prejudice or discrimination because they are female or of a sexual orientation, race, ethnic background, social class, or religion that tends to be devalued in American society. Oppression involves a systematic restriction of choices as well as direct subjugation or injury (Frye 1995). Whatever partners' level of self-esteem, it cannot be helped by encountering racism, sexism, homophobia, or other oppression on a regular basis. Understandable anger and anxiety can result. Unpleasant encounters can be almost as devastating when they are intermittent, because recipients may have let down their guard (Boyd-Franklin 1989). The African American man who has felt valued at work may be passed over for a promotion. Someone may overhear a racist remark from a service person with whom he or she had enjoyed bantering. Of course, the two partners may have different experiences with others. Especially when partners are of different races or ethnicities, one may encounter negative behaviors that the other does not. However, an interracial couple or an identifiable same-sex couple seen together still regularly face hostile responses in almost all communities.

Partners may disagree about how to handle problems encountered in their larger environment, thus generating more stress between them. When their differences have to do with how to cope with neighbors or unreasonable landlords, the problem is tough enough. When they encounter prejudice and discrimination, choices may be even more difficult. One partner's way of coping may be to ignore these insofar as possible. Another's may be to take a firm personal stand, fight back legally, try to involve others in the community, or engage in confrontations. Some partners wish to try to hide their ethnic background or sexual orientation. For example, a same-sex couple may disagree when one partner wants to be "out" more publicly than the other does. In some instances, partners have internalized society's negative responses to their race, ethnicity, gender, or sexual orientation and these negative self-beliefs complicate coping. The influence of partners' encountering prejudice and discrimination from others is discussed in more detail in Chapter 7.

Finally, *society in general* has an impact on a couple beyond that manifested in face-to-face contacts between partners and others. For one thing, the media conveys society's attitudes in movies, newspapers, and magazines and on TV and radio. For another, larger events in society influence most of its members, at least indirectly. The state of the economy influences people's job security and savings. Wars, even limited ones such as the 1993 Persian Gulf war, tear the lives of some couples apart. Events that have no direct impact can still affect couples through the publicity they receive. For example, many couples in which battering had occurred or threatened to occur experienced heightened tensions during the O. J. Simpson trials that stretched between 1994 and 1997.

PARTNERS AS INDIVIDUALS

Clinicians must always carefully assess partners as individuals. Attention can focus on each partner's physical self, personality functioning, sociocultural background, and individual history. Physical factors include gender, sexual orientation, age, health, and the like. To evaluate personality functioning, the presence of major psychopathology, substance abuse, or interpersonal violence needs to be considered first. Some assessment of the partners' autonomous ego functioning, as well as screening for specific symptoms and behaviors, discussed in Chapter 3, can help a clinician determine whether any of these three possible contraindications to couple treatment is present. Further personality assessment especially relevant to the work of couple treatment can then focus on the adequacy of the partners' coping with their lives in general, possible dysfunctional cognitions, and the way each deals with basic needs and feelings. Finally, it is important to consider how partners may be influenced by sociocultural factors and their own histories.

> Ron and Lynn were both 19 when they entered treatment complaining of frequent arguing, usually about how to deal with Ron's mother or money. Ron's mother had not approved of Lynn since Ron and Lynn "had to get married" a year before. She often called telling Lynn how to take care of Ron and their baby, now 7 months old. These conversations usually deteriorated into criticisms and put-downs started by Ron's mother but loudly continued by Lynn. Ron would tell Lynn to simply ignore what his mother said, as he did. When the couple disagreed, Lynn expressed anger quickly while Ron would remain quiet and sullen, then eventually explode with frustration. He had pushed Lynn on one occasion. Ron worked days as an auto mechanic and often took the baby to his parents' house at night. Lynn worked from 3:00 to 11:00 P.M. as a hospital aide. To Ron's consternation, Lynn had run up considerable debts buying things for herself and the baby and by frequently calling her family in another state. He was more frugal and wanted to keep to a budget, with the idea that doing so might allow Lynn to quit work. Ron was Polish and Catholic, Lynn of French background and no particular religion. Both loved the baby very much and wanted to try to save the marriage.

Ron and Lynn's ages may partly explain why they have not yet fully separated from their parental families to establish themselves as a couple. From what is known so far, they show no obvious psychopathology or trouble with autonomous ego functions. However, substance abuse and Ron's future potential for battering Lynn or the baby would need to be evaluated carefully, since evidence of any of these could contraindicate couple treatment. Seen in the context of their youth and enormous environmental stresses from Ron's mother, caring for a 7-month-old, money problems, and working different shifts, their individual coping may not be too inadequate. Both are holding jobs but little is known about how well they are functioning there, with friends, and as parents. Neither is coping very well with Ron's mother, but she is extremely difficult. Lynn's coping with money seems to be a problem. While her need for telephone contact with her family is understandable, she may also be dealing with anger toward Ron and getting self-esteem needs met through spending. In terms of dysfunctional cognitions, each is probably attributing the other's behavior to the other being uncaring and unreasonable. Clearly Ron and Lynn are meeting many affiliative needs with their parental families, a triangling pattern that contributes to, as well as results from, their couple problems. They have a lot to be angry about in their current situation, but anger management seems to be difficult for both. Lynn is probably mouthing off too freely and Ron is suppressing anger, then exploding.

Sociocultural and historical influences on Ron and Lynn can also be assessed. Based on jobs, both seem to be working class. Getting married young, with a child born soon after, is more often characteristic of working-class couples (Rubin 1992). Their continuing close connections with parental families may be influenced by their social class and Ron's Polish ethnicity (Folwarski and Marganoff 1996, Rubin 1992). Religion may be a source of conflict, particularly if Lynn does not want to raise the baby Catholic. While we know little about their personal histories, Lynn's self-esteem especially may have been damaged by the marriage being forced. Often both partners in such situations wonder if they would have wanted each other enough to marry without the pregnancy. Finally, a clinician must be concerned with strengths as well as problems in the partners' individual functioning. Ron and Lynn show strengths in their willingness to come for treatment and wish to save their marriage as well as their possibly adequate job functioning and love of their child.

Let us examine more closely these areas clinicians can consider in assessing partners as individuals.

Physical Selves

Of the various aspects of partners' physical selves that have an impact on their functioning, one of the most important is *gender*. Scientists are only beginning to understand which of the many differences between genders have biological roots and which are learned (Unger and Crawford 1996). Obviously, men and women look different and have inherent differences in sexual functioning, childbearing, and strength. They have, on average, different levels of pain tolerance and different propensities toward various illnesses. Research has found men more vulnerable to physiological arousal during interpersonal conflict situations (Weiss and Heyman 1990). Perhaps this vulnerability was one reason Ron had trouble talking about his and Lynn's problems when Lynn's level of anger increased.

Certainly gender has an immense impact on each partner's life experiences, sense of self, behaviors, self-expectations, and the expectations of others. From birth, one learns how people of both genders are to behave by observing others, receiving societal and interpersonal messages about gender-appropriate behavior, and seeing others' reactions to one's gender self (Unger and Crawford 1996). Such learning becomes so much a part of self that gender is perhaps people's most salient way of defining their identity. If asked to respond spontaneously to the question, "Who are you?" many people will say "a woman" or "a man." Most also want to live up to their own and their partner's expectations of what a woman or a man should be and suffer a serious blow to their self-esteem if they do not (Sheinberg and Penn 1991). Ron may have felt bad about himself as a man because his wife had to work, and Lynn may have thought less of him as well. Unfair as it may have been, in our earlier case example, Tina may have felt a sense of failure as a woman because she had not become pregnant. Individuals' expectations about how an intimate partner will behave also tend to be guided by the way a parent or other significant caretaking person of the partner's gender acted. Gender-linked beliefs, such as "men leave you" or "women fall apart," are generated from partners' childhood experiences.

In looking at partners as individuals, clinicians can try, without stereotyping, to assess characteristics that may be gender influenced. Many of these can be relevant to the way men and women approach couple treatment, communicate, problem solve, and deal with intimacy, as reviewed in Chapters 4 and 7. One key issue for assessment is each partner's belief about gender roles, including how much flexibility in roles each allows. Social class and ethnicity profoundly influence these beliefs. For example, African Americans have been found to have more flexible beliefs about what are appropriate male and female roles than do couples of many other ethnicities (Hines and Boyd-Franklin 1996).

Society significantly influences men's and women's self-valuations, worldviews, behaviors, and options. Women are far more likely to devalue themselves because of society's messages about gender. Feminists believe that society's awarding of more power to men is always reflected in some fashion in male–female relationships (Rampage 1995). Perhaps if Lynn had had the option of bringing in more money by working as an auto mechanic as Ron did, she might have felt more powerful in their relationship and would not have had to assert her views so aggressively. Both might have felt less stressed about their finances. On the other hand, Ron, as a working-class man of Polish background, might also have felt threatened by such a shift from traditional gender roles (Folwarski and Marganoff 1996).

Of course, two partners may be of the same gender. If so, they are men or women first but their identities also include being gay male, lesbian, or bisexual (Nichols 1994, Unger and Crawford 1996). Evidence to date suggests that people's *sexual orientation* is probably genetically influenced (Okun 1996). There are no other inherent differences that distinguish people with a homosexual or bisexual orientation from people with a heterosexual one. However, those having a same-sex orientation will have encountered societal prejudices and oppression, almost always including the oppression of having to keep their full identity hidden in many circumstances. Some partners who are lesbian, gay male, or bisexual have internalized society's homophobia as disapproval toward this core aspect of self, and perhaps toward their mates as well (Okun 1996). Many have experienced losses of relationships with family members or friends because of their sexual orientation. The influence of sexual orientation on partners' functioning and treatment is discussed further in Chapter 7.

Another important physical characteristic is each partners' *age* and life-cycle stage. Those under the age of 25 may still be struggling to establish a firm sense of identity, a place in the adult world, and greater separation from families of origin, as was seen with Ron and Lynn. Couples may face decisions about childbearing until female partners reach late middle age. Partners aged 45 to 60 must often deal with beginning to slow down physically, decreasing job satisfaction, and perhaps an "empty nest." Most people over 60 are facing or experiencing retirement and more persistent evidences of aging. A large disparity in partners' ages can mean strain as the two cope with different life-cycle tasks. A man of 60 wanting to retire at the same time that his wife of 40 is still strongly invested in her career is one example.

Appearance and *intelligence* have a strong impact on how people see themselves and how others regard them. Appearance also connotes someone's race, to be considered as a sociocultural influence below. People themselves as well as others constantly evaluate their height, weight, perceived feminine or masculine looks, perceived attractiveness, and so on. Partners may choose each other partly because they look somewhat alike, because a partner's looks evoke a positive stereotype such as that red-haired women have fiery personalities, or because one partner looks a little like a significant figure from the other's childhood. Changes in partners' looks over time may evoke disappointment or anger. Intelligence, while only partially physically based, is usually relatively fixed by adulthood. Partners' intelligence may have significant impact on their functioning if it is unusually high, low, or divergent between mates.

A crucial influence on partners' individual functioning and their relationship is the *health* of each. Good health is a blessing, however much it is taken for granted. Everyone has intermittent health problems and a sizable number of people have chronic ones, whether minor or more significant. Research has found the declining health of one partner to adversely affect marital quality (Booth and Johnson 1994), although some studies have produced contradictory results (Burman and Margolin 1992). Couple partners, unless elderly, usually do not expect to deal with major health problems in themselves or a mate. As noted earlier, doing so takes money and time. It provokes anxiety, frustration, anger, and fatigue. Medications can have unpleasant side effects. Partners often disagree about how to deal with health difficulties, especially how much to attend to them. Temporary or chronic health problems may also limit partners' abilities to help around the house, work, bear children, or function sexually (Booth and Johnson 1994). Ill or disabled partners often must be more physically and emotionally dependent on mates than either would like. Their self-esteem may suffer. Chronic pain or illness, permanent disability, or a potentially terminal condition hugely influences couples (Rolland 1994).

Finally, more or less minor aspects of bodily functioning can cause stress between partners. One may be a morning person, the other not. One may snore or have a tendency toward body odor. One may feel hot and the other cold at the same temperature. Most couples negotiate such apparently minor vicissitudes well; others find them a major irritant.

Personality Functioning

Assessment of each partner's personality functioning involves, first, ruling out serious psychopathology, substance abuse, and interpersonal violence, matters to be discussed in Chapter 3. However, examining partners' *autonomous ego functioning* may be part of doing so. What ego psychologists and object relations theorists call the autonomous ego functions encompass people's capacities for perception, memory, thinking, reality testing, and judgment (Blanck and Blanck 1994). Some theorists include the ability to learn or accept new information (White 1963). Clinicians can evaluate whether the partners' perceptions of each other are generally realistic, even though these may be somewhat distorted by selective attention or by the misinterpretation of what a certain behavior or characteristic means. For example, one partner may accurately perceive the other as doing some housework but underestimate the amount or interpret it as indicating how little the other values their relationship. Each partner's ability to remember events should be reasonably sound. Both should be able to think clearly except when under stress, and reality testing and judgment should be adequate. Serious defects in any of these ego functions suggest possible psychopathology or physical pathology that should be further evaluated. Partners' capacities for new learning are extremely important to the work of couple treatment. Barring low intelligence, mental or physical problems, or inadequacies in the way clinicians present information, partners' reduced capacities to learn in treatment are likely to be caused by fears or strong emotions defended against by denial or avoidance.

Also important to assess in cases appropriate for couple treatment are how each partner copes with life in general, any dysfunctional cognitions each may hold, and how each handles key needs and feelings. If there are problems in these areas, a clinician can try to assess the reasons.

Looking at partners' *coping in general* involves making some evaluation of how each partner deals with all the areas of the environment and self identified in our assessment framework so far. Any notable problems can be evaluated first, to determine whether a given situation is so stressful that anyone would have trouble coping with it, especially if few supports or resources are available. Different coping styles between partners may be causing additional stress. For example, a lesbian partner may feel overwhelmed and temporarily immobilized by her former husband's initiating a suit to take her children away from her. She may not have support from her parental family, coworkers may not know her sexual orientation, and her mate may favor an aggressive legal response while she would prefer calm negotiation. As a second possibility, problems in coping may stem partly from an individual's not having adequate information or knowledge of what to do differently. Finally, partners sometimes encounter internal obstacles to better coping, such as strong feelings or fears, or there may be external obstacles, such as environmental systems resistant to change. The lesbian partner threatened with the loss of her children might not know, for example, what legal options might be available or how to get more support from friends. She would certainly be dealing with strong feelings and a possibly antagonistic legal system. If need be, one could consider whether internalized homophobia was part of the problem, making her have some doubts as to whether she was a good parent.

A clinician may at some point seek to evaluate partners' *cognitions* about self, the mate, or the external world that seem distorted. Cognitions pertaining to the self may be skewed in the direction of being too negative, as when a partner thinks, "I can't do anything right," or "People never like me." They can be too positive, as in, "I'm always right." Cognitions pertaining to the partner or the relationship can be especially dysfunctional when they involve negative attributions, assumptions, or expectancies, or unreasonable or divergent standards, as discussed in Chapter 1. All four partners in our two earlier case examples (John and Tina, Ron and Lynn) probably thought that their mates not doing what they wanted meant they did not love them very much. Further, John interpreted Tina's requests as "unreasonable demands" and, probably due to selective attention based on negative expectancies, perceived her as "constantly" nagging him. Both Ron and Lynn probably saw their own beliefs about how money should be managed as right and the other's as wrong, rather than seeing these as normal differences to be negotiated.

Finally, clinicians can assess partners' *handling of key needs and feelings* in the couple relationship and elsewhere. First, they may evaluate whether the partners' needs for affiliation, self-esteem, sexuality, and stimulation, or their feelings of anger or anxiety, seem excessive. A caveat here is always to judge these in the context of whether partners' affective responses seem out of proportion to environmental and relationship events and whether adequate opportunities for meeting needs and coping with feelings exist. Still unexplained or apparently excessive needs or feelings often have to do with partners' unresolved issues from childhood, to be discussed further below. The next question is how the partners are dealing with each need or feeling. Some coping may be healthy or at least functional, but some may involve defense mechanisms that are unnecessarily restrictive or destructive. In some instances a need or feeling seems to be mostly pent up or unmet. And again, partners may be in conflict simply because their ways of coping with needs and feelings do not mesh well. Lynn wanted to cope with her anger toward Ron's mother by arguing with her while Ron wanted Lynn to stuff her anger and ignore his mother, as he did.

Healthy coping with affiliative needs usually involves meeting them partly through interdependence and intimacy with the partner and partly in relating to children, extended families, friends, and others (Hill 1996, Stiver 1991). Being overly dependent on any one of these relationships may be less healthy. Or partners may repress their own affiliative needs and perhaps project them onto the mate or others, engaging in excessive caretaking or exaggerated independence. Partners may have normal self-esteem needs or excessive ones, the latter manifesting in constant efforts to receive admiration or approval. Healthy coping involves meeting self-esteem needs through feeling valued and competent in the couple relationship and in work, parenting, friendship, or other roles. In dysfunctional coping, underlying low self-esteem may be defended against by putting others down or self-aggrandizing. People may also defend against low self-esteem by doing too much for others or by allowing exploitation in order to preserve a self-image of being "good."

Healthy ways to meet sexual needs are through the partners' consensual sexual relationship, perhaps along with masturbation, fantasies, and erotic media. Dysfunctional ways are through seductiveness with children or peers, affairs, or forced sex with anyone. All people have some needs for stimulation or variety in their daily lives. An excessive need for simulation may defend against underlying emotional emptiness or other feelings the individual cannot face. Normal stimulation needs may be met constructively in a variety of relationships and productive or recreational activities. Dysfunctional ways to meet such needs include, among others, affairs, gambling, and any other activities that endanger the self or others.

One partner's anger may be judged excessive if it is consistently out of proportion to what the other has done, persists at a high level in spite of a clinician's interventions, or surfaces often in other relationships outside the couple. Healthy coping with anger includes appropriate assertiveness and expressions of anger proportional to the amount one has been hurt, frustrated, or otherwise transgressed against. Such mechanisms as engaging in exercise or sounding off to a sympathetic listener can also help at times. Dysfunctional coping common in couple partners includes stuffing anger until it bursts out in verbal attacks, being unassertive and internalizing anger into depression or self-blame, acting out anger by displacing it onto someone whose actions did not really provoke it, or projecting anger so that it is perceived as emanating from the partner or someone else. Sometimes internally directed anger shows up in somatic symptoms such as headaches. Partners may also deal with anger passively, simply by failing to finish tasks they have agreed to do. One highly destructive way a person may deal with anger is to physically or emotionally abuse the partner or their children, as will be discussed in Chapter 3.

Feelings of anxiety are inevitable in any human being at times. If excessive, such feelings manifest as fears and worries out of proportion to the real situations a partner faces. Partners deal with anxiety most functionally by recognizing it, trying to figure out the source, doing what can be done to effect change or, if needed, expressing the anxiety verbally and asking for support. Some means of coping may be relatively functional unless they cause distress for a mate who copes in a different way. These include such mechanisms as lengthy processing of an anxiety-producing event, joking or humor, getting away from the anxiety-producing situation for a while, exercise, or nonproblematic levels of substance use. Usually least functional are denial, actions such as dangerous risk-taking that may discharge tension, or overuse of alcohol or other substances.

Many destructive actions serve as dysfunctional means to cope with a variety of needs or feelings or with different ones than may be apparent. For example, having an affair can be a way to meet affiliative needs, temporarily raise self-esteem, and express anger more than to meet sexual needs. As noted in Chapter 1, direct expression of one need or feeling is sometimes mainly a way of coping with another. A partner who is anxious about closeness may push the other away by expressing anger.

When encountering a partner's problematic coping with needs or feelings, clinicians can again wonder about the reason. Sometimes it may be that too many stressful needs or feelings have arisen at the same time, as is likely when one partner first learns the other has had an affair. Another possibility is that a partner does not know how to cope with a given need or feeling more functionally. Finally, partners can encounter internal or external blocks to coping differently, as when childhood learning or a too fragile mate make it feel dangerous to express anger openly.

Sociocultural Influences

People's *race, ethnic identification, social class, and religion*, if any, have an enormous influence on their life experiences and worldviews, learned ways of thinking and coping, and beliefs about themselves and the world (Ibrahim and Schroeder 1990). Much of this influence is not in conscious awareness. Because *race* affects how others react to an individual throughout life, it can profoundly shape peoples' attitudes toward self and others (McGoldrick and Giordano 1996). In American society, many whites of European origin see themselves as the normative group and feel superior, hostile, or awkward around people of other races. African Americans, Latinos of color, Asian Americans, and Native Americans know that others often relate to them based on racial stereotypes rather than as unique individuals. People may hold negative, positive, or ambivalent perceptions of their own racial identity (Okun 1996).

Everyone, including couple partners and clinicians, is also influenced by a singular or mixed *ethnic background*. " 'Ethnicity' refers to a social grouping sharing national origin and linguistic and cultural traditions, with which members may or may not actively identify" (Kliman 1994, p. 29). Ethnic minorities constitute about 28 percent of the United States population. The largest group is African American, followed by Latinos, Asian Americans, and Native Americans (U.S. Bureau of the Census 1998). All of these groups are heterogeneous in terms of national or tribal origin, social class, and religion. De La Cancela (1991) makes the important point that the values of an ethnic minority group may reflect not only its national origin but also its treatment by the dominant culture. For example, Puerto Rican men's "machismo" has probably been heightened by the difficulty they experience in obtaining adequately paying jobs in the United States.

People vary considerably in the degree to which they experience a sense of ethnic identity, although some authors (McGoldrick and Giordano 1996) see a sense of belonging and historical continuity with one's ethnic origins as a basic human need. Having a strong ethnic identity is sometimes related to more recent immigration to the continental United States, and being less acculturated to the dominant culture's values and lifestyles. Those who place a strong value on family and community or who have experienced prejudice and discrimination, including not only people of African, Latino, Asian, and Native American backgrounds but also Arabs (Abudabbeh 1996), Poles (Folwarski and Marganoff 1996), and others, have often maintained a strong sense of ethnic identity. However, many people who move into the middle or upper classes begin to identify less with their original ethnic groups (McGoldrick and Giordano 1996).

Especially when people's ethnic identity is not strong, they tend not to recognize how many of their worldviews, including their values and preferred ways of coping, are shaped by their ethnic heritage (Giordano and McGoldrick 1996a). A couple in which the partners' ethnic backgrounds are different may argue about what is right to do in some situation with no idea that their ethnicities have influenced their beliefs. For example, a Greek American man may suggest borrowing money from his parents while his German American wife strongly disagrees because "a couple should stand on their own two feet." In the Ron and Lynn case, Ron's valuing of stoicism is a Polish trait (Folwarski and Marganoff 1996) while Lynn's expectation that he provide her with affection and support her against his mother may have been partially influenced by her French heritage (Langelier 1996). Many ethnically based beliefs about what is right or wrong and encouragement toward particular styles of coping persist for generations. I must look back four generations to trace my part-Scottish heritage, but I still know how to pinch a penny.

Important areas to assess regarding partners' ethnicities include their sense of ethnic identity, acculturation to mainstream values and lifestyles, and which ethnic worldviews and coping styles have been retained (McGoldrick and Giordano 1996, Okun 1996, Zuniga 1988). Beliefs and coping styles that may especially influence couple functioning are those pertaining to gender role expectations, place of the extended family in the couple's lives, ways of dealing with needs and feelings (Zuniga 1988), and the handling of children and money (Okun 1996). When partners have encountered stereotyping, prejudice, discrimination, or oppression based on race or ethnicity, clinicians should assess the nature of these experiences and the partners' ways of coping with them (McGoldrick and Giordano 1996).

Assessment should also attend to either or both partners' experiences and coping with *immigration* and *culturally related losses*. Immigrants from other countries and Puerto Rican Americans who move to and from the mainland (Garcia Preto 1996b) may have had to leave extended family members or even children far away. Such losses are all the more compelling in cultures in which the maintenance of family ties is highly important (Zavala-Martinez 1988). Also frequently lost with immigration are old friends, a feeling of "place," the familiar customs and artifacts of home, a former higher social or economic status, and a sense of security with one's ethnic identity (McGoldrick and Giordano 1996, Mirkin 1998). For recent immigrants, these losses must be processed while people deal with the stresses of coping in a new and often unfriendly land (Javed 1995). Some culturally related losses may be due to genocide (Mirkin 1998). Within the last few generations, Jews may have lost family members to the Holocaust, while Native Americans may have seen children forcibly taken away and socialized to ways of the dominant culture (Sutton and Broken Nose 1996). Other partners may have immigrated from South American, African, or Asian nations where large segments of the population, including nuclear or extended family members, have been eradicated. These experiences will affect the partners indirectly even if they happened in their parents' or grandparents' generations.

People of different *social classes* tend to vary in values, beliefs, and practices as much as people of different ethnicities, although the two are cross-cutting influences (Kliman 1994, Langston 1998). The best indicators of current social class are partners' job histories and educational levels (Perry-Jenkins and Folk 1994). The poor may include those "who hold mainstream values about work and education" but are unemployed as well as an "underclass . . . who make their livings illegally or otherwise on the fringes of society" (Kliman 1994, p. 28). Now also recognizable is a large group of the working poor, those families with one or more employed members who nevertheless live below the poverty line (Newman 1998). In general, blue-collar or low-paid service jobs and a high school education are associated with being working-class. People identified as middle class usually have at least some college and white-collar or professional jobs. Higher paid professional and corporate jobs, or not working because of family money, tend to be associated with being upper class. Often, however, the values and attitudes gained in people's childhood social class remain in spite of later academic or vocational achievements (Langston 1998). For example, working-class women, as compared to women whose background is middle class, may want but not expect much intimacy, communication, or help with household chores from their mates even when their incomes increase (Perry-Jenkins and Folk 1994). Perhaps as testimony to often hidden social-class influences, couple partners are less likely to be of different social classes than of different ethnicities (Falicov 1995), although Hines and Boyd-Franklin (1996) note that it is not unusual in African American couples for the wives to be more educated. When partners' social-class backgrounds differ, some conflicts about value and lifestyle preferences are almost sure to occur.

Religion is a highly significant influence on some people, a small or nonexistent one on others. Any *religious influences* tend to be intermingled with those of ethnicity and social class. In most studies, religion is not strongly related to marital happiness. However, religion is a significant source of support for some couples (Booth et al.

1995). One large study found religiosity to be associated with increased happiness for African American wives but not for their husbands or for white spouses (Veroff et al. 1993). Religious influences from childhood may be strong even though partners negligibly practice any formal religion. The person raised Catholic may still harbor guilt about using birth control or contemplating an abortion. Partners of different faiths or those who differ in how much they wish to practice their common religion may experience considerable conflict (Lehrer and Chiswick 1993), especially if their extended families or others close to them take sides. People often want to return to religion in conducting family ceremonies around marriage, birth, and death (Aradi 1988).

In contemplating all sociocultural influences on partners, clinicians must be constantly mindful of the impact their own race, ethnicity, social class, and religion have on themselves and on the way partners may view them. Assessment and intervention as influenced by clinicians' and partners' sociocultural characteristics are considered more fully in later chapters, especially Chapters 4 and 7.

Interwoven with the influences of sociocultural factors on partners are the influences of their unique life histories, especially their family-of-origin experiences. We turn now to contemplate these.

Earlier Life Experiences

Earlier life experiences include all that has happened to partners up to the present, including the couple's history. However, what are likely to be the most important historical influences on the partners' functioning as individuals are their *childhoods* or *family-of-origin experiences.*

First, these experiences may leave partners with excessive or otherwise problematic needs and feelings. Optimally, children need parent figures who provide reasonable and consistent love, security, expectations, and limitations. When partners describe their parents as never having had time for them, having been emotionally ungiving or the like, clinicians can guess that some of their affiliative or nurturance needs were unmet during childhood unless another environmental figure, such as an older sibling or grandparent, met them. These unmet needs may appear as excessive in adulthood, or partners may defend against experiencing them because doing so is too painful or frightening. Partners with critical parents or parents whose expectations were too high to meet may have needs for self-esteem that were not adequately fulfilled. Even when partners successfully met too high parental expectations or were given praise or nurturance for being very "good," they may need excessive reassurance as adults that they are lovable. This need may manifest as partners paying too high a price to insure self-esteem supplies, such as by being overly giving or always performing so as to be constantly admired.

Children also need stimulation and opportunities to be successfully assertive on their own behalf. If they receive too little of either, they may give up on these needs and function as adults with a passive attitude. Overstimulated, they may engage later in thrill-seeking behavior or other anxious acting out to re-create such hyperstimulated states. Encouraged to assert their needs without considering anyone else's, they may become domineering or selfish. Excessive anger in adulthood can often be traced to childhoods in which partners were given too little love or praise or received adults' unwarranted anger or sexual advances, leaving them with justifiable anger in response. Excessive sexuality may be an attempt to deal with affiliative needs, or with anger if sex is used to control or put down the other partner. Sometimes it reflects a childhood in which inappropriate sexual advances by an adult told a partner that being sexual was the only way he or she could be loved.

Family-of-origin experiences in which important needs were not consistently met or painful hurts occurred can also leave partners with significant later anxieties. These may especially pertain to what might happen to them in close adult relationships. Partners whose parents or other caretakers were inconsistently emotionally available or who suffered significant losses because of death or desertion can have strong fears of abandonment (Siegel 1992). Some who experienced rejection if they did not conform to parents' or caretakers' wishes carry later fears of the same response from others, especially intimate partners. Those who received unwarranted anger or sexual advances in childhood often fear that others, especially partners, will brutalize them in adulthood. Many of these fears are unconscious, but perhaps can become conscious in treatment. A partner's expectations or fears of the mate that come primarily from childhood experiences constitute transference toward the mate. The woman whose father was critical fears her husband will be critical or reads criticism into a comment he intended neutrally. A man whose mother was overbearing perceives his wife as controlling when she is not. A lesbian partner expects her mate to abandon her as she feels her mother did when a sibling was born.

Children also learn much from their family-of-origin experiences about how to cope with their needs and feelings. Some of what is learned usually comes from parents' and siblings' modeling (Gerson et al. 1993). Positive models, such as a father who derived appropriate self-esteem from his children's accomplishments, may stimulate emulation. Or more negatively, a man who complains that his father was an angry bully bullies his own wife and son. A woman who experienced her mother as critical finds herself critical toward her partner and children. Parents may have an influence as models even when partners purposely strive to be unlike them. Gerson and colleagues (1993) have used the concept of "reversal" to point out this possibility. A partner will say, "I was determined not to be critical toward my children like my mother was toward me." He or she may then be too lenient. Sadly, a negative model gives no instruction on how to carry out more appropriate coping. Partners who reverse into too much leniency toward children may finally turn to being critical because they do not know how else to limit the children's behavior.

Another way in which children learn how to cope with needs and feelings is from other family members' responses to their emerging coping efforts (Siegel 1992). They will have learned very young which expressions of needs and feelings were acceptable and which were not. Some parents smile and ask more about the anger of a 2-year-old, encouraging verbal expression. Others hit or shame the child. Continued interactions convey which means are acceptable for dealing with affiliative needs, sexuality, anger, and self-esteem. The family that permits an abused child to abuse a younger sibling has both modeled and encouraged violence as a means of handling anger. Another child learns to be very independent and repress affiliative needs because overworked parents reward this mode. One way whole families encourage certain coping strategies is by meeting more of children's affiliative or self-esteem needs when they fit into a given family role (Gerson et al. 1993, Siegel 1992). A child who gains family approval by caretaking may later expect to have self-esteem and affiliative needs met primarily by caretaking the mate or their children.

Partly in their families of origin, children also learn how to cope with their physical selves, nonfamily members, and other aspects of the world at large. In addition, they pick up beliefs and standards about how people should conduct their lives. Parents or other caretakers may model hypochondriacal preoccupation or denial as ways to cope with bodily concerns. Children given love in the form of food may learn to equate physical with emotional nurturance. Families distrustful of outsiders implicitly convey that peers cannot be trusted. Parents who denigrate gay, lesbian, and bisexual people may create great shame in a child who realizes at some point that he or she is same-sex oriented. Family beliefs encompass everything from whether a big fuss should be made about birthdays to how important it is to respect children's sexual boundaries. As with sociocultural learning, which is delivered mainly by families (McGoldrick and Giordano 1996), partners' own families' beliefs usually feel like the "right" way to do things. One partner who does not make a big fuss about the other's birthday when birthdays were important in the other's family of origin is likely to be perceived as uncaring or worse.

Finally, *experiences outside the family in childhood and up to the present* influence all of partners' coping and beliefs. Children who achieve at school, work, or sports may learn to gain self-esteem through these means. A partner whose parental family moved around a lot or immigrated to the United States may have later sensitivity to separation and loss even though the family always remained intact. One man known to me dealt with feelings related to his family's frequent moves in childhood by periodically giving away the couple's dogs, causing his wife great consternation and anger. Someone whose first marriage ended in divorce because of a spouse's affair is likely to be more suspicious of the next partner. An individual's history of job functioning, experiences with extended family in adulthood, dealings with the couple's children, physical and psychological health, and any other significant events prior to the present will always affect his or her functioning.

THE COUPLE

While couples are profoundly affected by their environments and each partner's individual functioning, the couple as a system is also influenced by its own history, stage of development, the partners' communication, and interaction patterns that may or may not allow intimacy. In the Ron and Lynn case, the couple's history of having "had to" get married almost surely made both question their true commitment to each other. Their interaction had fallen into the pattern of Lynn emoting and Ron withdrawing, or both participating in escalating arguments. This couple's many communication problems and the work that was done with them in treatment are detailed in Chapter 5.

Couples' possibly dysfunctional communication, problem solving, and interaction patterns are significant in almost every case.

> Jan and Mike, both ethnically mixed European American, middle class, and in their early thirties had a sole presenting complaint. For the past year or so, Mike had been making mean remarks to Jan, mainly when the children were not orderly when he came home from work. Their children were 5, 3, and 18 months. Mike was an accountant, Jan worked part-time, and both took care of the children when Mike got home. Jan thought Mike was unreasonable to expect order with the children so young. Mike was sorry he was mean but said he was always exhausted and tense between work and home. These partners were bright, competent, and otherwise loving with each other. However, their inability to resolve this issue and sometimes others was beginning to interfere with their feelings of intimacy.

Jan and Mike's difficulties stemmed partly from the very real stress of dealing with three young children and Mike's demanding job. They were trying to manage the difficult developmental stage in which a couple functions as parents without having mastered necessary earlier learning about how to negotiate and resolve problems together. As more information became known, it also turned out that Mike, an only child, got much more nervous than Jan around the children's noise and high activity level. There may even have been a constitutional difference in his level of reactivity. However, a large part of their difficulties stemmed from the way they had tried to solve this problem. Jan kept pushing her solution, that "Mike had to accept that kids will be kids." Mike kept pushing his, that Jan should keep better order when he first got home. Both would begin to criticize and blame the other, and Mike would finally say something really mean. Other decisions or problems were approached in the same way, with each partner pushing his or her preferred solution and rejecting the one preferred by the other. Then their communication would deteriorate into blaming or criticism.

When a couple shows communication and problem-solving difficulties, clinicians must examine these to delineate specific strengths and deficits. A further question is to what extent any difficulties may be caused simply by the partners' not knowing what to do differently. It turned out that Mike was not used to thinking about and verbalizing his needs, a necessary communication skill. Jan tended to respond to his upset about the children's noise with blaming or critical comments or by trying to talk him out of his feelings. Mike would get angry and mean in response. The degree to which a lack of knowledge about how to change is causing such problems can be determined only by the clinician trying to provide new information, in ways discussed in later chapters, and observing the response. A further possibility, of course, is that couples are having trouble communicating or problem solving in given areas because of dysfunctional cognitions, strong feelings, or intimacy fears.

Clinicians must always consider how a couple's history and stage of development, communication and problem solving, interaction patterns, and efforts to deal with intimacy may be influencing them.

Couple History and Stage of Development

Any couple's history begins with the pair's first meeting. Almost always, partners experience the way they met and their early dating in positive terms. Often there were humorous events. Positive attributes and feelings drew them together. After a shorter or longer time the relationship became exclusive. Others began to perceive them as a dyad. They fell in love. This first stage in the couple's history and development may be called the stage of *becoming a couple*. It has also been called "the honeymoon phase" because partners often do not see any negatives or brush them aside (Kovacs 1994). This stage may push partners who have not yet resolved their gay male, lesbian, or bisexual identities to do so if the relationship is their first serious same-sex one (Okun 1996).

Couples who stay together at some point usually move to a second stage, the stage of *commitment* to each other. For some, the commitment is demonstrated via legal marriage or a public ceremony for same-sex couples. For others, a formal engagement provides a testing period during which commitment is anticipated but not definite. Other couples still more tentatively commit, perhaps only to continued exclusivity although they may be living together (Nock 1995). The commitment stage is important because it is here that a couple must establish an identity of "we-ness," defining a stronger boundary around itself and separating from parental families or the ghosts of past intimate relationships (Wallerstein 1994). Yet each partner must maintain an individual boundary and autonomy in meeting some needs with others as well. When compared with white couples in one major study, African American couples' early marital happiness was less tied to developing a sense of "we-ness" and more to maintaining individual autonomy (Veroff et al. 1995) and close but not intrusive extended family ties (Timmer and Veroff 1996). For some couples, this stage is complicated by the presence of children from earlier relationships. Same-sex couples who have not received family validation or who do not wish to have a public ceremony may feel uncertain at times about the security of their commitment. Couples who have difficulty making a commitment may seek treatment to determine what is holding them back or whether they should stay together.

A third stage, often overlapping with and sometimes preceding the second, can be called the stage of *upset and compromise*. Inevitably at some point, partners realize that they do not always agree and may have to modify their behavior. The shock this discovery brings reflects the naïveté with which many couples approach the task of establishing a relationship (Hof 1995). They usually try to resolve their differences amicably. Some manage to work out adequate communication and problem-solving strategies in this crucial developmental stage. Indeed, research suggests that successful relationships depend not on a lack of conflict, but on couples developing ways to resolve it (Kovacs 1997). When they cannot, normal and well-intentioned partners may fall into dysfunctional communication patterns, as Jan and Mike did. In treatment, many couples trace the beginning of their problems to what turns out to be the upset and compromise stage.

The fourth couple stage consists, if the couple is lucky, of both *intimacy and productivity*. Partners who have learned to manage conflict in their day-to-day functioning together may be able to enjoy secure closeness, unless intimacy fears and defenses against them interfere. Whether or not consistent intimacy is achieved, most partners carry on as productive adults through some combination of work, caring for children, and other creative or valued activities. In a good relationship, the couple negotiates to manage the new stresses these activities entail and to protect their relationship, including their sex lives, from being too diminished by them (Wallerstein 1996). Such productivity then enriches their lives by providing stimulation and self-esteem the partners can share. In a troubled relationship, the partners' immersion in work, child-care, or the like may both lead to and divert them from a lack of fulfillment with each other. Attention to these other activities may then become excessive. Some couples, like Jan and Mike, seek treatment at this stage because they are still not communicating well or miss the intimacy they had hoped to achieve.

Midlife and *old age* define couple as well as individual life-cycle stages. Those who form new couple relationships during these years, perhaps after being widowed or divorced, will have to cope with earlier couple developmental stages at the same time. At midlife, roughly ages 45 to 60, partners may be facing a diminution of work satisfaction and child-care responsibilities. If so, they are likely to look to each other for increased stimulation and gratification. Partners may also struggle with the wish to make midlife changes or with obligations to elderly parents that may upset the couple's balance (Anderson et al. 1995). If communication is poor or intimacy needs are unfulfilled, the midlife couple may seek treatment or break up (Kovacs 1994). At older ages, couples may find their ability to resolve problems together overwhelmed or at least stretched near the breaking point by new stresses, perhaps engendered by health problems or retirement (Sachs 1995). Successful relationships in the later years may rely on partners' abilities to hold onto their early idealization of each other and the relationship while still dealing with the new realities of their life together (Wallerstein 1996).

Of course, any couple's history is marked by unique events and fluctuations in how the couple gets along. Major illnesses, periods of substance abuse, the birth of children, job changes, moves, or illness and death in the extended family can cause ups and downs in the couple relationship. There may be affairs or separations. Some couples describe their problems as persisting almost from the start of their relationship or from the upset and compromise stage. Others trace their difficulties to a time of special stress or even a presumably positive change, such as one partner's job promotion. Any noticeable congruence between fluctuations in a couple's relationship and external events or partners' health may be highly important in understanding reasons for a couple's problems, as was illustrated earlier in the John and Tina case. Positive experiences in the couple relationship may also help partners overcome fears or dysfunctional learning from childhood, reducing the impact of these (Wallerstein 1996).

Communication and Problem Solving

Most people do not learn effective communication and problem-solving skills in their families of origin. To communicate constructively, people first must be aware of what they need and feel (Sayers et al. 1993). They must be inclined and able to constructively present needs, feelings, alternatives, and preferences to their partners and to hear and understand what the partners say. They must be able to balance reason and emotion in finding mutually compatible solutions to problems. Effective communication and problem solving also imply a willingness to share power at least somewhat equitably (Kovacs 1994). Sometimes one or both partners' strong negative feelings or distorted cognitions get in the way. Most couples who experience poor communication and problem solving are frustrated with their relationship and may, without help, be on the road to breaking up (Kurdek 1995). Studies have consistently found spouses' marital satisfaction to be positively related to the frequency with which each uses constructive conflict resolution strategies, such as compromise and humor, and negatively related to how much each responds to conflict with withdrawal, defensiveness, or the like.

Couples often present for treatment saying they are having trouble communicating or solving problems together. If so, they are usually right. Some couples describe instead that they "argue about everything" or about specific issues such as money, in-laws, disciplining children, or sex. As a third possibility, couples identify either or both partners as too critical, controlling, stubborn, or the like. In these instances too, some or all of the reason for identified problems may be ineffective communication. Even when couples cite intimacy problems or dysfunctional patterns such as one pursuing and the other distancing as their main reasons for seeking help, they are likely to have troubles with communication or problem solving that are contributing to these.

Perhaps the most common communication problem seen in treatment sessions or reported by couples is the use of words that blame or criticize the partner. *Blaming* may be direct ("you did . . ." or "didn't . . ."). It may take the form of character assassination ("stupid," "lazy," "controlling"), generalizing about the other ("you always . . ." or "you never . . ."), or red-flag words conveying implicit blame ("your excuse is . . ."). The partner's natural response is to blame in return. A more subtle form of blame is to punctuate a sequence of events such that one's own negative behavior is seen as a response to the partner's having done something negative first (Watzlawick et al. 1967). For example, "I only nag because you never pay any attention to me." While highly destructive, blaming or criticizing is not usually the way most couples' poor communication started. It is more often the result of months or years of trying to talk with each other more constructively and still not being able to find ways to resolve mutual issues. Each partner usually has become more frustrated and angry over time, feeling that he or she is trying hard yet positive outcomes are not being achieved. The person at fault therefore must be the other partner.

A more likely original and continuing difficulty is that in trying to settle differences, *partners each push their own solutions*. They usually do so without clearly understanding the other's needs and concerns. We saw this happening in the Jan and Mike case. In fact, this communication problem is far more widespread than most clinicians recognize. Every individual faces numerous situations on a daily basis in which he or she must take action. Perfectly normally, people evaluate such situations and make instant decisions about what to do. They do not usually think through each step in a logical problem-solving process. For example, let us say that someone's dog is whining. The owner rapidly and without conscious thought moves through consideration of: (1) What is the problem? "The dog is whining." (2) What additional facts are important to understand? "He wants to go out and I'm the only one here." (3) What are the possible solutions? "Take him out now or let him wet the rug." (4) What should I do? "I'll take him out now." A perception that the dog is whining leads instantly to a decision, "I'll take him out now."

Unfortunately, when one partner in a couple encounters a situation in which action needs to be taken, he or she tends to go through the same instantaneous process even if the situation or solution affects the other partner. The partner whose needs or preferences are not taken into account then feels angry, hurt, or controlled. For example, a woman who feels bored and lonely when her husband goes bowling with his friends may say, "You've got to give up bowling." This solution is one that may work for her but not for him. If he refuses, she may feel angry and unloved. Or he may offer his own solution to what he thinks the problem is, saying something like, "If you spent less on clothes, you wouldn't need to make me feel guilty about spending money on something I like." Neither has clearly identified what the real problem is: the woman's loneliness. Neither has tried to find a solution that might work for both. Each may call the other selfish, and a blaming cycle begins.

In such situations, partners may exhibit other well-intentioned but dysfunctional responses. For example, one partner may stuff feelings and go along with what the other wants at too high a cost to the self. Although such noble responses can work in some instances, they are not constructive on a regular basis even if both partners give in equally. The problem is that at each decision point one partner's needs and wishes are being stifled rather than true accord being reached. Sometimes partners even give in, at great cost to themselves, to do something actually minimally important to their mates. For example, people sometimes sacrifice a great deal to keep the house neat and clean or work long hours to bring home more income when their partners scarcely care about such "gifts." When recipients do not much appreciate these efforts, resentment grows.

Couples may show *other communication problems* that are not destructive on an occasional basis but that can significantly impede or even prevent problem resolution if they happen often. These include interrupting, mind reading, not listening carefully, not reflecting that one has understood, topic jumping, and rehashing the past rather than focusing on solving problems in the present and future. Chapter 5 reviews many such common difficulties couples have with communication and problem solving and gives detailed suggestions about how clinicians can help.

As an additional influence, partners' negative feelings sometimes block constructive problem solving. Such feelings may be a relatively minor but still pressing response to recent circumstances, such as when partners angry about having their needs disregarded must ventilate the anger and have it acknowledged before problem solving can occur. Sometimes a feeling is more intense and pervasive, for instance, anger at having been the recipient of long-term verbal abuse, or guilt about having had an affair. Some feelings may be stronger than warranted by events in the couple relationship because an earlier difficult feeling, perhaps from childhood, has been evoked. For example, a man who felt his mother never cared about him may be very reactive to his partner's occasional lapses of attention, such that he abandons all efforts to problem solve when these occur.

Also likely to interfere with constructive communication or problem solving can be either partner's distorted or inaccurate cognitions, as discussed earlier. Some of these can be the result of transference to the mate. One partner may be thinking, "He'll never find me lovable," or "She'll abandon me sooner or later." Less catastrophic inaccurate cognitions, such as the idea that "His watching the football game means he doesn't care about spending time with me," still tend to block good communication, partly because of the negative feelings they evoke. Partners may proceed based on believing things about the self, the mate, or the relationship that are not valid and may fail to check out these assumptions. They therefore end up feeling hurt, angry, or hopeless about the possibility that their problems can be solved.

Interaction Patterns

It is in the nature of human beings that much of their thinking and behavior becomes habitual. As discussed in Chapter 1, it is in the nature of couple systems that interaction patterns develop and tend to persist. When one partner criticizes, the other withdraws or criticizes in return. When one partner emotes, the other becomes more logical. When one jokes in response to talk about anxiety-producing topics, the other feels more anxious and tries to talk about the topics more. And so on. Of course, constructive patterns can also develop. When one partner emotes, the other may offer support. Unfortunately, couples who come for treatment are far more likely to be experiencing dysfunctional patterns. Partners may even describe themselves as "stuck" in such patterns, which they cannot seem to modify.

Some such patterns have begun because partners did not know how to communicate constructively about their differences. The example of mutual blaming has been suggested above. Nonetheless, once such a pattern has developed, it tends to be self-perpetuating. While any persistent pattern is likely to serve some function for the couple, many also preclude better coping. A mutual blaming pattern serves the function of discharging the partners' anger and is an attempt by each to salvage self-esteem. But it stimulates more anger and repeatedly jeopardizes self-esteem without allowing the pair to solve the problems they started fighting about.

Some interaction patterns seem to be developed as a way for partners to try to meet needs without arousing too many childhood fears. As an example, a man constricted and fearful of his own emotions marries a woman who is emotional. The partners were perhaps attracted to each other originally when she saw him as helping her feel more secure and he enjoyed her spontaneity, which seemed to give him a capacity to feel. She now complains of his rigidity and he describes her as hysterical. The wife may have hoped her husband would meet her affiliative and self-esteem needs without being critical and controlling like her father was. The husband may have hoped his wife would be able to give to him like his mother did but without his mother's frightening losses of control. Both perceive, rightly or wrongly, that their worst fears have been realized. One can also hypothesize the husband's projecting his own emotions onto his wife and her projecting her need for structure and security onto him, with each now rejecting in the other the unwanted qualities projected from the self.

However, as communication theory suggests, escalations tend to develop naturally within systems, leading to patterns that become more and more extreme. While a particular pattern may meet partners' psychological needs or serve defensive functions, it may also have become more pronounced over time simply because, when one partner's part of the pattern has occurred, it has triggered the other's automatic response in a slightly more exaggerated way. Because the husband in the above example is a little more rigid, the wife becomes a little more angry and emotional. Because she has become a little more emotional, he becomes a little more rigid. By the time the couple comes for treatment, the pattern may have become more extreme than either partner psychologically "needed" it to be. This notion is especially important because it implies that deep-seated intrapsychic conflicts are not always present and do not always need to be resolved before pattern change can happen. A sufficient treatment goal may be simply to interrupt such patterns and help couples deal with each other's needs and differences in more functional ways.

Dysfunctional couple interaction patterns often follow one of three general configurations. Probably the most common is that of *opposite styles*. Here partners each act in a different and often opposite way in a given arena of their life together. If the pattern has become more extreme, each carries out his or her part in a more and more exaggerated way over time. One emotes and the other constricts, as just discussed. One talks a lot and the other tunes out. One pursues and the other distances. One takes over more and more responsibility while the other becomes more passive. One becomes stricter with the children as the other becomes more lenient. One wants to save money, the other spends more freely. Often, of course, several interrelated patterns coexist. The partner who wants to talk more also wants to spend more time together while the other partner tunes out more and wants to spend less. If the distancer does come home, the pursuer is so full of pent-up talk, possibly blaming talk, that the distancer feels it necessary to stay away again.

Another common pattern, which may coexist with the first but usually in different arenas, is that of *parallel or competing styles*. In these escalations, partners each do more or less the same thing and again tend to spur each other on to more extreme behavior. Both blame, argue, or otherwise push to be one-up in having their own point of view prevail (Gray-Little et al. 1996). Both make decisions without consulting each other. Both spend too much money, drink too much, or have affairs. Parallel or competing styles can quickly bring couples to extreme actions, including a breakup, because the partners are both in a very real sense going more and more out of control. However, some couples who get into these patterns manage to find ways to de-escalate, such as by going through periods of emotional withdrawal, temporary agreements on budgetary constraint, or emotional closeness that happens only after fighting.

A third common interaction pattern, borrowing from Bowen's family systems model (Papero 1995), is *triangling* one or more other parties into the couple interaction. Again, ethnicity must be taken into account before determining whether a partner's doing so may be dysfunctional. Most often those triangled in are the couple's children, but they can be in-laws, friends, jobs, affair partners, or even pets

(Basham 1992). Triangling works because need-meeting can take place with whomever is triangled in when partners are not getting needs adequately met with each other or when tension arises between them for any reason. The external need-meeting is thereby reinforced as a coping method. Patterns involving triangling tend to be self-perpetuating because they serve a function not only for the partner involved but also, often, for the person triangled in. A child gains attention from being one parent's favorite even if the other parent resents their closeness and withdraws.

Some of the most complex interaction patterns clinicians may see are shown by narcissistically vulnerable couples (Lansky 1981). These partners often take opposite stands on issues or have opposite styles. However, most blatant are their parallel styles, often shown by extreme mutual emotionality and chaotic fighting balanced by intense but very temporary periods of closeness. At these different times, the mates tend alternately to devalue and idealize each other. Their children, affair partners, or others are often triangled in as well. In other narcissistically vulnerable patterns, one mate may be more prone to engage in the behaviors just described while the other functions in a less extreme manner. All of these patterns are presumably fueled by the partners' intrapsychic conflicts from childhood played out in the couple relationship, as will be elaborated in Chapter 8.

In many cases, it can be difficult to determine what is maintaining a couple's interaction patterns and how hard it will be to change them until clinicians try intervening. Patterns that exist mainly because the couple does not know how to communicate or problem solve more effectively are likely to be more open to change than those serving partners' deep-seated psychological needs, especially if the couple turns out to be narcissistically vulnerable. However, almost all long-standing patterns will show some resistance to change. When triangling occurs, the outside party's possible investment in the status quo must also be considered.

Intimacy and Its Vicissitudes

A number of couples present for treatment complaining of lack of intimacy or closeness. Occasionally this is the sole presenting problem. More often it is one among several, or is named after more pressing problems have been addressed. In such cases clinicians must seek to learn exactly what the couple means by "intimacy" and must assess what stands in its way. Doing so is not necessarily as simple as it sounds. Partners may say they want to feel closer but may not really have thought out how such a feeling could come about. As noted in Chapter 1, couples who have achieved intimacy are probably meeting needs for sexuality and many affiliative needs with each other, as well as some needs for self-esteem and stimulation. But how does such need-meeting occur? While partners must reach their own conclusions, Kersten and Himle (1990) suggest that for most, intimacy needs can be met in four major ways. These are *mutual self-disclosure, emotional support, sensual-physical contact, and companionship*. Self-disclosure should include sharing feelings as well as recounting day-to-day experiences, thoughts, opinions, and so on. Emotional support has to do with partners offering each other nonjudgmental acceptance and empathy when either is having a hard time. It may also involve one partner affirming the other's strengths and self-esteem. Sensual or physical contact includes affectionate touching as well as overtly sexual activities. Companionship means enjoying doing things together. Couples who self-disclose and enjoy doing things together often describe their partners as their "best friends" (Wallerstein 1994), and some studies have found self-disclosure the variable most often correlated with spouses' feelings of intimacy (Weeks 1995a). Research has shown partners' making positive or caring comments to each other also to be associated with marital satisfaction (Veroff et al. 1995) and most likely intimacy. Finally, intimacy is not unrelated to the achievement of communication and problem-solving skills. Finding that they can share information, listen to each other, and compromise fairly and sometimes generously to meet the needs of both helps partners establish an atmosphere of trust (Karpel 1994). Such trust serves as a foundation to support the other building blocks of intimacy.

Sometimes, part of what stands in the way of intimacy is that one or both partners do not understand what they need to do to achieve it. That is, they have not realized how important it may be to share thoughts and feelings, give support, provide physical affection and affirmation of love, or find time for companionship. Another possibility is that one or both feel uncomfortable trying an activity that might promote intimacy because they believe they do not know how to do it well. Many men, for example, feel they are not good at self-disclosure or that they do not know what to say to give emotional support (Stiver 1991). Sometimes these self-perceptions are accurate. If the partners' lack of knowledge about what to do or discomfort about lack of skills to do it are mainly what is preventing intimacy, such knowledge and skills can be learned in treatment (Kersten and Himle 1990).

Often, however, *blocks to intimacy* do not stem primarily from a lack of such knowledge or skills. Negative emotions, especially hurt, anger, and fears, may also prevent or stifle intimacy. Perhaps the most common sources of such negative emotions in a couple relationship are the old bugaboos: dysfunctional communication, inaccurate cognitions, or problematic interaction patterns. These immensely frustrate couples and almost always lead both partners to feel they are not being treated fairly, their mates are mean or uncaring, they are trying harder than their mates, or the like. Of course, partners do not feel like self-disclosing, offering emotional support, or saying how much they care when mutual blaming or other dysfunctional patterns are going on. The resultant hurt and anger also inhibit affection and the desire for sexual contact, especially in women (Stiver 1991). Even companionship can become uncomfortable when partners feel hurt or mad at each other. When intimacy activities decrease because of negative emotions, a vicious cycle begins because partners may feel more negatively about having been denied these activities.

Intentional actions of one partner that cause significant hurt, anger, or sadness for the other justifiably preclude intimacy. If the actions are still occurring, the rift cannot begin to heal until they cease. Examples include physical or verbal abuse, forced sex, substance abuse that has caused significant problems for the partner, and affairs. Even when such activities have stopped, the healing period may be extensive. It may be complicated as well by the offending partner's guilt. Later chapters consider such situations further. Partners sometimes feel significant hurt, sadness, or anger that have varied and less obvious sources. These feelings may range in severity but still preclude intimacy unless resolved. As an example, a man harbors hidden anger because his wife delayed childbearing to establish her career and then had fertility problems that could not be successfully treated. He might feel saddened by the loss of parenthood and blame her for it.

Major fears of intimacy can also spring from a number of sources. Past hurts or disappointments in the couple relationship tend to create fears of trusting or being vulnerable again. There may be fears that some form of abuse or an affair will recur, that arguing will again happen to disrupt closeness, or that one partner will again withdraw just when the other needs him or her the most. Anger, hurt, and fear of trusting coexist in many of these instances. Sometimes, hurts or disappointments suffered with earlier partners cause fears of intimacy with the current one. The partner who has had two earlier marriages end in divorce may have trouble risking closeness in a third out of fear of the same thing happening again.

Most commonly, at least some fears of intimacy come from the partners' having experienced in childhood that closeness can be dangerous (Weeks 1995a). As discussed earlier, these often unconscious fears can lead to adult behaviors or character patterns designed to keep closeness at bay. Couples' problems with intimacy are explored further in later chapters, especially Chapters 6, 7, and 8.

Based on their assessment of why couples' problems may exist, clinicians will be ready to present some of their ideas to the partners and negotiate treatment goals. It is always important that the clinician also see and explicitly identify strengths. These uses of assessment hypotheses will be discussed in detail in Chapter 4. First, let us examine a number of special issues that may surface during the assessment or treatment process and their influence on the way a case should proceed.

CHAPTER 3

Deciding When to See Couples

Whenever they learn that couples are having trouble getting along, not handling problems well together, or feeling unhappy with their relationship, clinicians can consider whether couple treatment might be indicated. The issue can arise in a potential client's telephone call or initial individual interview. A referral source may bring up a possible case. Clients being seen in some other form of treatment may reveal couple difficulties. Many couples ask to come in together, and some are required to do so by an agency or court. The existence of problems in the couple relationship is not a sufficient reason to recommend couple treatment, however. Clinicians may need to proceed in some other way if possible contraindications to couple work exist.

This chapter begins by reviewing situations in which couple work is usually indicated, whether alone or in combination with some other form of treatment. Ways to deal with confidentiality when one partner reveals information without the other present are briefly considered. Subsequent discussion focuses on how to assess special factors that may contraindicate couple treatment, or at least require clinicians to proceed cautiously. It is most important to consider evidence of possible physical or emotional abuse, substance abuse, or untreated psychopathology, any of which may require individual evaluation. Other situations in which couple treatment may or may not turn out to be indicated occur when a partner is suffering from a sexual dysfunction, having an undisclosed affair, or uncertain about wanting to save the couple relationship.

INDICATIONS FOR COUPLE TREATMENT

Many couples themselves initiate the idea of conjoint treatment. The possibility may also arise in other circumstances, most often when the partners have been coming for family sessions or when one partner has sought individual help. In all these situations, clinicians must consider the options carefully before deciding how to proceed.

Recommending Couple Work

Partners often ask for conjoint treatment for the stated reason that they are experiencing difficulties in their relationship. They may conceptualize these as trouble communicating, trouble handling certain problems together, disagreeing or arguing a lot, not feeling satisfied, not feeling close, not having a good sexual relationship, and so on. In general, barring any of the contraindications for couple work to be given below, couples who want to work on improving their relationship should be seen together (Bakely 1996). Even if one partner wants couple treatment and the other is uncertain or resistant, couples with no contraindications should usually be encouraged to come in together initially if it is at all possible.

Clinicians may believe couple treatment could be useful in some circumstances where partners are uncertain or do not ask for it. One of these can occur when children's problems seem to be adversely affected by their parents' or other caretakers' couple relationship. Perhaps family treatment has been undertaken and the need for couple work becomes apparent as it proceeds (Karpel 1994). The couple may persist in disagreeing about discipline, continue to form unhealthy alliances with children, or often fight in front of the children. Couple sessions may then be suggested to work on coparenting skills or other problems the partners have acknowledged in their relationship. If the partners agree, a new contract must be negotiated for the couple work. This possibility is reviewed as part of the discussion of initial couple sessions in Chapter 4. A combination of couple and family treatment may be offered, with the need for family work likely to decrease if the couple relationship improves. A more difficult situation, also to be considered in Chapter 4, occurs when parents have been required to undergo couple treatment against their wishes.

Another time clinicians may initiate the idea of couple work is when one partner seeks treatment or is already in treatment for distress that may be caused mostly by couple problems, may indicate both individual and couple problems, or may reflect a primarily individual problem but one not helped by the mate's response. Research clearly indicates that couple relationship quality affects both men's and women's levels of personal distress (Barnett et al. 1994). The clinician's ability to assess individual and couple functioning and circumstances, as discussed in Chapter 2, can assist in making an evaluation. Clinicians receiving an initial call or meeting with individuals who are in a couple relationship should routinely think about whether the couple might be seen (Karpel 1994). It is usually easier to begin with a couple and switch later to individual appointments or a combination of individual and couple appointments, if needed, than to begin with an individual and then try to get the partner in.

For example, a woman might call to say she has been feeling "down" in the past few months since her husband seemed to be withdrawing from her. While the clinician should inquire to make sure the woman's depression was not severe, it could be caused mainly by her marital distress and couple treatment might be appropriate. At least further questions could be asked and the possibility of an initial couple session raised to evaluate the situation further. As another example, a partner who calls or comes in for an initial individual session might allude to relationship issues by saying, "I get anxious when my husband is late coming home" or "I don't know how to handle my wife's family." The question would then be whether the anxiety in the first instance or the uncertainty in the second were primarily happening in response to couple problems. If problems in a couple relationship seem to be the major reason for an individual's distress, a couple session may be suggested unless there are contraindications.

Another possibility is that one partner has problems influenced both by the couple interaction and by his or her own biochemistry or individual issues. A partner's moderate depression or anxiety is often influenced partly by individual biological or psychological vulnerabilities and partly by couple difficulties. Seeing the couple together might reveal that the mate had some problematic symptoms or character traits as well (Karpel 1994). Or the two might have gotten into increasingly dysfunctional patterns as the couple failed to cope well with one partner's symptoms and the symptoms worsened in response (Prince and Jacobson 1995, Sayers et al. 1993). Here, treatment for both the individual and the couple might be indicated, or the couple might be treated first to see if amelioration of its dysfunction might sufficiently help the individual. There is research evidence that couple work is helpful in treating mood disorders (Beach et al. 1994, Prince and Jacobson 1995) and some anxiety disorders (Craske and Zoellner 1995, Sayers et al. 1993). Partners' wishes, the severity of the individual's disorder, and the apparent openness of the couple to change in treatment would be deciding factors (Karpel 1994). This type of case is further discussed in Chapter 9.

Perhaps most commonly encountered in general clinical practice are situations in which an individual who seeks help for personal distress also has relationship problems, as in the McKinney case.

> Joan McKinney, age 27, was seen for an initial interview after having called to ask for treatment for mild depression. She was struggling because the same pattern that had happened to her many times before was happening with her current boyfriend, Allen, and with some women friends. Joan would always hope others could see how much effort she had already put into doing what they wanted and would not ask her to do more. When they continued to expect her to do too much, she would comply but at the same time withdraw emotionally. Sometimes, when pushed too far, she would blow up or break down and cry, especially with Allen. Allen would then comment bitingly on her temper or lack of self-confidence. He did not put her down at other times.

The information learned so far should lead the clinician to consider the possibility of some couple work rather than solely individual help for Joan. Joan's pattern of not communicating clearly with others about her needs and limitations was probably contributing to her depression. These problems seemed her own in that they were longstanding and not just occurring with Allen. Although Allen was also a negative influence because he did not respond well when she got upset, one cannot simply assume he was an undesirable partner. He probably did not know how to react more constructively and might be a poor communicator himself. Even a supportive response on his part might not have helped if it simply reinforced Joan's pattern of feeling powerless. After further exploration in the initial interview, the clinician might have discussed the option of conjoint treatment if Joan wanted to improve her relationship with Allen and Allen was willing to come in, probably along with individual sessions to help Joan with her own issues. Joan could then make the final decision. In the actual case, only individual treatment was recommended and Joan and Allen soon broke up.

> A few months later, Joan became heavily involved with Mark. Although she experienced him as very nice, their relationship initially developed some problems similar to those that had happened with Allen. Over time, however, Joan became more assertive as a result of her individual work. Mark responded by saying she had turned from a dishrag into a tiger and he wondered where her "attempts to dominate him" would stop. Their relationship became shaky, and Joan was distressed because she loved Mark and had hoped that they would eventually marry. At this point, the clinician suggested adjunct couple sessions and Joan readily agreed. Mark turned out to have difficulty with assertiveness himself because he had had a domineering mother. But he and Joan were both willing to work on communication skills in an effort to ameliorate their relationship.

Even if an individual requiring or already undergoing his or her own treatment reveals negative couple influences, as with Joan and Mark, adjunct couple work may be considered (Karpel 1994). When a partner responds poorly to changes an individual client makes, clinicians too often assume that the relationship should end. Perhaps this conclusion is warranted when such partners show evidence of negative character traits not likely to yield to intervention. If they do not, and the individual client wishes to continue the relationship, couple work can be suggested unless there are other contraindications. Both partners may be able to make positive changes and grow. The mate who has not been in treatment may at least become more supportive of the one who has.

Issues in Moving to Couple Work

If partners seen individually might benefit from couple work, clinicians should thoroughly discuss with them why it might be desirable and what is likely to happen there (Karpel 1994). They may even help such partners decide how to suggest couple sessions to their mates in a nonblaming way. However, many clinicians prefer not to see the couple themselves when they have already been treating one partner (Siegel 1992, Weeks and Treat 1992). Doing so is rarely feasible if the partner already in treatment has a strong transference relationship with the clinician or shows any borderline or narcissistic features. In other cases, there are pros and cons. Advantages include the clinician's established relationship with one mate, significant understanding of the situation from this mate's perspective, and ability to have more control of the process. Often the partner who has not been coming has some level of trust in the clinician due to the other's treatment gains. Every case requires careful judgment. Even if the clinician is willing, the individual client and the other partner must be the ones who finally decide.

If the same clinician will be seeing the couple, the partner who has been in individual treatment may be concerned about information either the clinician or the other mate might reveal in conjoint interviews. The other mate may feel wary about being invited into an established treatment relationship. Extra work must be done to dispel the treated client's perhaps unrealistic expectations or fears of the couple sessions. Clinicians should explain clearly what they will do in couple work and suggest that the partner who already knows them may feel bereft at first as they reach out to and try to understand the newcomer. Clinicians can ask what information they already know they can feel free to share with the other mate. To help the new partner feel more comfortable, they can offer to talk or meet individually with him or her before a conjoint session, with their client's permission (Karpel 1994).

Confidentiality issues arise whenever a clinician seeing a couple has information only one partner knows. Perhaps one mate has been treated individually but now couple sessions will be held, as just discussed. Sometimes a partner in ongoing couple treatment reveals significant information in a telephone call or when seeing a clinician alone. In situations to be reviewed below, clinicians may talk with partners individually as part of an initial assessment process. Confidentiality then becomes a concern whenever the couple ends up coming in. Often confidentiality concerns are greatest when one partner is ambivalent about staying in the relationship or is having an undisclosed affair. Clinicians who work with couples take varied positions on confidentiality, each with its benefits and drawbacks (Karpel 1994). Whatever guidelines are used should be conveyed to a partner who comes in individually or speaks with the clinician on the telephone before the couple is seen, and to both partners as soon as possible.

Confidentiality must always be handled so as to protect a partner in danger. Therefore, clinicians should not reveal one mate's reports of being battered to the other. They should reveal the serious risk of suicide, homicide, or psychosis to the partner or another appropriate party. Beyond these immediately dangerous situations, some clinicians routinely hold all confidences. The difficulty here is that they may hear of one mate's affair, intention to leave the relationship, illegal activities, hidden substance use, or something else that is strongly affecting the couple. If they cannot then help this partner in individual sessions either to change or tell the mate what is going on, they are left with the choice of participating in couple treatment that is a sham or ending it without explanation. At the other extreme, clinicians may tell partners that they will not promise to hold any confidences unless there is danger to someone in revealing them. Here clinicians who see or talk to partners individually need not struggle in regard to confidentiality but the partners may not reveal ambivalence about their relationship, affairs, or even painful facts about themselves, such as childhood sexual abuse, that they are unwilling for the mate to know.

A middle position is to hold most confidences. Clinicians can tell partners that in general, neither may see or talk with the clinician without the other's knowing the contact has taken place, but what is discussed will be kept confidential if a partner wishes it to be. The exception to both rules will occur whenever holding to them could lead to immediate or long-term danger. These guidelines allow for protection of a partner who may be abused and for disclosure of suicidal or homicidal thinking, serious substance abuse, or a partner engaging in unsafe sex. However, clinicians can also say that if what is revealed is not dangerous but causes them to believe couple treatment cannot continue until further individual work is done, they will say so and suspend the couple sessions. Learning that one partner is having an undisclosed affair or is not really motivated to work on the relationship then gives the clinician a little time to work individually with this partner to decide how to proceed. Clinicians can still encourage partners to tell their mates about thoughts, feelings, childhood histories, or past behaviors relevant to the couple revealed in individual contacts. But because they have told both partners that they will hold such confidences, they need not force them to.

EVALUATION OF SPECIAL SITUATIONS

In an initial telephone call from a partner, an initial couple session, or even later in a case, a clinician may encounter circumstances that warrant careful evaluation to determine whether or in what manner couple treatment should proceed. Let us review assessment issues and options in these situations.

Partner Abuse

Abuse occurs when one partner in a couple relationship intentionally or recklessly does or says something that harms, frightens, or coerces the other. The harm may be physical or psychological. Even if there is not a clear-cut intent to harm, abuse may come from acting with reckless disregard for the other's well-being, such as when one partner carelessly breaks a prized possession of the other or exposes the other to a sexually transmitted disease. Physical abuse ranges from that which is extremely dangerous, such as stabbing, strangling, or beating up the partner, to that which may be less dangerous but still painful or frightening, such as pushing, pinching, or restraining. Forced or coerced sexual activity of any kind constitutes abuse (O'Leary and Murphy 1992). Threats and other forms of psychological abuse can be extremely emotionally damaging as they increase feelings of fear, powerlessness, depression, and low self-esteem (Tolman 1992). Most partners who engage in chronic physical abuse also psychologically abuse their mates. The latter often report the psychological abuse to be equally or even more damaging than the physical. There are gray areas as to what constitutes psychological abuse or coercion. For example, one partner may call the other stupid or put some pressure on the other for sex, but not actually force it. While never desirable, the more unpleasant and repeated such actions are, the more likely they are to constitute a pattern of abuse. Most often there is one abuser, at least with physical abuse, but sometimes both partners abuse each other. Mutual psychological abuse is probably considerably more common than mutual physical abuse.

Unfortunately, partner abuse is not a rare phenomenon (Bachman and Pillemer 1992). Even if the definition is limited to physical abuse, it has been found to occur at some time in about 28 percent of marriages and at roughly comparable rates for dating or cohabiting couples. Most studies have found male and female rates of physical abuse to be about the same. However, the consequences of women's violence are almost always less and it often occurs in retaliation for men's abuse or in self-defense. When psychological abuse is included in the definition, prevalence rates in couples may go as high as 65 percent. Partner abuse happens in all social classes and ethnic groups and in same-sex as well as heterosexual relationships.

A partner's propensity to engage in physical abuse can stem from many sources, and abusers are far from a homogeneous group. Many theorists believe that society's attitudes condone and even encourage violence toward women (O'Leary and Murphy 1992). Other contributing factors may be partners' experiences with violent parents in childhood, having a personality disorder associated with impulse control problems, alcohol abuse, low self-esteem, or inadequate knowledge of how to handle anger or conflict. The latter may include consistent use of aggression to dominate, or being unassertive and stuffing feelings until an explosion occurs (Saunders 1992). Physical or psychological abuse is often linked to the abusing partner's pathological need to be in control (Bula 1996), perhaps resulting from childhood experiences of physical or emotional victimization. Because any close personal interaction seems to risk putting the abuser in a similar vulnerable situation, he or she must be dominant at all costs. While couple interaction patterns may develop to incorporate abuse, the other partner's actions should not be construed as causing or justifying it. For example, the first incidents may have happened when batterers felt frustrated and inadequate during arguments, due to their mates' superior verbal skills. Once abuse has begun, periods of calm between mates may be followed by increased tension as both wait for more violence to erupt (Steinfeld 1997). Reacting to the tension, the mate who has been abused may do something, such as becoming more withdrawn, that again evokes the abusing partner's underlying feelings of low self-esteem, vulnerability, or powerlessness. The violence becomes a way for this partner to repeatedly regain total power and control.

Clinicians often fail to detect couple violence or psychological abuse and must make sure they screen every case to do so (Bula 1996, Holtzworth-Munroe et al. 1995). But they must exercise caution lest an abused partner be placed in greater danger by the assessment process. *A partner possibly at risk must be questioned out of the presence of the mate*. Someone who reveals abuse on the telephone can be assured of confidentiality and asked more questions immediately. This partner's legal options can be reviewed, a safety plan discussed, and a referral made to a local domestic violence program. If physical abuse is described or suspected in a conjoint session, a clinician may use part of the time to talk with each partner separately (Karpel 1994). However, when clinicians suspect abuse but believe the victim could be placed in greater jeopardy by an immediate inquiry, they may instead schedule an individual session with each mate as a part of the initial assessment process, even if they would not usually do so. As a last resort or if individual sessions are declined, a clinician might call a possibly abused partner later at a time the other mate is unlikely to be present.

A number of clues to possible abuse may warrant such separate assessment. One is very controlling behavior on the part of a partner who is physically stronger, usually the man in a heterosexual pair (Karpel 1994). For example, this mate may override anything the other says or keep the other isolated at home. Another is one partner seeming to be fearful of or overly acquiescent to the other. Physical injuries for which no satisfactory explanation is given or a history of emergency room visits for such injuries are an obvious danger sign. A partner who is being physically or psychologically abused may appear to be dominated by the mate or may show hesitation, fear, or quick evasions when clinicians ask about injuries or conflict situations. A partner showing possible signs of a depressive or posttraumatic stress disorder, such as excessive crying, suicidal thoughts, startle reactions, or nightmares, should be evaluated as a potential victim of abuse as well as for the presence of these disorders themselves. Since child abuse and partner abuse often occur together, any situation in which one type of abuse has been found should be evaluated for the other (McKay 1994).

Even when partner abuse seems unlikely, couples should routinely be asked questions or given standardized assessment questionnaires to try to make sure (O'Leary and Murphy 1992, Saunders 1992). Research has found that over half the couples requesting treatment at some clinics report abuse when specifically asked (Holtzworth-Munroe et al. 1995). Questions about how a pair handles conflict can lead to inquiries such as, "Has either of you ever pushed or shoved the other or done anything physical in the course of an argument?" (Karpel

1994, p. 245). Or, since not all abuse happens in response to conflict, "Has either of you ever been harmed by or found yourself harming the other, perhaps when you did not intend to?" Even when the answer to such questions is negative, partners may reveal fears of violence or near losses of control that warrant the clinician's attention.

If a clinician learns at any point about threatened or actual physical abuse, the first step is to evaluate the dangerousness of the situation. On the telephone or in an individual session with a partner at risk, the immediate relevant questions are what has happened, surrounding circumstances (including possible substance use), previous history of abuse in the relationship, new threats, and new stressors that could precipitate an exacerbation (Saunders 1992). An abusive partner's threats of homicide or suicide should be taken as very serious indicators of potential lethality, especially if weapons are available. Substance use and the abuser's obsessiveness about controlling the mate increase risk (Holtzworth-Munroe et al. 1995). The possibility of the mate's leaving often increases a batterer's desperate fear of losing control of the relationship and, therefore, potential lethality (Hart 1988). Likely to be very dangerous are situations in which a batterer has recently become more threatening, impulsive, suspicious, or controlling, or in which the abusive acts have resulted in increased physical harm. The mate is often in the best position to identify an escalating potential for violence. Whenever he or she expresses feelings of being in danger, these fears should be respected.

Partners in danger of serious harm should be helped to consider leaving the couple relationship if at all possible, even if temporarily (Holtzworth-Munroe et al. 1995, Karpel 1994). They should be given information about domestic violence, such as its probable impact on their children and themselves, how unlikely it is for the batterer to change without help, and their options for finding a safe place to stay (Call 1997, personal communication). In many communities some services exist to assist in the process. Another possibility is to encourage an abused partner to press charges, to force arrest and possibly a restraining order or mandated treatment. When partners at risk of serious harm choose not to leave, they must still be made aware of available resources and helped to develop a detailed plan to ensure their safety in the event of greater danger. All clinicians should be familiar with programs for domestic violence victims in their areas. Further individual or group help may be offered to partners being abused, but couple and family treatment are contraindicated because tensions aroused there may increase the risk of harm.

Sometimes an individual assessment conducted with a partner who has experienced less frequent and less severe physical abuse, such as restraining or pushing, reveals no apparent immediate danger of severe harm. However, there may still be other dangers, including escalation or psychological abuse (Bula 1996). The majority of cases in which partners have requested couple treatment without citing abuse as a primary problem are of this type (O'Leary and Murphy 1992). Here, a clinician should ascertain whether the abused partner wants to stay in the relationship if further abuse can be prevented and the relationship otherwise improved. Often this partner needs some sense of treatment options and likely outcomes before making the decision. If he or she wants to consider staying in the couple relationship, the clinician can assist in determining whether separate specialized treatment for the abuser is necessary or couple treatment alone may suffice.

Clinical evidence suggests that in many situations couple treatment alone will not help prevent further abuse and may place the mate at greater risk. Clinicians should insist on specialized battering treatment when there is any long-standing pattern of physical abuse (Karpel 1994), or when a batterer attempts to control the mate, is jealous of the mate's relationships with others, blames the mate for all the couple's problems, abuses substances, or is psychologically as well as physically abusive. Further indicators that a specialized program is needed are the batterer's denying that the abusive acts have been harmful or insisting that he or she can easily stop. Specialized treatment for a batterer and possibly later adjunct work with a couple who will be staying together or reuniting is probably always the combination most likely to be effective.

At times, however, couple treatment may be given alone if a couple prefers it and a *number of additional criteria are met* (O'Leary and Murphy 1992). There should be no chronic pattern of abuse and control, no substance abuse, no history of severe or life-threatening abuse, and none of the signs of lethal danger cited earlier. The batterer must not be in denial about the harm caused by prior abuse and must accept full responsibility for it (Holtzworth-Munroe et al. 1995). He or she must be willing to sign a no-violence contract and agree to participate immediately in specialized battering treatment if the contract is violated. The abused mate must have a safe exit plan and commit to using it in the event of actual or threatened further abuse. Both partners must be willing to use initial couple treatment sessions for learning immediate and long-term abuse prevention techniques such as are discussed in Holtzworth-Munroe and colleagues (1995) or Steinfeld (1997). Both must be willing to come or let the other come for individual sessions when these are recommended or requested. Finally, the clinician must have expertise in treating partner abuse or refer the couple to someone who does.

Clinicians must also be concerned with assessing psychological abuse in couples. Even with no physical abuse, a pattern of persistent one-sided psychological abuse can be emotionally devastating (Bula 1996). Different forms include, but are not limited to, verbal put-downs, threats to deprive the mate, coercion by other than violent means, extreme jealousy, isolating the mate from the outside world, demanding sex, consistently withholding emotional support or access to the couple's finances, or "psychological destabilization" in which the abuser commits "acts that leave the victim unclear as to the validity of [his or] her own perceptions" (Tolman 1992, p. 297). An example of this last is a man repeatedly telling his wife that he had not said things he did say, or that she had done things she did not remember. A number of checklists and formal assessment tools (Bula 1996, Holtzworth-Munroe et al. 1995, Tolman 1992) exist to identify such patterns. Clinicians can watch for signs of low self-esteem, confusion, and fear of being crazy in psychologically abused mates while the abusive partners may appear glib and self-confident (Bula 1996). Partners should be interviewed separately when serious one-sided psychological abuse is known or suspected. Such sessions can be used to validate abused mates' feelings (Tolman 1992) and determine the abuser's level of self-awareness, motivation to change, and possibly relevant personality dynamics or childhood experiences. Individual treatment may be indicated for both partners (Bula 1996), possibly combined with couple sessions. In some narcissistically vulnerable couples, to be discussed in Chapter 8, both mates may be psychologically abusive.

Problematic Substance Use

Many clinicians now see people's behavior in regard to substances as representing a continuum from nonproblematic use through that which is problematic intermittently or to varying degrees (Lewis et al. 1994, McCrady and Epstein 1995). Recreational use of alcohol, street drugs, medications, or other substances can be considered substance abuse when it occurs at a level endangering the person's health or impairing his or her functioning in major life roles (*DSM-IV* 1994). Sometimes both partners in a couple problematically use or abuse substances. Use of multiple substances, substance use occurring along with violence toward the partner, or a substance abuser having a comorbid psychiatric disorder are not uncommon. Any of these circumstances can magnify the dysfunction caused.

While a variety of factors may influence individuals to start using substances, factors that perpetuate problematic use are most important to understand. These almost always include the user's physical and psychological response to the particular substance. People can become physically addicted to some substances, as well as psychologically addicted when the substance of choice makes them feel immediately more relaxed, happier, less anxious, or whatever. These effects may be especially compelling if the individual has a coexisting psychiatric disorder. The responses of family members, peers, and others may encourage continued substance use or further it unwittingly. Substance abuse tends to be higher in some ethnic groups, such as Irish (McGoldrick 1996) and Polish (Folwarski and Marganoff 1996) Americans. Substance use may become a person's way of dealing with interpersonal stress. Continued problematic use frequently leads to health difficulties, increased psychological dependence, dysfunctional couple relationships, and problems with jobs and other aspects of life functioning (Kingery-McCabe and Campbell 1991, McCrady and Epstein 1995).

Complex patterns regarding problematic substance use can develop between couple partners. The two may participate in use together, burying relationship problems in the mutual enjoyment of, and eventual compulsive need for, their substances. Or a partner who abuses substances may be easier to live with as he or she becomes less demanding of relationship intimacy and more willing to settle for gratifications the drug provides. The mate may object only when the substance abuser's behavior becomes more extreme or begins to have further consequences, such as health or job problems. In other relationships, one partner's overuse of substances causes couple tension from the start. But the mate's protestations, anger, nagging, or withdrawal often simply arouse stressful emotions, such as anger or guilt, that are handled by still more substance use. The nonabusing partner may also take over more and more responsibility for maintaining the couple's or family's functioning, leaving the substance abuser feeling useless and isolated (Karpel 1994, McCrady and Epstein 1995).

While some partners may unconsciously seek out or tolerate substance abusers as mates because of their own intrapsychic issues, others apparently get caught up in such dysfunctional patterns out of normal caring about a partner who seems out of control and because they do not know what to do differently. They can also be guided by understandable wishes to protect themselves, the partner, and their children from the consequences of the substance abuse (Troise 1993). When a wife phones her husband's boss to say he has a toothache rather than a hangover, she is trying to save his income and job for the whole family's sake. The fact that she has thereby enabled his continued drinking may not seem so salient to her at the time.

Partners who call requesting couple treatment sometimes immediately identify concerns about their own or their mate's substance use. Sometimes such concerns are voiced at the time of the initial interview or later in couple work. However, partners do not always volunteer information about substance use that interferes with individual or couple functioning (Karpel 1994). To detect it, clinicians should ask within the first few sessions of every case about both partners' use of alcohol and recreational drugs. When they suspect or learn of substance use that may be problematic, further evaluation is needed. Usually, discussing the problem in both conjoint and separate individual sessions is warranted. Assuming the issue is first identified in a conjoint session, perhaps the initial interview, the couple's views of the extent and influences of the problem can be sought. The clinician can express nonjudgmental concern and the need for further understanding. He or she may do some education about dangers and perpetuating influences in problematic substance use (McCrady and Epstein 1995). Couching these discussions in terms that do not make the substance user feel blamed is important (Karpel 1994).

In a separate session with the partner whose use may be problematic, a clinician's attitude should again be of concern, not condemnation. Some clinicians do a substance use history or ask this partner to complete a screening tool such as the Michigan Alcoholism Screening Test (Heath and Stanton 1991, McCrady and Epstein 1995). Another option is to have this partner keep written records of use for a week or two, if there is no danger in prolonging the assessment (Karpel 1994). Sometimes such records persuade the partner that more use is occurring than he or she originally thought. If use is problematic, clinicians should assess the partner's level of denial and possible willingness to seek specialized help. Denial can take many forms. It is not unusual for a partner to admit the amount of substance use but not see it as a problem. Or he or she may admit problematic use but claim ability to change without any special attention to the matter in treatment.

A separate session gives the nonabusing mate a chance to tell safely about any physical or psychological abuse that may occur during substance use or about other dangers to be discussed below. The nonabusing mate, while likely to give a more accurate picture of the problem than the substance abuser, may participate in denial as well. This mate can also describe his or her own feelings, fears, and behavior in response to the problematic substance use.

Assessment sessions should yield enough information to answer a series of key questions. First, is the substance use posing any immediate danger to the user or others? Common immediate dangers include the possibility of overdose, lethality, or reactions to mixing certain drugs; driving or using other machinery while under the influence of a substance; use of a harmful substance during pregnancy; battering incidents that occur primarily or solely during substance use; and activities such as sharing needles or entering dangerous neighborhoods to obtain substances. Also dangerous is further use that will aggravate an existing physical condition, as when someone with cirrhosis of the liver is still drinking alcohol (*DSM-IV* 1994). Finally, clinicians must screen for the coexistence of substance abuse with a psychiatric disorder, which substantially increases the risk of suicide (Fawcett et al. 1993). Additional data to be evaluated are the history, current patterns, and severity of problematic substance use, and the partners' interaction around the substance (Karpel 1994). Prior attempts to control use should be determined, along with the extent of both partners' acknowledgment of any current problems and apparent motivation to do something about them. All this information is vital to treatment planning.

Faced with a level of substance use in which there is significant danger to the user or others, clinicians should take a strong stand that a specialized substance abuse treatment program is needed. An alternative that may lead to the same result is to refer the pair to a substance abuse specialist for further evaluation (Karpel 1994). If the partner dangerously using substances refuses further evaluation or specialized help, a clinician may see the mate separately to organize an "intervention." This is a planned session in which the nonabusing partner and others confront a substance abuser in a loving but very firm way and give a bottom line of repercussions that will take place unless he or she enters specialized treatment (Massella 1991). At the very least, the nonabusing partner can be helped to consider individual work or a program such as Al-Anon if the mate refuses to admit or deal with problematic substance use (Karpel 1994, Koffinke 1991).

Often assessment sessions reveal substance use that poses no immediate danger but that is still chronic and clearly problematic for the user and the couple. Here specialized substance-abuse treatment combined with adjunct couple or family work is still the preferred approach and should be recommended as such (Alexander et al. 1995, Karpel 1994). However, a trial of couple treatment, possibly along with the substance abuser's attending a self-help group like Alcoholics Anonymous, may be undertaken instead if the couple prefers it and certain conditions are met. Most importantly, the substance abuser must recognize his or her use as a problem and commit to doing something about it. A qualified physician should be consulted to evaluate this partner's health and determine whether substance reduction or detoxification may be done safely outside a medical setting (Heath and Stanton 1991). The substance abuser must agree either to abstain or to monitor his or her use and keep it at or below an agreed-upon level (Karpel 1994). Contingency agreements may be that failure at controlled use will be followed by abstinence or failure at abstinence will result in going to a specialized treatment program. Finally, the treating clinician must be qualified to deal with substance abuse. Descriptions of such treatment may be found in McCrady and Epstein (1995) and Wakefield and colleagues (1996). If couple treatment fails to combat the substance problem and the abusing partner does not follow through with specialized treatment, an "intervention" can still be held.

Sometimes clinicians learn in an initial assessment that one or both partners' substance use is under a certain amount of control but may still have long-term health implications or be a problem for the mate or family. Perhaps a partner drinks every night but not in the daytime and never misses work or becomes obnoxious. Or a partner uses marijuana regularly on weekend nights or overuses prescription drugs to fall asleep. Such use patterns may not concern either partner, or one partner may be concerned while the other denies a problem. The question here is what stance the clinician should take. Clearly the health hazards or any other dangers of a partner's use should be pointed out. The effects of substance use on the couple relationship and any children should be explored and clarified. The clinician should make clear that treatment will not help the couple achieve its goals if the substance abuse will interfere. For example, a clinician might suggest, "You say you want to communicate better and evenings are your only real time to talk. But if Pat has had too much to drink then, I don't see you being able to try out new ways to talk to each other."

Couples wanting to achieve greater intimacy can be told that significant substance use virtually always precludes this. Such discussions may lead to the substance user's agreement, however reluctantly, to focus on reducing or eliminating his or her use as a goal of treatment. A final possibility is that both partners are comfortable with the existing level of use and want to work on treatment goals it does not preclude. Here, clinicians must make a personal decision as to whether they feel they can ethically participate, perhaps with hopes of raising the substance use issue again at a later time.

Psychiatric Disorders

Sometimes, in initial contacts or later in treatment, clinicians become aware that a partner may be showing symptoms of an untreated psychiatric disorder. Clinicians must be able to determine when such disorders may exist and with what urgency they should be evaluated, especially when suicide may be a possibility. They must always take the partners' ethnicity into account in doing so, since they may otherwise either underdiagnose or overdiagnose psychopathology (Sue et al. 1995). When partners manifest severe or dangerous conditions or certain personality disorders, couple treatment may be contraindicated, at least until a later time. Couple work with milder-range disorders may be helpful, as discussed earlier, but the need for other treatment must still be assessed.

Causes of psychiatric disorders are diverse. The more severe conditions of schizophrenia, bipolar disorder, and major depressive disorder almost surely are biochemical illnesses in large part, although stress often precipitates symptom exacerbations (Prince and Jacobson 1995, Sayers et al. 1993, Yank et al. 1993). Suicide is a potential danger in all three (*DSM-IV* 1994). Some of the anxiety disorders, including generalized anxiety disorder (Cowley and Roy-Byrne 1991), panic disorder (*DSM-IV* 1994), and obsessive-compulsive disorder (Cooper 1996), are thought to have some physical basis. Borderline personality disorder may as well (Marziali 1992). One implication is that psychotropic medications may be useful in treating any of these conditions. Many theorists believe that childhood experiences that leave specific emotional vulnerabilities or teach coping that is problematic in adulthood can make people prone to mild- to moderate-range depression, some anxiety disorders, eating disorders, dissociative disorders, or a number of the personality disorders. Posttraumatic stress disorders are by definition caused by traumas outside the range of normal human experience, no matter at what age these occur (*DSM-IV* 1994).

Either partner's psychiatric disorder tends both to influence and to be influenced by the couple's interaction (Anderson et al. 1986, Craske and Zoellner 1995, Prince and Jacobson 1995). However, the influence is somewhat different depending on whether a partner has a personality disorder or some other emotional disorder. Persistent and dysfunctional character traits tend to give partners with personality disorders more power than their mates in the couple interaction. While the former may suffer with their conditions, their mates often suffer more as they are forced into helpless or caretaking positions. For example, the partner of someone with paranoid personality disorder may become acquiescent and watch every word so as not to fuel the mate's paranoia, and end up doing so anyway. Even more complex interactions develop when two personality-disordered partners get together. As noted earlier, narcissistically vulnerable couples often comprise partners who show features of borderline or narcissistic disorders.

When one partner suffers from a more symptomatic psychiatric disorder, such as an anxiety or mood disorder, the couple's interactions are usually quite different. Often, the other partner responds to the symptoms with denial, anger, fear, frustration, or labeling of the sufferer as "crazy" or "irrational." The partner with symptoms may have a great deal of concern and shame about them. He or she may deny anything is wrong, accept put-downs or labeling, or respond with anger to these. Even when a psychiatric disorder is diagnosed, these mutual reactions may continue or worsen if partners do not understand the possible causes, prognosis, treatment, and optimal management. Since dysfunctional couple interactions can make almost any emotional disorder worse (Anderson et al. 1986, Craske and Zoellner 1995, Prince and Jacobson 1995), vicious cycles can develop. For example, the nonsymptomatic partner may be angry or withdrawing, followed by an increase in the other's symptoms, followed by oversolicitous behavior by the nonsymptomatic mate, followed by anger or withdrawal when the feeling of burden becomes too great. Meanwhile, the partner with symptoms reacts to an atmosphere that feels highly unpredictable. Of course, symptoms of a particular disorder, severity of the condition, both partners' responses, and the interaction patterns that develop are idiosyncratic.

What is crucial for clinicians to notice and evaluate quickly is evidence that a partner may be suicidal, seriously depressed, manic, psychotic, or suffering from an eating disorder. Any of these can lead to serious danger. The partner may show a history of similar symptoms or prior normal functioning. At times, such symptoms represent a drug reaction or serious physical pathology. They always require medical or psychiatric evaluation and treatment. Couple treatment may be given at the time or later, but it will almost always be ancillary to the primary care (Anderson et al. 1986, Miklowitz and Goldstein 1997, Prince and Jacobson 1995, Root 1995).

Partners who are feeling suicidal often will not volunteer this information. There is too much shame or guilt attached, and some do not want to be stopped. However, they may describe feeling hopeless, depressed, or trapped with no way out (Fawcett et al. 1993). They may have mentioned suicidal thoughts to their mates or friends. Sometimes clues to suicidal thinking are even more subtle. A partner makes extremely negative self-statements, such as saying he or she is evil or has ruined others' lives. Apparent affects may be of hopeless resignation or self-hatred. Sometimes partners whose mind is made up demonstrate intent by giving valued possessions away or suddenly making a will. Some avoid talk about the future or begin to speculate about what happens in the afterlife. Suicidal thinking should always be suspected when a partner presents with symptoms of major depression. Besides or instead of depressive affect, these may include anhedonia, loss of interest in surroundings, low energy, trouble concentrating, and significant changes in appetite, sleep, or activity level (*DSM-IV* 1994).

Both the mate and the partner who may be depressed should be asked about the latter's possible depressive symptoms and indicators of suicidal intent (Fawcett et al. 1993, Karpel 1994). Clinicians should ask directly whether a potentially suicidal partner has spoken about or thought about self-harm. Some may admit these thoughts but claim they will not act on them. Others deny such thinking in a way that is not convincing, or admit to depression but not suicidal ideas. Clinicians need to be aware of their own anxiety around the possibility of suicidal intent. Otherwise they may either overreact and send someone to a hospital when outpatient help would suffice, or be too ready to drop the subject in response to the partner's immediate assurances that he or she will not take action. Instead, in further exploration of possible suicidality, clinicians should ask whether partners at risk have thought about a means of harming themselves, whether they have ever tried, and whether anything holds them back (Fawcett et al. 1993). Higher risk accrues when people have made specific plans, have carried out prior attempts, cannot see impediments, are impulsive, or use substances. Panic attacks or severe anxiety combined with depression are other significant risk factors.

In the presence of some suicidal risk, clinicians need to decide how much pressure to put on a couple to get emergency help. With clear dangerous risk at the time of a couple session, the clinician should secure both partners' promise that the couple will go immediately to an emergency room or doctor's office for an evaluation. With less risk, an alternative is to secure a no-harm contract in which the potentially suicidal partner promises to obtain a psychiatric evaluation within the next few days and the mate promises not to leave the partner alone for any reason until it is completed. The mate must also agree to remove from the home any items that could readily be used in a suicide attempt, such as guns or poison (Fawcett et al. 1993). Such a contract usually specifies that the person at risk will go to an emergency room or call the clinician's emergency number immediately if he or she fears at any point being unable to resist attempting suicide (Karpel 1994). Both partners' responses to these ideas must be monitored. If neither will act in response to serious risk, the clinician may have to institute commitment proceedings (Fawcett et al. 1993). Doing so should be a last-ditch option as it may destroy the possibility of work together thereafter.

Psychotic, manic, or eating disorder symptoms can also place partners in danger. The most obvious signs of psychosis are hallucinations, delusions, grossly odd behaviors such as ritualistic touching that the person does not see as unusual, and incoherent or otherwise disorganized speech (*DSM-IV* 1994). A manic episode usually includes grandiose thinking about the self, inflated and unrealistic plans that may be acted on, rapid and pressured speech, and decreased need for sleep. One danger of ignoring these emergent conditions is that they will almost surely get worse without treatment. Another is that partners in the grip of unrealistic thinking may place themselves or someone else at risk. Psychotic partners may walk in front of cars or go into dangerous neighborhoods at night because they are preoccupied with visions or voices telling them to do so. A partner who is manic may be promiscuous or spend large sums of money on reckless schemes. Finally, eating disorders are eventually dangerous unless treated. While unusually low weight signals possible anorexia, people with bulimia may be of normal weight and hide their binge eating and purging (*DSM-IV* 1994). Either disorder can be suspected when a partner seems to diet or exercise excessively, is secretive around eating behaviors, disappears into a bathroom shortly after eating, or shows loss of dental enamel that may be caused by repeated regurgitating of stomach acids.

Many partners showing psychotic, manic, or eating disorder symptoms resist seeking psychiatric help. If so, the mate can often be helped to see the dangers and force an evaluation. During or after treatment that may include a period of hospitalization, psychoeducational couple help may be given (Anderson et al. 1986, Brennan 1995, Prince and Jacobson 1995, Root 1995, Simon 1997). Such work is beyond the scope of our discussion here.

Often a partner shows a less dangerous condition that meets *DSM-IV* (1994) criteria for a depressive, anxiety, or dissociative disorder. Clinicians must watch for these conditions because partners may hide their symptoms out of shame or fear or may not recognize their significance. For example, people who suffer from excessive anxiety, panic attacks, phobias, obsessive thoughts, or compulsions may fear they are going crazy. Instead, these symptoms usually signal anxiety disorders that can be treated effectively with medication and cognitive-behavioral or behavioral psychotherapy (Butler and Booth 1991, Michelson and Marchione 1991, Roth and Fonagy 1996). Posttraumatic stress disorder symptoms include reexperiencing the traumatic event, perhaps in flashbacks or repeated nightmares; numbing of general responsiveness, with possible inability to experience feelings; and symptoms of arousal such as difficulty sleeping or hypervigilance (*DSM-IV* 1994). Not uncommon are partners' unrecognized posttraumatic stress disorder symptoms stemming from childhood sexual abuse, domestic violence, sexual assault, or wartime combat experiences. Symptoms of a dissociative disorder may include multiple personalities or personality states, but also feelings of depersonalization that can be misinterpreted as harmless "spacing out" (*DSM-IV* 1994). The dysthymia sufferer is chronically depressed and often shows low self-esteem, difficulty concentrating, and some eating or sleeping problems. Unless a partner's symptoms are prominent and under little control, couple treatment can be helpful in most of these instances, at least as an adjunct to individual work. However, such treatment may need to be modified in ways to be described in Chapter 9.

Clinicians must also recognize partners' characteristics warranting a diagnosis of a personality disorder. Most commonly presenting for couple treatment are partners who meet *DSM-IV* (1994) criteria for paranoid, dependent, obsessive-compulsive, borderline, or narcissistic disorders. Traits of the first three are more or less self-evident. Traits, dynamics, and treatment of couples in which one or both partners show borderline or narcissistic functioning are considered at length in Chapter 8. Many partners with personality disorders show lack of interest in separate treatment for themselves because they see nothing wrong with the way they are. Couple treatment, sought because such individuals almost inevitably experience relationship difficulties, may at times be more effective than individual work in starting the process of change. However, there are situations in which character pathology in a mate precludes couple work. These include one partner being a chronic liar, consistently engaging in antisocial acts, or showing such rigid and controlling behavior with the mate that the clinician cannot anticipate having any positive impact. An example of the latter might be a partner who shows severely paranoid traits.

Sexual Dysfunction

Many couples coming for treatment report problems in their sexual relationship. Most of these are appropriate to address as a part of regular conjoint work. Some, however, signal the need for further evaluation, possibly leading to some form of more specialized individual or couple help. Immediate issues to consider are whether sexual dysfunction in one mate may be caused by a physical problem, individual psychological issue, or the couple's problematic interaction. If both partners function adequately when they do make love, their complaints about frequency, lovemaking that is too inhibited, or the like usually reflect individual psychological issues or couple interaction problems. Environmental factors such as a crowded household can also be an influence.

Individuals' fairly consistent lack of sexual desire, arousal, or orgasm are sometimes physically based (LoPiccolo 1990, Weeks 1995b). Diabetes can lead to potency problems in men. Problems may arise due to use of prescription medications; for example, medications for high blood pressure or depression can decrease sexual desire. Recreational substance use can inhibit or promote immediate sexual expression, depending on the substance. Long-term use usually diminishes sexual desire and performance. Psychological reactions to health problems, infertility, or aging can lead to inhibited sexual desire (Weeks 1995b). So may significant weight gain in either partner.

A partner who is a survivor of sexual abuse or a sexual assault at any age will almost surely show sequelae in his or her sexual functioning. "Phobic or dissociative reactions during sexual interactions," perhaps combined with symptoms of anxiety, depression, or feelings of powerlessness in the couple relationship, should alert clinicians to the possibility of childhood sexual abuse (Talmadge and Wallace 1991, p. 172). Many anxiety and depressive disorders can inhibit individuals' sexual functioning (Weeks 1995b). Life experiences leading to anxiety, guilt, fear, or other negative feelings about sex can do so as well (Heiman et al. 1995). Because sexual desire, arousal, and orgasm are not under voluntary control, even fairly mild performance anxiety can inhibit these. Partners uncertain for any reason about their ability to function sexually may become anxious about failure, and therefore virtually ensure it. Strong religious beliefs that people should have sexual intercourse only in marriage or for procreation can lead to guilt that inhibits sex in unmarried partners or those who use birth control. An undisclosed affair often inhibits sexual expression in the primary relationship (Karpel 1994). Internalized homophobia may cause a same-sex partner to have negative, inhibiting feelings toward his or her sexual relationship with a mate. Or a partner with a same-sex orientation may hide it due to internalized or societal homophobia and remain in a heterosexual relationship, showing sexual disinterest there (LoPiccolo 1990).

Whenever physical or psychological factors inhibit one partner's sexual functioning, even if the dysfunction is temporary or minimal, either mate may compound the problem by responding negatively (Karpel 1994). Many women reach orgasm only some of the time but still enjoy sex. Many men have occasional problems with potency, especially at later middle age and older. If both partners take such events neutrally and, if needed, discuss how to adjust their lovemaking, positive sexual experiences can usually continue. If either person's response is to demean the other or become overly anxious, greater problems are likely. Often, without adequate understanding of whatever is the root cause of one partner's sexual difficulty, the mate may interpret it as due to, for example, anger or the mate's unattractiveness and respond negatively. A reciprocal negative response by the original partner may then begin a dysfunctional cycle around sex.

Sometimes a partner's sexual difficulties spring mainly from inadequate knowledge, poor couple communication about sex, or both (Karpel 1994, Weeks 1995b). Lack of accurate knowledge about sexual functioning and lack of good communication about sexual needs and preferences are far from unusual. Many people do not know a great deal about their partner's body, or their own, and are somewhat inhibited about finding out. For example, a woman may interpret a man's morning erection, caused by his needing to urinate, as an attempt to pressure her into having intercourse. Many partners are embarrassed to tell each other what they do and do not enjoy sexually, leading to frustration and disappointment. That women want more cuddling and other foreplay and that men move "too quickly" to intercourse are very common complaints in couple treatment.

Environmental circumstances can affect couples' sex lives. Many couples have trouble finding the time and energy to have much of a sexual relationship if they have young children or work long hours. A crowded house and lack of privacy can be factors. Any stressor that makes people more anxious and preoccupied, such as problems with extended family, can affect their capacity to be sexual at a given time.

Finally, sexual difficulties most often arise when partners with no significant individual dysfunction and a prior satisfactory sex life are involved in couple strife or fear emotional intimacy (Weeks 1995b). A sexual difficulty may also serve some system function for the couple, such as when it gives one partner power to defeat the other's control. Partners who are angry, frustrated, or otherwise filled with negative emotions because of frequent arguing are unlikely to feel loving and sexual toward each other. While men may find their physical need for sex can override such negative emotions, women rarely do (Hurlbert and Apt 1994). The exception is that some couples get into cycles in which strife repeatedly occurs to defend against fears of closeness, allowing periods of closeness with good sex in between. When female partners who are not being battered or psychologically abused have lost interest in sex, they are sometimes responding to male partners who frequently leer at or make demeaning remarks about other women. Finally, either partner's fears about closeness in relationships, often based on childhood experiences, can make opening up to the closeness of satisfying mutual sexual experiences difficult or impossible. For example, partners whose parents dominated or controlled them or those who experienced parental abandonment may be unable to let down their guard enough to be sexually free with a mate. Intimacy fears shared by both partners, usually representing a complex mixture of individual intrapsychic and couple dynamic factors, can impede sexual intimacy as well as closeness in other arenas.

When couples report sexual difficulties in initial contacts or later in a case, further assessment is needed. Both ethnicity and upbringing influence how comfortable partners feel talking about sex. Often, a partner with a problem of desire, arousal, or orgasm is best seen individually to promote frank discussion (Talmadge and Wallace 1991, Weeks 1995b). Most such problems that have not been medically evaluated should be unless they are couple specific, for example, the partner does not experience arousal with the mate but does during sexual fantasies or masturbation. It is highly important to identify problems that may stem from an undiagnosed physical or psychiatric disorder or prescribed medication (Heiman et al. 1995). Sometimes a recent desire, arousal, or orgiastic problem in one partner began with what might have been a temporary difficulty had one or both mates not responded to it so negatively. If a thorough assessment of how the problem started suggests this possibility, the clinician can try some education about how temporary sexual problems can arise in certain circumstances, such as when a couple is under stress, and can seek to facilitate the couple's more constructive response. If the dysfunction does not quickly cease, however, the partner should still discuss it with a physician.

In individual sessions, clinicians can also assess possibilities of partners' depression, anxiety, substance abuse, homophobia, an undisclosed affair, or history of sexual abuse or assault causing recent or long-term sexual difficulty. When evaluation confirms any such underlying problem, it should be further assessed and perhaps treated separately. The couple may or may not need help to deal constructively with any continuing dysfunction. Partners with significant anxiety or guilt around sexual performance may be helped by specialized procedures such as education, sensate focus exercises, and cognitive-behavioral techniques (Heiman et al. 1995). However, clinicians untrained or only slightly trained in the use of sex therapy techniques should refer the couple to someone more qualified (Karpel 1994). A sexual dysfunction clinic can be helpful for evaluation and treatment if partners can tolerate such a direct focus on this aspect of their relationship and are willing to work together to improve it (LoPiccolo 1990).

One partner's sexual functioning that has apparently been inhibited by couple discord or long-term intimacy fears usually requires further assessment to determine if individual treatment, couple work, or both are indicated. If partners prefer it, such assessment may be carried out for a time as a part of the couple treatment, as happened in the Carlson case.

> The Carlsons were a couple in their early thirties, both well educated and high-earning professionals. They had married two years earlier after a courtship in which Maureen, who was fairly sexually experienced, introduced sex to Dan, who had been a virgin. Dan was not religious or from a particularly strict background. Presenting problems were a general pattern in which Maureen had become more and more dominant and Dan more and more passive, while their sex life became almost nonexistent. Dan admitted he had never been highly interested in sex, but he felt their sex prob-

lem resulted from his feeling controlled and angry with Maureen.

Several months of work together achieved major changes in the dominant-passive pattern. Dan learned to tell Maureen what he was thinking and be more assertive rather than wait for her to take over. Maureen learned to hold back and welcome Dan's participation in decision-making and other activities. However, in spite of Maureen becoming much more responsive to what Dan said he wanted sexually, he remained uninterested. He finally admitted that even now when Maureen hugged him, he felt anxious and almost repulsed. At this point Dan agreed to a referral for individual evaluation and treatment.

Most couples whose sexual problems seem related mainly to lack of knowledge about sexuality, environmental stresses, poor communication, recent or long-standing couple strife, or mutual intimacy problems will report intermittently satisfying sexual experiences with each other. Sexual difficulties and their underlying causes can then usually be tackled as part of standard couple treatment. Some education about people's sexual functioning and efforts to improve the couple's communication about sex may help. General work on couple communication and problem solving to reduce day-to-day conflict may be needed. A vicious cycle in which one partner has come to feel obligated to have sex may need to be interrupted (Talmadge and Wallace 1991). Even insight-oriented work that tackles partners' fears of closeness in the context of couple treatment may lead to significant improvement in their sexual relationship. These possibilities are discussed in later chapters.

Undisclosed Affairs

Many couples seek treatment because one has just learned the other has been having an affair, a situation discussed in Chapter 9. However, sometimes clinicians suspect an undisclosed affair or hear about one in individual contacts with partners. Research suggests that up to 50 percent of married men and 26 percent of married women have had affairs (Karpel 1994). Men are more likely to see affairs as justified by a need for sexual excitement, whereas women are more likely to feel justified if affairs represent emotional involvement (Glass and Wright 1992). Some partners in heterosexual relationships have same-sex affairs. Some affairs are nonsexual but still emotionally intimate. A recent phenomenon is the Internet affair, in which participants may not even have met although they may develop an intense emotional involvement.

Couple partners have affairs for many reasons. They may be influenced by long-standing or more temporary individual factors, couple dynamics, peers, ethnicity, and the larger environment or society. Often most intransigent is a partner's pattern of having repeated affairs in spite of being married or in another supposedly exclusive relationship. This pattern usually represents the errant partner's handling of chronic intimacy fears by triangling in someone else. In partners with narcissistic personalities, affairs may defend against underlying fears of abandonment or exploitation in the primary relationship (Pittman and Pittman Wagers 1995). Other partners who have repeated affairs may be unable to meet intimacy needs with only one person because they cannot be overtly angry at someone on whom they are dependent, they fear being dominated, they fear experiencing a loss, or they have some other reason stemming from unresolved early life experiences (Westfall 1995). A partner's parent who had affairs also provides a role model for dealing with relationship problems or intimacy fears in this way (Pittman and Pittman Wagers 1995). Finally, repeated affairs can be influenced by long-term substance abuse that has dulled a partner's sense of morality (Westfall 1995), or by values in some ethnic groups that condone men's affairs as not too grievous a sin (Boyd-Franklin 1989, Garcia-Preto 1996b, McGoldrick et al. 1989).

A second set of reasons for affairs includes more temporary influences on individuals, usually in interaction with couple, environmental, or societal factors. Affairs may happen when a partner encounters a difficult life transition or anxiety-producing new life-cycle phase (Pittman and Pittman Wagers 1995, Westfall 1995). For example, an affair can allow someone to deal with loneliness after a move to a new city or to deny the aging process. A possibly related reason is low self-esteem (Glass and Wright 1992). A partner who has turned out to have fertility problems (Westfall 1995), lost a job, or reached middle age may begin to feel valueless. A variety of problems in the couple relationship can increase anxiety, decrease self-esteem, and heighten a partner's need for secure connection just when the mate may be least likely to provide it. Boredom with one's life or unmet needs for stimulation can be an impetus. In any of these circumstances, finding that a desirable person outside the couple relationship is willing to become sexually or emotionally involved can temporarily defend against anxiety or heighten self-esteem.

Anger at one's mate is a frequent precipitant for an affair. The anger may represent revenge for some real or imagined hurt perpetrated by the mate (Karpel 1994). Or anger may stem from one mate's feeling that the other is failing to meet his or her justifiable needs for affiliation, sexual expression, or stimulation (Glass and Wright 1992). Of course, communication or intimacy problems that are not one partner's fault more than the other's are often the real reason such needs are not being met (Slater 1994). In other situations, unmet needs without a great deal of anger at the partner can lead to an affair. For example, when one mate's chronic physical illness has left him or her unable to meet many of the other's affiliative, stimulation, and sexual needs for a long while, the other may stray. At times a partner who is too frightened or guilty to end the primary relationship has a long-term affair to meet needs elsewhere, perhaps partly hoping to get caught. Often, other factors tip the balance for or against an affair when one partner is vulnerable due to individual or couple distress. Thus, an eager affair partner, transient substance use, being in a conducive environment such as a business trip without the mate, having free time because of a job loss, or "permission" from tolerant peers can exert some influence (Glass and Wright 1992, Pittman and Pittman Wagers 1995).

Whatever the reasons for starting an affair, one that continues undisclosed takes on a life of its own. Some gratifications accrue from the new relationship. The affair partner may express guilt, make escalating demands, or be content because he or she also has intimacy needs being met by the affair. The partner having the affair must struggle to hide it while still maintaining the primary relationship. Lies usually become necessary to deal with the mate's suspicions or time taken up by the affair. The primary couple's balance shifts toward greater distance. Occasionally the mate is relieved by the withdrawal, perhaps to the extent of ignoring obvious clues that an affair is going on (Charny and Parnass 1995). More often this partner exhibits increasing anger, with the other responding either by increased withdrawal or hostile counteraccusations. The latter may serve to displace anger felt toward the self because of guilt.

When clinicians learn about an undisclosed affair before a couple has been seen, they can try to meet alone first with the partner having it. If they suspect an affair during a conjoint initial interview, they may ask to see both partners individually as a part of the assessment process. Based on such suspicions later in a case, clinicians can explain that they would like to explore some matters further with each partner individually. In the individual session with the suspected partner, a clinician can nonjudgmentally ask whether an affair is going on. A session with the mate of a partner who may be having an affair can be used for routine exploration of individual issues and support.

With partners having undisclosed affairs, clinicians must make clear their unwillingness to proceed with couple treatment until the affair is given up (Pittman and Pittman Wagers 1995, Westfall 1995). They can clarify that they are not taking a moral position, but that couple treatment cannot be effective and is not ethical to pursue if one partner has undisclosed loyalties to another relationship. This stance will rarely come as a surprise to the partner having an affair. However, he or she may be unable to decide whether to give it up or leave the couple relationship. Sometimes this partner may even want to give up the affair and not be able to. The reasons can range from threats by the other party to reveal the affair if it is ended, to being entranced by the affair's gratifications. It is appropriate for the clinician to offer to help this partner sort out what to do, or to make a referral to another clinician for this purpose. In the meantime, any couple work must be postponed.

Uncertainty about whether to break off the affair or leave the couple relationship usually calls for a clinician's help first, to figure out with the partner involved why the affair probably happened. If problems in the couple relationship contributed, the two can assess these at least preliminarily. The clinician can offer some judgment about whether and by what means identified couple problems might be remedied, assuming both partners would participate in further treatment. The possible future of an ongoing relationship with the affair partner can also be evaluated, partly by playing out whether its present gratifications might realistically continue if the original couple relationship ended (Pittman and Pittman Wagers 1995). For example, a clinician might point out that either party's fears of intimacy or commitment would be likely to surface in the affair relationship were it to become exclusive. Finally, when partners have affairs primarily because they are too frightened or guilty to break up a troubled couple relationship, clinicians may help them figure out how to proceed more constructively.

Partners who want to break off an affair but who have been unable to do so can also be given help in individual sessions once the reasons for their hesitancy are determined. Often the best way to deal with threats that a spurned affair partner will reveal the affair to the mate is to do so preemptively. The clinician can help the partner having the affair figure out when and how to confess it. Other possible concerns with which the clinician can help may be that the affair partner will fall apart, become enraged, claim sexual harassment if the affair began at work, or the like. If the reason for not being able to end the affair is that it is meeting the partner's strong personal needs, the clinician may be able to help the partner determine whether and how these might be met eventually in the original couple relationship.

> Donna and Rob, a couple in their mid-twenties, came for treatment when they had been separated for three months but wanted to see if their marriage could be salvaged. In the initial interview, the two described having dated since high school and "idealized each other" prior to their two-year marriage. Once married, Rob settled into a routine existence much like that of his parents, with expectations that Donna would be content working, doing most of the housework, watching TV in the evenings, and spending time with parental families. Donna had told Rob repeatedly that she needed more attention, affection, closeness, and companionship from him, but he more or less ignored her. When she had moved out three months before, he was shocked. He had since asked that they begin dating and was now trying hard to understand what she wanted from him. He was also willing when Donna suggested that they might need counseling.
>
> Donna disclosed in a telephone call just after the initial couple session that she had been having an affair with an attractive, high-powered lawyer she had met through her job as a paralegal. She was not sure what she wanted to do. The clinician suggested she tell Rob she needed some individual help before proceeding with the couple treatment. In these sessions, Donna said that the man

was in his forties, married with five children, and making her no promises. She did not expect him to marry her but had some fears about breaking off because he might tell her boss about the affair. Some discussion about how she might prevent this or handle it if it did occur led to her confession that she was "addicted" to the gratifications the affair was giving her. In the course of several interviews, she began to see that she was meeting needs for affection and recognition with the lawyer that she had not been able to meet for a long time with Rob, and was perhaps also punishing Rob for his inattention to her. However, she would never be able to learn if Rob could really meet her needs while she was denying him the chance. The clinician made clear that the choice was Donna's, and asked if she would regret giving up the affair if couple treatment did not rescue the marriage. She decided that she really wanted to resolve the marriage one way or another to be able to go on with her life. She was willing to give up the affair to do so.

Assuming an affair does end and couple treatment is to be undertaken or continued, the question arises as to whether a clinician should insist that the affair be disclosed. Often the partner who had the affair will want to do so. Sometimes he or she will want the clinician's advice on whether to confess or will be reluctant to. Clinicians can help such partners think through whether they can really enter fully into couple treatment without disclosure. If there seem to be valid reasons not to disclose and the clinician has worked individually only with the one who had the affair, the couple may be referred to someone else for treatment. It may be difficult for couple work to proceed honestly if the clinician and one partner share such a major secret. However, there are gray areas, and clinical judgment is required (Karpel 1994, Westfall 1995). For example, because Donna's affair had happened while the couple was separated and was over before the couple treatment began, the clinician working with the pair might not insist that it be disclosed.

Uncertainty about Wanting to Save the Relationship

Sometimes neither partner has been having an affair but one or both are unsure whether they want to work on saving their relationship.

Still, they may also not be certain they are ready to end it. This ambivalent situation is different from the common one in which couples come to treatment not sure whether their relationship can be saved or how much it can be improved. In these latter instances, both partners may be more ready to try a period of treatment to see if they can achieve positive change.

Partners are usually uncertain about even wanting to try to save their relationship when they are close to running out of hope that it can be improved (Hof 1995). While couple treatment could be a chance to find out, a partner may believe that significant change is unlikely and that investing more time, effort, and money in treatment while experiencing more vulnerability and pain may yield, at best, marginal results. Such partners may have almost no energy left for the relationship. They may feel a great deal of anger, guilt, or discouragement that makes the future seem bleak. Partners can be especially discouraged if they have already tried a period of couple treatment with another clinician and it has not been helpful. A partner who has emotionally withdrawn may be uncertain whether she or he still loves the other or would be able to again even if positive change occurred. Some partners have become emotionally invested in moving on to another life, perhaps in some other city or on a new job. However, they may still be ambivalent or too guilty to say so because if the primary relationship ends, the partner who is left, or their children, will suffer (Walsh et al. 1995). Finally, in some circumstances a partner probably does want to leave but hopes that a period of couple treatment will provide the mate with a clinician to lean on, lead to a more amicable breakup, or facilitate a more favorable divorce settlement. These motivations are not reprehensible if the partner can be honest about them with the clinician and at some point, one hopes, with the mate.

Sometimes partners reveal in an initial telephone call or conjoint interview that they are not sure they want to try to save the couple relationship. Or they may give hints, perhaps by wondering whether individual sessions should be held. If one partner's ambivalence surfaces before couple treatment has begun, individual sessions with one or both mates may be the only ones held until a decision is made about whether to work on the relationship (Siegel 1992). Clinicians dealing with either partner's uncertainty or possible wish to leave the couple relationship need to be aware of their own attitudes and feelings so as not to become judgmental. The prospect of breaking up a long-standing relationship, especially when there are children, evokes strong feelings in almost everyone (Wallerstein 1997). We have all experienced losses or situations where one partner in a relationship wanted to continue it more than the other did. Every such occurrence brings pain and often guilt or anger. Yet losses and disappointments are inevitable in life. It is important to remember that people cannot help how they feel. If hope for change or feelings of love cannot be rekindled, a partner who wants to leave the relationship does no good by pretending. What is owed the other partner is a concerted attempt to sort out mixed feelings, eventual tactful honesty, and a parting that is as humane as possible. On the other hand, the permission to be honest with the clinician in individual sessions sometimes helps ambivalent partners sort out their feelings and make some realistic investment in trying to save the couple relationship.

When partners openly voice doubts in early conjoint sessions, their ambivalence can be discussed there. Another possibility occurs when clinicians suspect hidden ambivalence, perhaps because one or both partners do not seem invested in the couple work (Walsh et al. 1995). The clinician may then try to surface the ambivalence by asking about it directly, perhaps adding that people cannot help how they feel but owe it to their mates to be honest. If ambivalent partners are not sure how they feel or are reluctant to talk further, a limited number of individual sessions can be offered. There, an effort can be made to help them sort through their feelings and decide what to do, as in the case of Donna and Rob. Meanwhile, their mates can be offered supportive help either in couple sessions or individually. In cases where partners will probably break up, the couple clinician should not continue to work individually with both. Some partners may wish to use further conjoint sessions to work out a separation or amicable parting, possibilities discussed in Chapter 9.

It is crucial, in assessing either partner's ambivalence about whether to work on the couple relationship, to determine why the uncertainty exists. Some of this assessment can take place in a conjoint session if the ambivalence has been revealed there and the partners' concerns are whether the relationship can be significantly improved. Here the couple needs to have a frank discussion about past and present positives, the nature of their problems, and what would have to change for both partners to feel satisfied enough to stay (Walsh et al. 1995).

If one wants the other to change in specific ways, the other's willingness and ability to do so must be considered. Often, clinicians' reconceptualizing what has gone wrong, in ways given in the following chapter, helps both partners feel less anger and more hope. They may then be less demanding about what changes might improve the situation. When there has already been a period of couple treatment with someone else and it did not help, the clinician should try to ascertain why and explain, if appropriate, how a new attempt might be different.

Also helpful when partners are uncertain whether they want to work on saving their relationship is to empathically accept their feelings about having already tried hard and their possible fears that further efforts could fail. With recognition that both have been trying and have fears of trying further, hope can sometimes resurface. The reason is that the partners sense the clinician's understanding and begin to believe they could rely on his or her support if they made the difficult decision to work together toward change. We see this outcome with Elise and Jerry.

> Elise and Jerry had been married for seven years, for the first five of which Jerry had been abusing alcohol. They had two children, aged 1 and 3. Jerry was now in recovery and attending AA meetings four to five nights per week, with Elise's support. He was working steadily. Nevertheless, the couple was frequently arguing and ready to separate. Both were openly uncertain whether they wanted to work on the relationship. Elise freely voiced criticisms of Jerry and felt he would just have to be less sensitive to these if the marriage were to succeed. Jerry tended to retreat but then blow up and yell. Both agreed that this had also been their pattern when Jerry was drinking and that, in fact, it was only Elise's criticisms that made him get moving and do things that needed to be done at that time.
>
> The clinician responded to their situation by recognizing the enormous turmoil they had gone through for the first five years of their marriage and the burdens Elise had carried during that time. He suggested they had probably thought their arguing would improve when Jerry stopped drinking. They had both undoubtedly tried hard and were feeling discouraged now. Yet what they were experiencing was not uncommon for couples after a long

period of substance problems. Both partners usually have a lot of feelings left over from that time—anger, hurt, maybe guilt—that never got sorted out. They find it's hard to change communication patterns that worked as well as anything could during the substance use, like Elise getting Jerry to do things by criticizing him. After more discussion, Elise acknowledged that Jerry's becoming less sensitive to her criticism might not be the whole solution to their problem. Perhaps both partners' ways of communicating would have to change.

On the other hand, when partners present for treatment with uncertainty about working on their relationship because of major, apparently irreconcilable differences in lifestyle preferences or values, there may be less possibility for salvaging the relationship. The chances usually decrease the more major the areas in which differences exist, the farther apart the partners' positions are, the less likely either seems to change, and the greater the number of such differences.

Joanne and Christian, a couple in their late twenties, came in to consider whether they should undertake couple treatment. Both were of German origin but Christian had been in this country only two years, whereas Joanne had been born here. They had married a year before after a whirlwind courtship of two months. Christian was finding life in America difficult because he missed his parental family and had not found as good jobs as he had hoped. He thought he might want to return to Germany, while Joanne did not want to leave America.

The couple was also arguing a lot about whether to have children, which Christian did not want, and about whether Christian should help more with the housework. Christian protested that his mother never expected his father to help her around the house, as Joanne did with him.

For Joanne and Christian, the hope of reconciliation seemed very slim. To achieve some compromise on dividing the household chores, Christian would have to change his conception of male–female roles that was strongly culturally supported (Winawer and Wetzel 1996). Whether to have children and whether to live in the United States are life decisions in which true compromise is hardly possible, yet the impact on partners' lives is monumental. In such cases, clinicians can state their opinion about the difficulty of resolving the couple's differences but offer a trial period of couple treatment to test out possibilities, if the couple wishes to undertake it. Or they may suggest individual or conjoint sessions to help partners decide what to do (Karpel 1994).

All the special circumstances just reviewed are most likely to become apparent in initial contacts with partners, assuming clinicians carefully screen for them. However, they may also begin happening later on in a case, or partners may only later be willing to reveal them. Clinicians should not relax their vigilance for possible occurrences of partner abuse, overuse of substances, or any of the other difficulties identified above. All may strongly influence or preclude couple treatment at any point, and some can be life-threatening if not addressed.

CHAPTER

4

Initial Contacts

Many couple cases begin with a call from one partner suggesting that the pair is having trouble and would like some help. Others follow individual, group, or family sessions with the same clinician or are initiated by a referral. In any of these instances, if both partners are willing participants and no contraindications to couple treatment are found, the clinician using this book's integrative approach can usually conduct initial telephone calls and interviews in a fairly standard way. This chapter offers general guidelines for clinicians in such initial contacts, and then considers ways they can respond helpfully to diversity in all three participants' genders, sexual orientations, and sociocultural characteristics. A final section suggests how clinicians can intervene when partners are reluctant to come for needed couple treatment.

Sometimes clinicians realize in initial contacts, perhaps because of one or both partners' apparent borderline or narcissistic personality characteristics, that a couple is probably narcissistically vulnerable. Or couples may turn out to be dealing with a recently discovered affair, a separation or possible breakup, or one partner's mild depressive or anxiety symptoms. Modifications needed in initial contacts and continuing treatment in these situations are covered in Chapters 8 and 9.

GENERAL GUIDELINES FOR BEGINNING CONTACTS

Assuming couple treatment may be indicated in a particular case, clinicians must seek to accomplish several key objectives in initial telephone contacts and interviews. One is to try to facilitate both partners' constructive engagement. Another is to gather enough useful information to decide how to proceed. As they do so, clinicians must also help couples identify workable treatment goals, often by reframing issues and problems the partners present. Finally, by the end of an initial interview if possible, clinicians can try to help partners to feel hopeful about treatment and agree on an appropriate plan.

Initial Telephone Calls

In some settings, initial telephone calls from couple partners are taken by an intake person. If clinicians handle their own initial calls, there are two schools of thought about how to proceed.

One possibility is to conduct a brief initial assessment on the telephone (Karpel 1994), gathering information and giving feedback along lines suggested below for initial interviews. By doing so, any unforeseen contraindications to couple treatment are likely to be discovered. One partner will tell his or her side of the story and probably feel accepted and understood. The major disadvantage is that a connection is made with only one member of the couple, except in the rare circumstance that both place the call. Often the caller is the partner already more comfortable with the idea of couple treatment or more likely to try to seek control of it, leaving the relationship between the clinician and both partners out of balance from the start.

Another way to handle initial calls, if the caller asks for a couple session, is to avoid probing the couple's situation and just proceed to schedule one. However, the clinician should add something like, "I usually prefer to hear about your relationship from both of you but I do ask two questions before seeing couples. Is there any situation going on that you consider an emergency, or has there been any violence in your relationship?" Most important is to give callers a chance to report any concerns about partner or child abuse, suicide, homicide, or psychosis that might warrant an individual session or emergency response. Other possible contraindications to couple treatment can usually be explored at the time of the initial couple interview or in additional individual appointments suggested then, without danger to participants. However, sensing a caller's hesitation, a clinician might probe further with, "Is there any reason you may not be able to speak freely in a conjoint interview?" Callers may then report an affair, uncertainty about whether they want to work on the relationship, or another problem that may warrant an initial individual session, or at least further discussion on the telephone. If they simply begin giving their version of the couple's problems, the clinician can encourage them to wait and tell about these in the later interview when both partners can offer input.

Some callers say at the outset or reveal later in the call that they are unsure whether they should come in alone or with a partner. Here, clinicians need to ask enough about the situation to facilitate an informed choice. While in so doing they form some alliance with the caller, it is almost surely not as deep as that likely to be forged in an individual initial session. If couple treatment is recommended after the caller is seen individually, getting the other partner involved will often be even harder.

Before setting up initial couple interviews, clinicians should always ask if callers have any questions. Common ones are about appointment times, fees, insurance, and transportation arrangements. Sometimes callers ask about the clinician's theoretical orientation or experience working with couples with particular problems, ethnicities, or sexual orientations. All these questions should be answered openly and honestly. It is desirable to schedule the first couple interview reasonably soon and at a time convenient to both partners. Most often an hour-long interview is appropriate, but allowing fifteen or more minutes' leeway before the next scheduled appointment can be helpful in cases where it turns out to be needed.

Barring any evidence of danger, when a caller has given significant information about the other partner or the couple, the clinician should usually convey that he or she will mention it briefly at the start of the initial couple interview or ask the caller to reveal it again with the mate present. The explanation can be given that it is important for both partners to know what the clinician knows about them. Any concern callers express about this plan should be explored and considered. Personal information about the caller, unless it is directly relevant to the couple, need not necessarily be shared. At times, however, careful judgment is needed. For example, a caller might reveal a childhood history of incest that the mate does not know about. While this information is clearly relevant to the couple, the clinician should certainly not insist that it be told during an initial interview.

Such a telephone revelation might well be a reason to ask whether the incest survivor is in other treatment, and if not, to suggest an individual appointment prior to a conjoint session. During this individual time, the clinician could explore why the partner has not been told and the risks and benefits of revealing the secret.

Some clinicians ask couples to complete open-ended questionnaires before they are seen for a first interview to learn things partners may not share in the conjoint session or learn more than time there will permit (Nichols 1988). The clinician may mail the questionnaires, asking partners to complete them and bring them in, or couples may be asked to arrive early to complete the questionnaires before the interview. The questions may tap such areas as partners' past and present physical and emotional health, substance use, treatment of any of these, any history of physical abuse in the relationship, partners' personal histories, the couple's history, or partners' perceptions of their relationship problems. In any instance, clinicians should explain the purposes of questionnaires, answer couples' questions about them, and offer them the option of not completing a questionnaire or of answering the questions orally. Some partners may need to complete the questionnaires in a language other than English.

The main advantage of such open-ended assessment questionnaires is the additional information they generate, especially the possibility of discovering problems that may contraindicate couple treatment or require modifications in it. There may also be some saving of interview time. However, clinicians must weigh possible disadvantages as well. Information one partner gives might be problematic or even dangerous for the other to learn, yet couples filling out the forms at home may have trouble ensuring secrecy. Illiterate partners or those with poor reading or writing skills may feel humiliated to admit that they cannot complete questionnaires. Others, such as those whose ethnic groups value warmth and informality in relationships, may feel alienated by being asked to reveal information about themselves in such an impersonal way.

A second possibility is the use of standardized questionnaires given before the initial interview to objectively measure couples' perceived levels of marital satisfaction, intimacy, or some other aspect of their functioning that couple treatment could be expected to ameliorate. An instrument might consist of statements such as, "We argue a lot," with partners to indicate on a five-point scale their level of agreement or disagreement with each. Reviews of such instruments may be found in Baucom and colleagues (1995), Karpel (1994), L'Abate and Bagarozzi (1993), and Sayers and colleagues (1993). Before using any instrument, clinicians should make sure its reliability and validity have been tested on sample populations of the particular couple's race, ethnicity, and social class (Alexander et al. 1995).

Clinicians who assess partners' levels of relationship satisfaction, intimacy, or whatever through standardized measures taken before and after treatment are being accountable to their clients and possible funding sources by measuring practice outcomes. They also have more chance to learn about the partners' specific areas of difficulty or growth through their answers to specific questions. The main disadvantages are those also occurring with the open-ended assessment questionnaires. Partners may be uncomfortable immediately encountering a written document, although a clinician's careful explanations may help. An additional problem lies in these instruments' very standardization. The dimensions of variables measured, such as relationship satisfaction, may not fit particular couples. The same things that lead to satisfaction in most couples may not in a unique case. Or a variable such as intimacy or overall relationship satisfaction may be less important to a couple than solving specific problems, such as being able to agree on how to deal with money.

As another option for measuring treatment outcomes, clinicians can ask couples in initial sessions to begin some structured form of daily or weekly self-monitoring. This possibility is discussed further below.

Beginning the Initial Interview

Interventions to facilitate engagement and assessment go hand in hand for most of an initial interview. Clinicians should begin by greeting couples warmly. They may engage in a few minutes of small talk about the weather or the couples' travel to the office. Assuming they have not met either partner before, they can start the actual interview by saying something like, "I'd like to use this session mainly to understand what brings you here and what you hope to get out of coming. As you know, Mary called last week to set up this appointment. Other than that, I really don't know anything about you." If a few things were learned in the initial telephone call, a very brief, perhaps sanitized review may be given. For example, "She told me you've been having some communication problems," when Mary actually said her partner never listens to her. Another possible opening statement, when the initial telephone call was longer or contained touchy information, might be, "Mary identified some concerns which, I assume, will come out in discussion here. I'm sure you [looking at the mate] must have some things on your mind, too." The clinician thereby conveys an expectation that the caller will bring up salient concerns mentioned on the phone but tries to suggest he or she will weigh both partners' perceptions of problems equally.

Without further instruction, the couple may be uncertain where to start or may begin helter-skelter to describe their problems. In either circumstance, they may feel awkward or uncomfortable. Clinicians can often better proceed by asking for some background information on each partner and taking a short history of their relationship. For example, a clinician may suggest, "Before I hear about what brought you here, if it's okay with you, I'd like to get to know a little about you as individuals." This may be followed by a series of questions directed first toward whichever partner wants to start, then the other. Information may be briefly sought about partners' ages, work, children, where they grew up, and any prior committed relationships or marriages. Partners' ages are not always apparent from their looks, yet can be important as a beginning basis for understanding them. Hearing about jobs and children gives the clinician a little information about the partners' daily lives as well as their likely social class or socioeconomic status. Clinicians can also follow up by asking whether a partner likes his or her job, which can reveal stresses and gratifications there, and can empathize with stresses from jobs or caring for children. A ballpark idea of the partners' functioning outside their relationship may be gained.

Finding out where someone grew up can suggest ethnic or socioeconomic backgrounds or allow clinicians to probe these tactfully. Also, partners asked this question often volunteer information about seminal childhood experiences. For example, they may say, "We moved around a lot because my father was in the army," or "We moved to Iowa when my parents divorced when I was 10," or "I was one of ten kids and didn't have much of a childhood." Finally, earlier committed relationships or marriages and any children resulting from them can be briefly discussed. A clinician may follow up on clues to any information that may be important. If the topic may also be threatening, questions can be prefaced with, "If you're comfortable telling me about this now . . ." or the clinician can acknowledge the natural discomfort of talking to someone the couple hardly knows.

Besides giving clinicians a smattering of information useful in understanding partners' childhoods and current environmental circumstances, questions about their lives apart from the couple relationship allow each to engage with the clinician as an individual. Clinicians can facilitate such engagement by showing nonintrusive interest, understanding, appropriate empathy or concern, and acceptance of what has been said. Use of humor can also be appropriate. For example, to a partner caring for two children, aged 1 and 3, the clinician might say, "I don't need to ask whether you get plenty of exercise."

A series of excerpts from the Jane and Richard case illustrate how a typical first interview with a cooperative couple may be conducted.

> Jane and Richard's first appointment was prefaced by a call from Jane in which she said they had been arguing about Richard's family. She felt he spent way too much time with them. After some brief small talk, the clinician began the initial couple interview by saying primarily to Richard, "As you know, Jane called to set up this appointment. She mentioned you two were having some trouble agreeing about how much time to spend with your family." Looking at both, the clinician continued, "I imagine you'll both want to tell me more about this, as well as any other concerns. But first, I'd like to get to know a little about each of you as individuals." She then asked who would like to start. They looked at each other and Jane said to Richard, "Why don't you?" He nodded and the clinician asked, "Do you mind telling me your age?" The two eventually revealed that Richard was 34, Jane 31. He worked as a supervisor in his family's small business and she baby-sat with two neighbors' kids as well as taking care of their own kids, 6 and 4. She grew up on a farm in another state, he in a Greek neighborhood in the city. He agreed, when asked, that he was second-generation Greek while Jane said she was "just American." Neither had been married before.

Generally, information gathering about the partners as individuals need take no more than perhaps ten minutes of the initial interview. The clinician may then ask about the couple's history, beginning with how long the partners have known each other and how they met. Especially revealing is to ask what first attracted them to each other or, as suggested by Satir (1983), why out of all the possible partners in the world they ended up choosing each other. These questions usually get the couple back in touch with positives about themselves, each other, and the relationship, at least those extant at an earlier time. The qualities that first attracted them to each other may later turn out to be the very ones frustrating them now.

As the clinician continues to ask about a couple's history together, other important information may emerge. There may have been communication or intimacy problems as soon as the relationship became serious. The couple may have been negatively impacted for periods of time by health problems or stresses from their environment. The time when couple problems began to emerge or the fluctuations in these problems over time may be significant. Often interaction patterns that started out as positive or innocuous have become increasingly extreme and negative. From learning the couple's history, their mastery of different developmental phases or problems with these can be inferred. In taking the history, clinicians should be careful to elicit positives and comment on strengths as well as hearing about major events and problems. They should also make sure both partners participate in telling their story by asking both such questions as, "Is this how you remember this period?" or "How do you see things having been at this time?"

Jane and Richard had met through her cousin shortly after high school when Jane's family had moved to the city. They dated and eventually fell in love. Jane was attracted to Richard's love of life and ease with people, although he had a slight reputation as a ladies' man. Richard thought Jane would be a calming influence and help him settle down. She seemed real nice and stable, especially in contrast to some of his wilder former girlfriends.

They had married about two years later, now ten years ago. Before their children came along, they enjoyed doing a lot together and didn't have many problems, although they spent more time socializing with Richard's family than Jane would have preferred. After their first child was born, Jane wanted to keep working but Richard didn't like the idea. They worked out the compromise of her keeping two other children in their home during the day to bring in extra money.

The couple history often takes up no more than ten or fifteen minutes before the partners begin to describe the problems that brought them in. In a relationship of many years' duration or when partners are giving too detailed a history, clinicians may encourage truncating it to get to the current problems and covering the rest at another time. Or they may offer partners the option of continuing with the history and perhaps taking two sessions for the initial assessment. Most will want to get to describing their current problems and discussing what to do about them in the first interview.

A standard initial interview can often begin only a little differently if the clinician has already seen one partner individually or both in family sessions. In the first instance, a slightly longer introductory statement may be needed to convey, briefly and in a nonblaming way, the reasons the clinician and the partner seen thought couple sessions might be a good idea. The clinician should ask what the two have discussed about coming in together and may say a little of what he or she knows about both partners and their relationship. If at all possible, some positives about the other partner or the couple should be mentioned. A special effort can be made to welcome and bond with the other partner, perhaps by acknowledging that it may be uncomfortable to begin talking with someone the mate already knows. The clinician will need to ask for more background information about the newcomer, but both can recount the couple history. When both partners have previously seen a clinician in family sessions, he or she will obviously know a good deal about them already. If they are now coming in as a couple to work on their relationship rather than just on parenting skills, learning more about the mates as individuals and their history together is still appropriate. Further discussion in cases involving prior individual or family work can then be similar to that in any initial interview.

Continuing the Interview: Assessing and Reframing Problems

As partners begin to describe their current situation and problems, clinicians must work hard to make sure the initial couple interview progresses constructively. Doing so begins to establish a safe environment for the work together. Couples usually come in bearing some amount of anger, shame, or guilt because they believe one or both of them have failed as a caring or competent partner. While some are able to present their problems in mutual, nonblaming ways, such as by saying they cannot seem to communicate well, many believe one or the other partner must be more at fault. With no active intervention by a clinician, partners' descriptions of their problems can quickly deteriorate into criticism, subtle or obvious blaming, and generalizations such as "you always" or "you never." The clinician must prevent or stop such negatives while at the same time trying to determine what the couples' problems and strengths really are.

One key intervention strategy is to catch accusatory words or phrases and say something like, "Wait, could you put that differently? Tell us what he does that you don't like, rather than calling him selfish." Underlying feelings may also need to be acknowledged, as in, "I know you're pretty frustrated, but it will help me understand why if you tell me specifically what happens." Clinicians may also suggest that partners say, "My perception of what happens is . . ." or they can imply this by asking each partner, "What is your perception of what happens between you?" In any case it is imperative that clinicians elicit both partners' points of view.

At appropriate times, clinicians can model good listening skills by reflecting back the gist of what partners say, asking if they have understood correctly, acknowledging feelings, and perhaps showing empathy or normalizing a partner's experience. Ideally, most empathic or normalizing comments can be directed to both mates, as in, "This sounds hard for both of you," or "A lot of couples have trouble agreeing on how to discipline their kids." Positives and strengths should also be elicited and noted, especially if they can be balanced between partners or found in their interaction. A clinician might say, "That was really a nice, supportive comment you gave her," or "You two have a nice way of giving support to each other."

Clinicians will observe many of the couple's dysfunctional communication or interaction patterns and strengths in the interview itself. But they must also probe for more details or examples of couple interaction at home to form beginning hypotheses about what goes on and why. With a couple who says, "We can't resolve anything," the clinician might respond, "What happens when you try?" Or "Give me an example of what happens when you disagree." If a couple says they do not feel close, the clinician might ask, "How do you try to be close?" or "What seems to happen to prevent it?" Any vague or overintellectual responses can be probed for more behavioral details.

In response to "She just seems to be afraid of closeness," the clinician might ask, "What does she do that makes you think she's afraid?" Any mind reading can also be gently discouraged by a comment such as, "Well, you can't really know what she's feeling unless she tells you. How about asking her right now if she's afraid at those times?" Whenever one partner offers amplifying information about a problem being described, the other's perception should be elicited as well. Both partners need not talk an equal amount of the time in an initial interview, but both must experience equal opportunities to contribute.

> The clinician told Jane and Richard it sounded like they had a pretty strong foundation in their marriage with all those good early years. She wondered if they could tell more, then, about the problems that had brought them in. When did they really start? Jane felt they had been there to some degree all along—Richard always spent too much time with his family, but this didn't seem as inconsiderate before they had the kids. The clinician said, "I don't know if Richard is being inconsiderate—could you maybe just tell us what bothers you about it?" Jane explained that Richard does help with the kids when he's home but he often goes over to help his mother and leaves her to cope with the kids alone. Then when he comes home and she's exhausted from dealing with the kids all day, he wants to make love. The clinician asked Richard how these situations seemed to him. He said his need to be with family was natural and he doesn't understand why Jane wants to sit at home all evening after being home all day. The clinician said she could see this has been a tough issue for both of them, and asked how they have tried to deal with it.

As couples describe their problems, it is highly important that clinicians make sure these are conceptualized, if at all possible, in mutual and nonblaming terms. Often clinicians must reframe the problems, that is, conceptualize them differently than the couple has. Instead of a problem being seen as "He's too strict with the kids" or "She's too lenient," the clinician may frame it as "You haven't been able to agree on how strict to be with your kids." Another useful intervention may be to suggest that all couples find they have some different preferences or personality styles. In these instances, neither is right or wrong; they are just different. This simple idea comes as a revelation to many couples, although it may have to be repeated several times before they take it in. Pejorative labels for each other's personality styles can also be reframed in more neutral terms. For example, a woman may present with the initial complaint that her husband is indecisive while he says she is impulsive. Having sought further information, the clinician might say that the man likes to be more laid back or cautious while the woman is more eager to move ahead and make decisions. The problem can then be defined as not having known how to coordinate or adjust these different ways of approaching life.

Several authors (Baucom et al. 1995, Hof 1995) point out that reframing changes partners' cognitions about their problems. For example, rather than attributing these to either mate's unreasonable behavior, bad character traits, or lack of caring, they can begin to see the problems as normal differences of the type all couples must resolve. At other times, reframing may draw the partners' attention to the positive aspects of each other's behavior when they have been selectively attending to the negative. Such cognitive changes then often bring affective changes, primarily reduced anger and a renewal of positive feelings.

Another possibility is that the partners' differences, which perhaps initially attracted them to each other, have crystallized into more extreme and dysfunctional interaction patterns as the relationship has gone on. Perhaps the more one partner is emotional or pursues the other, the more the other constricts or withdraws. Or the more one criticizes, the more the other stops listening and tries to escape. Also possible, of course, are parallel behaviors: both criticize more and more. Or triangulations happen: both withdraw toward greater involvement with jobs or children. Most couples who come for treatment have developed a great deal of frustration and anger around such patterns. Clinicians can reframe them by suggesting that the patterns may have gotten more and more extreme even though both partners find them distressing. Both partners are suffering and both are feeling stuck. Specific dysfunctional patterns can be spelled out, as in, "I suspect that the more Ellen talks with some emotion, the more you, John, feel uncomfortable and withdraw, and the more John withdraws the more you, Ellen, feel upset and try to get through to him. You both end up having more and more of a perfectly natural response, and it ends up that things get worse and worse." Couples usually agree with such conceptualizations with great relief. Clinicians may even offer reassurances such as, "I think you're both caring people and neither of you wants to get into these interactions. But you don't know how to get out of them. We can work here to make things go differently."

> Richard and Jane turned out to have been having terrible arguments about his need to be with his family, which Jane interpreted as indifference to her. The clinician first asked Richard if he did feel indifferent to Jane. He denied this, although admitting he was often angry and felt unappreciated. The clinician then suggested she had thought of two other possible explanations for what was happening between them. One was Richard's Greek heritage in which close family ties are expected and enjoyed, while Jane came from a different background. Another perhaps was more complicated. Maybe the more Jane felt angry and upset about his absences and told him so, the more he felt uncomfortable at home and found himself staying away. The more he was away, the angrier and more neglected Jane naturally felt. The clinician added she didn't think this was either of their faults. It was a vicious cycle they had somehow got stuck in. After some questions and discussion, the couple agreed.
>
> The clinician noted that they had worked out some other compromises in their marriage before, like Jane taking care of neighbor kids to stay home with their own children, and she thought this disagreement could be worked out too. But they probably could use some help doing it. She asked if there were other issues between them and they agreed that sex had become an area of conflict as well. The clinician proceeded to ask more details and said they might have to wait to talk more about this problem next time.

Another aspect of reframing is to place problems in a context that limits blame. Clinicians will have been forming their own preliminary hypotheses about why a couple may be having problems, perhaps using the assessment framework given earlier. Based on such understanding, it may be appropriate to point out the partners' different opportunities to meet needs in their environments. The clinician working with Tina and John, a couple discussed in Chapter 2, might have said, "Tina, you don't have friends and family here like John does, so I can see why you'd hope he'd spend more time with you." In another case, a clinician might identify stressors such as, "No wonder you've had no time to be close when you've both been taking care of your kids and Jim's ill father at the same time." If a couple is struggling with problems of a specific developmental phase, a clinician might suggest, "Now that you've taken the step of moving in together, you're finding out what every couple does at that stage: you need to learn how to communicate better." Another strategy, if a clinician has sufficient information, is to reassure couples that they may be having the problems they do because their childhoods did not help them learn how to solve them. For example, "Most people don't really learn from their parents how to communicate effectively," or "No wonder neither of you is comfortable talking about feelings when you tell me your parents never did."

More difficult to reframe in a nonblaming way is a situation in which one partner has emotionally hurt or dominated the other, with the other clearly more the sufferer. Mean or domineering behavior cannot be condoned, and partners who act in these ways without seeing their behavior as problematic will be discussed later in this chapter. However, many partners who have acted badly genuinely wish they had not. If this seems to be the case, clinicians may proffer a possible explanation, as in, "I wonder if you were still mad about what had happened the day before and it came out this way?" Or they may say something like, "I believe that you didn't intend to be hurtful. I think something else must have been going on for you, and maybe here is a place where you can figure out some other options for handling whatever it was." They must also attend to the feelings of the other partner, acknowledging the hurt or anger as valid. If there are considerable negative feelings from recent or more distant events in the couple's history, the clinician may suggest that some time in treatment will need to be set aside for the mate to hear these.

Finally, lest partners become overwhelmed or discouraged about negatives in describing their current situation, clinicians should always try to make sure some positives are identified. They should convey hope, if possible, that treatment can help. Negatives may also be placed in context. In an initial session where a husband was identifying a great number of negatives he had never told his wife, the clinician might say, "These aren't so many problems when you consider they've never been talked about before. They all seem like the kind of problems many couples have. They piled up because you two never had a chance till now to work on them."

Closing the Interview

A final benefit of reframing in an initial interview is that it allows formulation of a workable definition of a couple's problems. Framing problems in workable terms begins to suggest what will have to change for the couple to feel their relationship has improved. A problem defined as one partner being indecisive and the other domineering is unworkable. If the two are instead seen as struggling with two different styles of problem solving, there is hope that their differences can be negotiated. A conceptualization of a couple's problems mostly in mutual, nonblaming terms, whether it is initiated by the couple or by the clinician's reframing, therefore sets the stage for contracting near the end of the initial interview. If all have agreed on a workable definition of the problems, it is time to discuss treatment goals and how the work together might proceed.

> The clinician said she wanted to summarize briefly what she had heard from Richard and Jane. They seemed to have a marriage with many positives, including getting along pretty well in the early years and solving some problems together. What they hadn't been able to solve was their differences about how much time Richard should spend with his family, and sex had become something of a problem as well. She asked if she had understood correctly. The couple nodded. She then wondered whether they would like to work on resolving these issues in some continuing sessions together. They both said they would, but Richard had some questions about exactly what would happen and how long this was all likely to take. Discussion of these points continued for the rest of the interview.

A clinician generally signals the ending phase of the initial interview by beginning to pull together what has been said. This summary need not cover the entire interview content. It should briefly review the reframed versions of major problems discussed, strengths or positives, and any important contextual factors. The clinician can follow up by asking if he or she has understood the situation correctly or left anything important out. The next question is usually whether the couple would like to work on the identified problems in treatment. These may be "flipped over" into implied goals. That is, the clinician might ask, "Do I assume correctly that you would like to work on learning to communicate better?" Or "Would you like to work here on how to get together on disciplining your kids?" It is important to make sure the couple has verified or identified the treatment goals they would like to accomplish, and that they have a chance to add any realistic goals not yet covered. Very rarely, resistance that has not surfaced earlier in the session will surface here, and can be dealt with in ways described later in the chapter. Most often, if the clinician has been in tune with the partners all along and has sensed no reluctance on their parts, they will agree they wish to proceed. In some cases, clinicians or partners propose that another conjoint session is needed for assessment before treatment decisions can be made.

Certain questions should be asked in first interviews whenever the opportunity arises, but may sometimes be postponed to the second if there are no hints of significant issues in the areas covered. These include inquiries about both partners' health, use of medication, prior or current other therapy, and prior couple treatment. Partners who have had other treatment should be asked why it was sought and what happened there. If someone is currently in treatment, it should be ascertained that the other clinician condones the idea of couple work and that both partners will be willing for the two clinicians to confer. Occasionally, partners carry another clinician's unbalanced views of the pair's interactions or the mate's foibles into the initial interview. The couple clinician can say he or she sees their situation somewhat differently and proceed with reframing of their problems more heuristically. Finally, partners should always be asked at some early point about their use of alcohol or recreational drugs and any threats of violence, actual violence, or psychological abuse, as discussed in Chapter 3. These can be presented as routine questions the clinician asks of everyone.

Some clinicians always schedule individual sessions with partners to complete the initial assessment and do not plan treatment until they have done so (Karpel 1994). The advantage of such sessions is that the clinician can glean more complete information about individual perspectives, histories, and, sometimes, factors that contraindicate couple treatment. However, such sessions can also delay couple treatment and, of course, cost the couple additional time and money. Relevant information about the individuals' backgrounds generally will come up sooner or later in the couple sessions and can be highly useful for their mates to hear. Thus, another way to proceed is to see partners individually only when there may be a special reason to do so.

Such reasons can include any possibilities or revelations in the initial session of physical abuse, substance abuse, or other complications reviewed in Chapter 3. Occasionally partners ask to come in alone, or a clinician simply has a sense in the conjoint session that something important is not being revealed. In any such instance, both partners should be seen individually lest the clinician be perceived as allying with either one (Karpel 1994).

When treatment planning need not be delayed, details of the treatment contract can usually be worked out by the end of the initial couple session. Partners will want to know how treatment will be conducted and may ask how long it is likely to take. Fees should be settled and the scheduling of appointments, usually weekly to start, agreed upon. In cases where a couple wants to improve communication, the clinician may suggest they think about a problem they can work on next time to begin to learn to communicate differently. If the couple wants to resolve specific problems, such as disagreements about handling money, the clinician may suggest a similar beginning. It is often best to advise couples not to try to solve major problems on their own before the next appointment, since they have not yet learned the communication and problem-solving tools they will need to do so. If a couple's main goal is to improve intimacy, work may already have begun in the initial session to determine what is preventing it. The treatment contract may be to continue this exploration before defining changes needed, or to begin working on blocks to intimacy, perhaps poor communication or other issues, already identified. In some instances, goals may be set to figure out ways to reduce or cope better with stresses on partners from their environments or from physical factors such as poor health.

In general, motivated partners who do not show the problems identified in Chapter 3 and who are not narcissistically vulnerable can make significant progress on communication skills and resolving disagreements resulting from poor communication skills within a few months. Intimacy problems usually take longer. Still, in any case, there should be some shifts evident after four to six interviews, and couples who ask can be given this information. When only a limited number of sessions is available due to the couple's insurance plan or for some other reason, goal priorities should be clearly identified. Clinicians who know that treatment must be very short-term, perhaps six sessions or fewer, may truncate the information-gathering portion of the initial interview, help the couple identify limited treatment goals, and begin work on these in the first session.

Toward the end of a first interview, some clinicians suggest that couples self-monitor the problems they have decided to work on in treatment to keep closer track of any changes (Bloom et al. 1994). A first step is to help the partners define the problems more exactly than they otherwise might. For example, rather than simply saying they would like to communicate more effectively, couples may be asked to consider more specifically what such communication would look like. They might decide they would like to achieve fewer arguments, more discussions in which problems were resolved, or more words of caring or praise for each other. The couple would need help to define each goal in very clear terms; that is, what would constitute an argument versus a discussion in which problems are solved. Finally, they would be to asked to estimate how often each specified behavior had occurred in the past two weeks (or longer) and to keep track of it thereafter. The estimate of the past frequency, plus the data on the first week or so after the initial interview but before work to change the specified behavior had begun, would constitute a baseline against which future progress could be measured.

As a self-monitoring alternative, if partners cannot yet be so specific about what they want to change, they can be asked to keep journals of what happens that is problematic or positive in their communication, problem solving, or whatever for a week or two. Thereafter the clinician can help them identify and define key behaviors to be changed. Other options exist for partners monitoring their cognitions (Baucom et al. 1995) and even their feelings over time. For example, they may each devise their own 5- or 7-point self-anchored scales measuring variables such as their levels of anger, sadness, or anxiety or their feelings of closeness. Obviously, couples have to be fairly strongly motivated to do formal self-monitoring. The benefits include being able to track their progress and possibly determining reasons for fluctuations in their behaviors, and helping them carry communication and problem-solving skills learned in sessions into their daily lives. Clinicians who successfully encourage couples to self-monitor their behaviors, cognitions, or feelings and who also keep track of their own interventions are doing at least a rudimentary form of single-case research (Collins et al. 1994).

DIVERSITY CONSIDERATIONS IN INITIAL CONTACTS

Clinicians and partners form impressions of each other based not only on their behaviors in initial telephone contacts and interviews but also on each other's gender and perceptions (whether correct or not) of each other's sexual orientation, race, social class, religion, ethnicity, and socioeconomic status. Each may react based on life experiences with others with similar characteristics or other sources of knowledge, including prejudices derived from stereotypes. Clinicians must try hard to recognize and respond constructively to all such reactions they or partners experience throughout treatment, but especially in initial telephone contacts and interviews. All parties are more prone to misunderstandings and discomfort before they know each other well. For example, research has found clients more likely to drop out of individual treatment with a clinician of a different race but to have no different treatment outcomes than with a racially matched clinician if they stayed (Gregory and Leslie 1996). In one study of family treatment, African American women experienced smoother and more positive first sessions with African American than with white clinicians, but these differences had disappeared by the fourth session. However, African American families seeing white clinicians were less likely than those seeing African American clinicians to continue in treatment to the fourth interview.

It is also crucial that clinicians try to understand how partners' genders, sexual orientations, and sociocultural characteristics may influence their expectations of treatment. The clinician's use of interventions must then be tailored to take this understanding into account.

Initial Influences of Diversity

While misunderstandings and negative reactions are more likely between clinicians and partners whose genders, sexual orientations, or sociocultural characteristics differ, they can also occur when people have the same or similar characteristics (McGoldrick and Giordano 1996). In the latter instance, clinicians or partners may assume understanding and affinity when neither exist. Everyone's life experiences are a unique influence. A man may not be more comfortable with a male clinician if his father was critical and overbearing. Same-sex partners do not always prefer a clinician whom they know or suspect to be same-sex oriented, perhaps because of homophobia (Schwartz 1989) or fear of running into the clinician socially (Okun 1996). A clinician of Irish American and Catholic origin may have disliked these influences and have sought to eradicate all traces of them, while an Irish American, Catholic couple may find their parentage delightful and their religion sustaining. The clinician in this case might have more difficulty engaging constructively with the pair than a clinician more divergent from them would. Or if one member of the couple disdained their heritage and the other embraced it, the clinician with the same heritage might have more trouble not taking sides.

A common danger when a clinician and both members of a couple are known to share a same-sex orientation or the same ethnicity is of all parties embracing similarities, which tend to make people more comfortable with each other, and denying or minimizing important differences (Greene 1994). A clinician who identifies with a couple because all are of the same ethnicity may overlook differences in social class or socioeconomic status that might strongly affect the couple's attitude toward treatment. Or a clinician and couple may feel comfortably alike because all are known to be same-sex oriented while denying that differences in race or ethnicity need to be discussed. Ultimately, for either clinicians or partners to deny difference is for them to deny parts of themselves (Brown 1995a). The treatment relationship and the treatment itself will suffer if clinicians do not understand and seek to deal with such issues.

Relationship intricacies are especially likely with a clinician who is like one partner in gender, sexual orientation, ethnicity, religion, or social class background, and unlike the other (Ho 1990). Clinicians must take care not to identify with the partner more like them or to see the other as less or more desirable based on how the differences are perceived. For example, a lesbian clinician needs to be careful not to favor a partner who is lesbian and secretly disapprove of one who is bisexual. A Latino clinician may need to avoid identifying with the Latino partner in a bicultural relationship, especially if this partner and the clinician are of the same gender. In some instances, clinicians will tend to favor the partner who is different from them based on negative valuations of their own characteristics or in an exaggerated effort not to push away this person. Partners who perceive a clinician to be similar to one of them and different from the other in some important attributes are usually quite alert as to how the clinician is responding to them.

When a clinician differs from both partners in some combination of gender, sexual orientation, or sociocultural characteristics, any party may misunderstand or experience emotional reactions to differences. Misunderstandings based on stereotypes or prejudices are usually more dangerous than those based on simple lack of knowledge. But the latter, if not recognized, can be a considerable problem too (Brown 1995a). Even without negative biases, partners and clinicians may react to differences with fears that they will not be accepted or understood or that they will commit an unintentional faux pas. Same-sex couples, partners of color, and couples living in poverty often wonder whether clinicians who differ from them will look down on them. Usually all have encountered professionals who have done so, or who simply did not understand the stresses they encounter (Davis and Proctor 1989, Parnell and Vanderkloot 1994).

Partners' and clinicians' reactions to each other will be heavily influenced by earlier life experiences with people with the same characteristics. Usually gender is the main characteristic to which transferences and countertransferences stemming from childhood experiences are tied. However, good or bad earlier experiences with others with particular sexual orientations or sociocultural characteristics may also have an influence. A heterosexual partner whose sibling is gay may be less inclined to reject a clinician thought to be gay. An African American couple with many white European American friends may be more open to working with a white European American clinician. If the clinician has experienced close relationships with other African Americans, he or she will likely be more comfortable as well.

Besides being aware of possible reactions all the participants may have to each other's similarities and differences in initial contacts, clinicians need to take into account what the partners' responses to the idea of couple treatment may be. Clinicians cannot assume that partners will hold particular attitudes based on their genders, sexual orientations, or sociocultural characteristics, since people differ within any group. However, when they do not yet know a couple, clinicians should be aware of how these factors may influence both partners' approach to the idea of treatment. Interventions can then be adapted to have the best chance of facilitating engagement, assessment, reframing, and treatment planning. Constant vigilance to ascertain partners' responses to interventions and to gather further information when needed will help correct missteps based on this strategy.

Often—and again, it must be emphasized that these generalizations are far from applicable to everyone—women are more likely than men to regard the idea of couple treatment positively (Brooks 1991, Rampage 1995). Some of the reasons have to do with the fact that women are often socialized to be more comfortable talking about themselves, talking about feelings, and being in a less powerful position with an authority figure. As noted earlier, men may also experience more unpleasant physiological arousal during interpersonal conflict, a situation they are likely to anticipate happening in couple treatment. Partners' sexual orientation has no bearing on their attitude toward couple treatment except that same-sex couples presumably more often share the attitudes common to their gender. Thus, female same-sex partners are more likely to seek treatment than males.

While no ethnicity precludes the possibility of couple treatment, ethnicity may make it more difficult for some couples to seek help. Latino partners are likely to turn first to members of their extended families, seeing clinicians as a last resort (Garcia-Preto 1996a,b). They are more likely to seek help for children than for marital problems. Davis and Proctor (1989) note that Asian Americans and Native Americans also tend to believe problems should be kept within the family. Men who are Asian American or Latino may feel awkward talking about intimate matters with young female clinicians (Ho 1990), although in one study, Latino men preferred couple treatment with a female clinician (Powell 1995). Partners whose ethnic groups espouse self-sufficiency, such as German Americans (Winawer and Wetzel 1996) or Scandinavian Americans (Erickson and Sinkjaer Simon 1996), may feel insulted at the idea they cannot take care of things themselves. Boyd-Franklin and Franklin (1998) suggest that African American couples may be constrained by the cultural value of not talking about their personal lives with strangers. African American men who learned in childhood not to admit weakness, hurt, or pain and who have faced many difficult life experiences because of prejudice and discrimination may find it especially hard to come to treatment where they will be expected to talk about feelings (Boyd-Franklin 1989).

Social class and socioeconomic status can have a strong influence on couples' attitudes toward treatment as well. For example, middle-

and upper-class men are more likely to have favorable attitudes than working-class men. In my experience, the latter sometimes see any treatment as being for people who are weak or crazy and may fear that clinicians will criticize or bully them. When couples live in poverty, men may feel shame, believing they should be able to provide more financial support (Davis and Proctor 1989). Both partners may feel ashamed if poverty has kept them from marrying. Even when both mates willingly seek help, being poor can create severe obstacles. Finding low-fee or free services with hours available when partners are not working or watching children, or arranging for child-care, are just some of the likely problems. Many settings that offer low-cost services have waiting lists.

Moreover, the lives of poor and working-class people are often unbelievably stressful, with a great deal of time and energy needed to deal with poor transportation, inadequate health care, and the ubiquitous pressure of having too little money for family necessities (Rubin 1994). Finding the time and emotional resources to seek help with couple problems is bound to be difficult. Clinicians often do not understand the special stresses that couples living in poverty face. Perhaps some of these reasons explain the consistent finding that couples and families with lower income are less likely to continue in treatment (Bischoff and Sprenkle 1993). However, in one large study of family treatment cited by Bischoff and Sprenkle, *clinicians* initiated more of these terminations, apparently due to agency service limitations.

Responding to Diversity in Initial Contacts

In an initial telephone contact, a clinician and the person calling will usually know each other's gender and may infer each other's ethnicity or sexual orientation. Clinicians should bring up known or suspected differences if these could inhibit their ability to work with the couple or if they think partners may have concerns. As noted earlier, callers' questions, perhaps about the clinician's experience with same-sex partners or those of a particular ethnicity, should be answered honestly. Clinicians may also suggest that any concerns can be discussed further in the initial session. Those who are not very knowledgeable about the influence of partners' same-sex orientations, ethnicities, religions, or socioeconomic status should say so in the initial telephone conversation or, at the latest, in the initial interview. Clinicians can also indicate a wish to learn more and invite partners to educate them, but must also ask about partners' comfort with this arrangement (Hines and Boyd-Franklin 1996). One hopes all clinicians will be familiar with the influence of social class and gender, although blind spots in regard to both are far from uncommon (Brooks 1991, Rubin 1994). Finally, clinicians should try to help couples find workable solutions to any difficulties paying fees, arranging transportation or babysitting, and so forth.

The conduct of the initial interview can depend on what partners of particular genders, ethnicities, or social classes are likely to find most comfortable and helpful. Neal and Slobodnik (1991) suggest that because many men are leery about treatment and initially less articulate there, clinicians take special care to elicit and respect the man's experience of a couple's relationship and its problems. Even if a man's fears eventuate in efforts to control the session or other dysfunctional behavior, clinicians who set limits can empathize with the underlying discomfort (Brooks 1991). Men are likely to be more comfortable with a structured approach to initial contacts like that suggested earlier than with a more laissez-faire approach (Alexander et al. 1995).

African American, Latino, and Asian American partners usually also prefer an active, goal-directed approach to treatment (Hines and Boyd-Franklin 1996, Lee 1996, Sue et al. 1995). All three groups may prefer clinicians who offer a welcoming ambiance and who self-disclose (De La Cancela 1991, Lee 1996, Sue et al. 1995). It is important for clinicians to convey respect, for example, by not using African American or Latino partners' first names without asking and making clear the partners can address them similarly. While African American and Latino couples may prefer a clinician who conveys interpersonal warmth, traditional Asian American couples may expect an initial session with the clinician to be fairly formal, perhaps with last names only being used (Lee 1996). A clinician might need to defer to a husband speaking first, only then eliciting the wife's views. Clinicians with any of these couples should wait for openings to ask questions about sensitive matters that may seem like "prying" (Garcia-Preto 1996b, Hines and Boyd-Franklin 1996, Lee 1996). Correcting a couple's communication when they describe their problems, as was suggested for a standard initial interview, might need to be done more cautiously so as not to cause loss of face.

Clinicians working with Native American couples who are strongly identified with traditional ways would need to modify their initial treatment approach even more significantly from that presented earlier to accommodate to the couples' possible preferences for silences, use of storytelling or metaphors, and other methods of less direct interpersonal communication. The atmosphere of the session should be informal, perhaps with coffee and food being served (Sutton and Broken Nose 1996, Wasserman 1995). Native Americans may also hope for practical advice. Wasserman (1995) cautions that Anglo clinicians working with Native Americans in a reservation community are likely to be viewed as government representatives, with a great deal of underlying anger and suspicion not discussed because of adherence to tribal values proscribing interpersonal confrontation. Such clinicians must expect to spend time proving their genuine interest through a series of informal contacts before trust can be established.

The way a clinician conducts other aspects of an initial interview may also be influenced by partners' genders, sexual orientations, and sociocultural characteristics. Assessment should cover immigration experiences of partners not born in the continental United States, and coming-out experiences of same-sex partners. Clinicians may ask questions that will help them infer the strength of the partners' ethnic identity and their level of acculturation (McGoldrick and Giordano 1996). Reactions of extended families and friends to interracial, interethnic, interfaith, and same-sex relationships should be ascertained. Clinicians should be careful not to reframe any couples' problems so as to suggest goals aversive to the couples' cultural values. For example, Latino couples could consider a goal of dealing with disagreements more directly as advocating disrespect between mates (Alexander et al. 1995). A couple whose Hindu religion and recent immigration from an Asian Indian country made them comfortable with more traditionally defined gender roles (Almeida 1996) would probably prefer a clinician who does not reframe their problems as being due to the man's greater power over the woman. Partners who hold strong European American values of self-sufficiency may benefit from the clinician's emphasizing, during the contracting stage of the interview, that the couple will do most of the work of treatment. Any partners, but especially those who may have experienced oppression from people of the clinician's gender, sexual orientation, or sociocultural characteristics, can also explicitly be told that the clinician will offer new ideas, but that they will be free to use these or not in deciding how they will actually change.

Clinicians meeting with partners living in poverty may find it hard to understand the kinds of lives such couples lead. Yet questions must be asked with a great deal of sensitivity and support. It is important to convey respect and listen to the couple's version of their problems (Davis and Procter 1989). Special efforts should be made to help partners who may be ashamed of their poverty or unmarried status to feel accepted and welcome. Clinicians should notice partners' strengths in dealing with adversity and validate them. Compared to standard initial interviews, less time may be devoted to getting individual and historical data and more to learning about current stresses. Clinicians should inquire empathically about a couple's daily lives and express understanding of the problems their economic situation causes for them. It may be appropriate to immediately help partners obtain services or resources that will ease their stress (Davis and Procter 1989, Hines and Boyd-Franklin 1996). As with any couple, the most common treatment contract is likely to be for work on communication and problem solving, but some will benefit from insight-oriented help. Low-income couples may have difficulty keeping regular appointments when their situational problems become pressing. Partly for this reason, some help with immediate problem solving may be given in the first interview. In some situations, home visits may be offered (Boyd-Franklin and Franklin 1998).

Clinicians should be very tuned in to how partners who differ from them in gender, sexual orientation, or sociocultural characteristics are relating to them and to the idea of couple treatment. If partners have had bad experiences with helping professionals before, clinicians should say they would like to be more helpful and would appreciate the partners letting them know when they are not. In any instance, they should always ask whether partners different from them have any concerns about proceeding. An extensive review (Sue et al. 1995) of research on psychotherapy with clients of four ethnic minority groups revealed that African Americans and Latinos tended to prefer a clinician of the same ethnicity but rated ethnic matching as less important than several other clinician characteristics, such as level of education, values, and therapeutic style. There was also some evidence that clinicians' discussing clients' culture or undergoing cultural sensitivity training led to better treatment outcomes. Ethnic matching was more often important to Asian Americans and Native Americans, with individuals who were more acculturated to dominant cultural values in both groups more likely to be comfortable with dominant culture treatment approaches. Several authors (Ho 1990, Sue et al. 1995) recommend that clinicians discuss ethnic prohibitions about self-disclosure to outsiders when working with Latino clients, and possible concern about loss of face with African Americans and Asian Americans.

In many instances, it can be helpful to normalize partners' concerns in advance by saying something like, "Many men don't feel totally comfortable working with a woman," or "It would be natural to wonder if I'll understand you, since I'm not Latino." When differences are discussed openly, with a frank airing of any questions or concerns, partners usually begin to feel more comfortable. The clinician's explicit encouragement to discuss such concerns is especially important with Latino (Falicov 1996, Garcia-Preto 1996b), Asian American (Lee 1996), and Native American (Wasserman 1995) partners, whose respect for authority may otherwise make them withhold these. If partners deny any difficulty, clinicians can suggest that the issue can be raised later at any time. The partners will still appreciate clinicians' concern and the groundwork for discussions that may be needed later will have been laid.

Ho (1990) identifies a number of special issues and intervention strategies for engaging couples whose partners are of different ethnicities. First, one partner may be more reluctant to seek help due to his or her ethnicity. Using an approach compatible with this partner's most comfortable way of proceeding as well as surfacing any of his or her concerns can be helpful. Reframing using cultural values can be a useful tool. Ho cites the example of helping a reluctant Asian American wife engage in couple work by framing her willingness to participate as a demonstration of her loyalty and commitment to family. It is especially necessary for the clinician who is like one partner in ethnicity to open up discussion of this fact and ask the pair to speak up if they feel he or she is losing neutrality. If the clinician needs help to understand one partner's language, an interpreter should be brought in rather than the other mate performing this function. Finally, goal setting is especially crucial with an interethnic couple because the two may have very different perceptions of what their problems are. Ho suggests that some goals may be related to dealing with the couple's probable situational stressors and cultural differences and some to idiosyncratic couple issues.

When any couple opts out of treatment without discussion after the first interview or simply does not return, clinicians should call to try to find out why. It is especially important to do so when partners living in poverty or differing in sexual orientation, race, or ethnicity from a clinician may have felt concern about the clinician's attitudes or expertise. Some of the techniques to deal with initial resistance described below may be useful in such conversations, but a clinician should also open or reopen a discussion of the partners' possible reactions to any clinician–partner differences.

RESISTANCE IN INITIAL CONTACTS

Discussion up to now has assumed that couples have been motivated and cooperative. This section of the chapter considers situations in which one or both partners balk at coming in for a first interview, do not participate constructively, or resist continuing although couple treatment seems needed and appropriate.

Possible Reasons for Resistance

Reluctance to begin needed couple treatment or to participate constructively, no matter how it manifests, should be viewed as "puzzling . . . behavior that requires understanding" (Basham 1992, p. 248). One common cause is either or both partners' having negative preconceptions of what such treatment implies. Some simply see it as a costly and uncomfortable exercise that will not ultimately help. Some view those who use any form of psychotherapeutic help as being crazy or dependent. Even if couple treatment carries less stigma, it may connote failure to solve one's problems oneself. As just discussed, gender, ethnicity, and social class often influence such perceptions. In some ethnic groups, going to a clinician may also connote disloyalty to extended family members, who should presumably be the ones to help with problems. The attitudes of their peers and extended families toward couple treatment can have a strong impact on all partners' views.

Even without negative perceptions of couple treatment or feelings of disloyalty in seeking it, partners may experience what should be unwarranted concerns about what will happen there. They may fear they will be blamed for the couple's problems. Some anticipate being forced to change in the specific ways the other partner wants. For example, if a wife has been pushing her husband to be home more, the husband may think the clinician will try to badger him into complying. Partners whose knowledge comes from books, movies, or prior individual treatment may expect to be psychoanalyzed. Bad prior treatment experiences that partners have had or heard about naturally create expectations that what will happen with this clinician may be similar. Their own past couple treatment may have been ineffectual because many clinicians with no special training in couple work nonetheless conduct it. Partners who have experienced discrimination due to their sexual orientation or sociocultural characteristics may be worried that a clinician differing from them will be prejudiced, awkward, or lacking in needed expertise.

Some of either or both partners' fears about entering treatment may not prove unfounded no matter what the clinician does. Both may sometimes feel uncomfortable or ashamed in sessions. Both will have to look more closely at their behavior within the couple relationship and at thoughts and feelings that may be painful. Those made anxious by interpersonal conflict or talk about personal matters cannot help but find the idea of treatment disquieting. Justified in some cases too is the fear that something upsetting will be revealed, or that opening up discussion of their relationship problems will make things even worse. Close scrutiny of a couple's relationship in treatment makes it hard to hide affairs, painful past experiences, embarrassing sexual problems, and the like. What partners may not realize beforehand is that they will have the clinician's help in dealing with these difficult matters and that the benefits can be worth the pain. Of course, a clinician cannot guarantee that treatment will help a couple; it sometimes does lead to a stalemate or to breaking up. More likely, however, is that the eventual outcome of having no treatment will be worse.

Most partners will also experience some realistic fears of change that may or may not cause initial resistance (Astor and Sherman 1997). Change holds risks ranging from getting stuck with unwanted household chores to having to share greater closeness. It is always hard to give up the known, no matter how distressing, to travel to an unknown place. Participating in treatment means, to some degree, trusting the clinician, the partner, and the process enough to give up some control. While some fear of doing so is natural, the idea of couple treatment can arouse intense transference-based fears if a partner has been significantly hurt by caretakers when he or she was vulnerable in childhood, or by the mate earlier in the couple relationship. Some partners' character rigidities that may protect against extreme fears of being vulnerable can make it very hard for them to begin couple treatment. When both partners harbor deep-seated fears of being vulnerable, both may collude in resistance. Finally, highly likely to resist treatment initially are partners coming in more or less against their wishes, perhaps when required to do so by a setting treating their children. People forced to seek help are bound to feel angry and vulnerable.

In assessing why partners may be balking at the idea of treatment, clinicians should also consider realistic obstacles that do not spring from misconceptions or fears. These can range from parental families pressuring their offspring to leave the couple relationship to a lack of money to pay for treatment. Here may also be included clinicians who place unreasonable demands on couples, such as that they take time off from work for appointments when they cannot afford to do so, or who otherwise are not sensitive to the couples' needs. For example, research has found couples more often to prefer relatively brief, problem-oriented treatment and to experience higher dropout rates when clinicians nonetheless offered "long-term treatments oriented toward personality change" (Bischoff and Sprenkle 1993, p. 359). Before they consider how to intervene, clinicians must be very careful to assess whether couples' problems in beginning treatment may be related to the clinicians' own behaviors, the partners' environment, or specific influences of gender, ethnicity, or social class.

Handling Initial Telephone Calls

Resistance may become evident in an initial telephone call when a caller says he or she wants couple treatment but the other partner does not. Less commonly, the caller is the reluctant party or says both do not wish to come, but are being required to. In any of these circumstances, a clinician can first ask whether the caller is willing to explain what prompted him or her to call. Based on information the caller gives, couple treatment may turn out not to be appropriate because of substance abuse, battering, or some other contraindication. If it is appropriate, clinicians should try to help both partners come in, because addressing resistance in person usually has the best chance of success. They may ask if it is possible to defer any decision and schedule an initial interview as a consultation to help the couple evaluate whether or not to proceed. If couples are being required to undergo treatment, clinicians can express empathic understanding of how hard it must be to be forced to do so, but say they would like to hear the partners' views of their situation.

Some callers will need to talk more because they or their partners are reluctant to come in even once. Clinicians may then try to elicit more discussion of the reasons, perhaps adding that some people do have doubts. Partners' negative perceptions of couple treatment, past bad experiences with it, fears, or the conviction that the couple does not have problems requiring help may be revealed. Almost always when resistance surfaces, clinicians' initial response should be an accepting one. A clinician might say, "Many people do think that," or "I can understand that you [he/she] could feel that." If the issue raised is a couple's united antipathy to required treatment or their disagreement over whether they need help, clinicians need to avoid taking sides either with referral persons or with partners who do want to come in. The importance of responding by respecting the reluctant party's ideas cannot be overemphasized. Least likely to be effective in helping any partner through resistance is to engage in a power struggle. Acceptance and respect help people not to feel blamed or bullied and perhaps, therefore, to be comfortable revealing more. When the caller is not the reluctant partner, the clinician has modeled empathy and conveyed the even-handed stance to be taken throughout treatment. Often, too, a supposedly willing caller harbors some of the same misconceptions and fears the overtly reluctant partner does (Siegel 1992).

If a caller is expressing reluctance, the clinician will have a better chance to correct at least some of this partner's misconceptions or alleviate some of his or her fears, as in the following case.

> Leonard Johnson called to say his wife wanted them to have couple counseling but he was against it. He was calling just to get her off his back. The clinician said it sounded like a tough thing that they disagreed, and asked if Mr. Johnson was willing to tell him a little more about the situation. Mr. Johnson responded that he and his

wife argued a lot and that their disagreeing about the issue of treatment was typical. After ascertaining that the arguments did not turn violent, the clinician said some couples do find counseling helpful to work out better ways of talking to each other. But he understood that Mr. Johnson didn't think this was a good idea. Mr. Johnson said, "You're damn right! I don't need some shrink like you telling me what to do." The clinician countered that a lot of people think that's what happens in couple counseling, but he likes to think of it more as being a coach or referee to help a couple reach their own mutual agreements about what they want to do. After some further conversation, the clinician asked if Mr. Johnson would consider coming in for one session to see what it would be like and then make up his mind. He also pointed out that if Mrs. Johnson was unhappy enough to want counseling, not coming in at all might create even more stress between them.

In this fairly brief conversation, the clinician's use of Mr. Johnson's word, "counseling," was one way to try to reduce his reluctance. Many people do not see "counseling" as conveying illness and stigma as much as terms like "therapy" or "treatment" do. Also, while clinicians' roles obviously go beyond being coaches and referees, the analogy may help Mr. Johnson understand that the clinician will not side with his wife and tell him what to do. Effective clinicians pick up clues to partners' perceptions about treatment, and Mr. Johnson's comment about shrinks suggested a fair lack of sophistication. The more willing reluctant callers are to reveal their misconceptions or fears about treatment, the more likely clinicians can engage them to come, making clear that coming once does not mean they have to agree to proceed further. If callers have had bad experiences with prior treatment, clinicians can explain how this treatment could be different. They can promise to try to be impartial in hearing both partners' points of view. They can point out possible risks in the reluctant partner simply refusing to come in. When treatment has been required by an outside authority, the cost of noncompliance can be nonjudgmentally reviewed.

Sometimes callers express more realistic fears. For example, a caller may express concern that the partner will use the interview to ask for a divorce. The clinician cannot promise to prevent something like this, but can say that if it happens, he or she will try to facilitate a discussion about whether counseling might be able to save the relationship.

Some callers express fear that a clinician will lose control of the interview or be "conned" by the mate, especially if these things have happened in other couple treatment. The clinician can promise to try to prevent the feared problems and can say how he or she will deal with them if they do occur. If partners fear that couple treatment will not help them, the clinician can say there can be no guarantees, but the possible benefits as well as dangers of coming in can be discussed. It will then be the caller's decision how to proceed.

In the common circumstance of a caller reportedly wanting couple treatment but saying the other partner does not, a clinician eliciting both partners' concerns and trying to offer reassurance may not be enough. One further step may be to ask what discussion the couple has had of the need for treatment and to suggest the caller reframe the request in a more mutual and nonblaming way, as in, "We don't seem to be able to solve our problems, even though I know we both have been trying." Of course, the caller cannot pretend the conversation with the clinician has not happened. The clinician may propose saying, "I called someone and she would like to hear your side of the story," and perhaps, "She said we could try just coming in for one time." It is also appropriate for the clinician to offer to speak to the reluctant partner by phone, if this might help (Astor and Sherman 1997). Boyd-Franklin (1989) suggests that clinicians ask to talk directly with African American men who are reluctant to come in, lest the men feel that they are being put immediately into a position of lesser power. Garcia-Preto (1996b) notes that clinicians who call a reluctant Latino man may persuade him to come in out of respect for an authority figure even when his female partner could not.

In the final part of a conversation with a partner whose mate may end up still not wanting to come in, the clinician can suggest the caller consider how much pressure he or she is willing to exert. The caller may wish to think through the cost to the relationship should no couple treatment occur and decide whether to warn the reluctant partner of it. Such costs may range from the caller's emotional withdrawal to a threat of ending the relationship. The caller can also be offered an individual appointment to discuss what to do in the event of the partner's unwillingness to participate.

Let us now examine what may happen when a couple comes in for an initial interview and one or both partners resist the idea of needed further treatment.

Partners Who Admit Problems but Do Not Want Treatment

When clinicians hear before an initial interview about one or both partners' reluctance, they can start the session by telling what they know from the initial telephone call or referral source and expressing appreciation that both mates have come in. They can then ask if both would be willing to discuss the couple's situation. Usually both will want to give their version of the couple's story. A clinician may, if the couple is willing, seek some brief information about partners as individuals and the couple's history before getting to their views of what has been going on between them.

Probably the most common manifestation of resistance in initial interviews occurs when both partners admit that the couple has some problems, but one resists treatment as a means of solving them. In this instance, as the partners describe problems, clinicians can attempt as usual to convey empathy and reframe the problems in mutual and nonblaming ways. They may do extra "wooing" of a reluctant partner by being sure to credit his or her valid insights and strengths while not neglecting those of the other partner. These interventions sometimes lessen both partners' fears that they will be blamed, psychoanalyzed, or forced to change against their will. However, reluctant partners may resist reframing as they push to have their own view of the couple's problems prevail. Or they may ask something like, "What does it matter since we're not coming in again?" Sometimes reluctant partners participate in problem description and appear to accept reframing only to have resistance surface at the point of discussing treatment. Clinicians should be sure to leave enough time in the interview to address it at this point even if some usual beginning content must be truncated.

Sooner or later a partner may convey resistance with statements such as, "Treatment won't help," "People should solve their problems themselves," or "We'll take care of this ourselves." If possible, clinicians should accept at least part of what reluctant partners say, if only by some comment like, "Well, I respect your opinion, but I don't agree with it," or "You may be right. Treatment might not help. But what makes you so sure?" Then they may explore what makes reluctant partners think treatment will not help and cite their own perceptions of the couple's strengths and possibilities for achieving positive change. They can counter the idea that people should solve their own problems with an explanation that that is exactly what the couple would be doing in treatment. Indeed, their willingness to solve problems themselves will be a tremendous help.

Further, clinicians should try tactfully but firmly to explore concerns either partner may have about what might happen in couple treatment, if it should occur. The rationale for doing so can be that, while there is no guarantee treatment will help the couple's problems, it might, and so why not try it and see? When real reasons for reluctance surface they can often be dealt with without too much difficulty, whereas hidden sources of resistance will continue to cause problems. Often useful can be clinicians' empathically suggesting partners' possible concerns, based on what has been learned or can be guessed about the couple. For example, "You've told me you're a self-made man who doesn't like to talk things to death, and you may be wondering if that's exactly what will happen here." While a partner's fears of being blamed or bullied often dissipate during the interview, a common remaining one is that if the reluctant partner consents to treatment, he or she is agreeing to solve some of the couple's problems in the specific manner the other partner wants. To correct this misconception, clinicians may even say something like, "You may be thinking I'm going to take your wife's side and insist everything will be solved if you just come home on time each night. I won't do that. I believe strongly that couples have to find solutions that work for both of them, maybe even something neither of you has thought of yet but that you can figure out together."

As discussed earlier, reluctant partners of a different gender, sexual orientation, or ethnicity than the clinician should be encouraged to air concerns with a comment such as, "I wonder if you're a little uncertain about working with me because I'm [or I'm not] a woman [or whatever]. That would be understandable." This intervention was used in the Howell case.

> Jean Howell, 32, was African American, while her husband Ken, 34, was white and mixed European American. Ken very much wanted couple treatment because of perceived communication problems and lack of closeness. He felt his wife had been gradually withdrawing from him over the past several years. Jean agreed they had problems but felt they could cope by themselves. She at first denied concerns about how treatment might proceed. How-

ever, when the clinician noted that he differed from her in both race and gender and she was entitled to some concerns about that, Jean commented, "My husband doesn't understand my culture, why should you?" The clinician replied that that was a valid question. He went on that he might understand her husband more readily but he would also want to try hard to understand her. Perhaps she could help him and her husband could learn to understand her culture better at the same time. Ken chimed in with, "Jean, I do want to understand you."

If resistance persists, clinicians can ask couples to anticipate what will happen if they do not have treatment. Some partners issue an ultimatum outlining severe consequences, such as separation or divorce. Usually partners who want treatment simply predict that the problems will continue or get worse. Reluctant partners usually disagree, protesting that they or the couple will "try harder" to solve things on their own. Clinicians can cautiously ask for more specifics. Reluctant partners may respond with promises that have been made and not been kept before, usually because they are unworkable solutions to the problems (e.g., "I'll just stop yelling at her"). Clinicians can ask if these solutions have worked or express concern that they will not because they do not take care of both partners' underlying needs. For example, a clinician might say, "It's a good idea to stop yelling, but I think you're yelling when you get tense or don't like what your wife is doing. I'm concerned that you won't be able to give it up until you both figure out a better way of handling your differences. Just stuffing it and being unhappy doesn't sound like a good answer to me."

In further discussion, Jean's idea about how to proceed without treatment was that she would try to be more open to Ken's wishes for affection and recreational time together. The clinician suggested that this effort might work, but he was concerned it wouldn't. He asked how she had usually responded to Ken's requests for these things and she said, "I do try . . . for a while." The clinician said he believed she did, but he thought the lack of understanding she was feeling in the relationship, or perhaps other unhappiness about it she hadn't yet revealed, might be holding her back and that these needs of hers deserved attention. They shouldn't just be stifled.

If reluctant partners are still inclined to refuse treatment, clinicians can ask if they would be willing to come for a few appointments, perhaps three or four, before making up their minds. Or clinicians can try to help the couple work out a compromise wherein the reluctant partner will come back for treatment if both do not agree their situation has improved after a set time period, such as one month of "trying harder." If the reluctant partner's objection is to the present clinician, he or she can offer to help the couple find someone else. Jean Howell eventually agreed to couple treatment with an African American clinician, a stipulation Ken was willing to accept.

Finally, when no agreements can be reached about further couple treatment, clinicians can offer dissatisfied partners individual appointments to decide what to do.

Partners Who Resist in Other Ways

Sometimes in an initial interview partners resist treatment by denying that the couple has any significant problems. Another possibility is that partners say they want help but one or both insist on unworkable definitions of their problems, goals, or plans for treatment, or interfere with having a constructive discussion. In any of these instances, many of the interventions just suggested can be used but additional strategies may be tried as well.

When one partner believes the couple has problems and the other denies it, clinicians who elicit their story can sometimes reframe that the two simply disagree about what their problems are. For example, reluctant partners may acknowledge that their mate's acting unhappy, complaining, or withdrawing has become a problem for them. If this approach does not change the denial, clinicians can still elicit partners' ideas about how couple treatment works in order to deal with misconceptions or fears that may be fueling resistance. They can ask whether a reluctant partner would be willing to try a few sessions since the other mate is dissatisfied. Asked what will happen without treatment, reluctant partners usually say that things can continue as they are because there is no need for change. Their mates may express that they will go on being unhappy, withdrawing further, or moving toward ending the relationship. A clinician can encourage the unhappy partner to find ways to meet nonsexual needs in other relationships and activities, noting that doing so may ease the pressure on both. This intervention often has the somewhat paradoxical effect of increasing the resistant partner's interest in treatment, since his or her power to control the relationship by withholding is jeopardized. However, it should not be used if there is any chance of partner abuse. As a final possibility, clinicians may offer unhappy partners individual appointments to consider what to do.

Both partners denying their need for couple help is not unusual when a treatment setting or the courts require them to undergo it. Most often this circumstance occurs when a child is having problems or has been abused. Essential in such instances is that clinicians empathize with the couple's anger, frustration, or other feelings at being forced to come in against their will. Clinicians must also give a full and fair hearing to the couple's point of view about the situation that has resulted in their being called in. Often, doing so will reveal misperceptions of what the requirement for couple treatment is all about. For example, if a couple believes it means that a treatment setting thinks they caused their child's problems, the clinician might clarify that they are not necessarily the cause but can be part of the solution. In all instances, clinicians should validate such couples' strengths. They should seek to learn what goals, if any, the couple might like to try to achieve. They should discuss what might happen in couple treatment to clear up misconceptions and fears. They may suggest a couple try a few sessions, giving them time to learn the clinician will not humiliate or bully them. If resistance persists, clinicians may have to fall back on suggesting nonjudgmentally that it is the couple's choice whether to fulfill the requirement or deal with the consequences of not doing so. Of course, the consequences must be made perfectly clear if they have not been already.

Partners who say they want couple treatment but try to define it in destructive ways or otherwise prevent meaningful discussion are also showing resistance. Such resistance sometimes takes the form of one partner labeling the other as "the sick one," "the problem," or "the one needing help" when there is no real evidence of this mate's greater dysfunction. In one case known to me, a man proposed a treatment plan in which the clinician would work to cure his wife of her low self-esteem while the man supervised and assisted. A partner given a label may or may not agree to it. Or both partners may try to label each other. Such couples are less likely to continue in treatment than those who see their problems as relational (Bischoff and Sprenkle 1993), and probably less likely to benefit from it unless their views can be altered. Some partners find other ways to resist, such as by jumping from topic to topic, excessive joking, denigrating the clinician's expertise, or overtly trying to dominate or control the initial session. Here again resistance caused by misperceptions or not too deep-seated fears about couple treatment may be dissipated by intervention strategies already described. It is often a good idea to point out empathically that a partner seems not to be comfortable with the clinician's way of proceeding and to ask if he or she would be willing to discuss why. Sometimes, however, diversion tactics or inflexibility continue. A clinician's attempts to reframe problems may be met with persistent denial, as in a partner's statement, "You don't understand. She's the problem," or "I'm right and he's wrong." Men who have benefited from the power differential in traditional definitions of gender roles "may attempt to control therapy sessions or compete with the therapist for power" (Brooks 1991, p. 54). For example, a man may insist the goal of treatment be that his wife agree to do all the housework because "that's what women should do." Sometimes clinicians can find a way to frame a couple's problems that accedes partly to the controlling partner's way of thinking, but also gives a message to the mate that his or her point of view will not be ignored, as in this excerpt from a first interview:

> In the initial session with John and Rhoda Donovan, ages 60 and 58, John complained that Rhoda was getting too many ideas from her women friends about "fancying up her life." The couple had had a very traditional marriage with John working as a long-haul truck driver and Rhoda staying home to raise their five kids, now all grown. Their minister had suggested they seek couple treatment. John dominated the session with descriptions of how Rhoda was "challenging" him. She was complaining of boredom even though he brought in a good income. She wanted to do volunteer work, go out with her women friends, and sometimes eat out as a couple rather than cooking every night. Rhoda claimed, when the clinician helped her get a few sentences in, that John was a good husband and she didn't mean to challenge him, but she *was* bored with her life sometimes. The clinician's attempts to reframe the problem as the couple needing to have better communication, especially

during this new life-cycle stage, failed to have a noticeable impact on John. John wanted couple treatment so the clinician could "talk sense to Rhoda and make her stop asking to do this, that, and the other thing."

Finally, the clinician pushed Rhoda to identify how John had been a good husband. She said he didn't drink or hit her, brought home a good paycheck, and didn't criticize the way she handled the house or the kids. The clinician then suggested that maybe part of their problem was that they had always had a clear picture of areas that were Rhoda's domain, but with the kids gone her domain had gotten smaller and she needed to broaden it some way. Maybe John, as a good husband, needed to help Rhoda figure out ways to broaden it that wouldn't make him so uncomfortable. Then she might be happier and not constantly asking about possibilities that felt like a challenge to him. Both seemed to be thinking hard about this redefinition.

This interview excerpt illustrates another strategy sometimes helpful in influencing partners whose rigid efforts to control couple treatment seem to preclude its proceeding constructively or at all. The strategy is to try to appeal to the self-interest of the overcontrolling partner. The clinician pointed out that if Rhoda Donovan were given some of what she wanted, she might stop challenging her husband all the time, a behavior he obviously disliked. In another case, a clinician might point out that the less powerful partner might be more giving if the partner with more power gave up some of it, even if the latter still held onto more control.

If a clinician's best efforts fail to make much impact on such couples, the clinician may again be faced with the dilemma of how to proceed. One alternative is to suggest that the discussion of problems, goals, or a treatment plan continue for another session to see whether all can find a way to agree then. Another is to schedule individual interviews with each partner, hoping that a better connection will help both accept a more constructive way of beginning. This strategy may also help a partner who has been labeled or controlled gain enough power to make some demands in the relationship. In some cases, clinicians may refuse to continue with a couple, perhaps saying that they do not believe the proposed treatment will be workable (Karpel 1994). Individual appointments, a time period for the couple to think about the matter, or the option of seeking help with a different clinician may then be offered.

In the Donovan case, the clinician offering individual appointments, refusing to treat the couple, or confronting John directly on his sexist views could have been alternatives to continuing. On the other hand, any of these very likely would have turned the couple off to the idea of treatment altogether. Rhoda seemed far from deeply unhappy with her marriage, and John had redeeming features. The chances of helping John modify his views enough to make a difference for Rhoda would seem greater if the clinician continued with them together. Other options could still be considered later if John proved totally unwilling to change. In such cases, both partners' wishes, the potential for harm to either, the likelihood of any positive change occurring, and the clinician's ability to maintain a constructive but not overly acquiescent stance are factors to be weighed.

CHAPTER

5

Work on Communication and Problem Solving

Most couples who present for treatment have trouble communicating and problem solving effectively together. Many identify communication difficulties as their main complaint (Sayers et al. 1993). Some focus on the specific problems they cannot seem to solve, as in, "We argue all the time about money," or "We can't agree on how to discipline the kids." Others say they communicate adequately about day-to-day matters but cannot make certain major decisions, such as whether to have a child. Couples whose presenting complaint is lack of intimacy also usually require some work on communication and problem solving. If partners have complex intrapsychic reasons for communicating poorly, therapeutic attention must be given to these. But their dysfunctional communication will not usually disappear with attention only to intrapsychic matters; both insight and better communication skills are almost always needed. Even with narcissistically vulnerable couples, whose ability to deal with anger, emotional neediness, and self-esteem is clearly compromised by childhood difficulties, work on communication provides some of the tools needed to get to these deeper issues (Siegel 1992). Some clinicians view helping couples with communication and problem solving as too easy or basic to be worthy of extensive discussion. Such work is certainly not so easy that clinicians can take for granted that they know how to do it well. And it is basic only in the sense that it is the foundation for all couple treatment.

This chapter and the two that follow cover work with most couples on communication, problem solving, and insight using the book's integrative approach. Discussed below are treatment possibilities when couples have asked or agreed to focus on communication and problem solving. Considered are ways to understand common communication problems, help couples learn communication and problem-solving skills, facilitate the change process, and deal with possible obstacles. Chapter 6 discusses insight work to help couples cope better with their needs, feelings, and fears, in order to achieve greater relationship satisfaction or intimacy. The influences of clinicians' and partners' genders, sexual orientations, and sociocultural characteristics in all such work are examined in Chapter 7.

ASSISTING COMMUNICATION AND PROBLEM SOLVING

Work on communication and problem solving can often begin in the second couple session, after clinicians have checked out the partners' reactions to the first interview and clarified any data needed to complete the initial assessment. It may also be useful at this point to get some sense of the couple's day-to-day life, such as who does what on evenings and weekends, as a context for understanding any problems to be discussed. Then the clinician can explain the likely format for the ongoing work. Generally, a few minutes will be spent at the start of each session assessing what has happened since the last one, with special attention to positive changes the couple has made and difficulties they have encountered in carrying out agreements or using new communication and problem-solving skills. Thereafter the couple will be encouraged to select one problem they want to solve together or a decision they need to make, and to try to communicate constructively about it to achieve resolution. Sometimes more than one issue can be covered in a session, while other decisions or problems will take more than one session to resolve. The clinician will help by teaching, coaching, modeling communication and problem-solving skills, and giving feedback. It can be explained that the primary intent is for the couple to learn new ways to communicate and solve problems for later use on their own. At the end of this description, the couple can be asked if they are willing to proceed and can be encouraged to let the clinician know whenever they have questions or concerns about what is happening. Assuming the couple agrees, the actual work can begin.

Some clinicians prefer to start instead by spending a few sessions having partners do behavioral exchanges, such as those described in Chapter 1, to help them provide more gratification to each other and dissipate anger (Christensen et al. 1995). Others focus for a number of sessions only on specific communication skills, such as active listening, before getting to problem solving. The difficulty in these approaches can be the couple's frustration as they wait to deal with the problems that caused them to seek help. At the very least, partners should be given the choice of how to begin.

Identifying Communication Problems and Strengths

To help couples work on communication and problem solving, a clinician must be able to assess what the partners seem to be doing wrong as well as where their skills are adequate. Just letting the two talk about problems in sessions as they usually do at home will reveal many of their specific communication difficulties. But it may also discourage them and persuade them that treatment cannot help. Clinicians must therefore take responsibility for spotting communication problems as soon as they occur and intervening immediately, if necessary interrupting a partner to suggest he or she proceed differently. Good communication should also be reinforced. Besides observing the couple's interaction in sessions to evaluate their communication skills, clinicians can ask partners to report on their discussions at home. Some even ask them to tape these or, as discussed in Chapter 4, to do written self-monitoring. Self-monitoring can also be used to assess partners' dysfunctional cognitions or beliefs that may underlie some of their communication problems (Baucom et al. 1995).

In the second interview with Ron and Lynn, the working-class couple introduced in Chapter 2, their clinician let them talk at first without interrupting.

> Ron and Lynn came into their second treatment session upset. They had had a tremendous argument because Lynn had again yelled at Ron's mother on the phone. Lynn said that she got mad and yelled when Ron's mother bawled her out for not wanting to bring the baby over all day Sunday. Ron repeated that Lynn should handle his mother as he does, by just pretending to go along with

what she says. Lynn began crying and said Ron doesn't respect her because he doesn't back her against his mother. Ron said he couldn't understand why spending time with his family is such a problem anyway. After all, Lynn spends money calling her mother in another state several times a week even though she talks about silly, unimportant things and she and Ron have money problems. Lynn replied angrily that Ron is a tightwad and all their troubles spring from the fact that they were raised differently. She was raised not to take guff from anyone.

In what probably amounts to ten or fifteen minutes of their second interview, Ron and Lynn have arrived at a total impasse without solving anything. They have also demonstrated a number of common communication problems from the following list:

Topic jumping

Many couples who begin talking about a problem digress into areas that are tangentially related or that can be used to blame each other as ammunition against being blamed themselves. Such couples tend to report that when they argue or talk about problems at home, nothing gets resolved. Partners do not usually intend to topic jump, and most do not even realize they are moving rapidly from subject to subject. In the brief excerpt just given, Ron and Lynn have touched on the problems of how much time to spend with Ron's mother, how to handle her, Ron's possible lack of respect for Lynn, their different spending habits, and their different backgrounds. Virtually no movement on any topic has occurred.

Not really listening to each other

Partners communicating dysfunctionally about a problem rarely listen to what the other is saying in the sense of really seeking to understand it. They may hear the other's words and even be able to repeat most of them, but misunderstand or fail to register the main points. Certainly they do not give back any response of having heard and understood what has been said before they begin to speak themselves. Instead they may defend themselves or offer a solution to what they think the problem is. One couple known to me calls this form of interaction "ice skating." The couple is hitting the surface, moving fast, and only apparently getting somewhere because they will sooner or later turn back and skate over the same surface again. Ron and Lynn are clearly doing this.

Blaming, criticizing, engaging in "character assassination" or "red flag words" (Ables and Brandsma 1977)

While communication of this type sometimes serves deeper psychological functions for partners, it is probably as often influenced simply by their frustration, anger, insensitivity to each other's feelings, role models who communicated in this way, or past couple history in which each has learned to fight fire with fire. As noted in Chapter 1, distressed couples do less self-censoring of their communication, especially of negative messages directed toward the mate. Blaming or criticizing runs the gamut from clear accusations that something bad is the partner's fault to apparently holding the partner responsible for something the speaker may or may not perceive as negative. That is, there are gray areas as to whether some statements constitute blame or are simply "facts." Ron may believe he is simply relaying the fact that Lynn spends money calling her mother several times a week whereas Lynn may infer that he is blaming her for this. A subtle form of blaming can occur when one partner says things have become more positive because the other has begun to act differently. The implication is that the original negatives were solely the other partner's fault. In character assassination, partners impute each other's negatively perceived behaviors to character flaws. Lynn takes Ron's frugality to mean he is a "tightwad." A "red flag" word belittles or otherwise negatively describes something the partner has done, thought, or felt, as when Ron calls Lynn's talk with her mother "silly." Many times partners who are not sensitive to their mates' feelings use character assassination or red flag words without any conscious awareness that these will be hurtful.

Mind reading or proceeding based on inaccurate thinking about the mate

As the cognitive behaviorists warn, partners may act based on inaccurate perceptions, attributions, expectancies, or assumptions about their mates without even realizing they are doing so. They simply assume that they have correct information about what their mates are thinking or feeling or the reasons for their behavior when they do not. An example with Ron and Lynn is Lynn's belief that Ron's not backing her against his mother means he does not respect her. When the partners' communication during sessions suggests that such cognitive distortions may be going on, alert clinicians must ask about or catch them (Baucom et al. 1995).

Focusing on the past rather than the future

Partners understandably have feelings about past happenings between them and may need to describe some history or recent interactions to clinicians to figure out what has gone wrong. Still, at some point couples need to decide what they will do differently from now on. This shift to a future focus is the essence of problem solving. Ron and Lynn would very likely spend the whole second session describing events of the past few weeks and complaining, blaming, or justifying actions if the clinician did not intervene. There must clearly be a time in treatment for devoting attention to immediate feelings or looking at major events that have evoked strong feelings in a couple's past. But such times need to be deliberately set aside for ventilation, understanding, and support, as will be discussed below. In general, discussion of past events needs to be limited in sessions so the couple can move into problem solving. They also need to learn how to do the same thing at home.

Rushing to solutions

This is perhaps the biggest mistake most couples make when faced with problems they need to solve together. As outlined in Chapter 2, partners as individuals solve problems all the time. They tend to try to solve them the same way as a couple and it fails to work. Yet each finds his or her proposed solution a good one and cannot understand why the partner does not agree. One of the major problems Ron and Lynn face is how to deal with Ron's mother, who is realistically quite intrusive and controlling. Ron deals with her by disregarding what she says. He wants Lynn to solve the problem by doing the same thing. Lynn's solution is to yell back at her mother-in-law. She cannot understand why Ron will not back her solution and attributes his not doing so to lack of respect. Lynn is probably right that they were raised differently. She may be beginning to see their differences as insurmountable, yet some differences between two partners' ways of coping are inevitable.

Before considering interventions to help couples like Ron and Lynn, let us identify a few other common couple communication problems.

Generalizing, as in "you always . . ." or "you never . . ."

This communication habit is usually another version of blaming. However, partners' perceptions of what happens between them may also be distorted by negative expectancies such that they fail to register the positive exceptions that do occur (Baucom et al. 1995). What the partner supposedly "always" does is something he or she should not, such as leaving dirty socks on the floor. What the partner is accused of "never" doing is something he or she should, like getting places on time. The usual rebuttal, of course, is that one's frequency of transgression is not really so extreme. A woman I once saw in couple treatment managed to handle with humor her husband's accusation that she had "never" given support for his painful feelings about turning 60. Her response was, "Yes I have. Last December I said, 'There, there.' "

Offering the solution–response turnoff (Ables and Brandsma 1977)

Here, in response to one partner ventilating feelings about a problem and wanting support or empathy, the other offers a solution. Perhaps a partner complains about a bad day at work and the mate responds, "You ought to leave that job." The first partner in such instances usually feels cut off and misunderstood. The second, who has tried to be helpful, does not understand why his or her response was not appreciated.

Trying to talk the other partner out of feelings

Feelings arise in people without planning or volition. Yet partners will often suggest that each other's feelings are not valid or should not be felt. For example, one partner says, "You shouldn't be mad at me for doing [whatever], I just did what anyone would in the circumstances," or "Why do you get so upset at the post office? You know there's always a line on Saturdays."

Taking the stance of an authority figure

This is a catchall designation for the times one partner comments on what the other "should" think or do, or analyzes the reasons for the other's behavior. Sometimes the partner who takes the authority role is being critical. But often his or her intent is simply to set the other partner on the correct path or help the other toward greater self-awareness. Underlying beliefs or standards that the speaker views as unquestionably "right" sometimes motivate such comments, as when one partner tells the other, "You should call your mother more often." Often the impetus is conscious or unconscious frustration, anger, or a wish to be in control, as when a partner suggests, "I think you have a deep-seated fear of commitment." While the second partner occasionally accepts the ideas offered, more often the implied one-up message causes resentment.

Failing to comment on positives or qualifying positives with negatives

As noted in Chapter 1, distressed couples make fewer positive comments to each other than nondistressed couples do. They are more likely to react overtly to negative actions and to ignore positive ones, thereby inadvertently reinforcing the former. Selective attention based on negative expectancies may be the reason partners do not notice positives. Still, even when trying to be complimentary, partners often slip in negative messages. A partner may say, "Your hair looks nice. I'm glad you finally got rid of all those curls." Or "Thanks for paying some attention to me for a change."

Not asserting one's own needs, and dealing with anger inappropriately.

Partners' appropriate assertiveness in expressing their own needs and effectively problem solving how to meet the needs of both usually prevents a lot of anger from arising and needing to be dealt with in the first place. However, their management of whatever anger they still feel also can directly affect the couple's communication and problem solving. In inappropriate handling, partners may stuff anger at the point it is really felt and express it as an overreaction to some later event. Anger may be displaced onto the mate from some other relationship, projected onto the mate as discussed in Chapter 1, or handled by continually "forgetting" to do what the partner wants. Criticism or blaming gets anger out but not in a way to which the mate can respond constructively. Often a good way to deal with anger is to state directly that one is angry and why. But sometimes it is appropriate to let anger over small things go.

Interrupting, monopolizing, and speaking for the other

These can be relatively minor errors of communication if they do not occur too often. Some amount of interrupting and talking over each other is normal (Tannen 1990). Occasional speaking for the mate is not necessarily problematic if it does not involve mind reading. However, frequent occurrences of any of these need to be avoided as they can lead to disrupted problem solving and to partners becoming annoyed or passive.

Many of the above problems stem from partners simply not knowing how to communicate or problem solve more effectively. Some, as noted, are based on their inaccurate perceptions, attributions, expectancies, or assumptions about themselves or the mate. Communication is also affected when partners' beliefs or standards about how people should behave are used to judge the mate's behavior without awareness that their beliefs or standards may differ without one being right and the other wrong. Partners' problems handling anger as well as other affects, to be discussed further in Chapter 6, are also very likely to influence couple communication.

Focusing on a Specific Problem

A better way for Ron and Lynn's clinician to begin helping them would have been to suggest sooner that they focus on any one of the specific problems they were describing. The first step in constructive problem solving is for a couple to *choose and define a problem to be solved* (Christensen et al. 1995). Sometimes this process is relatively easy. Partners may already have identified a number of problem areas in which they have not been able to achieve agreement, and may choose to work on any one of these. Perhaps the issue will be how to deal with money, sex, in-laws, housework, or the kids. If each partner wants to tackle a different problem, the clinician can ask them to consider them in sequence, perhaps alternating whose issue is addressed. Some couples want to discuss a future event or decision rather than a recurrent problem. Such a focus is legitimate and may be defined as, "We need to decide how to deal with . . ." Clinicians may suggest breaking a large, multifaceted issue into a number of subproblems and then working to define and solve each one (Baucom and Epstein 1990). For example, a couple planning for a relative's visit might consider how to handle housekeeping arrangements, how much time each mate should spend with the relative, what the three might do together, and so on. In the first few treatment sessions, clinicians may also advise partners not to start working on their most difficult, emotion-laden problems or decisions if possible (Christensen et al. 1995). Or if such an issue is clearly the most pressing, there may be some way to scale it down a little, such as by suggesting the pair at first try only to find a partial or temporary solution. This is the strategy used by Lynn and Ron's clinician as their second session continues.

> The clinician finally suggested that Ron and Lynn try discussing one problem at a time. Since both seemed to be feeling scared and upset about the situation with Ron's mother, was this perhaps the most pressing issue to consider? She reassured them that all couples find they have differences of opinion or different ways of dealing with things, often based on how they're raised. Learning how to resolve such differences is a normal part of learning how to get along. Ron then told how his mother repeatedly called him at work after she and Lynn argued on the phone, placing his job in jeopardy. The clinician noted that there were many aspects to their disagreements about how to deal with Ron's mother. But maybe they should try at first just to work out a way such telephone arguments between her and Lynn could be avoided. How did this sound to them? The two readily agreed.

In some instances clinicians need to offer reassurance, support, or structure to help a couple move into a problem area, as with Ron and Lynn. They may suggest that the problem identified is one many couples have trouble solving, if this is true. They may identify contextual factors that have made resolution more difficult, such as the couple's having needed to deal with so many things at once or to deal with this problem while stressed out about something else. They may acknowledge that a problem has stirred up understandably strong feelings for one or both. When one partner has been more at fault than the other, a clinician may need to try to help this mate save face without necessarily condoning his or her behavior (Ables and Brandsma 1977). For example, the clinician might say something like, "Well, it looks like you were struggling with something this time and didn't do so well. You're each going to have this happen sometimes. Let's talk about how the two of you can handle a similar situation better in the future."

Couples often need some help from clinicians in order to define a problem in nonblaming and clear, specific terms, such as, "We can't agree on who will do what around the house," rather than "You don't do enough around the house," or "Housework doesn't go well," which could mean many different things. Sometimes a problem is disguised by a red herring (Ables and Brandsma 1977), as when a man says his wife always dresses up for company but not for him. Clearly the man's concern is not how the wife dresses for company, yet this part of his statement may be the one she focuses on if the clinician does not intervene. Asking how an issue affects the person raising it can usually help. The clinician might ask the man to describe, without using critical or blaming words, how his wife's casual dress affects him. The modified statement, perhaps even modeled by the clinician, might be, "When you wear sweat suits a lot of the time, I feel like you no longer care about being attractive to me. Can we talk about this?"

In fact, a generally helpful idea clinicians may introduce is that the basis for one mate raising an issue about the other's behavior must be its impact on the speaker. Obviously, the way one partner behaves toward the other does have an impact on the other, but the latter needs to identify his or her specific concern. For example, Lynn may need to say that when Ron does not back her in her discussions with his mother, she feels alone, helpless, and as though she is not part of a couple. This would be in contrast to her perhaps saying Ron "should" back her because it is the right thing to do or that he will back her "if he is any kind of a man." Clinicians may sometimes help partners identify their specific concerns by asking, "What is it that bothers you when this happens?" Or "What is your need in this situation that is not being met?"

A corollary to be suggested at some point is that mates have the right to protest what partners do outside the couple relationship when and if this behavior somehow impacts them, but generally not otherwise. It turned out later in the Ron and Lynn case that Ron spent a good deal of time fixing cars free for his parents, siblings, and other relatives. Lynn has the right to question this behavior if she wishes, on the basis that she feels Ron is not spending enough time at home. But the problem should then be defined as "disagreement about how much time Ron spends at home." If they decide it is fair for both to spend a certain amount of recreational time away from each other and Ron chooses to spend his time fixing cars for his extended family, this decision should be his. Many partners have developed the bad habit of bossing or criticizing their mate's behavior that has virtually no impact on them based on their own underlying beliefs or standards, thereby taking the stance of an authority figure. Clinicians can watch for such statements as, "You should . . ." or "Why don't you . . ." and say, "Wait, what's the impact on you? Otherwise, it seems like what he does with his [family, friends, job, or whatever] is his business."

Sometimes one partner will say in response to such a question that the other's behavior makes him or her uncomfortable. Clinicians can suggest that this discomfort be explored. Often doing so reveals the partners' different underlying beliefs or standards that it can be helpful to identify, or an underlying assumption about what the partner's behavior means that can be corrected. If the discomfort or concern is not reduced after such discussion, the couple may define this feeling as the problem and discuss that some compromise may need to be found. For example, Lynn might say Ron's working on his family's cars makes her uncomfortable because she feels like they are exploiting him. She might be helped to realize that in Polish families like Ron's, mutual help is expected (Folwarski and Marganoff 1996). Hearing that Lynn was raised differently, Ron might be willing to discuss changing somewhat to make Lynn more comfortable, if she would be willing not to keep pushing him to stop altogether.

Another issue that can arise in defining a problem for discussion is one partner's solution masquerading as a problem. A man proposes discussing the problem that his girlfriend will not watch X-rated videos. When asked why he wants her to, he says their sex life is dull and watching the videos could liven it up. Watching X-rated videos is his solution to their sex problem, not the actual problem itself. To learn how to avoid this difficulty when they attempt problem solving, partners can be taught literally to "give each other the problem, not the solution."

This example also illustrates another point, that something may be a problem for one partner but not the other. The girlfriend may or may not think the couple's sex life is dull. Clinicians need to explain in such instances that if something is a problem for one partner, the other still needs to understand and help try to solve it, although not necessarily in the way the first partner envisions. The first partner can return the favor by working on a problem the second is experiencing at another time.

Sometimes clinicians need to listen to couples' descriptions of their interactions and help identify potential problems to discuss. Or partners may describe an upsetting event or strong feeling they do not understand and need the clinician's help to define the underlying problem. It may be important to examine the circumstances in which strong feelings occur to determine what is eliciting them. A newly married wife describes her discomfort and anger when her husband asks her how much money she has spent on clothes. She finally realizes she perceives him as criticizing or not trusting her, whereas he simply feels he is keeping track of their budget. The two need to discuss the issue of how they will handle money together. While one or both partners may need to have the other hear their reactions to an upsetting event, the problem itself usually should be defined in terms of preventing a similar recurrence. Problem solving is always focused on how to have things go differently in the future. For example, a couple in a second marriage reports that when the wife's daughter misbehaved, the husband disciplined her more strictly than the wife would have. The couple had a big fight when the girl complained to her mother later. Further discussion in the session might reveal that the couple had developed no agreements on how much or in what situations the husband had authority over the girl, or on disciplinary guidelines. The clinician could suggest that the problem was that they needed to set guidelines, rather than get caught up in who was right or wrong in what had happened.

Another instance of clinicians' help being needed to identify important underlying issues occurs when partners complain of many problems that may have the same core theme (Christensen et al. 1995). A wife's complaints that her husband does not listen to her, falls asleep on the couch at night, and spends too much time at work may all be related to her concern about lack of closeness. Clinicians who suggest possible underlying concerns in such instances can sometimes help couples avoid spending a great deal of time on derivative problems. Even if an underlying issue is not clear at first, the couple's not making progress on the derivative problems, or producing a seemingly endless stream of them, is often an indicator that a more central aspect of the relationship is amiss.

Finally, couples may identify specific communication difficulties, interaction patterns, or ways they handle certain feelings as potential problems to discuss. For example, partners may say they often get into being critical. Couples can be told that much of the work on avoiding specific communication difficulties and building better skills will probably occur as they try to resolve other problems. A clinician might explain, "Usually when people get into criticizing, it's because they're frustrated and feel like they aren't getting what they need from each other. We'll be working here on ways you can both get what you need more often and on what to say that won't hurt the other when you don't." However, partners can also be given guidelines for avoiding specific destructive communication, such as, "When you find yourself about to criticize, think about why you're really bothered and try to just tell each other what you're feeling without using critical or blaming words. Say 'It upsets me when you do . . . because . . . ' rather than 'Doing . . . is stupid.' " Couples may also describe, or clinicians may identify, problematic interaction patterns such as one partner repeatedly nagging and the other "forgetting" to do chores, one getting more and more emotional while the other becomes more constricted, or one pursuing while the other distances. Defining any pattern as a mutual problem that both partners must work to solve is a constructive first step toward change. However, couples often encounter special difficulties around changing problematic patterns, as will be elaborated below. Problematic interactions around handling feelings, needs, and intimacy, which may require insight into family-of-origin influences, are considered in Chapter 6.

Understanding the Problem Further

Either after a couple has agreed on a problem to discuss, or as a means for partners to understand better why something needs discussion, the clinician can *help both give more information about the meaning, dimensions, and recent history of the problem for them.* For complex problems, such discussions may take several sessions. When couples have encountered more difficulty than usual solving a particular problem together, lengthier discussions are often needed because strong feelings or other underlying issues are likely to be involved for both partners. Even in briefer reviews, solutions may become more apparent as the true dimensions of a problem are understood. Partners can be encouraged to discuss what thoughts, feelings, or reactions each has been having in response to a problem and, if need be, why they feel as they do (Christensen et al. 1995). In one of my recent cases, a young wife proposed discussing the problem that she and her husband could not agree on when to have a baby. She could not understand why he was balking since both wanted children. Discussion revealed that he was worried the couple would not have enough time for closeness after a baby was born, a much more relationship-affirming reason than she had feared, as well as a realistic concern the two could then constructively address.

Clinicians may have to explain that, in trying to understand problems further, each partner needs to express where he or she is coming from in a nonblaming way. "I" statements may be suggested for this purpose. Each can be told not to speak too long at one time or try to get across too many ideas at once. If possible, a clinician can help a partner who gets overly emotional or angry to speak more moderately. The alternative is to set time aside for ventilation, with the likelihood that problem solving will be temporarily sidetracked (Baucom and Epstein 1990).

During and after speaking, a partner needs to feel that the other is listening and trying to understand. Positive nonverbal communication—such as looking attentive and nodding—rather than negative—such as turning away or rolling one's eyes—is important (Baucom and Epstein 1990). The mate and, if necessary, the clinician should ask questions for clarification and offer empathy when difficult feelings are expressed. The mate should be asked to paraphrase what he or she has heard and reflect it back, closing with a question, such as "Is this right?" or "Do I understand correctly?" Ideally the process is then reversed and repeated until each partner has a clear understanding of the other's position.

> In response to the clinician's coaching, Lynn described her frustration and anger at Ron's mother for trying to push her around and at Ron for allowing it. Lynn explained she couldn't just pretend to go along when Ron's mother made unreasonable demands or insulted her on the phone as Ron would like. She repeated that Ron's not backing her makes her think he doesn't respect her or maybe even love her as much as he does his mother. After ascertaining that Ron understood these feelings and perceptions, the clinician asked Ron whether Lynn had interpreted the meaning of his behavior correctly. Ron said no, he does respect and love Lynn, but he doesn't know what to do about the problem. When asked to share his own thoughts or feelings, he would say only that his mother has always doted on him and he doesn't want to hurt her. Lynn started to protest and the clinician asked her to try to understand Ron's concern even if she didn't agree with how he was dealing with it.

Sometimes when partners are trying to understand an issue, clinicians must spot their problematic cognitions or imposition of their own beliefs or standards and encourage questioning them, as Ron and Lynn's clinician does when Lynn attributes Ron's behavior to a lack of respect or caring. If one partner fails to perceive the other's positive behaviors, a clinician can point them out. He or she can suggest that a partner check out attributions or assumptions that may be mistaken. When mates express differing beliefs or standards, the clinician can normalize their differences. If a belief or standard is clearly unrealistic, such as an idea that partners should meet all of each other's needs for companionship, it often works better for the clinician to express doubt quickly rather than wait until the couple has polarized around the issue and it will be necessary to take sides. The clinician can help the mate who expressed the belief save face by saying something like, "That would be wonderful, but . . ." or "That may have worked in our parents' generation, but . . ."

Early in treatment, partners often have neither the patience nor the skills to share their positions totally nonjudgmentally and to fully use active listening techniques. Also, the need to arrive at some agreement on a given problem, at least temporarily, may be too pressing not to reach some fairly quick resolution, as Lynn's telephone arguments with her mother-in-law were for Ron and Lynn. In such instances the clinician may encourage more truncated discussions of why the issue is a problem for each and briefer reflections of having heard each other. However, partners still need to be restrained from topic jumping, criticizing, mind reading, trying to talk each other out of feelings, and rushing to solutions. If one tries to topic jump, the clinician can explain the importance of sticking to one problem at a time and suggest that the newly raised issue be kept in mind for later possible discussion. The exception would be when the couple feels the new topic is more pressing than the original one, and when both partners agree they would rather switch to discuss it. The clinician can interrupt criticizing, blaming, or generalizing to suggest that the speaker substitute words like, "I don't like it when . . ." or "It makes me mad when . . ." or "It doesn't work for me when . . ." However, underlying anger may need to be recognized too. Perhaps after inquiring what a partner was thinking or feeling when critical, the clinician might say, "It sounds like you're frustrated and feel like you haven't gotten what you need. Try now to tell her what you need in these situations." Clinicians should gently question mind reading with some statement like, "Wait, you don't really know what Bill is thinking. Why don't you ask him?" If one partner tries to talk the other out of feelings, the clinician can explain that people cannot help what they feel, but if the feeling may be based on a misunderstanding, the mate will have a chance to clarify it soon.

During this part of the discussion, a partner's rushing to solutions or offering a solution–response turnoff must be discouraged, even though the positive intent can be given support. A clinician might say something like, "Mary, I realize you're trying to be helpful but you're proposing a solution to the problem. It's really important to understand the meaning of the problem or the feelings involved for each of you first." Especially if solution–response turnoffs are a problem at home, the clinician may spend a few minutes explaining that when people are full of feelings, they may just need to express them and hear the other give understanding and support. Sometimes partners really do not know how to give this and may say, "I don't know what I'm supposed to do." The clinician can model some possibilities or suggest the person ask the partner what he or she would like to hear. It can be emphasized that support does not necessarily mean agreement, just that one cares and understands. The clinician should make clear that expressing feelings is often a needed part of the problem-solving process. It can be suggested that partners learn to tell each other when they need to ventilate feelings rather than be ready to look for solutions (Baucom and Epstein 1990).

It cannot be emphasized too strongly that clinicians must almost always be very active as couples are learning problem-solving and communication skills. Research supports this assertion (Bray and Jouriles 1995). Clinicians help keep the structure of the problem-solving process in place. They model, teach, gently but firmly interrupt and correct, normalize, offer support and empathy, and give positive feedback when good communication or problem solving happens. In this last, they must try to give balanced encouragement and support to both partners. If one partner has better skills or picks up new skills more quickly, the clinician must find positives to credit to the other as well. Skill discrepancies so noticeable that the partners comment on them can be handled by the clinician saying something supportive to the less skilled mate. Perhaps it can be pointed out that the latter is smart and will catch up, is better at something else important, or has reasons for not knowing as much yet about the skills, such as parental models who did not communicate much. The clinician's words and manner throughout need to convey optimism, respect, confidence in the partners, and easy comfort with the process along with a nonjudgmental stance. It helps if clinicians believe that most partners are decent, likable people doing the best they can, and convey this belief to couples implicitly or explicitly (Hof 1995). Humor and tact are also assets. As an example, after a couple had begun to learn how to express themselves in nonblaming ways, one partner might say somewhat jokingly, "He's a real dunderhead." Assuming the other partner smiled, the clinician might laugh and say, "Um, could you rephrase that?"

What should emerge from these first stages of work on any problem is that the clinician and the couple understand its major dimensions for each partner, some history, and the feelings attached. They should also have a sense of what each partner's needs in the problem area seem to be, because moving to work on solutions requires that these needs be understood. For example, with Ron and Lynn:

> After more discussion, the clinician asked what was the most important need Ron and Lynn each had in regard to Lynn's telephone calls with Ron's mother. Ron said for Lynn not to end up yelling at his mother. Lynn said for Ron to back her. The clinician summarized, "Okay, I understand that how Lynn should respond to Ron's mother in these phone calls has been a real tough problem for both of you. You really need to find solutions that will work for both. For you, Lynn, it's important to feel that you're not backing down and that Ron is supporting you. For you, Ron, it's important that Lynn not yell at your mother and your mother not get hurt. Have I got this pretty much correct?"

Assuming both partners feel reasonably well understood, they are ready to begin considering solutions.

Helping Couples Find Solutions and Solidify Skills

Here again, clinicians must be active in structuring the problem-solving discussion. The first time a pair tries *working toward solutions*, clinicians may explain how important it is not to reach closure too quickly, especially on major issues. The couple will usually need reminders of this point in many later discussions. Partners can be told that looking for solutions is often a matter of brainstorming. They should try to generate a number of possible ideas. They may have to look more specifically at what happens in the problem area to do so, perhaps to define more clearly where new solutions could be applied. Usually the first solution that comes to each partner's mind will work for him or her, but not for the mate. They will each probably have to compromise, but will often find a solution together that works better than the first either one proposed.

The pair can then be encouraged to put possible solutions on the table. They can try to be creative, even silly (Christensen et al. 1995). They may look at solutions that have worked for both in the past. Again the clinician must spot and interrupt topic jumping, partners' failure to listen to each other, blaming, mind reading, rehashing past negative experiences, and any other communication difficulties. The clinician can participate in suggesting possible solutions to the couple's problem as long as the couple is doing so as well. He or she may also do some education as to what it is realistic to expect in a love relationship, or may tell how other couples have solved similar problems. As possible solutions are put forth, or when a number have been put on the table, the partners should try to recognize each other's constructive efforts. They can say how proposed solutions might or might not meet their needs. In the process, these needs are often further clarified.

The clinician warned that Ron's proposed solution of Lynn ignoring what his mother says on the telephone and Lynn's of fighting back angrily might both have to be modified to take each other's needs into account. Part of being married is learning to compromise. She then suggested that they narrow in and get very specific about what happens when Ron's mother calls. Lynn explained that after asking how the baby is, Ron's mother usually suggests some time when she wants to see the baby. Or she may ask what Lynn is fixing Ron for dinner and tell her how to do it differently. She never asks how Lynn is or has anything pleasant to say, even if Lynn tries to exchange pleasantries. Ron started to defend his mother and the clinician commented that neither Ron nor Lynn can control what Ron's mother does. She asked Ron to understand again that such calls are upsetting for Lynn, and he said he did. He wondered if Lynn could just tell his mother she is busy and can't talk just then, or maybe that the baby is crying. Lynn said she is not going to become a liar. The clinician reflected that Ron is coming up with some new ideas, but it sounds like these possible solutions don't work so well for Lynn.

Lynn then suggested she could tell Ron's mother she doesn't want to talk to her and to call when Ron is home if she can't be polite. Ron started to protest and the clinician asked both for alternatives. They could not come up with any. The clinician wondered what happened when Ron is home when his mother calls. It turned out Lynn sometimes hands the phone to him but he just ends up giving in to whatever his mother wants, which makes Lynn furious. The clinician asked if they ever discussed together whether to do what Ron's mother wanted, before either one gave her an answer. They remembered they had done this once, when Lynn wasn't sure what she wanted to do and decided to let Ron make the choice. The clinician asked if it might work for Lynn not to make a decision either way when Ron's mother wanted her to do something.

After much discussion, the two finally agreed that when Ron's mother called to make any demand, Lynn would say she had to talk it over with Ron rather than just saying no. The couple could then discuss later whether they should do what his mother wanted. If not, either could tell the mother, but in any case it would be presented as a joint decision and Ron would back Lynn up. If Ron's mother began insulting Lynn for any reason, Lynn could say she did not like such talk and get off the phone. Ron would back her on this if his mother complained to him.

What happens while looking for workable solutions usually depends on how difficult and emotionally charged a problem is and how far apart the couple is on what they want to do to solve it. Problems that do not have too much emotional valence or on which the couple is not too far apart are often solved fairly easily. For example:

Rita and Ted, a young married couple in treatment, decided to tackle the problem that Rita wanted to have a holiday party for a group of her old friends while Ted did not. Discussion of where each partner was coming from revealed that these friends were very important to Rita and the holiday party was a tradition among them. However, the prior year, Ted (then Rita's fiancé) had felt very uncomfortable at this party because he did not know anyone, Rita and her friends talked about old times together, and the party went on late into the evening on a Friday night when he was exhausted from work. Rita's first suggested solution for the party was that Ted "just be nice and participate" and Ted's was that they forget the whole thing. However, after the clinician got them started toward compromise by asking if there was any way Ted's problems from last year's party could be lessened or avoided, they began examining better solutions. They finally worked out that they would get together with a few of these friends for an earlier social engagement so that Ted could get to know them better. Rita agreed she would try harder to include Ted in conversation at the party and try to end it by midnight; if not, he could go up to bed if he wanted. They also agreed that if the party did not go well this year, someone else would have to have it in the future and Ted would have the option to let Rita attend alone.

In some problem-solving situations, no solutions can be found that meet both partners' needs reasonably well. Even a quid pro quo, such as one choosing the movie one time and the other the next, may not be very satisfactory. A technique that can be useful in such situations is for partners to convey on a numerical scale of 1 to 10 how important their needs feel in this particular instance (Baucom and Epstein 1990). In the example just given, possibly no way could be found for Ted to be anything but bored or uncomfortable at the proposed party. Yet Rita might very much want him to come. A clinician might suggest each partner rate how strongly he or she felt about having a preferred solution happen. Ted might say it was a "7" for him not to have to go. Rita might say her wanting him there was a "9." The clinician can suggest that in such instances, the partner who feels less strongly may want to "give a gift" of complying with the other's wishes. It can be added that the one whose wish is fulfilled should be very appreciative because the other is doing something he or she does not really want to out of generosity and caring. Of course neither partner must make every preference a "10." With this technique, the partner who is given to usually feels very loved. The other may feel good about having done something nice that was appreciated, rather than angry and controlled as would be the case if the first partner had bullied or criticized to try to prevail. Such interactions tend to set up a positive cycle between partners or, as one couple put it, "emotional money in the bank." Partners who feel given to are also usually more able to give to the other or overlook the other's minor transgressions at another time.

The situation is more complex when one partner is repeatedly being asked to do something in the couple's daily life together more or less solely because it is important to the mate. For example, one may be asking the other to help keep the house neater than the latter considers needed. Such problems often represent partners' differing standards or expectations for how people should behave, perhaps stemming from their different ethnic, religious, or family backgrounds. Sometimes they are based on a partner's psychological coping mechanisms, as when someone raised in an emotionally chaotic home needs to keep physical order in the couple's house to guard against anxiety about things going out of control. In either case, the clinician's first task is to label such differences as expectable and state that no one is right or wrong. As noted earlier, this concept is often very freeing. Exploring the reasons for partners' preferences or suggesting that deeper issues may be involved, as will be discussed further in Chapters 6 and 7, may also help mates feel more empathy for each other's positions. They may then try to figure out compromises without so much defensiveness or rancor. Occasionally clinicians may suggest a compromise that seems fair or reasonable in a given situation. For example, if one partner has considerably higher housekeeping standards than the other, it may be fair for this partner to do somewhat more of the couple's housework. However, the other should probably do more than would have been required under his or her own lower standard. In most circumstances clinicians should offer their opinions only if the couple seems at an impasse and the opinion can be given without clearly favoring either partner.

Clinicians need to ensure some sense of balance between mates in discussing and trying to find solutions to their problems. Most often solutions should involve both partners changing their behaviors. Even when one primarily will change in a given area, the other can usually change by offering more appreciation, withholding nagging, and being the one to change more somewhere else. Clinicians can actively ask for such mutually balanced solutions. For example, when one partner has identified a problem that exists for him or her and the other has agreed to change, the clinician may ask the latter, "Now, is there any area in which you'd like to ask [the mate] to consider making some changes?" Clinicians may also question agreements that seem to favor one partner too heavily by saying something like, "Are you sure this is going to work okay for you?" or even "Are you giving up too much ground here?" Partners who tend to be overbearing can be told that their mates are not likely to want to meet their needs unless they experience some reciprocity (Ables and Brandsma 1977). Clinicians may also suggest it is not a good idea for partners to make agreements they will resent or not be able to keep later, just to satisfy their mates (Baucom and Epstein 1990).

In a sense, clinicians invoke their own values for couples when they suggest that partners work out agreements that are fair to both. Clinicians do, in fact, usually hold implicit values, such as that there should be some individual boundaries around each partner, that each should have a roughly equal share in deciding what will happen between them, and that neither partner should be mistreated. They believe that, in most circumstances, each partner must take ultimate responsibility for his or her own well-being (Christensen et al. 1995). Presumably these values are intended to ensure an optimal chance for healthy individual and couple functioning without clinicians imposing their own preferred ways of solving whatever problems couples face.

When a couple seems to have agreed on a workable solution to a problem, the clinician can *summarize and verify the agreement*, or ask the partners to do so. Each partner can then be asked again about his or her willingness to carry it out. A time period for doing so should be part of the agreement. The partners and the clinician need to consider as carefully as possible any obstacles that may arise and work to decide how to deal with them (Baucom and Epstein 1990). With complex agreements, it is often useful for the couple to write down in the session what each will do. The clinician can finally charge the couple with carrying out the agreement during the specified time period and reporting back on what happened. Some clinicians literally assign the couple the task of carrying out the agreement and ask them to keep track of the results as a form of self-monitoring. In either instance, clinicians must impress on couples the importance of working hard to carry out their negotiated agreements at home. They can reinforce that they will ask what happened, and they must do so. If glitches in carrying out agreements develop between sessions, couples can be given the choice of calling the clinician for help, working out a modified agreement on their own, or waiting until the next session to discuss the problem more. Clinicians can convey that "fine tuning" is often needed and can help the couple accomplish it. Even positive results should be checked out carefully with both partners, lest one be feeling secretly dissatisfied (Ables and Brandsma 1977).

In early work on problem solving, clinicians must often interrupt what partners are saying to get them to talk to each other rather than the clinician, phrase their comments more constructively, stick to one topic, stay in the right stage of problem solving, and so on. Frequent positive reinforcement for constructive efforts, reassurance, support, empathy, and normalizing where appropriate are also in order. So is encouraging partners to remark on positives to each other. Most couples will gradually begin to learn new communication and problem-solving skills and incorporate them into their discussions in sessions. Indeed, clinicians may first get a sense of a couple's progress in using the skills when they realize how much less often they are having to interrupt or talk.

While couples can be asked to carry out problem solutions at home as soon as these are agreed upon, their being able to *incorporate and use new problem-solving and communication skills* on their own may take longer. Clinicians must assist this process quite purposefully. At first they can help couples not to become discouraged by saying that, while they can try problem solving at home, it may not work on more than simple problems until their skills become more secure. Couples may be given written problem-solving and communication guidelines they can use on their own whenever they are ready (Baucom and Epstein 1990). In any case, clinicians must teach partners how to initiate problem solving away from sessions, by saying, for instance, "I have a problem I'd like to discuss. Is this a good time?" They can be told that, if the mate wishes to wait, he or she must either suggest another time and place reasonably soon or ask to delay discussion until the next treatment session.

After the first few interviews, clinicians should ask not only about how the couple has carried out prior agreements, but also about how their independent problem solving is going. Constructive discussions can be reviewed and praised. Clinicians can ask about how each mate was able to accomplish positive behaviors and how that felt to both. Continued reinforcement will help the two integrate the changes into their daily functioning. If a couple brings a problem they could not solve into the next session, they can tell what happened in discussion at home rather than starting from scratch. The clinician can critique some of the at-home problem solving or ask each partner to critique what he or she (not the mate) did wrong. Even more important is to reinforce whatever each did well (Christensen et al. 1995). If the two still wish to work on the issue, they can be helped to do so in the session, now avoiding their mistakes. When mates' habitual errors have been identified, perhaps with some humor, the partners can be encouraged to work very consciously on overcoming them. For example, a couple might be told, "Mary is great at expressing feelings and defining issues while John is great at looking for solutions. When we get you two working more as a problem-solving team, what beautiful music you will make together! Now, what are you each going to try to remember to do differently?" Further practice in sessions or exploration of partners' possible resistance to change, to be discussed below, may be needed as well.

SMOOTHING THE ROAD TO CHANGE

While couples themselves are responsible for achieving change in treatment, clinicians using this book's integrative approach must do all they can to facilitate it. They will further the partners' constructive participation partly by relating to both in a caring, empathic, and validating way. But they must also work hard to try to monitor the treatment process, keep it on track, prevent negative emotions or interactions that might impede progress, and help couples overcome blocks to change that nonetheless arise. Finally, clinicians must be aware of physical and environmental influences on the partners' efforts to change in treatment and may intervene in regard to these.

Helping Partners Maintain Constructive Participation

Clinicians usually monitor couples' movement toward treatment goals through a combination of their own observations and asking couples what is happening at home. Sometimes more formal questionnaires or self-monitoring tools are also used. Couples doing the work so far described may be making progress on three kinds of goals. They may be learning problem-solving skills, although one or another skill may be more difficult for a partner to use consistently. The same is true for positive communication skills and avoiding dysfunctional communication. Finally, couples may be making and trying to carry out agreements about how to function in major areas of their life together, such as how to deal with money or children. Clinicians should not only comment on any positive changes couples achieve in work on their goals, but also remind them of these when they feel bogged down. Couples may need to be told that it is usual for some treatment sessions to be less productive or to end with everything up in the air, and for partners to feel stuck or lose ground at times (Hof 1995).

Clinicians also need to monitor what is happening in sessions on a moment-by-moment basis, largely to help partners stay focused and working productively. Especially important is to do so early in treatment, before couples have consistently achieved what Christensen and colleagues (1995) call a "collaborative set." Early work on communication and problem solving finds some partners timid and tense because even talking about day-to-day problems makes them fearful of their mates' anger or rejection. At the other end of the spectrum, some partners show so much emotion so often that it is difficult to focus on anything else. But common throughout all work on communication and problem solving is that discussion can get off track and counterproductive emotions or interactions intermittently threaten to arise. It is the clinician's job to try to keep the sessions proceeding relatively smoothly and constructively.

Doing so requires, first, a good sense of when a given topic of discussion will be useful to pursue and when it will not. For example, partners arguing about what really happened in an earlier incident clearly should be stopped (Baucom and Epstein 1990), perhaps by saying there is no way to settle the issue. In the session with Ron and Lynn described earlier, the clinician cut off their digression into Lynn critiquing and Ron trying to defend his mother's telephone etiquette by saying neither could control his mother's behavior. Clinicians must often close off such apparently nonproductive side trips during problem-solving discussion without making couples feel stifled or resentful. Still, when partners describe happenings at home or interact during sessions, there are often a number of possibly useful issues to pick up. While partners should be the ultimate arbiters of treatment goals and problems to be addressed in particular sessions, they often need the clinician's help to know which foci are most likely to be productive.

For example, a gay male couple describes an incident in which they got into arguing when one partner stayed out late without calling the other. The mate says this partner has been partying a lot lately with friends the mate does not like. They may report that they tried to talk calmly but still ended up saying mean things to each other, with one threatening a breakup. Should the clinician encourage the couple to focus on the issue of when the two should call each other, the frequent partying, the disliked friends, or their communication? Even if he or she reinforces their having tried to talk calmly and asks which issue they would like to address first, the clinician would need to decide whether to explore the threat to break up. In general, to respond most helpfully, clinicians need to have a sense of the focus most salient to a couple's possible growth, how pressing given issues are, the couple's eadiness to get into certain discussions productively, and the need to reinforce positives to solidify them. Clinicians can sometimes help partners pursue a few related matters sequentially, if they can do so without causing confusion or overloading the couple with new ideas. What they must not do is let sessions lose structure and direction.

As a second major responsibility, clinicians must attend to, and sometimes seek to influence, partners' emotions during treatment sessions, including their positive feelings of mastery and hope and any negative ones of anger, discouragement, or anxiety. A calm atmosphere and positive feelings tend to facilitate couples' ability to engage in work on problem solving and communication while negative ones may impede it. When strong negative feelings are present, they usually need to be expressed and dealt with before treatment can move forward, as will be discussed below. Otherwise, clinicians may try to nurture partners' positive feelings and reduce, prevent, or at least not stimulate negative ones in order to facilitate their constructive participation. The intent is not to create a Pollyanna atmosphere in which nothing unpleasant can be faced, but to ease discussions that may otherwise become dysfunctionally difficult.

One intervention strategy that often helps partners feel more optimistic and capable consists of a clinician continuing, when needed, to reframe their characteristics or behaviors in positive terms. When a man calls his wife "willful," the clinician refers to her as having a good ability to assert her needs, adding that the man certainly is right to do likewise so they can work out their differences. Or behaviors may be reframed as less purposeful or immutable than partners may have feared. When a woman tells her partner, "You did that to hurt me," a clinician expresses doubt or asks her to ask her mate whether her assertion is true. When a man says his girlfriend is more emotional than he can handle, the clinician suggests that perhaps she can be less emotional if she begins to experience him as more responsive to her. If a partner's trait is unlikely to change a lot, the clinician can still connote it positively or neutrally. A man who tends to forget details of daily life might be called an "absent-minded professor," as long as both mates viewed this label as relatively benign.

A closely related intervention is to highlight similarities between partners, such as their common goals for the relationship or their mutual love, at times when they may be feeling discouraged about their differences. Or the positives inherent in their differences may be pointed out (Christensen et al. 1995). In a situation in which one mate tended to be somewhat impulsive and the other to procrastinate, the clinician might note that the two can learn to balance each other well because the first can provide an impetus for action whereas the other can slow them down long enough to make a careful decision. Clinicians reminding partners of their understandable reasons for being different from each other and the pain both have felt about their disagreements can also induce empathy and a collaborative set.

Clinicians may point out positives in what partners do in sessions and at home not only to reinforce them, but to encourage the couple's sense of mastery and caring and to counteract what may have been their prior selective attention to negatives. The way clinicians ask their questions may help couples attend to positives as well. A couple who tried to solve a thorny problem at home might be asked, "Did you feel you did some things well in the discussion?" rather than just "How did it go?" Further, while they should not sweep partners' significant negative emotions under the rug, clinicians need not always ask about milder ones they think may dissipate as the session goes on. They may also avoid asking a question when they are pretty sure the answer is going to make partners feel anxious, hurt, or angry, unless the topic is pressing. For example, when one partner says in passing, "Sometimes I think he doesn't even like to talk to me" and the other may not be sure he does, it is not always necessary for the clinician to clarify the issue immediately.

Clinicians may try to keep partners from getting unproductively anxious in sessions by staying in tune with the pace of discussion, evocativeness of material, and intensity of emotions each can handle and trying to "regulate the flow" accordingly. They must themselves take care not to move too fast. They may sometimes help partners slow down or ask if they are okay about proceeding with a difficult topic. They may ask whether a partner whose strong emotional expression is making the other anxious can tone it down a little. Part of the problem may be the way the mate is interpreting the emotion. I recently stopped a young couple who were trying to discuss a difficult topic because the wife kept crying even though the discussion was going well. Exploration revealed that she was not upset but had cried easily her whole life, while her crying often made her husband anxious or angry because he thought it meant he had done something wrong. The husband was encouraged to inquire in any ambiguous future situation and to tell himself his wife's crying often had nothing to do with him. Partners should also be urged to tell their mates if any discussion is making them too anxious. Whether in sessions or at home, it is far better to handle anxiety this way than to withdraw or attack, their likely responses otherwise.

Finally, it is usually dysfunctional to couples' problem solving and communication work for either partner to take or to be placed in a more favored or powerful position. A clinician can often maintain equity between the two by trying to give attention and positive feedback fairly equally to both. In the rare instance that he or she sides with one partner, a careful explanation should be given and the clinician should seek to validate something for the other at about the same time. Another means to balance partners' power positions in sessions is the clinician's selective use of self-disclosure. When a focus on one partner's negative behavior implies a one-down position that seems to be taking the two too far out of balance, some equity can usually be restored by the clinician sharing that he or she also has been known to talk too much, get places late, or whatever, especially if the disclosure can be made with humor. Of course, nothing should be told that is untrue, too personal, or embarrassing, and the clinician should be careful not to seem to be allying with anyone.

In spite of clinicians' efforts, however, all couples are bound to encounter some resistance or obstacles to change in work on communication and problem solving. Resistance should be viewed as a normal event in treatment and one that often offers special opportunities for growth (Astor and Sherman 1997). Sometimes couples openly raise doubts about or objections to the way treatment is going at a given time. But often clinicians must be attentive during sessions to partners' facial expressions, voice tone, apparently unwarranted anger or anxiety, inability to move forward, or seeming disengagement from the work of treatment. A partner may block in constructive discussion of a problem and become defensive, avoidant, or attacking. Or, away from sessions, partners may seem to get stuck and not be able to change in a given area, as perhaps shown by their failure to carry out solutions negotiated in session at home. At an extreme, a couple may question continuing in treatment although they have not achieved their goals, or may miss appointments when they realistically could have come in. Such difficulties can be caused by a variety of factors. Some ways to help when clinicians' interventions, partners' dysfunctional cognitions or negative emotions, persistent individual or couple patterns, or couples' reality circumstances become obstacles to change are considered below. Chapter 6 discusses insight work needed when resistance is caused by partners' transference reactions to each other or clinicians, or by their deeper fears of change.

Blocks Due to Interventions, Cognitions, Affects, or Patterns

No matter how skilled, all clinicians sometimes move too fast, jump too far ahead, say things that are unclear, or otherwise intervene unhelpfully. If they sense that they have done so, simply realizing it and taking a more useful path is sometimes a sufficient response. In addition, as noted earlier, all couples should be told to raise questions they have at any point about what the clinician is doing or not doing. The explanation can be given that they will thereby help keep the treatment process on track, because clinicians sometimes do things that are not useful without knowing it. Clinicians can also directly elicit a partner's reactions when they do something that might have caused a negative response, or when they think they see such a response on a partner's face. Partners who for reasons of social class, ethnicity, or other upbringing believe they should not challenge authority figures may especially need encouragement to reveal any negative reactions to interventions. Clinicians sometimes can suggest that a partner seemed to have a negative reaction and can propose a possible reason, as in, "I wonder if what I just said touched a raw nerve on the subject of your daughter . . ."

If partners do voice *negative reactions to what a clinician has been doing*, the clinician should take what they say very seriously. When an intervention may have been inappropriate or ill-timed, even if the clinician could not have known beforehand that it would be, the best course of action is to apologize and intervene differently thereafter. Sometimes a clinician needs to explain more clearly and carefully why interventions used should be helpful and ask a couple's indulgence to continue trying them. Sometimes a negative reaction has been caused by a partner's fear of proceeding, or cognitive distortion as to what an intervention implied. Often distortions can be elicited and corrected. Or partners' fears may dissipate if they are expressed and the clinician or mate offers reassurance. For example, one partner may hesitate and, when asked, say he or she fears saying something that might upset the other. The clinician may suggest this partner ask the other whether it is all right to proceed or may inquire how he or she thinks the mate might respond. Partners' deeper fears or distortions in response to interventions, perhaps caused by transference reactions to the clinician or the mate, may require insight-oriented attention.

Often, partners' negative reactions during treatment are caused not by interventions but by *cognitive distortions* in regard to something the mate has said or done. Since partners frequently are not aware of the cognitions on which they are operating unless they are asked to explore and evaluate them, clinicians must make sure such a process happens. The first step may be to notice that a partner seems to be having a negative reaction in an instance when a positive or neutral response might have been expected. The second is to direct attention nonjudgmentally to the possibility that something worthy of attention is going on (Baucom et al. 1995). For example, in response to a woman saying that she values her husband's friendship, her husband might frown or offer a put-down. Or the couple might report such an interaction at home. The clinician could suggest that the husband seemed not to like what the wife had said and ask how he had interpreted it. If he asserted that she thought of him only as a friend, not someone she loved, the clinician could respond that this might be so, but why not ask her? The first time such a discussion took place, the clinician might add that everyone operates based on assumptions about what other people's behaviors mean but it is worth checking their accuracy, especially when they seem hurtful. If the couple can later explore their own or each other's underlying cognitions when glitches happen, they will have learned an important skill.

Clinicians may sometimes guess aloud at mistaken perceptions, attributions, or assumptions that may be blocking couples' efforts to communicate or solve problems, based on their knowledge of the couple's history or other influences on their functioning. Even if their guesses are not quite accurate, suggesting them can often help partners get in touch with what they are really thinking, as in the following case.

> Ellen and Beverly were a same-sex couple in their fifties, Ellen being lesbian and Beverly bisexual. While talking about the problem of whom to hire to fix their broken fireplace, Ellen became increas-

ingly argumentative, starting just after Beverly said, "It's times like this we need a man around the house." Beverly had begun to respond in kind when the clinician interrupted. She said, "You two have usually been so well able to solve problems like this lately that I think something unusual must be going on this time. Ellen, I know you've felt criticized by Beverly in the past." Ellen nodded. "I wonder if you thought her saying, 'It's times like this we need a man around the house' was a criticism?" Ellen said "No," but then blurted out, "She means she really wishes she was with a man." Beverly quickly asserted that she did not, adding that she loved Ellen very much. Ellen smiled although she was also tearful, and said, "I'm sorry I'm such a chump sometimes."

Sometimes strong affects are caused by distorted cognitions but dissipate when the latter are corrected (Baucom et al. 1995). Ellen almost surely had been feeling hurt and angry in response to what Beverly probably intended as a semihumorous, throwaway comment. When its meaning was clarified, these negative feelings were apparently eliminated or at least significantly reduced. Obviously, partners' negative cognitions that clinicians elicit are not always distorted. The mate may confirm them or equivocate. In such instances, an important problem that may need to be addressed in treatment has surfaced and can be given attention. If Beverly were ambivalent about being with Ellen, reasons for her ambivalence would have to be faced and dealt with at some point.

Negative affects not based on cognitive distortions often block couples' progress in treatment until they are ventilated or otherwise handled (Weeks and Hof 1995). Many couples enter treatment experiencing anger and hurt because they have been engaging in blaming, criticizing, petty meanness, spite, or the like. Often these feelings dissipate when the clinician reframes what happened by saying they did not know how to communicate or problem solve more effectively. Strong negative affects occurring when past hurt was significantly one-sided are more difficult to let go, and rightly so. For example, a mate who has experienced psychological abuse or whose partner has had an affair is entitled to feel hurt, anger, and mistrust for a significant period of time. Treatment of such couples is covered in later chapters. Still, even lesser transgressions that one partner performed more often than the other can leave the latter with residual negative feelings. A pair in which one mate was more critical or carried considerably fewer responsibilities for couple or family functioning are examples. When one mate's behavior has disproportionately hurt the other, clinicians may validate the latter's feelings. They can suggest that the offending mate was probably troubled or hurting but his or her way of responding was apparently problematic. If at all possible, it can be very helpful for partners who have hurt their mates to listen fully to the mates' feelings and say they are sorry. Clinicians can explain how such a discussion may be healing and offer encouragement and support for engaging in it.

In work on communication and problem solving, partners may also do something in sessions or at home that arouses their mate's immediate anger or other negative feelings although there is no cognitive distortion involved. Perhaps what was done would produce a negative response in almost anyone. Or, one mate's words or actions may aggravate an area that is personally sensitive for the other for some reason. In general, clinicians' course of action again is first to direct the partners' attention to the fact that something is going on. Then the affected partner's thoughts and feelings can be probed or the clinician can guess what they may be. It can be important to elicit or suggest the "soft feelings," such as hurt, disappointment, or fear, that are often lurking below anger (Christensen et al. 1995). The clinician can usually normalize the feelings, ask if the mate understands, and explore why the latter acted as he or she did. However, partners may also need to be taught to handle each other's sore spots with care.

> Later in the same interview with Ellen and Beverly, Beverly said Ellen was really not very handy around the house. Ellen exploded, saying, "You know I'm sensitive about this issue but you keep bringing it up." At first Beverly protested that she was just stating a fact. The clinician said, "Maybe so, but can you understand Ellen gets hurt about this?" Beverly said yes, but did she have to always walk on eggshells to be careful of Ellen's tender feelings? The clinician responded with, "Well, people who love each other usually try to do that for each other." The clinician then clarified that she did not mean to blame Beverly, that she knew they were both frustrated over the expense of hiring someone to do household repairs. Beverly said she did want to learn not to push Ellen's "hot" buttons because when she did, they both suffered.

As with partners' reactions to interventions, their distorted cognitions or negative affects in response to each other that do not dissipate when ventilated or corrected may need to be explored further in insight work. Often, these stem from a partner's transference reactions to the mate.

Partners may also show resistance during work on communication and problem solving because *couple interaction patterns*, as well as *habitual individual ways of coping*, tend to take on a life of their own. This tendency toward persistence may be understood using the systems concept of homeostasis as an impediment to second-order change, behavioral theories of learning and reinforcement, or object relations theories suggesting that change can be threatening to people on both conscious and unconscious levels. While some partners will need to examine the functions of such patterns in insight-oriented work, clinicians may first see if a couple can benefit from direct efforts to alter them (Baucom et al. 1995, Christensen et al. 1995). The first step, as discussed earlier, is to define the habit or pattern as a problem. A couple may agree one partner has difficulty with the other continually leaving dirty socks on the floor, both criticize each other too much, one gets emotional and the other withdraws. The pros and cons of keeping the habit or pattern versus giving it up can be honestly examined during the stages of defining and understanding the problem. Often, short-term reinforcers and longer-term costs will be discovered at this point. The partner who leaves dirty socks on the floor does not have to bother with throwing them in the hamper, but is likely to incur the mate's wrath for hours or even days. If all goes well, the partners will agree to try to replace old behaviors with new solutions and will proceed to do so.

It is at this point, however, that preparing couples for how resistant the problem may be to change is often wise (Christensen et al. 1995). Clinicians can warn partners that old habits or patterns die hard. They may say, "You'll find the words coming out of your mouth before you even realize it," or "You'll find the socks wafting toward the floor . . ." Partners can be told they will have to work very hard at home to realize they are about to embark on habitual or patterned behavior and stop themselves. Often, at first, they will already have begun it and will need to try to stop themselves midway into the old behavior and regroup. Each partner may be helped to engage in conscious self-talk, such as, "Is it worth doing what I feel like doing now when it's going to lead to the same trouble it always does?" A slogan sometimes helpful for them to remember when both participate in dysfunctional patterns is that "the pattern is the enemy" rather than "the partner is the enemy." Couples often report stopping themselves by saying to each other, "We're getting into the pattern again." Clinicians should be careful to give positive attention to such efforts even if the habit or pattern is not conquered consistently at first. They should ask partners to plan beforehand how to reward each other for making positive changes and should make sure such rewards are forthcoming at home. If partners' conscious efforts do not work to interrupt bad habits or patterns, insight techniques can still be initiated.

A common instance of a bad habit persisting occurs when one partner promises in session to do something, such as no longer throwing dirty socks on the floor, but makes few or no efforts to change at home. This response is especially likely if the partner has developed a habitual pattern of promising to do things to pacify the mate and then rarely following through. The first interventions to deal with such situations can be to seek to prevent them. As detailed earlier, clinicians should warn partners during problem solving not to agree to anything they will later be unwilling to do, help them to anticipate obstacles to carrying out agreements, and say they will ask in the next session how an agreement went. If one partner nonetheless fails to follow through, clinicians should devote significant attention to the situation. They may first ask what went wrong. If the partner who reneged tells about something reasonable interfering, the clinician may suggest revising the agreement and in the future renegotiating at home when such events happen. If this partner says he or she decided not to follow through because the agreement was not fair or had some other flaw, the clinician can reiterate that partners should always voice such perceptions at home and renegotiate. The clinician may also indicate at some point that treatment will not help if partners do not follow through on changes worked out in sessions.

When a partner repeatedly fails to follow through, the clinician should nonjudgmentally wonder if perhaps agreeing to do things he or she does not really want to do has become a habitual way of coping. Often the history of such a habit goes back to family-of-origin experiences with a controlling parent. Or it may date from a period of couple interaction in which the more one mate demanded, the more the other placated without following through, leading to increased demands, less following through, and so on. In both instances, the clinician can label the habit as an earlier attempt at coping when no other approach seemed workable but one that is now causing problems. The partner who does not follow through can be asked to make a clear decision either to change or not, and to stick to it. An overly demanding mate must, of course, be asked to work on changing his or her role in the dysfunctional pattern as well.

A different situation occurs when both partners fail to carry out agreements reached in sessions. Again, clinicians may try by means discussed above to prevent such events, explore what happened, and emphasize the importance of following through. Repeated failures may indicate that the couple has deeper reasons for resisting the changes they have agreed on. Whenever change efforts seem stalled, it is worthwhile to ask couples whether they believe something is going on that is not being addressed. Perhaps underlying issues such as a lack of intimacy are the real problem. Clinicians can also try interpreting what they think may be the reason. These techniques are further discussed in Chapter 6.

Physical and Environmental Influences on Partners' Abilities to Change

Couples attempting to learn new communication and problem-solving skills do not operate in a vacuum. Partners are always influenced by their health and other physical attributes and by their environments, especially children, extended families, friends, jobs, financial situation, other treatment, and possible experiences with prejudice and discrimination. With the exception of prejudice and discrimination, to be discussed in Chapter 7, any of these influences may be positive. However, when they are negative or mixed, such influences may create obstacles to couples achieving needed change in treatment. The clinician using this book's integrative approach will seek to assess all relevant physical and environmental influences on partners and, if needed, to intervene in regard to them.

Partners who are intelligent, healthy, and energetic can bring these *strengths* to bear in the treatment process as well as in their daily lives. Some have *environmental resources* such as children, friends, or extended families who help meet their needs and offer support in times of difficulty. Religion or spirituality can be a significant help to some (Hof 1995). Having sufficient money constitutes an important resource. Other clinicians working with partners may considerably enhance their growth. The fit or balance between stresses and resources in a given case is critical. For example, a couple without much money but with a network of extended family, neighbors, and friends who can help them in a variety of ways usually do much better than couples wrenched by poverty who do not. The availability of community resources such as subsidized day care, food stamps, neighborhood recreation centers, and so on might also positively affect the balance for such a couple.

A frequent negative influence on partners' functioning and capacities to change in treatment is that they may be under considerable *physical or environmental stress*. Often one partner does not realize the stress the other is under or neither fully recognizes their stress levels from health problems, caring for young children or elderly parents, dealing with high-pressure jobs, struggling to make ends meet on inadequate income, or the like. Continuing stress from any of these sources can cause greater health problems or a buildup of anger, anxiety, or depression that then add to the stress (Conger et al. 1990). When poor health or environmental problems cause distress, partners' different ways of trying to cope with them can lead to conflict that is stressful as well.

Clinicians should identify and explore stresses from health problems or environmental influences that couples may not have fully recognized. At the very least, doing so may offer support to partners who have been blaming themselves or enduring blame from their mates for not coping better. Partners may also gain more empathy for each other. Just being reminded that they are under stress and coping reasonably well can strengthen both in persevering. Clinicians may also normalize and empathize with feelings that result from stress, such as anxiety or discouragement.

Another outcome of such discussions may be that partners decide to work in treatment toward better coping with health or environmental problems causing stress. If the other mate will not react negatively, a clinician may offer a partner who is more affected by a particular stress, such as a parent's illness, a few individual sessions to discuss coping. However, some joint problem solving is virtually always in order. Perhaps a pair will decide to cope differently by arranging for some respite from child-care responsibilities, or work together on how to handle the demands of one partner's former spouse. Even if not too much can be done about whatever is causing the partners' stress, they may find better ways to handle the stress itself. For example, perhaps stress from an in-law's visit can be reduced only to a certain point, but the couple may decide they will prepare to unwind afterward by having a quiet evening together rather than planning further activities.

Clinicians can often encourage partners' use of environmental resources to meet some needs or help them cope with stress. Christensen and colleagues (1995) note that helping partners engage in better self-care often cuts down on pressures for the couple relationship to fulfill so many individual needs. For example, mates may be helped to connect with others, such as constructive friends or extended family members, to meet some of their needs for emotional support, companionship, self-esteem, or stimulation. Clinicians can inquire whether partners would consider asking others in their environment for emotional, financial, or physical help when needed. Or they may ask whether religious institutions to which partners belong or other community resources might be of assistance. Often clinicians have more knowledge of the latter resources than couples do, and they should freely share it. For example, couples dealing with one mate's serious illness might be helped to find a support group.

As outlined in Chapter 2, *serious financial problems*, especially those that result in living below the poverty line, are among the greatest sources of stress couples can face. Not having enough money tends to create or be associated with a number of other problems that also cause stress, leading to a buildup that can wear partners down. Their health, energy, and self-esteem are likely to suffer. Couples who must depend on very low-paying work or welfare programs may experience crowded housing or even homelessness, hunger, dangerous neighborhoods, poor medical care, and other severe stresses as a direct result of their financial straits (Newman 1998). Yet poverty limits their coping options. Couples struggling with severe poverty are also well aware of society's prejudicial perceptions that they are a burden and that their problems are of their own making (Parnell and Vanderkloot 1994).

The stresses associated with economic hardship may reverberate throughout the couple system. Some of the ways partners cope with such difficulties are likely to be constructive but others may not be. Partners are likely to fight over how to handle money. Further, each may tend to handle anxiety over money differently, with perhaps one inclined to avoid discussing the problem and the other obsessing about it. There may be shame or conflict about using resources such as financial aid from extended families or welfare. One study of couple communication found that economic pressures seemed to have their effect by "promoting hostility in marital interactions and curtailing the warm and supportive behaviors spouses express toward one another" (Conger et al. 1990, p. 643).

A clinician conveying continued respect and acceptance is especially important with low-income couples, who may be more concerned than others about being judged negatively. Clinicians must acknowledge the impact of such couples' many stresses and recognize partners' strengths in coping with them. They may assist partners in working together to change whatever aspects of their environment they can modify (Parnell and Vanderkloot 1994). One way clinicians can offer help is to share their knowledge of resources and how to access them. Their direct assistance might range from helping a partner write a résumé to locating low-cost day care for a couple's child. Advocacy and efforts to coordinate services among different settings may also be appropriate when couples cannot obtain needed assistance by themselves.

To separate the partners' financial and related problems from their emotional reactions to them may be helpful in trying to foster better coping, as the following case excerpt shows.

> Rosa and Ernesto, both in their forties and born in Mexico, were seen together in a setting that had earlier helped them with a problem with one of Rosa's children. They had learned to trust the clinician, who was also Latina, at that time. In a brief telephone interview, Rosa now described arguing and verbal but not physical abuse by Ernesto. She had lost her job, Ernesto was earning below minimum wage, and Rosa's family had given as much financial help as they could. The couple was afraid to seek welfare help because Ernesto was in the United States illegally.
>
> After greeting them warmly and seeking more details, the clinician noted how hard Ernesto was working and how hard both were trying to deal with a difficult situation. She empathized with

> the anger and frustration both must feel. In telling more about their fighting, Ernesto tried to placate both Rosa and the clinician with promises to do better, but said Rosa should be trying harder to find another job. Rosa began crying and saying she was doing the best she could. She then began to get mad and say Ernesto gets mean. He should leave so she could get financial help. The clinician urged them to stop blaming themselves and each other. She said she knew people do this when they're mad and don't know what else to do. Maybe by the three putting their heads together, they could figure out a better plan. Both agreed that this was what they wanted.

In this instance, a sort of reframing has taken place. The clinician makes the financial problem rather than the partner the enemy, a variation on a strategy suggested earlier. The clinician has also joined the pair in fighting against the difficult problems they face. Clinicians need to be very aware of their own reactions in dealing with couples in poverty. They must neither glorify the partners' strengths nor secretly judge them, perhaps as defenses against feeling overwhelmed themselves. Usually some parts of couples' difficult situations can be improved even if the rest cannot. And partners' communication, problem solving, and coping with their emotions in response to stresses must not be neglected simply because the reality problems are more pressing. Even having a clinician who understands and who is with them emotionally can help ease some stress and enhance partners' self-esteem, giving them a little more energy to cope.

Another cause of many couples' difficulties in changing may be that *people such as their children, extended families, or employers resist* when partners want to deal with them differently. To try to prevent such problems, clinicians should always ask partners to anticipate how others might react to any changes planned. Clinicians can also give their own opinions or at least ask questions to highlight possible difficulties. For example, once Ron and Lynn presented his mother with joint decisions in response to her demands, the mother would very likely protest. The couple should be encouraged to think beforehand about what they would do if so. When partners agree on how to discipline their children, the children often test their unity in a variety of ways, a circumstance the couple can be helped to anticipate.

When others may or do react adversely, it can be useful for clinicians to recognize the strong feelings possibly evoked in partners. Guilt, anxiety, or anger may be felt toward the outside person or displaced or projected onto the mate. Partners may backslide in their handling of the situation or legitimately ask to adjust their prior agreements. Clinicians need to normalize any of these feelings or behaviors and support partners in figuring out how to proceed. Sometimes defining the other parties' resistance as a new problem to be addressed facilitates finding new and better solutions. Sometimes the problem may have to be recognized as more complex than originally thought because of one or both partners' feeling responses, perhaps requiring insight work or some other intervention strategy before much change can be expected.

Another option is to consider involving resistant outside parties in some treatment sessions. When children are reacting adversely or are failing to improve problematic behaviors in response to couples' positive changes, family sessions may be indicated. Even partners' parents or entire extended families can sometimes be invited in (Astor and Sherman 1997, Ho 1990). However, the clinician and the couple must be able to anticipate that doing so may help the couple or at least cause no harm. For example, partners' parents who do not believe in counseling or do not want a couple to stay together are unlikely to be helpful even if they consent to come in. Still another option is for a couple, or the clinician with the couple's permission, to enlist the help of a supportive outsider who may have some clout with a recalcitrant environmental figure. For example, perhaps a priest might have some positive influence with Ron's mother if the situation were explained.

Finally, not to be overlooked as a potential source of stress or interference with partners' efforts to make positive changes are *service institutions* (Basham 1992) and, in some instances, *other professionals*. For example, the clinician's own setting may not be open enough evening or weekend hours to accommodate partners who cannot take time off from work, or it may lack a sliding fee scale. Another clinician treating one partner individually in a way that counteracts what couple treatment is trying to accomplish can occasionally be a major obstacle to change (Siegel 1992). In such instances, a clinician's efforts to change policies, advocate on the couple's behalf, or mediate tactfully with another treating person are indicated.

As clinicians help couples work on communication and problem solving, they must continually update their assessment hypotheses about environmental, individual, and couple system influences on partners' functioning. Partners' growth in treatment may confirm that their original problems were probably caused largely by inadequate information about how to communicate and solve problems effectively together, since they seem to be taking in new learning in these areas and benefiting from it. Over time, environmental stresses may have changed or the couple may be dealing with them differently. Clinicians should always elicit partners' input on how treatment is going and consider it seriously in thinking about how to proceed. Some couples terminate after achieving new communication and problem-solving skills in specific areas, as will be discussed in Chapter 10. Most, however, need to do at least some insight work.

CHAPTER

6

Insight and Intimacy

In this book's integrative approach to couple treatment, insight work represents a continuum. Most couples need to develop some insight into the ways partners deal with key needs or feelings in order to achieve their treatment goals. Couples themselves may ask to work on better coping with anger, sexuality, or intimacy needs. Or partners' difficulties coping with these or other needs or feelings may be discovered during work on communication or attempts to solve other problems. A couple's efforts to learn new ways of coping then sometimes proceed in a relatively straightforward way. Often, however, they are facilitated by partners gaining at least a beginning awareness of the childhood sources of their learning about how to deal with needs and feelings, and possibly of some of their fears of coping differently.

In many cases, more of an insight focus is needed to help couples change. Here clinicians may try to help partners gain access to needs, feelings, or fears of which they have been less aware, including some that are transference-based. When deeper, perhaps unconscious individual or relationship dynamics block changes couples wish to make, still more intensive insight work may be useful. The goal most likely to require that couples develop deeper insights into themselves and their relationship dynamics is that of greater intimacy.

This chapter begins by explaining how some couples may be helped fairly directly to understand and change the ways they handle needs and feelings, including the need for intimacy. It then discusses increasingly deeper insight work. Part of the following chapter addresses ways to help couples gain insights into the deeper influences of their genders, sexual orientations, sociocultural characteristics, and any related experiences with oppression or loss. Treatment of narcissistically vulnerable couples, to be discussed in Chapter 8, almost always requires partners to achieve insight into their coping with needs and feelings and the influence of their pasts.

INSIGHT INTO COPING WITH NEEDS AND FEELINGS

Couples can often work to change their coping with needs and feelings by following the progression of problem-solving steps outlined in Chapter 5. However, completing each step may take more time and rely more heavily on the clinician's input than before. One reason is that couples may not realize that their problematic coping with a specific need or feeling is an influence on their communication or on other problems with which they have requested help. Another is that they may need more assistance to understand their current coping and possible ways they could change. Side trips into dealing with partners' fears of change are also more likely to be needed than in other problem-solving work.

Let us first consider how couples may do relatively straightforward problem solving to change their coping with particular needs or feelings, using the example of intimacy. Then the progression of problem-solving steps in somewhat more complex cases will be addressed.

Problem-Solving Steps to Change Coping with Needs and Feelings

Couples themselves sometimes identify their coping with a particular need or feeling as a problem for discussion in treatment. That is, they accomplish the first step in the problem-solving process on their own. For example, both may ask to discuss their handling of anger or sexual needs. If only one does, the rule of thumb can be invoked that if something is a problem for one partner it must be considered so for both, at least to the extent of understanding the problem better. This tactic is often needed when only one mate wants to work toward greater intimacy. In any instance, in beginning to examine a couple's coping with a particular need or feeling, a clinician should try to create balance between partners, usually by explaining that it will be important to look at the ways both cope. If partners still resist such discussion, the reason is often that they fear being blamed or pushed to change in an uncomfortable way. The clinician may need to gently elicit or suggest these fears and offer reassurance that the problem-solving work may simply give them some new options to consider. Listening to the other partner explain why the current way of coping is problematic for him or her may also create more empathy and a willingness to proceed.

While couples' search for new ways to cope with a need or feeling is often a complex process, sometimes it is not. For example, mates may fairly easily work out how to adjust their different approaches to meeting sexual needs, with men perhaps coming to better understand their female partners' usually greater needs for affection, time, and foreplay. A couple may realize that their habit of storing up anger and then exploding is dysfunctional and may readily work out more constructive means of assertiveness.

Even figuring out new ways to deal with intimacy needs can sometimes proceed without a great deal of difficulty. The first problem-solving step involves helping partners define what they mean when they say they would like more intimacy. Some equate sex and intimacy. Many think of intimacy mainly in terms of how they might feel when they have it, such as "closer" or "happier together." The appropriate question then is what might need to be happening differently for them to feel more this way. If the answer is something like "stop arguing" or "figure out how to deal with Joe's ex-wife," direct work on these identified problems may be undertaken to see if changes accomplished bring the partners the closeness they desire.

When asked to consider what might help them feel closer, partners often suggest one or more of the intimacy activities identified in Chapter 2: mutual self-disclosure, emotional support, sensual-physical contact, or companionship (Kersten and Himle 1990). Or clinicians may introduce discussion of these or similar intimacy tasks. The mates may then address which of such changes, if any, they wish to attempt. Couples themselves must determine how much intimacy they want and what they are willing to do to achieve it (Weeks 1995a). Different preferences between the two may have to be negotiated. If partners cannot figure out what keeps them from achieving intimacy or cannot agree on changes needed, deeper exploration may be undertaken to try to help them by means discussed later in this chapter. The case of Ginger and Ralph demonstrates one couple's fairly direct problem solving to achieve greater intimacy.

> Ginger and Ralph, a working-class couple in their late thirties, had already done some successful work in treatment to decide how to cooperate better in housework and care of their kids. Their communication and problem-solving skills in general had improved. Still, Ginger did not feel totally satisfied with their marriage. She thought she wanted to feel closer to Ralph, a wish that puzzled him because they were seldom arguing anymore. The clinician asked if Ginger could clarify what seemed to be missing for her. She wasn't sure, but felt it had something to do with Ralph spending so much time watching TV. Ralph protested that he often took the kids out in the evening to give her some break from watching them (one of their agreements from earlier problem solving), and that they were doing something as a family almost every Sunday. The clinician reminded him to slow down and try to understand what Ginger was saying. Ginger agreed he was helping with the kids a lot but noted that they almost never had any time together without the kids or "just to talk." Ralph said he still wasn't quite sure what she meant. The clinician noted that Ginger seemed to be talking about finding activities that might help them feel closer. Was Ralph willing to consider working on more closeness that might come in such ways?

Ginger and Ralph's clinician first seeks to help Ginger define the nature of her concern about intimacy and then tries to make sure Ralph is willing to work on it, or at least enter into a discussion about it. If the idea of achieving greater closeness or attempting a related change raises any difficulties, these may need to be addressed. Otherwise, work to understand the problem further may proceed.

> Ralph did not answer directly but said he had liked doing things just with Ginger before the kids were born. Still, he had kind of thought these weren't possible now, given the cost of babysitters. The clinician suggested that if both would like to spend more time doing things together, they could try to work on this just like any other problem to be solved. In further discussion, Ginger told how

much she had missed such activities. Ralph said it would be fun to do even a few of them again. They agreed that the hard part was to find the time and money. Eventually they worked out some tentative solutions, including that Ginger and her friends could trade babysitting to allow occasional nights out as a couple. They thought of some inexpensive things they could do together. Ginger also said she would rather have gift money (such as for her upcoming birthday) used to "buy" time together than expensive jewelry as Ralph had planned. The two seemed eager to begin trying out their new solutions.

Some couples are not achieving intimacy tasks mainly because partners do not have the needed skills (Kersten and Himle 1990). They may, however, be willing to attain them if asked to do so and helped with any fears that arise. Such proved to be the case with Ginger's second idea about what might lead to greater intimacy, that she would like more times when she and Ralph could "just talk." When Ralph questioned working on this goal, the clinician explored the reasons and also noted that many men do not feel comfortable "just talking." Ralph explained he did not know what to say about himself and was not too sure how to respond when Ginger talked about herself, especially about her feelings. However, he was willing to try to learn.

A few sessions later, Ginger and Ralph decided to work on Ralph talking more about himself and discussed some possibilities. Ginger said she would like to hear about what he does at work. Ralph protested that his work was boring since he did pretty much the same thing every day. The clinician asked if he talked to the other men at work about anything. He said they might talk about sports, their kids, or something funny that happened to one of them. He knew Ginger didn't want to hear about sports. Ginger protested that she is interested in some sports, for example, basketball because she likes Michael Jordan. This information came as a surprise to Ralph. The clinician asked if Ginger would also be interested in hearing about the funny incidents or the other men's kids and she said, "Sure, if it was interesting to Ralph."

The clinician suggested Ralph might have to work at the habit of talking more to Ginger, and that Ginger would have to remember to appreciate what he did say even if he was awkward or didn't talk too long at first. They also agreed, after further discussion, that both needed some time to unwind in the evenings and wouldn't want to spend them all talking. With the clinician's help, they worked out that they would try to spend twenty minutes or so each night talking after the kids went to bed, except Tuesdays when there were two TV shows on that Ralph especially liked. The clinician promised to ask for a report on how this was going and reminded them that Ralph had said he would also need help with how to respond to what Ginger said in their talks.

Clinicians suggesting that old habits die hard and that these must be very consciously addressed at home is again in order in work on intimacy tasks. Further interventions, as with Ginger and Ralph, may be assigning couples homework, promising to check up on progress, and suggesting that mates give each other positive reinforcement. However, any homework needs to grow out of a couple's discussions of how they might achieve greater intimacy, represent incremental change, and have a realistic chance of success for the particular couple at the particular time. The once-popular intervention of immediately assigning a struggling couple the task of talking together for one hour every evening, when they had not yet learned to talk without arguing or were terrified of the closeness involved, is an unfortunate example of what *not* to do.

It may also be necessary at times to focus on helping partners increase their more subtle intimacy-enhancing behaviors. Weeks (1995a) discusses some of these as validating each other's positive behaviors and attributes, showing respect for each other, looking out for each other's well-being in the relationship, protecting each other and the relationship from harm, taking each other's side with outsiders, and otherwise showing loyalty. Successful intimate relationships also involve both partners being able to apologize when needed (Karpel 1994) and forgive each other for occasional lapses (Weeks 1995a). When some of these capacities are lacking, they too can sometimes be encouraged and taught. Often, however, behaviors such as not showing respect or not looking out for the well-being of the partner signal deeper problems with intimacy.

When couples have trouble trying to achieve intimacy tasks or increase intimacy-enhancing behaviors, a clinician may explore or suggest what might be holding them back. Some partners respond well when helped to unearth inaccurate cognitions, buried but reality-based anger, or readily accessible fears of change. Ginger and Ralph's clinician suggested a possible fear of Ralph's when she said he might be hesitant to work on "more talk" because many men are uncomfortable with talking a lot. But if partners consistently do not follow through on efforts to achieve intimacy, the blocks may be more significant. Perhaps the two keep making excuses not to spend more time together. Perhaps one keeps being overly critical about small or nonexistent flaws in the other. Or both pick a fight or stimulate a child to act out just when they have been feeling close. Clinicians can interpret such behaviors as possibly reflecting partners' deeper intimacy fears and suggest further work to try to explore what these may be. If one partner is more the instigator of these blocks to closeness, the other may be told that he or she is likely also to have some intimacy concerns that may become apparent as the work proceeds.

Later sections of this chapter consider further insight work to help couples move past obstacles to change, including blocks to greater intimacy. Let us first examine other situations in which partners may need more of the clinician's help to identify, understand, or find solutions to their problems coping with specific feelings or needs.

Helping Partners Identify Their Problematic Coping with Needs or Feelings

When partners do not realize that their coping with a particular need or feeling may be at the root of another problem, the clinician may need to infer this component and push further to identify it. The assessment framework suggested in Chapter 2 can provide guidance for such inferences. It is always important for clinicians to think about how both partners seem to be dealing with their needs for affiliation and intimacy, self-esteem, sexuality, and stimulation, as well as their anger and anxiety. The next step can be to develop hypotheses as to how such coping may be related to the problems a couple wants help with. Often, doing so requires further exploration of an issue a couple cannot seem to resolve even when their communication skills have improved.

> Rhonda and Eleanor, a lesbian couple in their mid-thirties, sought treatment primarily because they could not agree on how to manage money. They had pooled their resources several years before

when their relationship became permanent. In initial problem-solving work they compromised on a budget, but Rhonda again went on a shopping spree that ran up serious credit card bills. She could not fully understand Eleanor's outrage since most of the items purchased were for their home. An argument ensued about whether the purchases were "selfish" or Eleanor's anxiety about the debts "silly." When the clinician tried to probe why Rhonda broke their agreement, she became defensive and down on herself, saying she didn't know.

The first necessity in such situations is to establish, if at all possible, a benign and unpressured atmosphere in which to try to understand what might be happening. In this case, the clinician might say she believed that Rhonda did not know what was compelling her and that she could not help not knowing. Perhaps a supportive comment about Rhonda or both partners' having worked hard so far to understand their different ways of handling money and be responsive to each other's needs would also be helpful. Then the clinician might explain, if she had not already, that when partners run into a block in understanding themselves, it is important to back off and come at the issue in some other way. Only if the person who has blocked can be helped to feel reasonably comfortable and curious rather than embarrassed, pressured, or attacked should discussion proceed. Such efforts also depend to some degree on the partners being "psychologically minded," a capacity many can attain with clinicians' help.

Clinicians have several choices of how to help couples "come at the issue in some other way." One is to encourage the partner who has blocked to try to be self-aware—literally to stop and turn inward to notice what thoughts and feelings are there—the next time an impulse to engage in the behavior under examination arises (Baucom et al. 1995). Another is to explore past occurrences of the behavior to see if any influences are suggested by the events that took place around it, perhaps even asking partners to review in detail what happened most recently to try to get in touch with what they thought or felt. Clinicians may also cautiously air their own speculations about possible needs or feelings influencing a partner's behavior.

The clinician suggested that Rhonda seemed genuinely perplexed as to what might have pushed her to spend money after they had agreed to another plan, and added that in such instances people were often responding to thoughts, feelings, or needs of which they were unaware. After securing Rhonda's permission to pursue the issue, she asked for more details about what had happened in this last experience. The couple felt that they had been under no unusual stress although Eleanor had been working long hours for several weeks. The clinician wondered if Rhonda had been angry or lonely during that time. Rhonda didn't think so, but Eleanor remembered she had complained about the evenings seeming empty. At this point Rhonda had a "flash" thought that she was annoyed one night that Eleanor went out with a friend after work instead of coming home to be with her. But she didn't think this feeling lasted and was able to pursue it no further. The clinician suggested that she try hard to be aware of what she was thinking and feeling if an impulse to spend a lot of money recurred.

The following session, Rhonda reported that when Eleanor again took time after work that week to go out with a friend, Rhonda found herself wanting to go to the mall. The first thought of which she had been aware was that with some new pots and pans she could be a better cook and perhaps please Eleanor more. Eleanor interjected that she'd rather be free of debt and that Rhonda was already a good cook. The clinician asked if anything else had gone through Rhonda's mind. She said well, she had really felt a pull to go to the mall. She realized she was thinking, "I'll show Eleanor I can take care of myself without leaning on her." The idea that quickly followed was, "To hell with the budget, I'm going to do what I want!" Eleanor interposed, "Now wait a minute!" Rhonda went on that she then felt guilty and ashamed of herself. She finally turned on the TV and managed to get involved in some program. The clinician said Rhonda had done a lot of good work to be aware of so much of her thinking. It sounded like she been mad that Eleanor had again chosen not to spend time with her. Rhonda said sadly, "I guess I was, but now I just feel bad that she doesn't love me enough to want to be with me. She'd rather be with her friends." Eleanor responded with, "Oh, for heaven's sake. How could you possibly think that?"

Only at this point could the focus of treatment shift from the problem of how Rhonda and Eleanor dealt with money to the problem of how both might be handling affiliative needs and anger. Rhonda's apparently distorted cognition about what Eleanor's behavior meant, and perhaps their divergent beliefs about how much time partners should spend together, would warrant attention as well.

A clinician may need to make special efforts to prepare partners who have not asked to deal with needs or feelings differently to move into further discussion. Both can be told that everyone has needs for human connection, everyone experiences anger at times. The clinician can explain that most people are not fully aware of how they deal with such needs or feelings and that many different ways of dealing with them are normal. An atmosphere must be established in which neither partner will put the other down, in session or later, because of what is revealed (Scharff and Scharff 1991). It can be reiterated that people cannot help how they feel although they can be responsible for how they deal with feelings. Clinicians must also watch for partners feeling bad about themselves because of a need or feeling they have experienced or think they have handled badly. The clinician may help by normalizing or suggesting that a partner perhaps did not know better options for coping at the time.

To establish motivation to work on coping differently with a particular need or feeling, it is sometimes important for the partners to examine, or the clinician to suggest, the damage done by the current means. In the case of Rhonda and Eleanor, the damage was clear because the couple saw their differences about money as a problem. An example in which neither partner might immediately recognize damage might be, for instance, one in which a partner stuffed feelings of anger. The clinician might point out that sequelae the couple did not recognize as connected with this coping method, such as this partner's later outbursts or withdrawal from the other, were in fact a likely result.

Helping Partners Understand Their Problems Coping with Needs or Feelings

When partners are ready to try to understand how they cope with a particular need or feeling, clinicians may first ask whether they usually know when they are experiencing it and, if so, how they usually respond. Often partners need help to gain greater self-awareness. They may not usually experience a need or feeling directly. They may not have realized some of the less obvious or more defended ways in which they have been coping. Their coping may be influenced by mistaken perceptions, attributions, or assumptions, as when one partner uses criticism instead of expressing anger directly because "that's the only way she'll listen to me." Hearing about how partners handle a particular need or feeling in different circumstances can also be instructive, as in, "I do enjoy sex but not when I'm exhausted after a day at work and then dealing with the kids." When partners' coping is dysfunctional, it may be useful to help them explore its possible roots in their childhood experiences. Finally, two mates' different ways of handling needs or feelings have often stimulated each to move into more and more extreme positions, eventuating in highly problematic interaction patterns. We see this situation with Sue and Eric, a couple in their early forties.

> In their first interview, Sue and Eric described as one of their problems that when they got mad, their opposite ways of responding drove them both crazy. Eric tended to "sulk and withdraw," according to Sue. He might stay distant for days, making Sue angrier every hour. The impasse might be broken by Sue yelling that he was a coward or didn't care about her since he wouldn't try to work things out. Then they would both criticize and blame each other. Eric admitted he carried his anger a long time but felt Sue's habit of immediately dumping it on the nearest bystander, usually him but sometimes the kids, was equally destructive.
>
> After work on resolving several other problems reduced the level of the couple's anger somewhat, the issue of how to handle anger itself was tackled. While each felt he or she was usually justified in getting mad, both could readily agree that the escalations they got into were destructive. And they seemed to be getting worse over time. The clinician suggested beginning to discuss this problem as they would any other, by further defining the problem and trying to understand where each was coming from before trying to solve it. Both saw the problem as not knowing what to do when they got mad, and so doing what they always did. Handling anger didn't arise so much with friends or at work, but Sue admitted she yelled too much at the kids and Eric added that, to be honest, he tried to avoid conflict in all his relationships. The clinician said she thought more information would be useful and asked

both to describe what they had learned about anger and how to handle it as kids.

Sue said she had seen her father yell at her mother a lot and her mother give in virtually all the time. Sue gave in too as a kid, because her father was frightening and sometimes hit them if they didn't obey. But she vowed she would never be controlled by a man as her mother was. In her perception, ironically, Eric could now control her by his silence and withdrawal. Eric started to object to this characterization but the clinician suggested that instead, he try to understand and reflect back what Sue had learned about anger growing up. After a few moments he said, "I guess she learned you can either yell or stuff it to avoid getting hurt." Sue looked thoughtful and the clinician wondered if she might have identified with her father's way of asserting himself, since her mother didn't seem to have found any way of asserting herself at all. Sue was somewhat uncomfortable with this idea. The clinician said it seemed Sue had had no good role models for how to deal with anger or get her legitimate needs met.

Before proceeding with Eric's part of the interview, let us comment on the use of family-of-origin material here. The insight both members of a couple may gain from realizing how each learned to handle a given need or feeling in childhood is relatively superficial but important. It is not based on delving into unconscious material or very complex aspects of psychodynamic functioning, but on the simple and usually easily grasped idea that people learn how to manage needs or feelings just as they learn many other things growing up (Zimmerman and Dickerson 1993). Recognizing the origins of such learning can make partners less defensive and less angry toward their mates because both have "good" reasons for doing things the way they do. A clinician may also point out that partners' ways of coping may have been needed and worked well in childhood. But as adults, they can choose to learn other ways.

When Eric was asked to speak about his childhood experiences with anger, he at first said he didn't have any because he never expressed it. His mother would have killed him. As it was, she was cold, critical, and controlling. His father was more affectionate, but passive, and he worked long hours. Eric was ashamed of the fact that he reacted to Sue much as his father had to his mother, but he had also experienced that being more assertive toward her in their arguments made him very uncomfortable and got nowhere. Once Eric had given his description, the clinician commented that it was pretty easy to see that he had not had good models for coping with anger either. Both he and Sue may have ended up taking parents they did not admire as models, probably without even realizing it.

A useful method for reviewing family-of-origin material to see how it may have contributed to current functioning can be found in an article by Gerson and colleagues (1993). As reviewed in Chapter 2, these authors suggest that partners may be influenced by "frames" each brings from childhood experiences. These frames include learned ways of coping with anxiety and other needs and feelings; modeling of family members' behavior seen in childhood; repetition of the role a partner played in the parental family; efforts to reverse behavior seen in an identification figure, such as when a partner whose parent was too strict becomes too lenient with his or her own children; and proclivities to react in terms of loyalty issues or definitions of reality experienced in the family of origin. Frames relevant to a particular couple can be suggested and explored further with them, as when the clinician spoke of their parents' modeling with Sue and Eric. Given Sue's discomfort with the idea that her present handling of anger was modeled after the way her father had handled it, the clinician might better have suggested a different frame, perhaps that Sue was trying to reverse her mother's acquiescence into a more assertive means of coping.

Sometimes there is little need to look at childhood influences on partners' coping with needs or feelings because they are ready to learn new methods without doing so. Sometimes partners do not wish to look at childhood influences, perhaps because this time was painful or they fear their mates misusing what is revealed. For example, one partner may fear that negative facts learned about his or her parental family will become the other's justification for not being so involved with them. Clinicians who suspect such fears can try inquiring or guessing what they are about. However, backing off at least temporarily may be best if partners' fears may be realistic or more preparation may be required before tapping into considerable underlying pain, a possibility to be addressed later in this chapter.

Helping Partners Find New Ways to Cope with Needs or Feelings

Once both partners have explored their coping with a given need or feeling and experienced the mate's understanding, they may be ready for the next problem-solving steps of developing and agreeing to try new solutions. However, it is likely that a clinician will have to offer some suggestions about how to cope differently, since neither partner may have much idea of the possibilities. As with any search for solutions, partners can be told that what works for one may not work as well for the other, and each may have to compromise. They can also be warned that changing long-established ways of coping with a particular need or feeling may take a while, partly because each may encounter fears that must be examined before proceeding. Let us see how Sue and Eric begin this phase of problem solving.

> Sue said she felt almost helpless about what to do with her anger besides yelling at Eric because if she didn't say anything, she just boiled inside. Often she also found herself yelling without having any intention to do so, out of habit and frustration. The clinician first suggested that both would have to put conscious effort into changing the ways they were handling anger that had become so destructive for them. Sue would probably have to "lower the volume" and Eric to "raise it." The clinician suggested Sue ask Eric what he would want Sue to do if she is feeling angry at him, if neither yelling nor stuffing it were options. Sue did so and Eric said, "I don't know, maybe just try to talk with me calmly somehow?" Sue pointed out that even when she did that, he tended to withdraw and get silent. She would then yell to get his attention and they'd be off to the races again. The clinician countered that this was where Eric would have to change by making a strong effort to stay "present" and hear her. Eric thought he could try to do this.
>
> The pair seemed to feel that a solution had been reached, but the clinician suggested they needed to work further. What was Sue going to say to describe her anger in a way that Eric could hear it? How was Eric going to let her know he had heard? And what about when Eric was mad at her? The clinician reminded them of communication techniques learned in earlier sessions and suggested they practice here and now with a real or anticipated situation. They

did practice replaying in a somewhat stilted way a minor incident in which Sue had been mad from the prior week.

In most cases, as with Sue and Eric, clinicians will be able to find ways to help both members of a couple work to modify their coping with a particular need or feeling. Again, as with other problem solving, a necessary part of working out solutions is planning what will be done in a detailed way, rehearsing in session if possible, and assigning couples the task of trying out the new coping at home. Clinicians must often help partners figure out how to realize when they are experiencing the need or feeling in question so they can initiate new efforts to cope with it differently. Otherwise, they will react automatically in the same old ways. Mates should be taught to notice and compliment each other for carrying out any steps toward new coping, even if awkwardly at first. Finally, the couple can be warned that they may find themselves having difficulty using the newly devised solutions. Some of the reasons can include the partners not really understanding or remembering what they are supposed to do, the threat that underlying feelings or fears may surface, or simply the resistance of patterns to change. Clinicians can emphasize that partners must put their best efforts into changing and that further work will be done in sessions to understand any difficulties they encounter.

When Sue and Eric returned for the following session, they reported an even worse argument than in the recent past. It turned out they had gotten stalled in doing problem solving on some other issue, Sue had felt discounted, and her anger had mounted. She tried saying she felt discounted, but now admitted that her voice tone was angry and that she had added sarcastically, "So what else is new?" She did not feel she was yelling, though. Eric said he had tried to keep from withdrawing but had experienced near terror in doing so. He ended up saying, "So you had to be a bitch after all," and the fight began.

This brief interview segment illustrates how difficult partners may find modifying their ingrained ways of coping with needs or feelings. The clinician should praise Sue and Eric for trying to change their pattern and each taking one step toward doing so: Sue to talk about the feeling prompting her anger and Eric to hang in and listen. Both had also been aware of their feelings at the time, an important prelude to changing how they coped with them. As noted earlier, the clinician's noticing such efforts reinforces partners' first small steps toward change and reduces their feelings of failure or blame. The clinician can then ask the two to look within themselves to see what might have made it hard to carry out new coping. Sometimes they have simply fallen back into old habits or fairly surface-level cognitions or affects have interfered. Sometimes feelings or fears blocking change are more buried and further insight work is needed to gain access to them, as will be seen with Sue and Eric below.

INSIGHT INTO BLOCKS TO CHANGE

More of an insight focus may be useful in couple treatment when partners cannot seem to improve their coping with needs or feelings or make other desired changes in response to interventions so far discussed. If clinician error, people in the partners' environments, or other factors described in Chapter 5 are apparently not causing such blocks, the reasons may have to do with feelings or fears of which the partners are not fully aware. Often these spring from transference reactions to their mates deriving from family-of-origin experiences. Use of defense mechanisms such as projective identification may be involved as well.

Clinicians can use education, support, exploration, empathy, and interpretation to help partners begin to develop increased insight into feelings or fears causing blocks to change. They must also establish a treatment ambiance conducive to partners' self-examination. Couples may have varied responses to any insights gained. As insight work increases, partners are more likely to experience transference to clinicians and clinicians' awareness of their own countertransference is especially necessary. Increased insight work is usually possible only when partners are not too emotionally fragile or stressed out by their life circumstances.

Promoting Increased Insight

Sue and Eric, in the interview excerpt given above, reported what is a common occurrence for many couples. Just after a session in which they had achieved some insight into their pattern of Sue yelling and Eric withdrawing and had tried to work out better ways of coping with their anger, they had a bad argument in which the pattern reasserted itself. It was certainly possible that they had not tried hard enough or had not really understood how to proceed differently. However, a comment by Eric suggested that for him, at least, a fear of handling anger differently had been evoked. Let us continue with the same session to see how their clinician began to help.

> After praising Sue and Eric for having tried to change their old ways of handling anger, the clinician said it was important to look at what was going on inside them when they ended up arguing again. She went on, "I'm not trying to make either one of you more responsible than the other for the argument. But, Eric, I want to pick up on something you said a few minutes ago. You said you felt terror when you tried to listen to Sue's anger. What was that about? Do you know what you were afraid of?" Eric was at first a little embarrassed and said he wasn't sure. The clinician added that people didn't always have totally rational thoughts at such times. Eric hesitated and finally said sheepishly, "I think I felt like I was about 6 years old and about to be humiliated." Sue began to protest that she doesn't humiliate him but the clinician stopped her to say, "Let's just hear what was on Eric's mind for now." Eric, however, picked up Sue's challenge and said she did humiliate him at times. Sue countered that she knew she criticized, but surely "humiliation" was too strong a word.

Here the clinician was trying to lead the couple into a more insight-oriented process. Some teaching, reassuring, and restraining of interruptions is frequently required because most couples are not used to talking to each other in such an open-ended way. If a partner does not readily come forth with underlying material, the clinician may need to make sure a comfortable enough atmosphere for self-revelation has been set. Explaining the need for exploration, making sure the other partner does not assert blame, and offering support can help. Fears of exposure can be explored or reassurance offered by saying something like, "Does it feel odd to be thinking this way?" or "I know it's hard to risk talking about what may seem like silly thoughts or feelings." Mates will frequently interrupt, as Sue did, when they hear something they think implies blame of them. A clinician needs to try to restrain them if at all possible and get back to the original train of thought.

> The clinician broke in and said, "Wait, let's not get into the reality yet of what does or doesn't happen. I'm assuming that since you both made honest efforts to change, something we don't understand was affecting the process. We'll do this in a few minutes with you, too, Sue. Can we go back to what Eric was feeling, whether or not it was totally realistic to the two of you?" The couple agreed and the clinician again pursued: "Eric, can you get more into the feeling that you were about to be humiliated? Tell us more about that." Eric said doubtfully that he wasn't sure where the feeling came from and anyway "it was just momentary." The clinician prompted, "Maybe the '6-years-old' part is a clue. Were you humiliated sometimes when you were that age?" Eric could not get into any specific memories. He did know that he had a visceral reaction when Sue got mad at him and he remembered having that feeling a lot as a kid when his mother criticized him. The clinician suggested, "Maybe when you hear anger in Sue's voice, it takes you back to that earlier time and you feel like you just want to run and hide." At this point Sue could hold herself back no longer and blurted out, "Don't tell me I remind you of your mother! I am in no way critical and controlling like she is!"

Again Sue interrupts due to feeling blamed, but here the concern is that Eric thinks she is like his mother. And, of course, in many ways she is. Object relations theorists would conceive that he married her to rework his relationship with his mother, hoping finally to receive love and praise but fearing he would again be put down and humiliated. Marrying an assertive woman also allows him to cope with his anger by projecting it onto her. She is the angry one, he is not, and therefore he does not deserve rejection. One may even argue that he stimulates Sue to be angry at him in a form of projective identification, to reassure himself that she is the angry one. None of these ideas will be useful to the couple as yet, however. The beginning-level interpretation most likely to help them at this time is to conceptualize Eric's transference reaction to Sue as what Siegel (1992) calls "a bruise on a broken bone" (p. 98).

> The clinician again stopped Sue and said Eric is probably very sensitive to the possibility of being humiliated because of his experiences with his mother. She added that everyone brings forward

from childhood some fears of being hurt or let down in the ways their parents hurt them or let them down. So Eric is probably going to be more reactive to Sue's anger than someone else might be, even if the anger isn't unreasonable. Did this make sense to them? They said they thought so. The clinician went on that she also wanted to hear what Sue had been thinking or feeling during the argument, when she found herself getting sarcastic in spite of good intentions [reported earlier]. When Sue drew a blank, the clinician volunteered that perhaps coming across less assertively felt frightening to her because she was so scared of being like her mother and getting walked on. Sue said maybe so, but could not take this idea further.

Here the clinician tried to induce insight for Sue by two different methods. After exploration of Sue's underlying thoughts and feelings proved fruitless, she gave an interpretation of a possible connection to a fear from childhood. In this instance, the interpretation did not work either. If neither of these interventions produces insight at a given time, partners must not be made to feel that they have failed. The clinician should make use of what has already been produced, if anything, and can try to induce future insights by these same means as well as others to be described below.

Partners' Responses to Insight

Any insights a couple gains in a given session may lead to a number of possible outcomes. These include problem solving in regard to how to use the insight, immediate change, an openness to more insight, and resistance.

A common outcome is that an insight does not lead to immediate growth, but can be used to work out better solutions in the area of a difficult problem. This was the first change accomplished with Sue and Eric.

The clinician suggested they talk about what to do for now about the fact that Eric felt unusually sensitive to Sue's anger because of his mother's being domineering and critical. She added that they would undoubtedly find out Sue had some sensitive areas too, and would also talk about how the couple could handle these together.

Sue asked, "Why do I have to change what I do since it's Eric's problem?" The clinician said, "I have a couple of answers for that. One is that Eric can't help feeling this way now, although he may feel differently later after we work on this issue more in treatment. Sometimes you do something for the person you love because they're hurting or sensitive in a given area just like you would take care of them if they were sick or carry something for them if they had a back problem. The second answer is that when it comes up, I hope Eric would also be sensitive about something special or unusual you need from him." The two then agreed to proceed.

With the clinician's help, they worked out that when Sue was mad, it would help Eric a lot if Sue warned him she was upset and needed to discuss something rather than just starting in with an angry tirade. He would then have time to "steel himself." The clinician suggested that while "steeling himself," Eric also engage in some self-talk, perhaps that he was grown up now and not powerless as he may have felt as a little boy. Sue agreed that if Eric needed to take a time-out from a difficult discussion, he could do so by saying that he heard her, but needed to back off for a few minutes. She did ask that he reassure her he wouldn't just leave, but would return to talking at a specific time. The clinician praised their efforts and suggested they practice these techniques in session. She added that it would still be important for both to keep track of feelings or fears aroused, and that Sue might find herself having trouble slowing the discussion down as they had planned due to issues of her own.

The importance of working out what are in some ways stopgap or pragmatic measures to cope better with partners' fears or sensitivities cannot be overemphasized. With these in place, the fears often decrease and further progress can be made. Even if not, the change can reduce a couple's level of stress, perhaps leading to less frustration, anger, and tension, and a salutary effect on their functioning. One partner's careful attention to the other's sensitivities often involves the sensitive partner clueing the other in as to when care is needed, or the other, having learned where such sensitivities usually arise, simply adding a few key words to an interaction. For example, many partners are sensitive to feeling abandoned or unsupported if their mates do not want to talk about an issue for as long as they do. The mates can mitigate many of these feelings by saying something soothing like, "I love you but I can only listen for a few minutes more, because I'm getting restless." Having been warned that a withdrawal is about to occur, the talker can take a few minutes to end the conversation on his or her own terms, therefore feeling much less helpless.

As some other possible responses to insights gained, partners may experience immediate change, access to feelings or fears that can lead to further insight and change, or both. Couples often report small positive changes after gaining insights, though possibly not recognizing the connection. In the latter instance they tend to say things like, "We don't know why, but we just seem to be less angry at each other." One reason for such changes may be that expressing previously hidden feelings often relieves them somewhat. Fears exposed to the light of day also tend to lose some of their power. Or partners' increased awareness that their present-day fears are based on childhood learning or misperceptions of their mates because of parental transference may make the fears less compelling. The partner who has expressed them and understood their roots may realize that he or she is not as helpless as in childhood and that the mate is not as powerful as the parent or other caretaking figure was. This process can be assisted by conscious self-talk, such as the clinician encouraged for Eric. If the mate can incorporate changes in his or her behavior that make it less evocative of the parental figure, perhaps after having learned to be careful of the other's sore spots, the fears may be still further reduced.

If needed, clinicians may help by highlighting real differences between an earlier caretaking figure and the mate. In a case known to me, a young man whose mother had suffered from a bipolar disorder was married to a woman who was somewhat emotional, but well within normal limits. As an only child, the man had had to call the police when his mother was suicidal or became manic and ran down the street naked. His father had left long before. The young couple presented for treatment at a time when the wife had lost her job and the husband was responding to her anxiety and upset by put-downs that were making her feel much worse. Not more than a few sessions into the case, the clinician told the man that his wife's strong feelings in response to her job loss were normal, but it was understandable that they scared him. He must wonder if she was going to go crazy like his mother did. The clinician added that the wife did not show any signs of such instability. The man did not say much in response to this interpretation—naturally he had learned to be in tight control of his emotions—but his negative behavior toward his wife changed appreciably. His wife also seemed to become more empathic about his touchiness and moderated her emotional expression somewhat. A more positive cycle began, with her needing less support and him giving more. They were able to terminate treatment soon after.

While the quick resolution in this case was unusual, gradual change based on a series of small or large insights is not. Importantly, the more partners expose their needs and feelings and *find their fears not to be realized in the mate's or the clinician's response*, the more likely the fears will significantly dissipate (Johnson and Greenberg 1995, Siegel 1995). A partner may then have less reason to defend against further self-awareness (Astor and Sherman 1997). Clinicians' and mates' acceptance of what is revealed can also lead to further self-acceptance, less energy tied up in unnecessary defense mechanisms, and more capacity for closeness and growth. It is also not at all unusual for one partner's insights to stimulate those of the other. In a later session, Sue recognized that just as Eric was afraid of her anger, she was too because she often felt like she was close to going out of control as her father had. She was especially concerned about the influence her yelling might have on their children, who sometimes seemed as fearful of her as she had been of her father. She finally realized she had married Eric partly because it seemed he would help her keep her anger in bounds. When partners become aware of their similar or complementary issues, whether spontaneously or after a clinician points them out, they are often even more motivated to try to resolve the issues together (Siegel 1992).

However, another response to insight likely to occur with every couple at times is resistance (Scharff and Scharff 1991). After all, insight by definition can uncover painful or frightening feelings, unacceptable needs, or unwanted memories in either the partner experiencing the insight or the mate. It threatens to disrupt defense mechanisms such as projective identification that have protected both partners from painful self-awareness. The partner who exposes needs, feelings, or fears is more vulnerable to being hurt either by the clinician or the mate (Astor and Sherman 1997). Further, changes one partner is making or trying to make are likely to stir up fears in the other exactly because their underlying issues are almost always similar (Kissen 1996). Before addressing deeper insight work and the attention to such resistances it requires, let us examine important issues likely to arise in clinician–partner relationships whenever partners are being asked to expose painful or difficult underlying needs, feelings, or fears.

Clinician–Partner Relationships in Insight Work

While a constructive relationship between clinicians and partners is important in every type of treatment, it becomes more crucial the more insight work is undertaken. Partners being asked to take the risk of revealing their vulnerabilities must be able to rely on a secure clinician–partner bond (Johnson and Greenberg 1995). In general, the acceptance and empathy a clinician conveys in sessions may counteract partners' possible transference-based fears, such as that they will be controlled or made to feel helpless, criticized, or otherwise hurt. When clinicians also prevent each mate from having such responses to the other, as just described, both may feel still less frightened and more secure (Scharff and Scharff 1991). Clinicians' abilities to maintain safety in the treatment sessions while showing genuine empathy with both partners' pain and fears creates an emotional ambiance that object relations theorists call a holding environment (Siegel 1992). While transference fears may emerge to cast doubt on either or both partners' safety, their reality experiences in sessions must continue to demonstrate that these fears are unfounded.

Partners are less likely to experience transference distortions toward a clinician than toward each other (Siegel 1992). However, there are times when clinicians' keeping of a safe treatment environment and benign provisions of empathy fail to dispel, or may even stimulate, partners' transference wishes toward or fears about them (Scharff and Scharff 1991). These reactions are more likely in insight work than in most work on communication and problem solving because partners' self-exposure may evoke nurturance needs insufficiently met in childhood, or fears that clinicians will take advantage of their vulnerability in whatever ways significant caretaking figures did. Transference wishes toward clinicians may manifest as a partner wanting special attention or even showing sexual interest. Transference fears may show in resistance to proceeding or in more direct negative reactions, such as a partner accusing a clinician of not caring about the partner's well-being. Clinicians can anticipate what some of partners' transference reactions might be by being aware of how the partners' parents or other caretakers, especially those of the clinician's gender, acted toward them.

As discussed earlier, couples in any type of treatment should be told that they may have negative reactions to a clinician or to interventions used and that, if so, they should bring them up. In treatment focused more on communication or problem solving or when partners are not very psychologically minded, a clinician may simply try to forestall distortions by acting less like the original caretaking figure than he or she might have otherwise. For example, to avoid evoking transference in a partner whose parent of the clinician's gender was seductive, the clinician might bend over backwards not to say or do anything that could be construed as seductive. Or a clinician might try to be even more tactful than usual in talking to a partner with a critical parent. If such a partner nevertheless felt blamed, the clinician might just try to correct the distortion by responding, "I'm sorry. I didn't mean that as a criticism. I think anyone might have acted as you did under the circumstances."

When transference to a clinician may interfere with the work of treatment if it is not addressed more directly, the clinician may need to explore the reaction or even suggest what it might be, as long as the interpretation is worded so as not to cause embarrassment. An explanation can be given that a partner having feelings toward or fears about a clinician is not unusual. Transference fears are usually easier to handle than transference wishes. Clinicians may explore a specific fear, perhaps suggest that it is understandable based on the partner's childhood experiences, and offer reassurance. For example, a clinician might say, "I can understand, Richard, why you might wonder at times if I'm thinking you're not working fast enough here since your father was always giving you messages that you didn't measure up. I want you to know that's not what I'm thinking at all—I know you're working hard and that people can't snap their fingers and quickly make the kind of changes you're working on."

Partners may be more threatened or embarrassed to have their transference wishes spoken aloud, but tact often makes such interpretations possible. For example, a clinician might say, "I think that because you see me as caring about you, you're beginning to want more closeness and caring from me. That's understandable since you've said you didn't always get what you needed as a child. I think these are normal needs, but [your partner] is the one who can fill more of them." If clinicians' efforts with both partners present do not dispel transference fears, some individual sessions can be suggested. It may be necessary for a partner to see a different clinician to deal with strong or persistent transference wishes. Such difficulties seldom arise with couples who are not narcissistically vulnerable.

All of the clinician's responses discussed so far are intended to dispel partners' transference feelings or fears in order to maintain a constructive therapeutic alliance. However, probing of transference distortions toward a clinician can also be undertaken to try to produce more insight into a partner's intrapsychic functioning or childhood issues. Usually some amount of education and reassurance is needed before taking this step. A clinician might say something like, "Barbara, I'd like for us to look more at the reaction you're having toward me, if you don't mind. I think it might help us understand some of the issues in your relationship with Dale. If Dale has a strong reaction to me at some point, of course we'll try to understand that too." With the partner's permission, some deeper analysis or interpretation of his or her reaction toward the clinician may proceed, as will be illustrated in a later case example.

Crucial in insight treatment, even more than in other types, is that clinicians be aware of their countertransference reactions so as not to act them out destructively (Solomon 1997). They must make the partners' emotional safety and growth rather than their own comfort of uppermost importance by remaining open to genuine empathy with the partners' pain and fears (Mojas 1995). Yet insight work is especially likely to stir up clinicians' own needs and anxieties. Countertransference can spring from many sources within their own current lives and backgrounds as well as be a response to couples' behaviors and dynamics (Siegel 1997, Solomon 1997). Clinicians may find themselves liking one partner more than the other or even fantasizing or dreaming about partners (Siegel 1995). They may become fearful or angry at things partners do. They may cope dysfunctionally with their own anxiety aroused in sessions, such as by talking too much (Scharff 1995), offering premature reassurance, asking distracting questions, avoiding affect, or even escalating couples' anxiety to avoid dealing with their own (Hill 1996). While some of clinicians' thoughts and feelings in response to couples may be realistic in the sense that anyone would be likely to react in the same way, partners may also unconsciously pick up on and evoke countertransference in particular areas of vulnerability (Siegel 1997). Clinicians must therefore always try to be in touch with personal components of their reactions and their possible source. If their own efforts to be self-aware do not sufficiently uncover countertransference that may impede their couple work, further consultation or even personal therapy may be sought.

On the positive side, clinicians' countertransference may be a unique pathway to deeper understanding of a couple: "It is almost certain the dynamics defined through the . . . countertransference already exist in the couple's relationship" (Siegel 1995, p. 63). A clinician known to me dreamed about her brother and realized the dream content was similar to content being discussed in a particular couple's treatment. She then saw for the first time that in spite of his charm, the husband in the couple was quite passive with his wife, as her brother had been. Clinicians may use insights gained though an awareness of their own countertransference in the same way as they would any other, to guide them in exploring or interpreting partners' underlying issues. Or they may choose to share the personal reaction that evoked the insight (Siegel 1995). In the latter instance, clinical judgment can dictate whether a couple may respond better to sharing a reaction directly or more indirectly, perhaps through use of a metaphor. For example, rather than saying, "I realize I was just now feeling afraid of your anger and steered away from it," a clinician might share that, "Your anger a minute ago reminded me of a big dog that barked at me once when I was a kid. I was scared but I think now the dog was barking because he wanted to keep me out of his space."

DEEPER INSIGHT WORK

When partners may benefit from access to still less conscious feelings or fears blocking their progress, perhaps toward a goal of increased intimacy, deeper insight work may be in order. Before proposing that it be undertaken, clinicians should ascertain that both partners are willing to proceed and have sufficient capacity for such self-awareness (Siegel 1992). Also necessary is the continued maintenance of constructive clinician–partner relationships and a treatment ambiance in which both partners feel safe. A couple may need some educational help to understand how to participate in more intensive work. And finally, the clinician must have sufficient expertise to help them develop deeper insights and the emotional capacity to stay with what can sometimes be an anxiety-provoking process (Scharff 1995).

Strategies to Move Deeper

Before undertaking deeper insight work, clinicians often need to explain to couples why it may be helpful to use treatment sessions differently than before. For example, they may suggest that discovering why a couple is having trouble achieving greater intimacy or other desired goals is more likely if the partners can try not to look directly for answers but simply talk about themselves and their inner experiences in a more open-ended way. They can explain or reaffirm the importance of maintaining an atmosphere in which both partners can safely talk about whatever is on their minds. Clinicians also usually need to help partners find ways to access new self-awareness. These may be chosen based on what a clinician has found useful with other couples as well as what turns out to work with a particular one.

In virtually every case, a clinician needs to gather more complete information about each partner's family of origin. Some do so by taking a lengthy history at an opportune time, perhaps using a genogram (Weeks 1995a). Others ask about specific aspects of partners' histories at a time when these seem affectively relevant to something being discussed (Scharff 1995). Some clinicians suggest that couples working on deeper insights bring in their dreams, as in a case example below. Some ask partners to sculpt a tableau of their current and desired relationship dynamics, write letters to each other, or speak to an empty chair in session to reveal painful feelings more readily (Astor and Sherman 1997). Another possibility is to suggest to partners that they notice both in session and at home when they are having unusually strong reactions to something or behaving in ways they do not understand. They are to try especially hard at such times to tap into private thoughts and feelings that may have been stirred up.

> Paul and Sharon came into treatment asking to work on intimacy. They were a likable couple in their early thirties who always treated each other respectfully in sessions and at home. They had no no-

ticeable communication problems and seemed to have worked out amicably the mechanics of their mutual life, with each giving in when needed. Their friends considered them the ideal couple and could not imagine why they needed counseling. However, their sex life had gradually declined and they did not feel very close, although they self-disclosed fairly freely and did a lot together. They were so far childless, both having busy and gratifying careers. Neither had been in treatment before.

After establishing rapport and gathering the above information, the clinician suggested the two perhaps needed to look deeper to see what might be impeding intimacy. Over the course of several sessions, she encouraged a leisurely sharing of each partner's family history and of the couple's relationship over time. Sharon reported that she was a middle child of two very busy parents. Her older sister was "the student," Sharon was the "little mother," and her brother turned out to be the rebel. Still, Sharon did well in school and ended up working in the insurance industry. Paul had a mentally retarded sister who was cared for at home, although she was older so he wasn't involved much in her care. He had always been independent, did well in school and at sports, and felt good about his work accomplishments. Both partners knew their parents loved them and gave them all the time they could. Both felt they had grown up to be pretty confident and secure. The couple had met when they worked together at a former job and had first developed a friendship, then began dating. They found each other compatible in virtually every way. They had been together for five years, married for three. When the clinician asked about their plans regarding children, they said, "Definitely later."

The clinician's probing about both partners' parents' marriages revealed that they seemed to be close. Neither Sharon nor Paul could remember much about their childhood responses to their parents' busyness. They could recall superficial feelings that it would have been nice to have more time with them, but it wasn't possible. The clinician's tentative interpretation that it seemed like they had learned early to take care of themselves and not ask too much from others led to some acknowledgment that they probably had, but this intellectual insight did not go much of anywhere.

While most couples do not come in with such a singular problem with intimacy as Sharon and Paul, it is not at all unusual for those who try to work on intimacy to experience resistance to achieving it. There is most often no conscious intent to avoid changing, but an inability to do so based on largely unknown or unconscious fears (Weeks 1995a). As always, it is important to try to unearth such fears, whether they be of the mate's responses or of what partners may learn about themselves. The clinician can start by telling the couple that most people have some fears of intimacy (Weeks 1995a). Mojas (1995) offers reassurance about these fears by explaining "the tendency for couples to be drawn together to heal and to work out . . . themes from childhood" (p. 84). She then uses an interesting exercise to help partners gain access to the fears and try to modify them. She asks each to draw a circle representing his or her current capacity for intimacy, a larger one in which each is to list his or her conscious fears of intimacy, and a still larger one encompassing the defenses each probably uses against such fears. For example, some of the latter might include picking a fight just after a time of intimacy, being critical, withdrawing, or workaholism. The next step is for each partner to begin to "replace the old defenses with a new way to cope with the old fears" (p. 87), initially by slowing down habitual reactions long enough to become more aware of what fears are being evoked.

Sometimes techniques such as these, or clinicians' encouraging careful exploration of occasions when fears arise, reveal partners' fears and perhaps offer an opportunity to resolve them. However, neither the partners nor the clinician may suspect what the fears really are. In this instance other strategies to uncover underlying feelings or fears can be helpful.

> The clinician suggested that Paul and Sharon keep track of their especially strong or "odd" reactions to anything during or between sessions and that they try to remember and bring in dreams. She explained that any of these might give clues as to what was preventing the intimacy they both so strongly desired. In the meantime, the clinician began taking a genogram of their extended family histories.
>
> Paul brought in a dream two sessions later. In it, a woman he knew from work was drowning and he felt he had to rescue her. To his horror, when he reached her he was overcome by the waves himself and felt them both submerging. He woke up in a cold

sweat. Both partners immediately asked the clinician what the dream might mean. She suggested that dreams do not usually reveal their significant meanings by directly looking for them. Instead, she suggested Paul talk more about what the dream brought to mind. Was anyone else present in it? What did the scene look like? What was his emotional tone before and after he noticed the co-worker drowning? Who was this co-worker—what was she like? Paul could not remember much more about the dream. He had a vague sensation there might have been someone like a lifeguard in the background, but he didn't think about the possibility of being rescued when he felt he was drowning at the end. The woman from work was a very strong woman, someone he respected and would certainly want to save. Thinking about it now, he couldn't imagine that she couldn't swim. He then suddenly remembered that in the dream he had felt somehow responsible for her plight.

When partners bring up material that may reveal unconscious content, whether from dreams or other sources, clinicians must make careful decisions about what to do with it. Unless the partner has already made the connection to a deeper feeling or fear, the clinician must decide how to open the door to such a connection without causing the partner to retreat and close over. Exploration is usually the best first step (Blanck and Blanck 1994). Empathic interpretation of what are likely to be the most accessible feelings or fears is also possible, especially if exploration does not work.

The clinician asked if there had ever been a time in Paul's life when he felt overwhelmed and scared as he had in the dream. At first Paul said he was a good swimmer, never near drowning, and had not witnessed anyone else who was. The clinician clarified, "I was thinking of when you might have felt emotionally overwhelmed." Suddenly the clinician became aware that Sharon was crying and gently asked what she was experiencing. Sharon said she was thinking of the miscarriage the two had suffered in the first year of their marriage. She had felt so overwhelmed and helpless at that time. The clinician, who had not heard of the miscarriage before, suggested that Paul's dream might or might not relate to this time but she could imagine they both had painful memories and feelings. Could they tell about them?

Staying with Deeper Insight Work

While the ultimate goal of insight is the achievement of whatever positive change a couple is seeking, the pathway to that goal is usually through the surfacing of feelings and fears that have not been processed constructively when the events that caused them first occurred. These may include childhood experiences partners did not have the maturity or support to deal with at the time, or difficult adult experiences one or both may have faced. When such feelings or fears do surface in treatment, discussing them in a supportive atmosphere usually goes a long way toward healing them. However, one or both partners may resist such discussion because the content is too painful or frightening. If one partner talking about difficult, emotion-laden topics stirs up uncomfortable feelings in the other, clinicians can offer a constructive way of coping by suggesting the partner can interrupt to say he or she is getting anxious and would like to slow things down. If partners still react destructively out of their own anxiety or other difficult feelings, the clinician can limit the negative behavior but empathize with and try to explore the feelings that have been aroused.

> Paul became noticeably anxious at Sharon's revelation and asked if it was really necessary to discuss something that happened two years ago. The clinician said she thought it might be, not only because Sharon seemed to be hurting but because burying painful feelings often meant they didn't go away. It might even be that not fully processing their loss at the time was contributing to their difficulties feeling close to each other now. The clinician reassured the couple that they could go slowly with this painful content if they needed to and that she would be there to help. Paul still seemed reluctant so the clinician asked if talking about what happened was a little frightening for Paul or for both of them. Paul said he was only worried about Sharon enduring further suffering. She had suffered so at the time.

As noted earlier, two factors that may facilitate deeper insight work are an educational one, as when the clinician explains to Sharon and Paul why discussing feelings connected with the miscarriage may be helpful, and a relationship one, as when the clinician is not only empathic but also conveys that she will be emotionally with the couple during the process. Also frequently needed is direct assistance to move past resistances that nonetheless occur. The means usually used to do so are to stop pursuing the content originally being discussed and explore or interpret one or both partners' fears of proceeding, as the clinician does when Paul still seems reluctant to talk. Partners will be able to get through resistance only if they do not feel pressured or judged. Instead, clinicians must seek to encourage the same feelings of safety accompanied by curiosity about themselves needed in all insight work. If these cannot be achieved at a given time, it is better to back off and suggest not moving forward until partners' concerns can be better understood, perhaps at a later time. The latter intervention is a form of paradox in that it tells partners that they need not change just then. The result may be that they become free to do so.

When a clinician probes a partner's fears of proceeding, the response is often a symbolic or disguised expression of what the fears really are (Scharff and Scharff 1991). Paul revealed what were probably his fears of his own painful feelings by expressing concern about his wife's. Clinicians have the choice of addressing what is expressed on the reality level or exploring beneath the surface. Often starting at the first level, then moving to the second, is best.

> The clinician turned to Sharon and asked how she felt about continuing the discussion. Sharon said it might help to talk more about what had happened. The clinician wondered if doing so might be harder for Paul. She added that a miscarriage is often almost as difficult for the husband, yet he has to be strong and help his wife with her feelings. He often doesn't have time for his own. Paul looked stricken and hesitant to continue. The clinician said gently, "In the dream, *you* were in danger of drowning too." At this point Paul put his head in his hands and began sobbing. Sharon immediately put her arms around him and held him. They remained this way for several minutes while the clinician murmured, "I know, it's okay," and, "You must have both felt so much." When Paul's crying subsided, the session time was almost over. Noting this, the clinician said that unfortunately, they could not continue just now. It had taken courage to let themselves experience some of the pent-up emotions, and she thought they would feel some relief when they had time to process them more. But were they okay now? Would they prefer not to wait a full week for another

session? Sharon said she was okay but that she definitely wanted to talk more. Paul added that he guessed they needed to.

Worth noting is that the clinician finally helped Paul reach through to his feelings with an empathic reminder of his affect from the dream. The connection with the dream content was an emotional, not an intellectual, one. She also chose to forgo a number of interpretations of the dream content that could have been valid, but that would not help Paul get to the most relevant emotional meaning at the time. For example, the distant lifeguard figure in the dream may have been the clinician, in Paul's unconscious mind a possible future resource but not yet one to be fully relied upon. There were also a number of possible connections to deeper intrapsychic or family-of-origin issues, such as Paul's possible fears that his feelings could overwhelm and "drown" people and that he must be on his own in dealing with them. The clinician would presumably keep all these clues in mind. If the themes were significant, they would emerge again (Scharff and Scharff 1991). The clinician might also refer back to the dream content at another time. The symbolic content to be pursued first, whether from dreams or some other source, is that which seems most accessible and emotionally meaningful at the time to the partner expressing it (Blanck and Blanck 1994).

In the case of Sharon and Paul, a number of sessions discussing the miscarriage brought the couple somewhat closer, but their intimacy problem was still far from solved. Interestingly, what did begin to change was that Sharon began to be more irritable toward Paul. Both were rather dismayed by this development and the clinician began to realize how very civilized the two had always been with each other. The occasions on which Sharon was testy with Paul seemed not to have much connection to realistic concerns or anger with him, however, as Sharon was the first to admit. Let us pick up the case again at this point, a little over three months into the treatment.

The clinician suggested looking more closely at some of the times Sharon "got picky" (their words) with Paul but didn't know why she was doing it. It turned out the most recent occasion happened when she had wanted him to help her move the sofa and he had asked if it could wait till he finished what he was doing. After Sharon had become impatient and snappy, Paul dropped his activity but felt annoyed himself. Sharon had apologized later and did again in the session, saying her impatience was clearly unjustified. The clinician said something deeper within Sharon that they didn't understand might have been going on. She suggested trying to stick with what the annoyance was about. Maybe the situation had reminded Sharon of something from an earlier time. Sharon couldn't think what, and the clinician asked her to try not to self-censor. Sharon retorted with an uncharacteristic, "That's fine for you to say, but I just can't do it."

The clinician responded with, "Okay. But what were you thinking or feeling just now when you felt pressured by me?" Sharon began to apologize for getting snappy with the clinician and said she didn't know what was wrong with her lately. The clinician replied, "I'm fine, don't worry about it. You were right to tell me to back off if I was pushing too hard. But maybe your psyche is also trying to tell us something. Let's keep looking at what you were feeling." Sharon said she *was* sort of tired of always having to "produce." It's "go, go, go" on her job and for a minute, it felt like that here. The clinician asked, "And in your family growing up?" Sharon said she did feel like she had to be perfect as a kid, not because anyone pushed her but maybe because that was her way of getting some attention from her parents. And it was hard at times. The clinician asked if she ever got mad at her parents, even deep inside. Sharon said, "Well, sometimes momentarily. Usually when they wouldn't help me when I was really trying and couldn't do something myself." The clinician softly asked, "Like you were trying to get in touch with your feelings and I wasn't helping much?" Sharon looked chagrined and said, "Maybe so." The clinician went on: "Or like you were trying to move the sofa and Paul wouldn't help you?" Sharon immediately cut in, "But that's not fair to Paul at all." The clinician explained that people do have feelings left over from childhood that get expressed with their mates, but understanding them and talking more about the childhood experiences often helps. She bet Paul had some issues left over from that time too.

Again the clinician made a choice as to which material to pursue and went for what was probably most salient: first some of Sharon's transference to her, then to Paul. Not being able to pursue both fully and probably believing the transference to Paul was more important to grasp at that point, she did not extensively explore Sharon's reaction to her. Also worth noting is that one likely reason Sharon could begin to experience her anger openly enough to get in touch with some of its sources was the earlier experience with the clinician discussing the miscarriage. Both members of the couple learned from it that the clinician, unlike their parents, could give them more of the attention they needed. The clinician was also nonjudgmental and reassuring when Sharon expressed annoyance toward her. As discussed earlier, transference feelings and fears ultimately can be exposed because partners experience both the clinician and each other as being different, or different enough, from the earlier transference sources.

Over almost a year of treatment, Sharon and Paul gained a number of insights that allowed growth and change. They became aware that both had been frightened of being overwhelmed by "bad" feelings, such as neediness and anger, that they had learned to repress in childhood. In their relationship, Paul was most afraid that his neediness might overwhelm Sharon and "drown" her. These fears were rooted in his childhood worries that his mother might "drown" and therefore not be available to him at all if he asked to have his needs met when she was already so overburdened by those of his retarded sister. Sharon was afraid that if she asked for too much or expressed anger she would be rejected, a fear based on transference from both her parents. Rightly or wrongly, she had felt their love to be conditional and had learned well to keep her part of the bargain. The couple found in each other the continued confirmation that being "good," independent, and not asking for too much would ensure a secure relationship. They had unknowingly colluded in keeping more dangerous needs and feelings from consciousness, to the detriment of achieving closeness.

Many partners experience one or more of several common transference-based fears of expressing needs and feelings to their mates (Mojas 1995, Weeks 1995a). They may fear that expressing neediness or dependency will make them vulnerable to being controlled, abandoned, rejected, criticized, or otherwise hurt or that they will overwhelm the mate. Fears of expressing anger commonly have to do with being rejected, losing control, or damaging the other. Intimacy fears may encompass any of these, as well as fears of being overwhelmed or trapped themselves (Mojas 1995). Men's and women's fears tend to be somewhat different, as will be described in the following chapter. In couples who are not narcissistically vulnerable, partners' fears usually turn out to be unfounded in the sense that they are based primarily on childhood experiences and are not likely to be realized if the risk is taken to be more open in the couple relationship.

However, each mate may indeed have some proclivities toward acting in just those ways that the other fears. Not only must clinicians try to assist partners in not doing so, as discussed earlier, but they must help both become aware of their "unconscious [childhood] struggle which is re-enacted, and how each is induced into playing out the necessary reciprocal role" (Siegel 1991, p. 75). Otherwise one partner's fears of change may prevent change in the other, stymieing both. I recall a couple in which the wife, who feared being inadequate and needy as her mother had been, projected these aspects of herself onto her husband. She would frequently and angrily point out his inadequacies, and she remained much too busy to meet what she saw as his excessive dependency needs. When the wife began to change in treatment, the husband became more anxious. He had been projecting onto her much of the anger that he thought had caused his parents to reject him, and her new reluctance to carry this affect for him frightened him. His anxiety turned out to have arisen also because he had experienced her constant criticism as more consistent attention than he had received as a child, and therefore as a reassurance that she remained invested in him. If treatment had not addressed this couple's interlocking dynamics, neither would have been able to change.

One final point needs to be made here. Sometimes partners in couple treatment cannot surface or sufficiently deal with influences from the past that are impeding their relationship functioning. Individual treatment of some duration may then be indicated. It may be with the same clinician if the individual work will apparently not induce significant transference to the clinician, if partners are not likely to become competitive or jealous, and, usually, if both partners will be seen individually while the couple work continues. An example of such a case is given in Chapter 10. The safer course in any other instance or when there is doubt is to refer elsewhere partners needing insight-oriented individual help.

CHAPTER

7

Diversity Considerations in Ongoing Treatment

Couple partners cannot ever be totally like each other in the influences that gender, sexual orientation, race, ethnicity, social class, and religion have on their lives and functioning. Nor can a clinician be totally like either partner. In this sense all couple practice, including all work on communication, problem solving, or insight, requires clinicians' understanding of and constructive responses to diversity. Clinicians using this book's integrative approach to couple treatment must be aware of how their own gender, sexual orientations, and sociocultural backgrounds are influencing them. Only then can they assess these influences on couples and try to tailor their treatment strategies to be as helpful as possible.

This chapter considers gender and a number of sociocultural factors as they may affect clinician–partner relationships, work on communication and problem solving, and insight treatment. A final section examines clinician–partner relationships and other important issues in work with same-sex couples. The significant impact of poverty on couples and their treatment has been discussed in Chapters 4 and 5.

GENDER AND SOCIOCULTURAL INFLUENCES ON CLINICIAN–PARTNER RELATIONSHIPS

The influence of clinicians' and partners' genders and sociocultural characteristics must be taken into account in understanding and treating every couple (Okun 1996, Rampage 1995). The case of Mary and Tony suggests why.

> Mary and Tony, aged 38 and 42, sought treatment after a marriage of sixteen years. The two had met at the bank where both had worked and where Mary had stayed except for a several-year hiatus when their two boys were young. The precipitant for seeking help was Tony's being told his current job at another bank would be "downsized" in about six months. According to Mary, he had become argumentative and overbearing in response, although there had been no physical or emotional abuse. The two had experienced similar problems during a period of Tony's unemployment two years before. At that time, he had also been reclusive and wanted no visitors because someone might find out he wasn't working. The boys had become rebellious under this regime and now, aged 15 and 13, they were increasingly defiant toward their father. Tony had a good job history except when working for female bosses, with whom he always seemed to get into arguments. Mary also felt Tony put his elderly mother before her and the kids. Tony and Mary were both Italian American, second and third generation, respectively.

A clinician who was not familiar with Italian American culture and not aware of his or her own cultural biases could form the conclusion that Tony had serious personality problems, perhaps even paranoia in his earlier fears that others would find out he was not working. Yet his gender and ethnicity might explain a good deal of his behavior. Giordano and McGoldrick (1996b) advise that the Italian American father must "provide for and protect the family" (p. 572). Most of all, he should never disgrace it. No wonder then that Tony's job problems and threatened unemployment are so shameful for him. Further, these authors note, "Traditionally, the father has been the undisputed head of the household, often authoritarian . . . in his rule-setting" (p. 572), which may be hard for adolescents exposed to dominant American values. Also, "There is virtually no such thing as a separate nuclear family in Italian culture" (p. 571). The Italian mother plays a very powerful role even in her adult son's affections, with daily contact not at all unusual. Mary's being one generation more removed from the original culture may make a significant difference in her loyalty to its values, although she may still uphold many of them. The point is not to take sides between Tony and Mary about these areas of conflict, but to see the extent to which they may be culturally influenced.

We will return later to this case to discuss treatment. Let us first consider some important influences of a clinician's own gender and sociocultural characteristics in couple treatment, partners' possible concerns about these, and constructive ways clinicians can respond.

The Influence of Clinician Characteristics

To understand their own inevitable biases with couples, clinicians may first look at their own worldviews—as influenced by gender, race, ethnicity, social class, and religion—on issues likely to arise in couple practice. It is perhaps most important to examine one's own concepts of appropriate behavior for men and women in relationships. A clinician may not hold the same values about male–female roles, such as Tony's probable belief that it is his primary responsibility to support the family, as partners of a different culture or social class do. Another issue for many couples is the partners' appropriate relationship to their extended families and communities. For clinicians and partners highly acculturated to dominant American values, the boundary around a couple may typically open to include the extended family only at limited times. But in many ethnic groups, including Tony and Mary's, the extended family and community may be much more involved in a couple's daily lives. These ties are not pathological and can be significant resources for partners in meeting affiliative needs and dealing with stress (Hurtado 1995, Turner 1991). Social class can also have an impact, with close extended family ties more often valued by clinicians and partners whose backgrounds are lower class or working class (Langston 1998).

In fact, whenever couples do problem solving, clinicians may hold gender-based or socioculturally based biases as to what good solutions may be. A few common examples among many possibilities include how money should be handled, how children should be reared, the appropriate balance between work and play, what constitutes appropriate couple sexual activities, and how important it is to practice one's religion. Even the particular communication and problem-solving modes with which clinicians are most comfortable as well as their beliefs about intimacy can be strongly influenced by gender, ethnicity, and social class. A clinician of British American background may hear a partner's verbal intensity as "yelling" while a clinician who is Italian American or Greek American may not. The concept that partners should meet so many affiliative or intimacy needs with each other comes from Western European culture. It is a cultural value, not a proven requirement for good partner mental health. Again to quote Giordano and McGoldrick (1996b), in traditional Italian American families, "Marital intimacy is not a high priority" (p. 572). Nichols and Schwartz (1995) have speculated on gender influences in the fact that Virginia Satir developed a family treatment model focused on helping family members talk more about feelings in order to become more emotionally connected, while Salvador Minuchin's model focused on changing family structures to reduce enmeshment and Murray Bowen's sought to foster members' differentiation through increased intellectual control.

Clinicians can have trouble finding "ground to stand on" to become aware of gender and sociocultural influences from their childhoods and other sources of learning, especially if they do not have a strong sense of ethnic or religious identity. Still, they must catch themselves up short if they realize they are seeing couples as influenced by such factors but thinking they themselves are not (Siegel 1997). McGoldrick and colleagues (1989) found that even after several generations in America, family therapists' own ethnic backgrounds still influenced their expectations of appropriate male-female relationships. Boyd-Franklin and Franklin (1998) warn that clinicians' awareness of cultural influences on their own views about gender in relationships is important even in treating couples from their own ethnic group. Indeed, increased self-awareness about their own gender-based and socioculturally based biases must be a continuing quest for clinicians. They should always keep in mind that partners may find many different ways to meet their needs and forge fulfilling relationships, with the ultimate choices belonging to couples themselves. Perhaps the only absolute values to which clinicians should adhere are that all human beings have worth and deserve fair and humane treatment from each other. Therefore, cruelty or oppression of any person or group by any other is wrong.

Further, clinicians need to understand how stereotyping, prejudice, discrimination, and oppression based on gender or sociocultural characteristics have influenced them as well as their possible participation in perpetuating these on groups to which partners belong. Many clinicians enjoy "White privilege . . . an invisible package of unearned assets about which [we are] 'meant' to remain oblivious" (McIntosh 1998, p. 148). Clinicians aware that they are part of an oppressor group may feel guilt (Garcia Coll et al. 1993). When partners are members of groups who have oppressed people of the clinician's gender or sociocultural characteristics, the clinician may quite naturally feel anger (Jackson 1995). Clinicians must take care not to deal with their own feelings or prejudices in a variety of dysfunctional ways, including trying to ingratiate themselves with partners or needing reassurance from them (Jackson 1995), finding racist beliefs surfacing when frustrated with couples' behaviors in treatment (Wasserman 1995), or avoiding discussions of partners' feelings about privilege or oppression as a way of defending against their own feelings (Garcia Coll et al. 1993). In regard to these issues more than any other, self-awareness is crucial. Workshops, continuing education courses, consciousness-raising groups, or talking with knowledgeable colleagues may help.

As an additional factor to consider in some instances, clinicians as well as partners may have experienced culturally related losses because of immigration or genocide. They too may have been influenced by earlier generations' losses. The sequelae are especially important to understand in insight work, lest clinicians resist dealing with partners' reactions to similar losses.

Finally, a clinician may experience countertransference reactions to partners of the same gender, race, ethnicity, social class, or religion as one of the clinician's own past or present significant figures. For example, a clinician holding negative feelings toward a French American father or male partner might have more trouble relating to a French American man being seen in couple treatment. A clinician whose parents experienced stress because one rejected the other's working-class background might have more trouble not taking sides with one member of a couple dealing with a similar conflict. Even a clinician who has enjoyed knowing a kindly Greek American neighbor woman might resent a woman of the same ethnicity not being nurturing to her partner in couple treatment.

Partners' Relationships with Clinicians

As noted in earlier chapters, partners often have concerns about gender or sociocultural differences, and sometimes even about similarities, between themselves and clinicians. Any concerns about being misunderstood or judged may recur, persist, or even be intensified during the work of ongoing treatment. Such issues may also be complex. If the clinician working with Tony and Mary were female and not Italian American, Tony might be angry if she questioned his shame about his job problems, with the perception that she did not understand. On the other hand, if she were Italian American, he might be even more ashamed, believing that she too might condemn him for his difficulty in supporting his family.

Partners' concerns are likely to be deepest when they perceive a clinician to be of a gender, race, ethnicity, social class, or religion that has oppressed or been oppressed by theirs. When partners' own groups have been oppressors, they may feel guilt or fear of saying the wrong thing (Jackson 1995). Some may fear that a clinician from an oppressed group will not be motivated to help them or will want to hurt them now that he or she is in a position of greater power. Any such feelings may cause partners to be overly guarded or to have even more dysfunctional reactions in treatment. In the opposite circumstance of the clinician being part of an oppressor group, partners who have been subjected to oppression may experience intermittent fears or negative feelings even if the clinician has seemed accepting and helpful. A Latino partner may see that an Anglo clinician does not recognize the job discrimination the partner is experiencing and may suddenly feel bitter that the clinician has not had to face similar obstacles. Or partners who are being asked to expose more of their inner feelings and reveal more about their childhoods in insight-oriented work may suddenly balk at the increased vulnerability to a clinician they are not sure they can fully trust. An African American woman exploring the source of some of her intimacy fears once told me that she hesitated to talk about her father's limitations because she did not want to confirm my possible stereotypes about irresponsibility in black men. Of course, being able to voice this concern itself showed an amount of trust that boded well for resolution.

The constructive handling of partners' reactions to such relationship issues must rely on accurate assessment of what is going on. Besides asking partners to bring up any concerns about the clinician or the treatment at any point, clinicians can directly address gender or sociocultural differences. For example, a clinician working with Tony and Mary might say, "Please tell me when it seems like I'm not understanding you. Because I'm not Italian American, I really may sometimes not understand fully what you're feeling or going through." If she were a woman, she might even lessen Tony's possible reluctance by evoking the cultural value of a man being protective, as in, "You'll keep me from just spinning my wheels here if you do." A further help, as discussed in Chapter 4, can be to offer couples reassurance in advance that any concerns would be understandable and that the clinician will not be upset by a partner sharing them. Besides asking about such reactions directly, clinicians can watch for further clues. The more they are aware of when partners' reactions to differences might arise, the more likely they are to spot them. For example, knowing that Tony might wonder whether a non-Italian woman could possibly understand his feelings about his children's defiance, such a clinician could watch his facial expressions as they talked about this issue.

When one partner is of the same gender, race, ethnicity, or religion as the clinician and the other is not, an additional danger is that the partner who is different will perceive the clinician as siding with the one who is the same. Again, open discussion of this issue can help. Boyd-Franklin (1989) suggests that female clinicians always ask African American men in heterosexual relationships whether they feel the clinician is siding with the woman. Clinicians may also need to make extra efforts to maintain their connection with partners who differ from them, without neglecting to affirm connections with the other mate. A female clinician working with Tony and Mary should ask Tony's help in understanding him as a man, but add, "Mary, just because I'm a woman, I know I won't always understand you and I want to know if that happens too."

Even when clinicians ask partners to share their concerns and offer extra reassurances, many will not do so. A value of their ethnic group may be to avoid confrontation. They may fear hurting the clinician's feelings or feel awkward themselves. If they have been mistreated by the group to which the clinician belongs, they may not want to reveal anger (Greene 1994) that they fear cannot be handled without damage to the treatment relationship. Or they may fear being pathologized (Brown 1995a). Faced with denials of feelings or concerns they are fairly sure are there, clinicians must make judgments about how important it may be to surface and deal with them. The answer usually depends on which choice is most likely to facilitate the couple's progress in treatment. As discussed in Chapter 4, one option is for the clinician to say, "Please let me know if you do have such feelings or concerns later," and then elicit them at a later time when partners might be more comfortable talking about them. In the meantime, the clinician can try insofar as possible to show understanding and not act in ways dystonic to partners' likely ethnic, social class, or religious values.

In the face of denials, other possible interventions are to ask gently whether partners would admit to such concerns if they were there, probe or suggest what might be stopping them, or explain why discussing such concerns is important. For example, faced with the likelihood that Tony had had a negative reaction to something a non-Italian female clinician said, the latter might suggest, "I wonder if you're trying to be polite and protect me by saying I didn't upset you, Tony, because you had a sort of upset look on your face a minute ago." When working with an African American partner or couple, a white clinician might say, "I wonder if you're thinking our relationship will be spoiled if you talk about reactions to my race. You certainly have the right to have a lot of feelings about it, but I believe we can deal with them together." In any case, but especially when partners belong to groups that have been oppressed by those of a clinician's gender, race, or ethnicity, clinicians must leave to partners the final choice of whether to discuss such issues. The last thing needed is for clinicians to assert power and demand that partners talk about something they do not wish to (Garcia Coll et al. 1993). However, clinicians can share their expert opinions as to whether such discussions might help the work of treatment.

When partners do want to discuss differences or similarities between themselves and clinicians, clinicians should welcome what they have to say. If the concerns are that the clinician will not understand a partner or couple well enough, he or she can ask for the couple's help in doing so and can offer to undertake other remedies if they are needed, such as reading or consulting with a clinician of the couple's background. If the concern is of being judged, or pushed to change culturally supported values, clinicians can promise to respect a couple's values or to say so openly if they hold different ones. In response to partners' feelings of anger, guilt, fear, or awkwardness based on gender or sociocultural differences, a clinician can encourage fully airing these. In all instances, talking out the concerns will usually help. If the concerns or feelings remain a serious obstacle to the work together, a clinician can offer to refer the couple elsewhere. However, too quickly suggesting this option may reflect the clinician's discomfort more than a real necessity.

Another possibility at times is that a clinician's gender or perceived sociocultural characteristics may evoke partners' transference reactions. Such reactions are most likely when a parent or other significant figure from a partner's past was of the same gender or sociocultural background as a clinician. For example, a partner with one Asian American parent might expect an Asian American clinician to react as this parent did. I once encountered an interesting transference reaction of this type when a partner who had been adopted, but told the ethnicity of her biological mother, thought I was of the mother's ethnicity and developed some transference feelings and fantasies based on this idea. Such transference reactions, while triggered by perceptions of clinicians' gender or sociocultural similarities with significant past figures, can usually be handled by techniques already discussed in Chapter 6.

An important final idea about clinicians' and partners' reactions to gender or sociocultural factors in the treatment relationship is that these may happen at any time. All parties may be relating comfortably and productively over a number of sessions only to have some misunderstanding, distortion, or concern arise. Such happenings need not be dysfunctional, and in fact may provide an impetus for clinicians' or partners' growth if they can be noticed and discussed. Only when problematic reactions cannot surface and be resolved are they likely to be destructive.

GENDER AND SOCIOCULTURAL FACTORS IN WORK ON COMMUNICATION AND PROBLEM SOLVING

Gender is an important influence on the ways partners communicate, their preferred solutions to problems, their handling of needs and feelings, and their expectations of themselves and their mates. Race, ethnicity, social class, and religion can also influence all of these. When partners encounter prejudice or oppression in their daily lives, the couple may need to work in treatment on how to cope with this problem. Clinicians using this book's integrative approach must be prepared to understand these different influences on partners in work on communication and problem solving and respond constructively.

Gender Influences in Work on Communication and Problem Solving

Gender can influence the ways partners go about talking with each other and their preferred solutions to problems, including their coping with needs and feelings, largely because of gender socialization experiences. When partners in heterosexual relationships encounter these differences, their own ways of thinking, feeling, or behaving are likely to feel natural and right. Anger at the mate's inability to see things "correctly" may be the result. Partners are also likely to have stereotypical expectations of their own and their mates' characteristics and behaviors based on gender. For example, they may think, "Women are emotional" or "Men can't ask for directions." Even when such notions are true about an individual, they contribute to assumptions as to what traits go together that may be totally inaccurate. The partner who thinks "women are emotional" may also believe, "therefore they can't handle money wisely." Finally, gender oppression between mates or of one partner by an outside party requires attention in some couple cases.

In work on communication and problem solving, clinicians first need to be aware of partners' characteristics that may be influenced by their genders without themselves stereotyping individuals. According to a review by Canary and colleagues (1997), "research suggests far more similarity than differences in men's and women's communication" (p. vii), especially when the two are in an intimate relationship together rather than being strangers. The degree to which men's and women's communication differs may also vary depending on how much their own gender role beliefs are sex-stereotyped. One study found up to 75 percent of husbands' and wives' communication in dealing with conflict to be similar, with both tending to respond in kind to their mates' prior acts. When there were gender differences, wives did more complaining and criticizing whereas husbands made more excuses and were more withdrawn. More than gender, the power balance in relationships may influence communication differences. Studies of same-sex intimate relationships have found that several communication styles thought to be gender related, including the use of reasoning, emotional expression, and interruptions, were related to which partner was perceived to have more power in the relationship rather than to gender (Peplau 1993).

Still, a number of studies have shown that the structure of men's and women's conversation may be different, with women more likely to give listening responses such as "Uh-huh," look at their partners while talking, and in general try to facilitate communication (O'Donohue and Crouch 1996). Women have been found to ask more questions while men are more likely to respond by making statements or challenging what has been said (Maltz and Borker 1982). Tannen (1990) summarizes both other research and her own observations as a linguist to suggest that women usually want comforting when they talk about troubles whereas men tend to give advice or solutions. Women tend to see talk as a way of connecting and interacting while men believe it should be used primarily to exchange information and are sometimes annoyed when women tell them "useless" things. A number of authors conclude that men are usually socialized to be competitive in conversations as well as in jobs (Brooks 1991, Tannen 1990, Walsh 1989), making the process of compromise and collaboration during problem solving more difficult to accept.

In no area may men's and women's differences be more profound than in the way they deal with needs and feelings. Studies of couple relationships have found that men have more difficulty expressing fear, women "more latitude in expressing their feelings including fear" (Canary et al. 1997, p. 31). Both tend to communicate anger similarly except that women are more likely to cry when angry and men to express anger nonverbally. Women often believe they should suppress anger to keep peace in the relationship but do not end up doing so. Men seem not only to experience more negative physiological arousal in conflict situations, but to take longer to recover a sense of well-being. When women are sad, they are more likely to continue experiencing the feeling and express it nonverbally, while men who are sad are more likely to engage in activities to distract themselves (Canary et al. 1997).

Gender can also influence partners' dealing with intimacy needs.

Women may define intimacy more in terms of "*being* together and engaging in . . . personal talk" whereas men may define it as "*doing* things together . . ." (Astor and Sherman 1997, p. 14, italics in original). Prohibited by their gender socialization from expressing feelings or needs for closeness except through sexual contact, men may attempt to convey caring through such means as providing financially or doing chores around the house (Stiver 1991). Men also tend to be more indirect than women when talking about problems and may "protect" women by not telling them about unpleasant life experiences, whereas women may believe that such sharing promotes intimacy (Tannen 1990). One study of marital communication found women more likely than men to be comfortable "admitting nervousness, telling personal problems, saying sorry, and showing anger" (Weiss and Heyman 1990, pp. 484–485), apparently because men feared expressing emotions they viewed as showing vulnerability and saw talking about problems as driving relationships apart rather than drawing them closer. Yet research has consistently shown that when men withdraw in response to couple conflict, both partners' relationship satisfaction decreases (Kurdek 1995, O'Donohue and Crouch 1996).

In fact, men may need emotional connections within the couple relationship more than women do because they tend to have fewer significant outside relationships and, unlike women, usually do not share feelings with close friends (Veroff et al. 1995). Brooks (1991) suggests men often feel disadvantaged with women because they "are enormously dependent on women for validation and emotional expressiveness" yet cannot acknowledge these needs (p. 71). Although in many ways men have more power in heterosexual relationships, their hidden needs can also make them feel more vulnerable. Women may be more likely to fear being discounted or ignored in intimate relationships while men are more likely to fear being "unappreciated, demeaned, or made to feel failure, with loss of face or power" (Astor and Sherman 1997, p. 14). Stiver (1991) has found men's fears of intimacy to center on the danger of entrapment, being smothered, or humiliated, while women's usually have more to do with being left alone. Women have often been raised not to ask directly for their needs to be met or to be otherwise assertive. They may therefore continue caring for the emotional needs of their male partners without receiving very much credit for it.

One implication of male–female differences in communication and the handling of needs and feelings, to the degree they exist in particular couples, may be that partners feel frustrated and misunderstood when they try to talk to each other or work out intimacy in their relationship. To try to deal with this issue, one choice is for clinicians simply to validate each partner's strengths and cite their differences as normal individual variations. A clinician might say, "John, you seem to be good at looking for solutions," or "Peggy seems to want more acknowledgment that you hear her whereas you, John, don't see this as so important. Let's talk about how you can adjust these differences." However, especially if John protests that Peggy "shouldn't" need so much acknowledgment, the clinician might consider adding, "Women are generally used to giving and receiving more acknowledgment than men." Is such an addition likely to be helpful or harmful? Almost surely the answer depends on the particular case. If John and Peggy seem content with their own and each other's gender identities and do not tend to stereotype their own or each other's characteristics as gender-linked, the clinician mentioning the possible gender association may make each less defensive. Peggy can see her wish for acknowledgment as natural, since she is a woman. John can see it similarly but also not feel bad about himself for not having given acknowledgment before because as a man he "didn't know." Each can perhaps understand the other's needs or ways of communicating rather than seeing the partner as unreasonable, hostile, or stubborn (O'Donohue and Crouch 1996). They may then cooperate to help each other learn how to give at least some of what they need (Rampage 1995). Brooks (1991) and Neal and Slobodnik (1991) agree that clinicians' externalizing gender-linked behaviors as reflecting learned but unnecessary constraints can free partners from blame but also leave them responsible for trying to change.

On the other hand, some partners do not like the suggestion that their own communication styles may be gender-linked, perhaps feeling they are being stereotyped. Some may use the idea of gender-linked traits destructively or feel hopeless about being able to change them. In the example just given, if John will jump to the conclusion, "Women make unreasonable demands and so does Peggy," or Peggy will think, "Men aren't able to give support," the intervention of drawing attention to gender differences will have contributed to greater anger and distance. A clinician may decide how to proceed based on whether a particular couple can seem to use the idea of a gender-linked trait as a reason for nonjudgmentally working to adjust to differences, or whether it will become another weapon in a battle to determine who is more right or competent. Although the clinician can express that neither is right or wrong and that gender differences can be negotiated, sometimes the only way to tell how partners may respond is to venture a comment about a possible gender link and see.

Another implication of male–female differences in communication and problem-solving styles is that couple treatment focused on learning particular skills, such as listening before moving to solutions, may feel less comfortable for some men while a focus on skills such as being assertive may be uncomfortable for some women. When partners do show discomfort, the question again arises as to whether clinicians should try to help by exploring or acknowledging the possible gender link. Several authors (Neal and Slobodnik 1991, O'Donohue and Crouch 1996) suggest doing so. The other choice is simply to discuss the feelings empathically and perhaps attribute them to the individual's background or lack of experience with the specific skills. Again, the decision can be made based on how the clinician thinks both partners will use the information, or on trying such an intervention and seeing how it works. In either case, both partners can be asked to compromise on their preferred communication styles. For example, a woman may agree to tone down her emotionality if her male partner will hang in and listen to her longer. The man may agree to listen longer and give more feedback if he is allowed to say at some reasonable point that he is about out of listening stamina.

Clinicians may also want to challenge partners' stereotyped expectations about their own or their mates' supposedly gender-linked traits when these are viewed negatively or are a constraint to needed change. One reason for raising questions is that gender-stereotyped views about mates may lead to inaccurate perceptions, attributions, or assumptions that serve as impediments to constructive communication and problem solving. Another is that if the clinician goes along with such views, both mates are more likely to accept them as valid. The challenge need not be made in a judgmental way. A clinician might say something like, "Well, I don't know if that fits Julie. Why don't you ask her?" A later section of this chapter considers insight work in regard to partners' gender-linked expectations and perceptions of themselves and their mates.

Men and women may also differ along gender lines on some issues that are the focus of problem solving. For example, it is highly likely that women will want more cuddling and emotional closeness than men may need before they feel like becoming sexual. Other areas in which gender preferences are likely to differ are the handling of housework and money (Rampage 1995). Often it is helpful for clinicians to conceptualize such differences as common between males and females, but to vote for working out solutions equitable to both. However, sometimes this strategy does not work, as we find when we return to the case of Mary and Tony.

> The first issue Mary and Tony tried to problem solve in treatment was how to handle their kids. Mary expressed feeling very frustrated with Tony's insistence that their teenagers should be expected to obey him without question. Tony countered that this was the way he was raised and it worked very well for him. Mary wanted to use a softer, more reasoning approach and natural consequences when the boys disobeyed. The clinician tried framing her preference as more of a woman's way and Tony's as more of a man's and wondered if the two could compromise. Tony would sometimes seem on the verge of being willing to do so, but then would become irate and accuse Mary of undermining him if she asked for any change.

Some men may have problems with clinicians' value position that both partners should have approximately equal power in making decisions or solving problems together, as Tony seems to. More often the partner having the advantage and trying to maintain the existing power balance in a heterosexual pair is male. The clinician's response can differ depending on how severe the imbalance is and whether or not the reasons for it have to do with sociocultural influences, to be discussed further in the case of Tony and Mary. Sometimes simple reframing is useful when a male partner may see the accommodation necessary in problem solving as "yielding to her control" (Walsh 1989, p. 278). Instead, the clinician may label it as being the behavior of a considerate partner who is willing voluntarily to give a "gift" the mate needs or desires.

A related issue may be partners' views on men's and women's roles, a matter on which clinicians may hold strong opinions as well. An ideal touted by feminist theorists is androgyny, in which no trait or role should be seen as belonging more to one gender than the other.

The reality at this historical time, however, is that most men and women see themselves and each other through a lens of what they consider gender appropriate. One or both mates in a given couple may believe, for example, that men should earn more of the family income while women should assume greater responsibility for the housework and children even if they are working. As feminists note, both genders are constrained by such beliefs, but men usually benefit more (Rampage 1995). Clinicians may at least gently challenge partners' ideas about gender-linked roles on the basis of how limiting these ideas may be. Such a challenge is trickier if the partners themselves disagree because the clinician will most likely be perceived as taking sides. Here, the value position that partners should have equal power and try to reach agreements that are fair to both may be the touchstone. The clinician should not become fixated on the personal value of androgyny if partners can agree on differing gender roles but ones that they consider equitable. Walsh (1989) suggests that happy couplehood relies not necessarily on both partners carrying out similar roles and functions, but on both feeling that agreements between them are fair and that their contributions are equally valued.

Finally, clinicians must take a stand against one partner oppressing the other based on gender, and must try to help with gender prejudice or oppression that partners encounter in their environments. Oppression in the couple relationship occurs when one mate, usually the man in a heterosexual pair, holds significantly greater power whether or not there is other abuse. As discussed in Chapter 4, clinicians may attempt to work with such partners for a few conjoint sessions to see whether their power balance can change in response to interventions. If it does not, seeing one or both in individual sessions may give the clinician a chance to have some impact at least in making the less powerful partner aware of options. In situations where outsiders are oppressing a partner because of gender, clinicians can help this partner and the couple work out how best to respond. They may buttress the idea that the oppressed partner does not deserve what has happened and offer to help access needed resources. For example, a clinician might help a partner obtain legal advice on how to deal with sexual harassment on the job. Clinicians' help to partners facing prejudice or oppression based on their sociocultural characteristics is discussed below.

Understanding Sociocultural Influences on Partners' Communication and Problem Solving

Partners' sociocultural characteristics may also influence their communication and problem-solving modes, their preferred solutions to problems, and their handling of needs and feelings. Generally race, ethnicity, and social class bear the heaviest influence, but religion is a major force in some individuals' lives. When partners differ on any of these characteristics, their different worldviews and ways of coping may cause conflict. For some partners, repeated encounters with prejudice and discrimination from others are an important source of stress. Clinicians must try to understand these possible influences on couples before they intervene.

First, clinicians need to become familiar with the likely communication and problem-solving styles of the ethnic groups to which partners belong and these groups' possible preferences about handling needs and feelings, gender roles, extended family relationships, child-rearing practices, and the like. For example, in traditional Latino couples, both mates may prefer to avoid conflict, valuing positive emotional expression, while assertiveness may be viewed as rude (Falicov 1996). Sex roles may be clearly delineated and interdependence between the nuclear and the extended family likely (Zuniga 1988). However, Latino couples often share decision making and show role flexibility in response to environmental conditions (Powell 1995, Vega 1995). Other Latino values that may influence partners' problem-solving preferences include the importance of family and community, honor, spirituality, and respect for authority. To deal with poverty and discrimination as well as other stresses, support from extended family, community, and church can be highly important (Falicov 1995, Vega 1995).

As with many other couples, African American women often complain that African American men cannot talk about feelings, and both partners may report not having witnessed parental models who communicated constructively (Boyd-Franklin 1989). African American couples have been found to have, in general, more egalitarian relationships than white couples (Orbuch and Custer 1995). However, this power balance may be influenced by black women's frequent higher education and greater ability to earn money in a racist society (Boyd-Franklin and Franklin 1998). One study (Orbuch and Custer

1995) found that being married to a wife who defined her work as a "career" was related to lower marital well-being for black but not for white husbands. Other research (Blee and Tickamyer 1995) has found black husbands to be more liberal than whites in regard to their wives working but more traditional in other aspects of gender role expectations. Highly important to most African American partners are bonds to extended families, which may include individuals not technically related (Hines and Boyd-Franklin 1996). While such kinship networks can give considerable support, they can also be a burden in that reciprocal help must be offered. How to deal with these obligations may be a source of conflict between partners. Many African American partners regard spirituality as central to their lives. The church may provide not only spiritual sustenance, but also emotional support and recreation. Finally, many African Americans experience a strong sense of connection with their ethnic community.

Traditional Asian American partners do not usually express love or conflict openly (Lee 1996). They may place a great of emphasis on emotional restraint and on saving face. Often men expect to hold greater power and sex roles are traditional, although less so the more middle class the partners and the more generations in the United States (Ho 1990). Extended family relationships are often hierarchical and considered extremely important. Hard work is valued. In times of stress, the extended family and community can be relied on for support (Lee 1996). Many Native Americans also avoid direct confrontation in their communication (Wasserman 1995). While most place an emphasis on spirituality, communal sharing, and harmony with nature, particular partners may vary widely based on their allegiance to different tribes and their differing degrees of acculturation (Sutton and Broken Nose 1996). A Native American couple may even seek help primarily to deal with conflicts in their two tribes' worldviews.

Partners' European or Slavic backgrounds must also be taken into account in treatment. For example, in regard to gender roles, German (Winawer and Wetzel 1996), Polish (Folwarski and Marganoff 1996), and Greek (Tsemberis and Orfanos 1996) men may expect to be dominant, while men of English (McGill and Pearce 1996) and Scandinavian (Erickson and Sinkjaer Simon 1996) origins are often more egalitarian but highly invested in their work. Partners of these latter backgrounds tend to control their anger by remaining silent and distant, while Italian American (Giordano and McGoldrick 1996b) partners may express emotions more openly. Confusing to clinicians of other ethnic backgrounds can be that Irish Americans (McGoldrick 1996) are often facile and colorful talkers and German Americans (Winawer and Wetzel 1996) readily express emotional warmth, but both tend not to be comfortable with other emotional expression. Irish American partners may expect a woman to hold more power than a man. Tannen (1990) argues that what she calls "high-involvement style" communication, with frequent interruptions, rapid speech, and loudness, tends to occur more often in people of some cultural groups, such as Russian Americans. While such speech is not intended to dominate others, listeners of a different ethnicity may think it is.

As a second major consideration, social class affects couples' communication and problem solving primarily in differences between working-class and middle-class couples. Beyond the influence of ethnicity, working-class couples have been perceived as likely to demonstrate more male-dominant decision-making (Boyd-Franklin 1989, Rubin 1992). However, some studies suggest that working-class couples espouse egalitarianism and are more likely to remain married if they achieve it (Davis and Proctor 1989). Rubin (1994) found that working-class wives are often caught between wishes that their husbands be less dominant and feelings that they should not challenge their men beyond a certain point. In one study, white-collar wives dissatisfied with their marital relationships were more likely to show negative affect than were dissatisfied blue-collar wives (Canary et al. 1997). Working-class couples may find it harder to bridge male–female communication differences than middle-class couples do (Rubin 1992). In my own experience, working-class men in treatment seem to have less tolerance for discussing feelings than middle-class men, and working-class couples often feel a more pressing need to reach agreements about issues on which they have differed, such as how to discipline their children, than to learn new communication strategies.

Religion is occasionally a major influence on how partners communicate and problem solve. For example, communication in Jewish couples can be highly expressive, leading non-Jewish clinicians to think the mates' feelings are stronger or more troublesome than they actually are (Tannen 1990). More often religion significantly affects partners' beliefs about male–female roles and other aspects of their lives together. In general, closer adherence to fundamentalist Christian, Catholic, Hindu, or Moslem religions increases the likelihood that partners will endorse strong family allegiances and males holding greater power (Almeida 1996). But there are many exceptions, with ethnicity, social class, and acculturation to dominant American values and lifestyles often overriding factors. Traditional Jewish culture tends to espouse strong family ties and male dominance, but assimilated Jews in the United States usually enact more egalitarian decision-making (Rosen and Weltman 1996).

When partners differ in ethnicity or ethnic background, they must often cope with differing modes of communication or problem solving and different solutions to problems that are influenced by these without necessarily recognizing the source of their differences (Okun 1996). For example, if one partner comes from an emotionally expressive background and the other from an ethnic group that avoids open conflict, a couple is likely to have many misunderstandings during problem solving. In general, greater adjustments are required the more the values of the two groups conflict, the partners have differing degrees of acculturation, and there are religious or racial differences as well as ethnic ones (McGoldrick and Garcia-Preto 1984). Acculturation differences even for partners of the same ethnicity may be problematic, especially when either has more access to the dominant culture through work or friendship groups (McGoldrick et al. 1989). I recall the case of a Mexican-born woman, in the United States for ten years, whose more acculturated husband and children were pressuring her with many demands for change. At the same time she was feeling lonely and frightened because her entire extended family, which would have been a source of support, was back in Mexico.

Partners aware of significant differences in their ethnicity or acculturation may see these differences as bad rather than enriching to the couple (Falicov 1995). One may be angry that the other has not lived up to "positive" ethnic stereotypes, such as that a first-generation Italian American woman will be all-nurturing or a white European American man will be a good provider (Okun 1996). They may cope by leading "parallel lives, each holding on to their culture and/or family of origin" (Falicov 1995, p. 239), or may minimize or deny differences rather than accepting, valuing, and negotiating about them. They may use ethnic stereotyping to cover over other problems or deal with anger or other feelings (Okun 1996). For example, a woman whose Latino husband has cheated on her says, "All Latin men have affairs" to protect herself from recognizing that he no longer cares about her (Falicov 1995, p. 244). Familiarity with others of the mate's ethnicity or level of acculturation, extended families' reactions to the relationship, and the reactions of partners' friends can also influence couples' abilities to accept and cope with differences. In some situations, one or both extended families may be so negative on a continuing basis that partners must either face constant struggle or significantly cut off from them (Falicov 1995). The mate who cuts off from his or her own family, and perhaps from others of the ethnic community, may experience considerable guilt (Okun 1996). Ho (1990) recommends use of an "eco map" to determine the available supports for interethnic couples, who often suffer from social isolation.

Social class differences are often a touchier issue for couples than ethnic or acculturation differences. Many of the two partners' values and behavioral preferences may differ. The partner from the lower of the two classes often feels ashamed of any indications of this background (Erkel 1994). Sometimes two partners have started out in the same social class, but one now aspires to move up or has already done so. Both mates may reject extended families perceived to be of a lower class. The partner with the higher class status often dislikes any presumed evidence of the disparity because it may pull his or her standing down with others or be a reminder of a lower-status past.

Partners who come from different religious backgrounds can find this fact a varying influence on their lives. If the adherence of both to their religious upbringing is minimal and their religions have not led to significantly different communication or lifestyle preferences, the dissimilarity may cause little stress. However, parental families may have difficulty accepting the partner of a different religion, or the differences may become more problematic around the religious training of children (Sirkin 1994). The more pervasive an influence either partner's religion is, the more their differences may need to be negotiated openly to avoid conflict or hidden resentments. Research has found marriages between partners of different faiths to have a higher failure rate than intrafaith unions, but less so when the beliefs and practices of the two faiths are similar and neither has a doctrine that strongly excludes outsiders (Lehrer and Chiswick 1993).

Finally, prejudice and all its sequelae are a severe source of stress on many partners belonging to racial, ethnic, or religious minorities. One price these partners may pay is greater difficulty earning a living wage. They are also highly likely to experience forms of oppression such as other discrimination, stereotyping, personal harassment, and more limited access to most of society's resources and services, including couple treatment. In an interracial relationship, a white partner encountering discrimination without the preparation the mate is likely to have received in his or her parental family may have an especially hard time dealing with it constructively (Okun 1996). All of these are stresses with which partners must find some way to cope. Often they can do so together, as will be illustrated by a later case example.

Dealing with Sociocultural Influences in Work on Communication and Problem Solving

Clinicians should never assume they fully understand ethnic, social class, or religious influences on partners but should ask partners to tell about these, whether or not the partners' origins differ significantly from their own (Ibrahim and Schroeder 1990). Each person's heritage is unique to his or her own background and experience. Clinicians can also learn more about possible sociocultural influences from sources such as readings, workshops, or consultants, since they should not rely on partners alone to educate them (Greene 1994). Interventions can then be used with sensitivity to ethnic and other sociocultural influences. New ways of communicating or problem solving a clinician is presenting can also be given as additions to culturally influenced methods, not replacements for them (Ho 1990). Helping couples who are experiencing prejudice and oppression may require use of additional intervention strategies.

Clinicians may show sensitivity to partners' ethnicity, for example, by slowly encouraging Latino couples to communicate needs and feelings more directly so as not to violate their possible values of saving face and respect (Alexander et al. 1995). More extensive use of cultural materials might include incorporating Latino cultural metaphors or poetry into treatment (De La Cancela 1991). Because Asian American couples are likely to respect authority and value a rational approach, clinicians may first explain the usefulness of particular communication and problem-solving skills, then educate the couple but let them translate the clinician's ideas into their own more indirect style (Lee 1996). Problem-solving discussions with Italian American or Jewish couples may need to involve more emotion and stronger language than a British American clinician would ordinarily use. With partners of British, Irish, or German backgrounds, clinicians may consider offering detailed guidance about how to get in touch with a range of feelings and may empathize with the partners' likely discomfort in doing so.

Clinicians may also use reframing to take couples' cultural values into account. With Mary and Tony, our continuing case, this intervention proved useful.

> After several unsuccessful attempts to help Tony feel comfortable compromising even a little on discipline with the couple's teenaged sons, the clinician asked more about his growing-up years. It turned out Tony's father was not home a lot but maintained strict disciplinary rules. His mother sometimes helped Tony get around these, especially as a teenager. The clinician suggested that Tony was denying Mary this mother's prerogative with their sons that he had enjoyed with his own Italian mother. This intervention seemed to make Tony more thoughtful about his stance. Later, when Mary was saying again that her method of dealing with their boys might be better or more effective than Tony's, the clinician suggested Mary present her method as something that would make her more comfortable rather than as necessarily a better or more effective way. The clinician also supported Tony's wanting to be involved in his sons' lives, such as by participating in sports together. Tony finally gave in a little, perhaps partly because taking care of his wife's happiness felt like a suitably protective male role.

Even if a male partner does not have total power over a female one, clinicians may have difficulty with men's greater power within a heterosexual relationship in some ethnic groups. Each clinician must determine whether he or she can accept particular partners' values on this issue enough to proceed in a given case. If not, it is only fair to say so from the outset, or at least to do so if discussion suggests mates are not open to considering much change. A clinician might point out possible advantages of at least some changes, such as increased relationship satisfaction for the woman, increased role flexibility allowing for more coping options, or a better fit with the dominant culture. Some clinicians may choose to go along with differential male–female power with which a female partner seems comfortable but to try to influence change when she is not.

Clinicians who do not themselves necessarily use spirituality, extended family, or community as sources of guidance or support should nonetheless consider encouraging couples to use such resources that might be helpful to them. For example, with couples of ethnicities that value strong extended family ties, clinicians may ask about possible use of family help to solve some problems (Falicov 1996, Lee 1996). Ho (1990) suggests that partners cut off from their extended families by immigration may benefit from a clinician's help to link up with an ethnically matched social network in the new location. Spiritual readings or the guidance of a religious leader may be useful in some cases (Hof 1995), although it is usually best to bring up these options cautiously unless clinicians feel fairly sure of where they might lead. I once encouraged a young Jewish couple to talk with a rabbi, who cited religious law to help the woman feel less guilty for placing loyalty to her husband before ties to her overbearing mother. Given the power of a close-knit Native American community in influencing the beliefs and practices of its members, Wasserman (1995) advises sometimes providing helping services indirectly through the tribal community itself rather than through direct treatment modes.

An educational approach is often helpful when partners' different ways of communicating or differences in preferred solutions to problems are influenced by their differing ethnicities, religions, or levels of acculturation (Falicov 1995, Ho 1990). The first step is to clarify again that no one is right or wrong. The problem may be reframed as due not to partners' differences, but to their "mutual difficulty in dealing with difference" (Waller and Spiegler 1997, p. 91). Each partner may be asked to explain how his or her ethnic group, parental family, or others of the same religion do things. When levels of acculturation differ, partners may be asked to reflect upon their experiences with exposure to dominant American values and lifestyles. Clinicians need to convey that partners' differences in any area provide a richness and opportunity for learning and to frame the functioning of each in neutral or positive ways. For example, the traditional Jewish love of emoting can be seen as a useful prelude to problem solving in that it clears the mind of emotional overload. A further comment can be that an ability to express and enjoy emotions can be a major asset in a couple's quest for closeness. The clinician should take care to value the couple's complementarity as a strength (Okun 1996). Partners may need to be given specific help with cognitions that are ethnically biased in regard to the mate. The British American Protestant wife of a Jewish man can learn, "When he's complaining, my first thought is he's weak. I tell myself that no, he is just Jewish and I love the fact he's so free with his feelings." Partners' strong reactions to differences in acculturation levels, which are often related to issues of loyalty, identity, and loss, may need to be handled through careful exploration of these underlying concerns. Perhaps each mate has faced similar issues but resolved them differently.

Another way to assist couples' reconciling of differences influenced by ethnicity, religion, or acculturation is to help them problem solve how to cope with times when the differences may especially come to the fore. One of these is likely to be around holidays and significant family events, such as births or weddings. As a possible rule of thumb, the partner who has stronger feelings or whose extended family is more involved in an event may be allowed more say in how it should be handled, as long as the mate is not left out or made to feel uncomfortable. When both are equally affected, the preferences of both cultures or religions may be honored or the two melded insofar as possible. Most important is that the couple make the decisions together and in fairness to both. They may also need to work out how to deal with and present a united front to extended families in regard to whatever compromises they achieve (Waller and Spiegler 1997).

In some instances, emphasizing differences in partners' sociocultural characteristics can be contraindicated, or at least caution is warranted. For one thing, clinicians should not trace so many problems to such differences that partners are stereotyped, their individuality is negated, or they feel overwhelmed by the newly perceived chasm between them. Sometimes couples who themselves have focused a lot on their differences may become unrealistically pessimistic about the possibility of change. Or they may use these differences to put each other down or create distance. In such situations, the clinician may wish to focus more on similarities or consider using insight work to uncover the defensive purpose the couple's emphasis on differences serves (Falicov 1995), as will be discussed below. Another difficulty with enhancing couples' awareness of sociocultural differences can occur when partners have negative or ambivalent feelings about their own or their mate's heritage. Because partners may not want their differences highlighted for this or other reasons, clinicians should raise the issue carefully at first to see how both partners respond.

If a couple's differences seem hard to reconcile because of a partner's strong religious beliefs or loyalty to his or her culture, other interventions may be possible. One is use of an outside party of this partner's religion or ethnicity to help the clinician or the mate understand the issues more clearly or to give the partner permission for more flexibility. Markowitz (1994) cites the case of a religious leader from a local mosque encouraging a Middle Eastern Islamic father to give less severe corporal punishment to his children, while Ho (1990) describes a Hopi elder giving a husband permission to provide more parenting to his daughter than Hopi custom normally would allow because he was married to a Latina wife. A bicultural "clinician helper" who is a friend or extended family member with credibility to both partners may sometimes be brought in to help a couple negotiate differences stemming from their different ethnicities or acculturation levels. Both Ho (1990) and Okun (1996) recommend that clinicians at times meet with extended families to try to reduce any stresses they may be putting on interethnic or interfaith couples. Also possibly helpful may be support groups composed of similar pairs.

When either or both members of a couple encounter prejudice or discrimination in their daily lives, clinicians can help the partners acknowledge the stress these experiences cause them and can offer empathy. More important, they can also work with affected couples to devise means to combat both the problems and the stresses these cause, perhaps by use of an empowerment approach (Lee 1994). Direct interventions to provide referrals and to facilitate couples' use of resources to fight prejudice and discrimination, such as legal assistance, are appropriate. As will be discussed and illustrated with a case example below, clinicians may also need to help some couples in such circumstances deal with ramifications in the couple relationship.

INSIGHT WORK WITH GENDER AND SOCIOCULTURAL INFLUENCES

When partners encounter difficulty making progress in work on communication and problem solving or show unexplained blocks to intimacy, the reason sometimes may be related to deeper influences of gender, race, ethnicity, social class, or religion. A woman who believes women should not be assertive may have a great deal of difficulty overcoming her tendency to acquiesce to her male partner. A German American man may have trouble letting himself show vulnerable feelings. Clinicians who suspect gender or sociocultural factors as influences first need to understand what these might be. Their interventions may then promote partners' insights into these origins of their difficulties.

Understanding Deeper Gender and Sociocultural Influences

As one important possibility, partners' negative self-valuations based on gender or sociocultural characteristics can be a hidden but problematic influence on their functioning. People's gender, race, ethnicity, and often their religion are part of the very core of who they are. To the degree they feel good about these, they will usually have a foundation for feeling good about themselves. To the degree they do not, they may feel bad. Even a partner's social class background becomes integrated into feelings about the self; witness the notion of being "from the wrong side of the tracks." Some partners learn negative valuations of these core aspects of themselves from their families of origin. Many have had to deal with others' negative valuations of their gender, race, ethnicity, or religion, even if their parental families tried to help them learn that these views were wrong. People may deal with such experiences in ways ranging from acceptance of the negative valuation to successful rejection of it, but even with good coping, some negative self-feelings may remain. There can also be other costs. For example, in an effort to disprove others' negative perceptions that an African American man may have gotten a job due to racial preference, the man may feel he has to work harder and perform better than his white co-workers.

Partners will also harbor a number of self-expectations influenced by their gender and ethnic learning, and sometimes by their religion, whether they realize it or not. They may try to hold themselves to these expectations and feel guilty or bad if they violate them. Sheinberg and Penn (1991) note that partners who believe they have not lived up to society's prescriptions for their gender frequently experience "secret feelings of gender failure" (p. 33). For example, men who show overt dependency needs may feel unmanly, whereas women may believe that seeking to meet any of their own needs is selfish (Stiver 1991). Partners may also fear that they have not lived up to expectations of their ethnic group, such as an African American partner always helping out family (Hines and Boyd-Franklin 1996). McGoldrick (1996) suggests that Irish American Catholic partners may have "intense feelings about religious issues" and a "sense of sin and guilt" even if they have left the church (p. 548).

Further, partners often have expectations of each other based on gender or sociocultural characteristics and may act to try to ensure their mates' conformity. A man and his wife may both uphold traditional gender expectations by describing him as weak if he shows sad feelings. A Jewish wife says to her Jewish husband wearing an article of clothing she does not approve, "You look like a *goy* [gentile]." Kupers (1997) makes the interesting point that men may be furious if their female partners speak openly about the men's dependency on them, since dependency may be allowed but recognizing it is not. Partners may invoke expectations based on their mates' gender, ethnicity, or religion whether or not they necessarily share these, as a homeostatic mechanism to try to influence their behavior. A European American man who does not want his Asian American wife to challenge him asks, "What would your parents say?"

The case of Tony and Mary illustrates many of these points. The two were probably experiencing some strain even before Tony's impending job loss was known. Tony may have felt Mary was violating the expected behavior of an Italian American wife by holding a good job and challenging his ways of relating to his mother and children (Giordano and McGoldrick 1996b). Mary probably felt Tony was being too stubbornly adherent to Italian norms and values for male behavior, although she may not have conceptualized the problem in this way. Once Tony knew he would lose his job, he may have reacted to his self-perceived gender failure in ways that made him seem even more stubborn and unreasonable to Mary. Hence the two sought treatment.

Partners must deal with both their own feelings and with those of their mates aroused by their expectations based on gender or sociocultural characteristics. Either may feel anxiety, guilt, or shame. There may be anger at the mate's failure to meet such expectations or at his or her attempts to invoke these. Even when partners have tried to reject gender stereotypes and no longer identify strongly with their ethnic group or religion, modification of earlier learning can be difficult. Moving away from ethnic or religious values can feel like a rejection of parents, childhood friends, and a partner's whole community. It sometimes is exactly that. Tony would have to go against his mother's values to comply with Mary's wishes that he not put his mother first.

Experiences with discrimination or oppression based on gender or sociocultural characteristics almost surely must leave partners with difficult feelings. A clinician who has not personally encountered such experiences, or known well those who have, cannot possibly be aware of the likely strength of partners' feelings in response to personal affronts, limitations of job and housing opportunities, the suspicions and ill will of others, and the like. Even if partners do not internalize negative valuations by others, knowing that others carry them is a constant source of anger and pain. Negative valuation and oppression by others can cause feelings of vulnerability and powerlessness as well as anger (Boyd-Franklin 1989, Greene 1994).

As noted in Chapter 2, some partners may also be struggling with intense feelings of loss because of experiences with immigration or genocide (Mirkin 1998). Losses even in parents' or grandparents' generations can affect partners by leaving a legacy of abandonment fears and ways of coping with them. A partner's own history of immigration, besides implying the immediate loss of people and places, can eventually entail losses of the native language, of children (to acculturation), and of power at home for men who cannot find jobs as easily as their wives (McGoldrick et al. 1989). Chow (1994) suggests that denial of one's ethnicity as the price to pay for assimilation means denial or loss of part of the self. Erkel (1994) makes a similar point in regard to social class when he describes that movement from his working-class roots into the middle class left him wondering, "Who am I?" and "Where do I belong?" (p. 46). Immigrants who experience significant discrimination may find their original sense of identity replaced by an uncomfortable new one as "the stranger" or "the other" (Javed 1995). Continuing discrimination can then prevent establishing a comfortable bicultural sense of self.

What a clinician may see when partners are struggling with deeper issues related to their genders or sociocultural backgrounds are anxiety or depression (Javed 1995), psychological defenses against their feelings or experiences, or, less often, the painful feelings themselves.

As individuals, partners may show an exaggerated version of characteristics they believe to be appropriate to their gender or ethnic group in order to deal with anxiety about not being able to meet their own self-expectations (Powell 1995). They may deny the defining importance of their gender, religion, or ethnicity (Zuniga 1988) but continue to be bound by constraints stemming from their self-expectations based on these. In response to negative self-valuations, there may be such compensatory behaviors as violence or self-abnegation (Boyd-Franklin and Franklin 1998, Sheinberg and Penn 1991). Partners may deny or otherwise defend against feelings in response to culturally related losses, perhaps by a "conspiracy of silence" (Lee 1996, p. 242).

The couple relationship also offers the potential to deal with any such feelings interpersonally, making them a significant force in a couple's lives. In projection, one mate perceives the other as having needs or characteristics unacceptable in the self. Some theorists (Sheinberg and Penn 1991) believe men may project dependency needs they consider unacceptable in themselves onto their female partners, while women may project their aggressive or independent strivings onto men. Partners' negative feelings related to their own gender or ethnicity may be handled by putting the mate down for characteristics denied in the self. Preoccupation with potential abandonment by the partner can be a way of displacing feelings about earlier losses. Finally, several authors (Boyd-Franklin and Franklin 1998, De La Cancela 1991, Powell 1995) warn that when partners from ethnic minority groups encounter oppression and discrimination in their daily lives, they may deal with resultant feelings of powerlessness by trying to exert more power in their couple relationships, resulting in heightened power struggles or excessive male dominance. In the latter situation, female partners may acquiesce so as not to join society in "beating their men further down" (Hines and Boyd-Franklin 1996, p. 70).

Part of the complexity of treating couples whose reactions to deeper gender or sociocultural issues is affecting their functioning is that mates' other intrapsychic issues become commingled with these, as seen with David and Mirella.

> David was a 25-year-old graduate student in a science field and Mirella a 26-year-old divorced mother working as a teachers' aide when the two came in for premarital counseling. Both were Afri-

can American. They had been having some difficulty agreeing on coparenting rules with Mirella's 5-year-old daughter, but Mirella also felt threatened by what she perceived as David's "militancy" about race. When the couple had trouble finding housing on their limited budget in an area David considered safe for Mirella and her daughter, David wanted to file complaints against several landlords who were apparently discriminating. Mirella, whose father had been killed in a race-related incident, objected.

This case example illustrates a number of points. First, David and Mirella were experiencing a current stressor a white European American couple would not have had to face even if they were poor, and were disagreeing about how to handle it. Complicating any efforts at problem solving in regard to this difference of opinion was most likely the anger both felt in having to deal with it at all. Further, Mirella was probably struggling with both realistic and transference fears due to the earlier loss of her father. Since his death had to do with racial strife, the reason for their current stress was that much more painful and her fears that much more terrifying. At the same time, both partners' gender-linked expectations might be that David, as an African American man, would have to find some way to fight back even if doing so might place him in danger. Many African American couples struggle with this dilemma, in which the black man should "be strong but not too strong" (Boyd-Franklin 1989, p. 227). Discussion of this case will continue below.

Working with Deeper Gender and Sociocultural Influences

As a first consideration, any couple's comfort with undertaking insight-oriented treatment may be affected by the partners' gender, ethnic, religious, or social-class learning. In general, men may be more reluctant than women to look at their deeper feelings or more painful life experiences. Partners belonging to ethnic groups that are more oriented toward family and community than individual well-being may not move readily into the individual introspection required. Asian Americans may see the direct expression of feelings expected in insight work as inappropriate or even dangerous to their mental health, but may express their feelings through metaphors (Sue et al. 1995). African American and Latino men may have special difficulty showing vulnerable feelings that could be considered signs of weakness (Boyd-Franklin 1989, De La Cancela 1991). Insight-oriented treatment may go against some lower-class or working-class partners' conceptions of what couple treatment is all about, and financing the usually somewhat lengthier process required may be difficult for them. Nevertheless, many partners who may need to engage in insight work to reach their treatment goals can be helped to move past such restrictions if clinicians explain the possible benefits and constructively address their concerns.

In some couple cases, partners' expectations of themselves or their mates based on gender or sociocultural characteristics, any negative self-valuations, and related experiences and feelings may themselves be explored to promote insight and growth. This process, as with all insight work, relies on constructive clinician–partner relationships and the clinician's use of empathy, support, and interpretation. Sometimes other interventions may be introduced. Because all participants are likely to have feelings about their own gender, ethnicity, social class, and religion as well as each other's, clinicians need to be highly attuned to everyone's responses to the treatment relationship during such work.

One possible focus for insight is to help partners examine more closely their self-expectations based on gender and, sometimes, those they hold for their mates. Sheinberg and Penn (1991) first probe couples' gender norms or expectations with questions about how the partners define masculine or feminine behavior for themselves and their mates. They may then ask how these norms were defined and enacted in partners' families of origin and discuss gender expectations in the larger society. A final step is to ask whether these norms fit the partners' inner experiences of self and what might be "the relational consequences of changing them" (p. 37). Questions are tailored to specific couples' situations, such as when a man who has criticized his wife for talking on the phone is asked what his underlying feelings were and whether it is permissible for a man to say directly that he "needs" his wife. A further possible technique suggested by Sheinberg and Penn is to construct a "gender mantra" for partners to repeat to themselves when their anxiety about not conforming to gender stereotypes might otherwise compel them to act dysfunctionally. For example, a woman might learn to say to herself, "I'm not letting my mother down if I'm more assertive. Times are different now."

Other authors suggest similar interventions to heighten the partners' awareness about the ways they may be constrained by gender stereotypes and to help them move beyond these. Brooks (1991) may directly challenge men's rationality, emotional self-control, denial of their own needs, and tendencies to overextend themselves. However, he also helps men avoid self-blame by emphasizing that they are operating based on the value system with which they grew up. Neal and Slobodnik (1991) make sure to help men identify constructive as well as limiting specifications for the masculine role, lest they feel they are being asked to give up their masculinity. These authors note that men may need support even to talk about such matters since part of the male role is "avoiding self-awareness, self-expression, and the sharing of our experience as men . . ." (p. 107). They focus further on strengths by exploring instances when men have been able to act differently than their own gender constraints would usually allow, for example, when they have shown feelings, and validate their capacity to act in these less stereotypical ways. The men may then realize they have choices whether to follow gender prescriptions or not. Similar techniques can be used with women in regard to assertiveness, self-care, and the like.

After helping male and female partners understand how their gender beliefs have constrained both, Rampage (1995) suggests they teach each other how to change. However, it is also important for clinicians to be empathic about the difficulty of doing so. Rampage notes that gender consciousness-raising groups can further enhance partners' self-awareness and growth. Papp (1988) uses metaphors, structured fantasy, humor, and exercises to help couples move out of gender-stereotyped behaviors that are dysfunctional for them. They may then realize they have choices whether to follow gender prescriptions or not. Mates may have to be helped not to stifle each other's new learning out of their own fears of gender failure. For example, both men and women may continue to deny men's normal dependency on their female partners, so strong is their gender socialization that such dependence may be allowable but talking about it is not (Kupers 1997). Men who are threatened by their female partners' becoming more assertive may have to be helped to examine what fears their mates' changing arouse in them.

Clinicians can also help partners examine their experiences related to ethnicity and religion through insight techniques. Several authors (Garcia Coll et al. 1993, Okun 1996, Waller and Spiegler 1997) suggest that, to help partners process ethnic learning and their mates to understand them better, they be encouraged to tell "stories" of their life experiences and the learning it entailed. Personal recollections, such as an African American woman recounting her shame as a child when a service station attendant included a racial epithet in his refusal to let her use a public restroom (Garcia Coll et al. 1993), bring the feeling component of ethnic experiences out in a way no other discussion can. It is also highly important that partners be able to speak about losses endured because of immigration or genocide, including airing feelings they may never have fully processed before (Cobb et al. 1995, Falicov 1996, Garcia-Preto 1996a, Javed 1995, Mirkin 1998).

A significant part of such reviews is to help partners deal with negative valuations others have placed on their ethnic or religious backgrounds and the various oppressions that have resulted from them. The steps in doing so are to move from discussing the experiences themselves to exploring the partners' responses, in an attempt to reveal underlying anger and perhaps the ways it has been handled (Boyd-Franklin 1989). Negative self-evaluations that may emerge can be interpreted as a natural but invalid response to oppression and, sometimes, as a defense against legitimate anger. When partners have directed anger about racism onto each other, clinicians may help them unite to fight oppression by reframing what they have been doing as "tearing each other apart and letting racism win" (Boyd-Franklin and Franklin 1998, p. 275). The partners' possibly stereotypical gender expectations of themselves and their mates, and the effects of racism on these, may then be explored. De La Cancela (1991) asks Puerto Rican men to look at their machismo to determine "whether what they previously defined as part of their culture might better be understood as a response to oppression . . ." (p. 201) and economic fears. Support may be given to directly voice their fears of not being able to fulfill their responsibilities to their families. Similarly, in couple treatment, African American women who have grown up believing that they must be strong because black men will not be available when they need them and African American men who fear showing weakness by expressing their feelings can be encouraged to talk about oppression, pride, vulnerability, and the pressures and demands on each (Boyd-Franklin 1989). Doing so may help partners to better hear, accept, and support each other.

Some of these intervention strategies were used in the case of David and Mirella. However, the clinician, who was white and female, first needed to attend to ethnic differences in her relationship with the couple.

> When David and Mirella wanted to do some problem solving about their difficulty finding housing, the clinician asked for more background information. They described the frustrations of their continuing search and their major disagreement about possible solutions. David felt they might be able to rent one of the places they had looked at if they pursued their complaints about discrimination with the city. Mirella did not want to live in a place where the landlord was already against them. For a while they discussed alternatives, such as looking in a different area of the city that was more expensive and less convenient for them. David was becoming visibly frustrated and finally said to Mirella, "Why won't you just let me solve this for you? Why do you always have to over-control the situation?" The clinician commented that it sounded like there were some underlying issues or feelings here. David remarked in a somewhat snide tone, "With all due respect, what do you know about all this anyway?" The clinician responded, "You're right." The couple then continued arguing about what they should do.

It is not constructive in the long run for clinicians of a different race or ethnicity than partners to simply withdraw when issues about the difference are raised (Garcia Coll et al. 1993), as the clinician does here. Yet their own anxieties about pursuing an area that is emotionally loaded for everyone may cause them to do so. As Greene (1994) suggests, partners themselves may fear the depth of their feelings, especially of anger, and clinicians who respond as if personally attacked or who defend against expression in other ways simply confirm that the feelings are too hot to handle. On the other hand, clinicians' anxieties can make them overly intrusive and insensitive to nuances when in other areas of discussion they are much more skilled. Part of the answer is for clinicians to seek consultation or some other venue for reviewing personal feelings. But ultimately they must simply try to help clients by hanging in and making a commitment to stay with the process (Garcia Coll et al. 1993).

> In the following session, David and Mirella were still at odds about their housing situation. The clinician suggested she would like to discuss something from the prior week. She had pulled back when David said she didn't really know what they were going through. She knew what he said was true, but she also didn't want her lack of having had this experience to keep them from talking about something they might need to talk about on a deeper level. Mirella responded that she was very embarrassed when David said what he did. The clinician regretted that her own discomfort might have heightened that. She wanted to be respectful of David's anger about her not having had to suffer the same stresses they did from racism. David said, less angrily this time, "I just don't think you can possibly understand." The clinician responded, "Probably not fully, but I can try. And maybe explaining it will help the two of you sort out your own feelings and experiences more." The two asked if this was really a good use of the treatment time. Again the clinician said, "I'm not sure. But my clinical experience does tell me that when a couple is having so much trouble solving something, deeper feelings are usually involved, and it usually helps to back off from trying to solve the problem and talk about them."

In the continuation of this case, the pair did talk about many of their life experiences with racism, their anger, what their parents had taught them about being African American, and eventually the gendered aspects of some of their learning. Doing so seemed to help both understand more fully why David felt he had to take a stand on the housing and why Mirella was so fearful about it. He did agree, based on her fears, that they would not try to live in one of the places about which he made an official complaint. The clinician also suggested that it might help Mirella to know David would be willing to talk with her in the future before doing something she might consider dangerous, since she got so scared due to her father's death. David denied in one session that he had any fears himself. But in the next, Mirella told that he had confessed sheepishly later, "Well, maybe a few." It seemed to help Mirella to feel he might be aware enough of his fears as well as hers not to act rashly in some future situation.

Such discussions can also go beyond immediate experiences of the partners themselves to examine what is known or can be learned about their family or ethnic group history. Genograms that cover possible learning from prior generations (Hines and Boyd-Franklin 1996, Okun 1996) are one possibility. Visits to families of origin to discuss parents' ancestors and their own gender and ethnic learning may reveal that parents do not hold the norms experienced in childhood as rigidly as partners think. Reviews of ethnic history from sources such as libraries or museums may be helpful. A focus on how partners' ethnic groups or religions have responded to oppression in the past and present may be a part of such reviews (Garcia Coll et al. 1993). Such approaches may especially fit the needs of Native Americans, who tend to value storytelling and may need to have the depth of their grief due to genocide acknowledged (Sutton and Broken Nose 1996).

Finally, a deeper exploration of religious or cultural norms and the way they influence partners can often be indicated with partners who differ in ethnicity, level of acculturation, religion, or opinions about how religious or cultural expectations should be carried out. This process may help individuals sort out confused loyalties and enhance mutual understanding and empathy. Insight work may also be needed to sort out the ways partners are using ethnic differences defensively. Ho (1990) recommends asking couples to monitor the circumstances under which each partner culturally stereotypes the other to detect their possible use of stereotyping to deal with anger or other feelings not really related to ethnicity. When a focus on differing ethnicities serves the function of allowing partners to remain overly tied to their families of origin, this dynamic may be uncovered through exploration, interpretation, or even the use of paradox. As an example of the latter, a clinician might call an "unhappy marriage a necessary and valuable sacrifice to the families of origin" (Falicov 1995, p. 241). Exploration or interpretation may also uncover that couple relationships of which parents do not approve serve a partner's defensive purpose of distancing from the parental family (Aradi 1988), while this mate perhaps holds the other responsible for the split.

PROBLEM SOLVING AND INSIGHT WORK WITH SAME-SEX COUPLES

Gay men, lesbians, and bisexual men and women usually communicate and problem-solve more or less as others of their genders do. Some authors argue that they are likely to be less bound by gender stereotypes than heterosexual partners, but this position is debatable. Couples composed of two women may be more likely to have difficulty with assertiveness while male couples may be uncomfortable discussing feelings (Brown 1995b). Certainly not an accurate stereotype is that in same-sex couples, one partner necessarily takes on more of a male role and the other more of a female one (Peplau 1993). Same-sex partners are, of course, influenced by their race, ethnicity, social class, and religion, just as partners in heterosexual relationships are.

There are, however, at least four ways in which same-sex couples differ from most heterosexual pairs. Clinicians' understanding of these differences is crucial whether such couples need help with communication and problem solving or insight treatment.

Understanding Special Issues of Same-Sex Couples

One difference stems from the simple fact that both partners are of the same gender (Brown 1995b). Whatever each mate's gender learning and self-expectations, similar learning and expectations will usually be true of the other unless they are differently influenced by their sociocultural characteristics or family backgrounds. Laird (1994) sees research findings that same-sex couples tend to differ from heterosexual ones on role division and uses of power and money as "more related to differences in gender socialization than to differences in sexual orientation" (p. 121). The potential for boundary confusion and mutual projection may be greater for same-sex pairs because of their similarity, but so may their potential for intimacy. Same-sex couples often do not have models for how two partners of the same gender should function together (Okun 1996), but may therefore be freer to work out what works well for them.

Much has been written about the gender-based expectations female partners may have of each other because both are women, such as the expectation that each will receive perfect love because women are expected to be good at nurturing (Schiemann and Smith 1996). Female gender socialization, combined with the need to create a rigid boundary around the couple because their bond is not validated by others, has sometimes been thought to increase female same-sex partners' fears of fusion, leading to greater distance as a defense. Many female same-sex couples report infrequent sexual relations (Metz et al. 1994), perhaps as a distance regulator. Gay and bisexual males, on the other hand, may be expected to have somewhat more trouble than heterosexual pairs holding their relationships together, since women are more socialized to take responsibility for doing so (Brown 1995b). They may also be more competitive with each other or more concerned about salary inequities between them than female same-sex couples are (Okun 1996). Part of the difficulty in making such generalizations is that much of the available literature is based on same-sex couples who seek treatment (Brown 1995b). Couples who are happy with their same-sex relationships tend not to be represented. In studies using community samples, men in same-sex couples and in heterosexual relationships have reported equal levels of relationship satisfaction, while women in same-sex relationships have reported more satisfaction than women in relationships with men (Metz et al. 1994, Rosenbluth and Steil 1995). In fact, Slater and Mencher (1991) report that female same-sex couples have expressed satisfaction with the same relational features that have been interpreted in the treatment literature as demonstrating fusion. These authors advise seeing lesbian or bisexual women's relationship closeness as constructive except when it is at extremely high or extremely low levels.

A second difference with same-sex couples is that the partners may have significant connections to a community of same-sex oriented individuals for friendship, social or political activism, or religious activities. These connections, which are more likely to be available in some geographic areas than others, can be an enormous resource for interpersonal support, validation, and role modeling (Brown 1995b, Carlson 1996, Laird 1994). As a corollary, partners may expect themselves to adhere to the cultural norms of these same-sex communities (Laird 1994). For example, one such norm is that ex-partners will remain friends and socialize with each other, even if one or both are in new relationships (Schiemann and Smith 1996). Mates may invoke these norms to influence each other or feel guilt if they want to disobey them.

A third difference is that same-sex couples must always deal with society's negative valuations, whether these manifest as prejudiced attitudes or outright discrimination, oppression, or violence (Brown 1995b, Carlson 1996, Okun 1996). Not only cannot same-sex couples legally marry and benefit from tax breaks available for married couples, they have no legal say in each other's medical treatments and usually cannot participate in each other's retirement programs or health insurance (Ellis and Murphy 1994). They often cannot legally adopt children and may be denied custody of children from prior heterosexual marriages. Any children living with them are likely to be stigmatized by others (Carlson 1996). If known to be same-sex oriented, they will often be denied access to housing or jobs. But same-sex partners who choose not to reveal their full identity in at least some settings to avoid discrimination deny a core aspect of themselves and their couple relationship as well.

Direct and indirect results of society's negative valuation of gay males, lesbians, and partners who are bisexual may influence couple dynamics in myriad ways. At the very least it is an almost constant source of stress. The partners may disagree on how to handle this stress, as for example when one is "out" to more people and believes the other should be too. Partners not far apart in age may be at very dissimilar stages of establishing their identities as gay male, lesbian, or bisexual. Normal couple issues such as whether to move to a new community or have a child must always be considered in light of the additional difficulties societal homophobia will create (Okun 1996). Some degree of internalized homophobia or negative self-valuation is common (Carlson 1996, Schiemann and Smith 1996), partly because those with a same-sex orientation, unlike people growing up in ethnic groups who experience societal devaluation, rarely have had help from parents or anyone else to deal with it (Brown 1995b). Lesbians and bisexual women have to cope with the additional devaluation of being female. As with any partners who experience negative self-valuation, the ways it is handled are sometimes dysfunctional for the individual or couple. For example, a same-sex partner may project responsibility for having this orientation onto the mate, as in, "I'm only in a lesbian relationship because of you and look at all the trouble I'm having because of it." This defense is especially available if the partner using it is bisexual and believes he or she could just as easily have ended up with an opposite-sex mate. Brown (1995b) suggests that when same-sex couples present for treatment with a single problematic issue, the primary problem may in fact lie in the couple's "self-oppressive beliefs and values" (p. 279).

Same-sex partners' experiences with prejudice and discrimination can also interact with other individual or couple dynamics, as the following case illustrates.

Lucille and Ann were a lesbian couple who had been together about three years when Ann's father became seriously ill. Lucille was African American, Ann was white and Irish American, and both were in their middle twenties. They had sought treatment because of intimacy fears. Lucille's fears centered on the concern that Ann would eventually reject her because of their relationship being biracial and bicultural as well as lesbian, although the lesbian community was more accepting of the racial difference than most heterosexual ones would have been. Ann readily admitted to abandonment fears because her mother had died when she was 12 years old, always a difficult time but more so because at this age she had begun suspecting her lesbian orientation.

When her father became seriously ill, Ann went to his side and Lucille accompanied her. However, the pair were not out to Ann's extended family, some of whom gathered to help. Ann's siblings, who did know about the pair's relationship, felt that having Lucille there was difficult to explain to the others and an unnecessary imposition on the family at an otherwise troubling time. Therefore, they were barely civil to her and kept suggesting she might need to get back to her job. Lucille and Ann could not spend much time together without arousing suspicion or ill feelings.

Apparent later, as will be shown below, was that this experience confirmed both partners' worst fears: Lucille's that she would be rejected and Ann's that Lucille would abandon her emotionally just when she needed her the most.

The fourth important difference from heterosexual pairs is that virtually all partners in same-sex relationships have had significant experiences of loss (Carlson 1996, Okun 1996). Some have lost their children from earlier marriages in custody battles. Many have totally lost relationships with members of their parental families who have rejected them for their sexual orientation. Those family relationships that continue are often strained, or feel incomplete and false if the other family member does not know the truth. The same-sex mate may not be accepted in either circumstance, leaving the pair with stress around family visits and the loss of family validation (Ellis and Murphy 1994). Childhood friendships and other past relationships may also have been lost or feel hollow because the same-sex orientation has not been revealed. Finally, there are the many lost freedoms that others take for granted. Same-sex couples usually do not even feel free to walk down the street holding hands, a joy most heterosexual pairs can experience whenever they choose.

To these almost inevitable losses must be added, in recent years, the awful specter of AIDS. While this terrible illness has struck others, it has so far taken its greatest toll on the gay and bisexual male community (Brown 1995b). Most gay and bisexual men older than 30 have seen their friendship systems decimated by AIDS-related deaths. Many have lost partners and many are themselves HIV positive or already symptomatic. Having to practice safe sex to protect uninfected partners from AIDS as well as dealing with the emotional and other stresses of one or both partners' being seropositive are significant challenges (Brown 1995b). Female same-sex partners are no more prone to be HIV positive or have AIDS than the female population at large, but many have lost gay or bisexual male friends to the illness (Schiemann and Smith 1996). While treatment of couples dealing directly with HIV and AIDS is beyond the scope of this book, the losses most same-sex partners have suffered from this illness must be acknowledged and addressed.

Ongoing Treatment of Same-Sex Couples

Clinician–partner relationship issues have added dimensions in work with same-sex couples. Neither heterosexual nor same-sex–oriented clinicians should work with such couples if they share society's negative views or expect same-sex relationships not to last (Brown 1995b, Ellis and Murphy 1994). Same-sex–oriented clinicians must be aware that partners' experiences will not duplicate their own. Partners will also wish to deal with the stress and self-feelings about being gay male, lesbian, or bisexual in ways that work for them, not necessarily in ways that have worked for the clinician (Schwartz 1989).

Even if not condemning of the partners' relationship, heterosexual clinicians may feel guilt over not having been similarly oppressed, discomfort with a couple's sexual activities (Ellis and Murphy 1994), or uncertainty that they can understand the partners' life experiences or same-sex culture. In response, they may idealize such relationships (Brown 1995b) or be "too light-handed or too heavy-handed" in their use of interventions (Carlson 1996, p. 73). Another danger is to defend against their feelings by avoiding discussion of partners' possible concerns about the clinicians' understanding and views. Again, self-awareness and efforts to learn more are key. Consultation, reading, course work, or talking with a same-sex–oriented peer may help (Brown 1995b, Carlson 1996, Ellis and Murphy 1994).

Besides whatever relationship concerns they may have based on a clinician's gender, race, or ethnicity, same-sex partners will certainly wonder whether their sexual orientations and related experiences will be accepted and understood. As always, the more openly clinicians can address these concerns, the better. As part of doing so, clinicians may have to face the issue of whether to reveal their own sexual orientation, especially if the partners ask. Sacrificing their privacy can feel like a risky venture to those who are same-sex–oriented themselves (Ellis and Murphy 1994). While same-sex partners may feel more comfortable with them and see them as positive role models, some may devalue them based on their own internalized homophobia (Schwartz 1989). Carlson (1996) speculates that work with a known heterosexual clinician can heal same-sex partners' feelings of having been rejected by heterosexual parents. Schwartz (1989) suggests that if partners ask clinicians' sexual orientation, clinicians may choose to say simply that they do not see homosexuality as pathological and are experienced in work with same-sex couples, assuming these assertions are true. Met with further questions, clinicians may explore what either answer will mean to the partners, or may give a direct answer based on the belief that doing so will strengthen the therapeutic alliance.

Same-sex couples usually need to do the same kind of work on communication and problem solving that other couples do, with the caveat that the nature of their communication difficulties may be somewhat influenced by their particular genders. In addition, however, it is likely that some problems a same-sex pair wishes to resolve will be influenced by societal homophobia. For example, where and how much to be out as a couple is a frequent issue for problem-solving discussion (Schiemann and Smith 1996). It is common that partners prefer to handle this issue somewhat differently. Earlier in the case presented above, Lucille and Ann had disagreed about whether Lucille should present Ann to co-workers even as a friend, since Lucille was not out at her job. Clinicians knowledgeable about unique issues facing same-sex couples can often help by normalizing a particular couple's struggles and offering information on constructive solutions others have found (Brown 1995b, Okun 1996). For example, couples who feel they cannot be out in some situations can devise ways to affirm their connection surreptitiously, such as by the use of an agreed verbal or behavioral signal (Laird 1994). Clinicians may also encourage couples to get more involved with the same-sex community for support and validation of their relationship, perhaps by holding a bonding ceremony (Schiemann and Smith 1996). Advocacy by a clinician can be in order at times, such as when the courts threaten to take away a same-sex partner's child.

Insight work in regard to same-sex partners' negative self-valuations or feelings of not living up to their own or their partner's gender expectations (Ellis and Murphy 1994, Schiemann and Smith 1996) may be desirable in some cases. Brown (1995b) suggests the importance of exploring for subtle manifestations of such negative self-feelings, partly by probing partners' experiences of external events that may trigger or evoke them. Some partners may need insight work to deal with emotional cutoffs from their families of origin or other losses (Carl 1990). Finally, the interaction of life experiences with prejudice or discrimination and unique partner issues from childhood may need attention, as with Lucille and Ann.

> The two agreed they had returned from their visit to Ann's father's home with their relationship damaged. Ann had withdrawn from Lucille and seemed listless and discouraged beyond what might have been expected since her father's illness had turned out not to be terminal. Lucille felt angry and bitter that Ann's relatives had treated her badly. After hearing about, recognizing, and empathizing with the bad experiences both had had, the clinician suggested trying to sort out further where their very upset feelings were coming from. In doing so, Ann repeatedly said that Lucille could have given her far more support than she did even in the context of having to disguise their true relationship from the relatives. Lucille readily acknowledged that Ann was going through a hard time but felt she had, too, because of worry about Ann and dealing with her own anger at her treatment by Ann's siblings. Ann reacted tearfully with, "Don't you criticize them. Soon they'll be all I have left." Lucille wondered how Ann could say this when Lucille very much wanted to be there for her. Ann retorted, "Well, you weren't, were you?"

At this point the clinician stopped Lucille from responding and suggested gently that she thought a lot of other things had gotten pulled into this situation for both of them. She would like to explore these. After acknowledging Lucille's hurt feelings and promising to return to them, she said gently, "Ann, I know you feel very sensitive to loss since your mother died so young, and here your father almost died too." Ann nodded. The clinician went on, "You've also said in the past that your sister Sally was the one who helped you the most to handle your mother's death." Again a nod. "It must be so hard for you that Sally, especially, was so cool toward Lucille and pretty much gave you the message she wasn't acceptable as a family member." Ann responded, "Yes, and I'm going to need Sally more than ever after my father goes." Lucille asked, "But is Sally more important than me?" Ann thought a moment and said, "Not necessarily, but I don't know how long I'll have you and family is always there." She then added, "Why do I have to make a choice between you and them? They'd accept you if you were a man." Lucille could not help but smile, adding, "Only if I was white, too, I'll bet." The clinician suggested seeing this as a problem they both shared, since both were worried about keeping their strong connection to each other and not losing the love of their families. Lucille's family didn't even know she was lesbian.

This brief case excerpt illustrates the many levels at which being a same-sex couple may create unique issues. The pair confronts a stressor any couple might face: a parent's severe illness and a caretaking visit. However, the relatives' homophobia, possible racism, and lack of validation of the couple relationship make the situation more tense and give the couple less time together to figure out how to cope with it. At a deeper level, gender socialization may have left both partners with the expectation that Lucille could be the perfect nurturer in a situation where she clearly could not. Negative self-valuations or other-valuations based on homophobia, sexism, or racism may have played a role. All this on top of Ann's loss of her mother at age 12, making transference of her abandonment fears onto a female partner highly likely.

The presence of a racial difference in this couple is also notable, and one wonders if the clinician in the case is dealing with it. While perhaps less often than elsewhere, "racism does exist in the lesbian community" (Leslie and MacNeill 1995, p. 162). Also, ethnic minority groups are often more homophobic and rejecting toward same-sex–oriented members than European American whites are, perhaps partly because they believe these individuals will bring further negative attention to them (Leslie and MacNeill 1995). Ethnic minority same-sex partners may suffer greatly from such rejection because they usually have a stronger ethnic identity and feel more connected to their ethnic communities than white partners often do. Lucille may be in a great deal of pain because she is not out to her family. She needs the clinician's encouragement to express this pain as well as justifiable anger at her treatment by Ann's relatives.

As clinicians, we can never know all of partners' worldviews and life experiences stemming from their genders, sexual orientations, ethnicities, and other sociocultural influences. Recognizing our own biases and areas of inadequate knowledge are first steps toward understanding and being helpful. We must then learn more from the couples we see as well as from other sources and must integrate such learning into our practice in meaningful ways. While this chapter may serve as an introduction to working with diverse couples, more knowledge must always be sought.

CHAPTER

8

Narcissistically Vulnerable Couples

In the past few decades, theorists have applied the term *narcissistically vulnerable* to couple relationships in which partners show intense escalations of anger, hypersensitivity to criticism, neediness, abandonment fears, poor boundaries, and extensive use of projective identification (Lansky 1981). Often one partner fits many of the characteristics and dynamics of borderline personality disorder while the other is more narcissistic, although either may show mixed features (Bader and Pearson 1988, Lachkar 1992, Slipp 1995). Other possibilities, in which couples' behavior patterns may be different but the underlying dynamics are similar, include someone with a borderline or narcissistic disorder paired with a healthier mate (Koch and Ingram 1985, Nelsen 1995) or with a schizoid partner (McCormack 1989, Seider 1995, Siegel 1992). Of course, many narcissistically vulnerable couples cannot be neatly categorized, and some show only a milder version of the characteristics to be elaborated below.

These couples are far from rare. Yet without awareness of their unique dynamics and treatment needs, clinicians who encounter them may fail to be of help. This chapter attempts to further such awareness. It begins with material on understanding and treating what may be called "classic" narcissistically vulnerable couples, in which both partners show borderline or narcissistic features, if not sufficient symptoms to warrant a personality disorder diagnosis. Further discussion considers narcissistically vulnerable couples in which a partner with borderline or narcissistic functioning is paired with either a somewhat healthier or a schizoid mate.

UNDERSTANDING CLASSIC NARCISSISTICALLY VULNERABLE COUPLES

The classic narcissistically vulnerable couple usually demonstrates characteristic interaction patterns and dynamics within the first few conjoint interviews. Clinicians must recognize and understand these as soon as possible so as to be able to intervene appropriately.

Recognizing the Classic Narcissistically Vulnerable Couple

Most characteristic of these couples is that their fights in session and as reported at home show rapid escalation, mutual rage and devaluation, and an imperviousness to therapeutic influence (Bader and Pearson 1988, Lachkar 1992, Lansky 1981). Partners may describe their arguments as "like World War III." Much of what they say at these times borders on or constitutes verbal abuse, usually dealt out equally by both. They readily criticize each other's most sensitive or painful areas, something healthier couples do much more rarely and only if extremely provoked. Neither the couple nor the clinician may be able to slow down the escalation once it starts. I have stood up between such partners to try to stop their fighting when a verbal interruption did not work, only to have them lean around me to continue the argument. Occasionally these arguments end with one partner running out of the session. At home, they may end in a partner temporarily leaving or, for some pairs, in hitting or pushing that is often mutual. In the latter cases specialized battering treatment may be necessary.

The arguments frequently start over what seem like very minor precipitants, and the partners may not even be able to remember how they begin at home. One couple I know argued for an entire session because, just before it, one had said to the other, "You're parked awfully far from the curb." While many couples who have poor communication and problem-solving skills present for treatment with the complaint, "We fight about everything," and narcissistically vulnerable pairs may say this too, only the latter will usually say, "We fight about nothing." Further careful exploration may reveal that most arguments start when one partner has felt criticized or blamed, needy, abandoned, threatened by too much closeness, or anxious for reasons unrelated to the couple, as will be elaborated below.

Partners in these couples are extremely sensitive to criticism or blame (Slipp 1995), both from each other and from a clinician. They often perceive blame even when it was not intended. Since the partners do often criticize each other, their reading blame into much of what their mates say is to some degree understandable. But it usually turns out to happen in their other relationships, such as with friends and at work, as well. Partners who seem to have reasonable self-awareness and reality testing at other times may almost totally lose them when blame or criticism might be happening.

> Ruth and Len, a couple in their forties, presented with the classic narcissistically vulnerable pattern of arguing. They worked together in their own business, in which Ruth produced artistic items and Len sold them. Many of their fights were about business procedures, with Ruth wanting more careful presentations of her work to customers and Len being more impulsive and sometimes cutting corners, for example, letting business letters go out with typos. Often they would end up arguing all day and get nothing done. Although in reality both worked very hard, each had sometimes complained that he or she worked harder. In one session, Len was preparing to tell about an incident that had occurred between them and, to set the context, said, "While you were doing *your* work . . ." Ruth immediately verbally attacked him. Careful probing revealed she thought he was being critical and implying she didn't work as hard, because of his slight emphasis on the word "your." In spite of Len's patient explanation that he was only setting the context for what he wanted to say and was not being critical, she continued to feel criticized. The clinician tried saying empathically that perhaps she felt criticized because Len had criticized her on this point before, but that it seemed he was not now. Ruth still could not relinquish her belief. (This case continues later in the chapter.)

As a third common characteristic, both partners in a classic narcissistically vulnerable couple tend to want the clinician's undivided attention more than partners in other couples do (Lachkar 1992). The corollary is that if one mate gets what the other considers too much attention, the latter can be angry and demanding. The week after a later session in which Ruth talked about very painful childhood experiences and gained considerable insight into their current impact, Len came in angry. He stated that Ruth had gotten more of the prior week's session time and that this was not fair. Such partners often show envy or jealousy of their mates' involvement with their children, friends, co-workers, or even pets. Yet when they receive attention from each other for too long, they retreat or attack. Both partners may describe having entered other relationships, including with past clinicians, with high expectations and then being disappointed (Siegel 1992).

Apparent at some point in work with such couples is that both have strong reactions to perceived abandonment (Lachkar 1992). Their response is usually rage. A mate who arrives home later than usual, leaves an argument before it escalates into its most virulent form, or even looks away during a conversation may provoke an intense reaction, usually without either partner understanding why. One or both mates may exploit the other's intuitively sensed vulnerability to abandonment by threatening repeatedly to leave the relationship. Yet often these relationships continue more or less unchanged for years (Slipp 1995). Strong reactions can also occur in response to perceived abandonment by clinicians. Partners may become furious or regress in response to a clinician's vacation, a session canceled because of illness, a break in empathy, or even a change of appointment time. However, often their anger is displaced onto each other rather than directly expressed.

Another characteristic of classic narcissistically vulnerable couples is the partners' poor individual boundaries (Bader and Pearson 1988). There may be fantasies of closeness almost amounting to merger. Partners may express that their mates should understand their every need without being told or should be endlessly giving as a parent would be with a young infant. In the brief good times such couples may have together, they may idealize each other, perhaps describing what sounds like perfect love and understanding. These idyllic interludes are always interrupted by an argument or some real or imagined transgression on the mate's part, since actual merger is highly feared. Poor boundaries are also apparent in the contagion of needs and affects these couples tend to show. If one is anxious, he or she may do something to make the other anxious or the other may become equally anxious without any clear reason. One's neediness, anger, or fear of abandonment can evoke the same need or feeling in the other, usually with no awareness of why.

Excessive use of projective identification is perhaps the most obvious and repeated example of such boundary confusion (Slipp 1995). If one partner is angry, he or she may perceive the anger as emanating from the other and may do something to make the perception a reality. Projective identification can be used as a defense against experiencing other needs or feelings as well. When Len was anxious about a sales call, he would begin harassing Ruth by saying that her anxiety about money undermined his self-confidence. While Ruth *was* often anxious about money, in the particular instance she may not have mentioned or showed this anxiety in days. In response to his accusation, she would become more anxious but label her anxiety as his fault because he was so often careless about some detail of his sales pitch. Thus, she would take on his anxiety, undermine his self-confidence, and validate his projection.

Partners in classic narcissistically vulnerable couples still show many strengths. When not feeling criticized or too needy, angry, or anxious, their capacity for self-observation may be adequate to good (Goldstein 1995, Lansky 1981). They may be quite charming, intelligent, and attractive people who give extravagantly to their mates at times. Sometimes they can even be very supportive and empathic, though usually not for long. Len always remembered Ruth's birthdays with highly original gifts tailored to her special liking. Ruth would tenaciously stick up for Len if any outsiders criticized him. Classic narcissistically vulnerable partners may be successful in their work, have friendships that persist, and even be reasonably good parents in some instances. While they may have problems with these other relationships or areas of functioning, they usually seem more emotionally disordered in the couple relationship than elsewhere.

As individuals, both partners in a classic narcissistically vulnerable couple may meet some of the diagnostic criteria for borderline personality disorder. For example, they may show "frantic efforts to avoid real or threatened abandonment," "alternating . . . idealization and devaluation" of others, "intense anger or difficulty controlling anger . . ." or "affective instability" (*DSM-IV* 1994, p. 654). However, in many pairs, one partner displays these characteristics more obviously than the other. This mate is also more likely to struggle with other traits typical of a borderline disorder, such as an unstable self-image or impulsivity that results in self-damaging behavior (*DSM-IV* 1994). Len sometimes seemed confident but often felt he was a failure, and he had lost several earlier jobs by talking back to the boss. The number and severity of such partners' symptoms may or may not be sufficient to warrant a borderline personality disorder diagnosis. Even if they are, the partner is likely to be in the healthier range of individuals with the disorder, since those in the sicker range cannot usually sustain a long-term love relationship.

Partners who show more narcissistic characteristics, possibly along with some borderline ones, may be somewhat grandiose or seem to need constant attention and admiration. Full diagnostic criteria for narcissistic personality disorder may or may not be met (*DSM-IV* 1994). These partners are also likely to feel rage in response to criticism, have fears of abandonment, and often idealize or devalue others (Slipp 1995). They usually have a fairly stable sense of self (Siegel 1992) and function more successfully in the world when compared to a more borderline mate. Ruth had a more stable job history than Len since she had never had a problem with impulsivity, and her friendships were more long-lasting.

Understanding Individual and Couple Dynamics

One may look to research and theory on borderline and narcissistic disorders as well as on narcissistically vulnerable couples to understand more fully why these couples function as they do.

Research suggests that physical factors, such as a neurological impairment or a biochemical proclivity to depression, may contribute to the development of borderline personality disorder (Marziali 1992). Also found associated with this diagnosis are childhood histories of losses, physical or sexual abuse, and chaotic parental families (Kroll 1993, Links 1992). Many of the parents have suffered from severe psychopathology themselves. Links (1992) speculates, based on available research, that a childhood environment conducive to borderline personality disorder may include parental overinvolvement combined with hostility or malevolence toward the child.

Further ideas are provided within the context of ego psychology and object relations theories. Masterson (1981) proposes that people suffering with borderline disorders have encountered difficulties during the important separation-individuation stage between about 1 and 3 years of age. At this time, when children experience an enormous internal push toward independence but still need to seek periodic reassurance and nurturing from a parent figure, the child who will later develop borderline functioning presumably receives different messages. The mother or other caretaker may be repeatedly physically or emotionally unavailable, or may reward regressive behavior but threaten to withdraw when the child tries to individuate. In either instance, the child experiences emotional needs that are not reliably met and feels significant anxiety and rage in response. The anger causes further anxiety because the child is likely to perceive it as one of the reasons for the caretaker's rejection. The lesson learned is that needing someone leads to being either abandoned or engulfed and exploited. Continuing neediness, rage, and anxiety about closeness are the result.

While Kernberg (1975) sees the origins of such a child's rage somewhat differently, both he and Masterson suggest that it is handled by the persistent use of splitting (Goldstein 1995, Siegel 1992). As described in Chapter 1, splitting is a defense mechanism in which bad feelings toward another person are kept separated from the good and the person is experienced as either all good or all bad. This mechanism, thought to be common in all children at an earlier stage, may continue in the child who will show later borderline functioning in order to protect the "good" relationship with the mother or other caretaker from being damaged by the child's intense anger. While splitting allows this relationship to continue, it also prevents the child from seeing the caretaker as a whole person who is good, or need-meeting, at some times, and bad, or need-denying, at others. The child who cannot put these two images together presumably cannot develop object constancy, or the ability to hold onto the image of a significant person who is away and take comfort from it. Hence for the child, and later for the adult, every separation feels like an abandonment. These individuals also do not stably integrate good and bad images of the self. They may therefore be prone to feel that if they do anything bad or inadequate, they are all bad. They are so vulnerable to criticism because it evokes "all-bad" self-feelings. Feelings associated with the all-bad self, such as anger and dependency, may be defended against by projecting them onto someone else, later including their mates.

Children who may later show a borderline disorder not only struggle to manage heightened anger, dependency yearnings, and fears of expressing these. Their parents or other caretakers also may not sufficiently soothe them when they are upset or affect-laden (Goldstein 1995, Siegel 1992). Hence they do not learn, as normal children do, to bind anxiety by soothing themselves when they are full of affects or fears. Instead, they act on these impulsively without thinking, leading to real-life experiences in which the dangerousness of these feelings is again confirmed. What they do not learn is regulated, healthy need and affect expression.

Before examining how these childhood influences play out in the adult relationships of people who show borderline functioning, let us briefly review theory about the development of narcissistic disorders. Here Kernberg and the self psychologists, primarily Kohut, are major contributors. Kohut's key ideas are that deficits in parenting have left narcissistic individuals with unmet needs for being admired or mirrored and for connecting with an idealized caretaking figure (Kohut and Wolf 1986). When parents or other caretakers have not provided soothing, empathy, and validation well matched to the child's needs, the child and later the adult must constantly look to others to provide these (Siegel 1992). Kernberg (1986) suggests that people who show narcissistic disorders had parents or other caretakers who were generally cold and hostile, but who may have treasured particular characteristics in the child. For example, the child's beauty, intelligence, charm, musical talent, or ability to take care of a parent might receive great praise and be shown off to others. On the other hand, the child's emotional neediness, anger, or possible weaknesses of any kind presumably elicited parental rejection or indifference. The child therefore organized a sense of self around the "grandiose self," consisting of those real qualities that had been perceived as valued plus other idealized aspects of the self and parents. The devalued parts of the self were split off, repressed, and projected onto others.

In adulthood, the narcissistic individual may prominently display valued parts of the self and feel entitled to others' continued admiration for them (Lachkar 1992, Siegel 1992, Slipp 1995). But no matter how much such admiration is forthcoming, he or she never feels truly validated since the split-off bad self must always be hidden and denied. Such individuals presumably experience great underlying neediness, rage at not being fully loved, and deep fears of being abandoned if the bad self were to be exposed. Rage is handled by splitting, in which others are either idealized or devalued, while projection or projective identification defends against awareness of dependency needs, anger, and any other unwanted needs or feelings. Real closeness in relationships is avoided, since needing the parent or caretaker in childhood led to being exploited and controlled. Although criticism and blame may threaten to expose the bad self, the narcissistic individual usually holds onto the grandiose sense of self and simply reacts with rage. Threats of abandonment may elicit a great deal of anxiety, likely to be defended against by projection or some form of acting out. Sometimes real losses may bring bad-self feelings to the surface, along with considerable depression.

When mates who show borderline and narcissistic personality dynamics get together, a synergistic pattern develops (Bader and Pearson 1988, Lachkar 1992, Siegel 1992, Slipp 1995). Both partners have desperate needs for love and attention evoked in the experience of the couple relationship. Yet both are extremely fearful of what intimacy may mean. Their dependency needs make them want closeness with the partner as a possibly giving parent figure, yet their childhood experiences tell them that closeness leads to being engulfed, controlled, exploited, or abandoned. A more borderline mate may even fear total merger and loss of self (Lachkar 1992). Both may experience rage at what their transference fears make them believe their mates will demand or do to them. And, of course, the partners cannot fulfill each other's hopes for perfect nurturing, leading to further rage. Since both partners' anger and dependency needs also arouse unacceptable bad-self feelings, they must try to defend against awareness of these. Splitting, projection, and projective identification are the inevitable result. Each mate sees the other as all good at some times and all bad at others. Through projection, each often views the other as the angry or dependent one, and criticizes to try to keep these bad-self feelings securely elsewhere. In projective identification, one mate lures or provokes the other into expressing the unwanted affect or need to show indisputably whose it is, as in the example with Ruth and Len given earlier.

One might think that each partner attempting to project unacceptable parts of the self onto the other would lead to a breakup of the relationship, but both mates' abandonment fears are also very strong. What eventuates when these couples stay together is collusion in a never-ending cycle that allows for partners to meet some emotional needs while staving off real closeness. In one part of the cycle, the two join in making up an idealized "good self–good other." They may have an idyllic weekend, wonderful mutual support during a crisis, or great sex. During this time, signs of imperfection are minimized or denied (Siegel 1992). Dynamically, each experiences that he or she is all good, as is the partner, and the needs of both are being met. This idealized period never lasts, and not only because the mates cannot perfectly meet each other's needs for long. Both become quickly frightened by the upsurge of neediness they feel and the extreme dangers they perceive in being so vulnerable. One then begins to see the other as bad and attacks or otherwise pushes him or her away. Of course the attack, which may be carried out initially by either partner, is quickly met by the other's counterattack and therefore confirms the dangers inherent in closeness. The fight also serves to control both partners' levels of expectation that needs will be fulfilled and allows projection of bad-self feelings elsewhere. Each partner cannot readily regulate his or her own self-esteem. But the mate can, by giving praise or by losing in competition (Siegel 1992). Thus the fights are also desperate attempts to "win," that is, to be the one who is good, while the mate is the one who is bad.

When fighting has gone on too long, each partner's abandonment fears become aroused enough that it temporarily ceases and—sometimes immediately and sometimes after a period of withdrawal—the whole cycle begins again. In a lengthy relationship, the "good" times often become shorter or nonexistent and only the fighting and withdrawn periods seem to alternate. In spite of the predictability of their patterns, these partners do not feel stable and secure. The repeated splitting, with the mate being seen as all good at some times and all bad at others, contributes to a sense of discontinuity and near chaos (Siegel 1992). The partners' continued boundary confusion and conflagration in feelings also mean that anxiety, anger, or neediness are rampant in the couple system much of the time (Bader and Pearson 1988). Such feelings can be further heightened when health problems or external events stir up partners' increased anxieties.

In some couples in which partner differences are more pronounced, with one clearly more borderline and the other clearly more narcissistic, a more continuous pattern of rage by the first and withdrawal by the second may be evident. Borderline partners in such pairs may originally believe that their stronger narcissistic mates will nurture them and contain their rampant emotions (Slipp 1995). Their more obvious dependency may fulfill the narcissistic partners' needs to feel superior and admired. When they become disappointed and rageful, their narcissistic partners may withdraw. In the long term the more borderline partners, by continuing to display more obvious anger and dependency needs, express these for both mates, allowing narcissistic partners to maintain their facade of independence (Lachkar 1992). Borderline partners may stay in such relationships partly because their mates' withdrawal helps control their neediness and protects them from extreme fears of fusion. If such couples' interaction is very skewed, their initial treatment needs are more similar to those of borderline-codependent pairs, to be discussed below, than to those of classic narcissistically vulnerable couples.

Any of the above patterns may be more complex when third parties, such as children or extended families, are triangled in. These individuals may become at least the intermittent focus of projected bad-self feelings, protecting the couple relationship somewhat (Siegel 1992). Or they may meet some of the partners' needs, allowing the couple's fighting to proceed almost endlessly. Of course if their children develop problems, the partners are likely to blame each other, adding new fuel to the fire. But they may also blame the children, their teachers, or other environmental influences, deflecting negative affects from each other.

The dynamics in classic narcissistically vulnerable couples are not always so dysfunctional as the above discussion may suggest. The intensity of the partners' needs and fears, and the recalcitrance of the patterns to change, vary from couple to couple. Many partners are competent, intelligent people who do have some self-awareness, perhaps gained during periods of prior individual treatment. But to whatever degree these narcissistically vulnerable patterns and dynamics prevail in the couple relationship, the clinician must almost always be prepared for a longer and more difficult course of treatment than would be the case with healthier couples.

TREATING CLASSIC NARCISSISTICALLY VULNERABLE COUPLES

Much of the work with classic narcissistically vulnerable couples is similar to that with other couples. At each treatment phase, however, some modifications are needed. Clinicians must also be especially aware of countertransference, which may be more troublesome than usual since such couples almost inevitably stir up clinicians' own issues with anger, dependency, self-esteem, and intimacy (Siegel 1992). The following discussion addresses treatment of couples showing the common, classic, narcissistically vulnerable pattern of persistent arguing alternating with brief periods of closeness or longer ones of withdrawal. It is assumed that couple treatment rather than family work is indicated, and that substance abuse and violence have been ruled out.

Early Treatment

In early sessions with most classic narcissistically vulnerable couples, as in any initial interviews, clinicians must try to engage both partners constructively in treatment, gather information needed for assessment, establish a mutual and nonblaming conception of presenting problems, offer realistic hope, and contract for the ongoing work. Constructive engagement and a nonblaming conceptualization of the couple's problems, however, will often be more difficult to achieve than with healthier pairs. Both partners are likely to enter the treatment relationship with strong transference wishes and fears and to project blame for problems onto their mates. These issues become commingled as partners are highly attuned to whether the clinician prefers one of them over the other or is seeing either as more in the right.

If one partner has told anything about a couple's problems in an initial telephone call, the clinician must be careful in sharing what was said with both, lest the caller feel his or her point of view is not being presented correctly or the other mate feel ganged up on. Probably it is best to allude very briefly to the conversation and say the clinician is eager to hear both mates' points of view. The early parts of an initial interview can follow the standard format of gathering information about both partners as individuals and their history as a couple. In fact, these discussions provide a crucial opportunity for the clinician to bond with each partner by listening empathically and commenting on strengths. Reviewing the couple's history up to the present allows the clinician to begin to interrupt splitting (Siegel 1992), in which the partners may either have forgotten about positives in their relationship or idealized its past, to help them create a more balanced picture.

In describing why they have come in for treatment, classic narcissistically vulnerable couples, left to their own devices, may engage in rapidly escalating arguments just as they do at home. Clinicians must do their best to keep structure in the session by stopping them decisively but with empathy for both (Lachkar 1992, Siegel 1992). A comment might be: "Wait, you're hurting each other. I don't want that to happen here. Is this what your arguments are like at home?" Or if one partner attacks and the other has not yet responded: "Wait, you must be hurting [upset, angry, or whatever] to be saying something like this, but tell us instead what the feeling is about. What happened?" Although the partners may not be able to stop themselves or say what has precipitated an attack, they will still get the message that the clinician wants to protect them both from blaming. He or she is also beginning to "encourage reflection and exploration of what lies beneath manifest problems" (Seider 1995, p. 371). In providing structure, clinicians must not come across as controlling or manipulative, which could evoke or reinforce negative transferences (Slipp 1995). They must control the session in a way partners can experience as being for their benefit rather than as serving the clinician's needs. The stance of a caring parent, who can clearly but empathically set limits, is a possible one to keep in mind.

Further, in initial sessions and throughout treatment, clinicians must "take an evenhanded approach, be nonjudgmental, and not side with one [partner] against the other" (Slipp 1995, p. 463). When offering empathy to one mate, it may be necessary to convey overtly that this does not mean the other is at fault. Clinicians may make statements such as, "I can see that you [looking at one partner] were still feeling upset about what had happened the day before but when you expressed some of that anger, I do understand that you [looking at the other] felt blindsided and were hurt." The clinician must try to give roughly equal attention to each partner. If focusing more on one for a while, it can help to keep checking back with the other. Or before beginning a more one-sided focus, the clinician may ask for the other mate's permission. Part of the reason is that lack of attention from a clinician can evoke a partner's feelings of being abandoned; a partner who gives permission beforehand for the other to receive attention is far less likely to feel helpless and left out.

If at all possible within the first interview, and continuing thereafter, clinicians can try to help narcissistically vulnerable partners conceptualize the patterned nature of their interaction. They must not get too caught up in the content argued about or in the disputes as to who is right (Bader and Pearson 1988). The couple is likely sooner or later to agree that they get into endless arguing. They may say that the fighting alternates with brief periods of togetherness or longer ones of withdrawal. However, they are very likely to differ on whose fault the arguing is, each perhaps saying the other starts the fights. In early sessions, clinicians must work to disengage them from this preoccupation with blame by verifying that their recognition of their pattern seems correct and that it is less important who starts the arguing. Both participate, but it can be quickly added that both do so unwillingly. They both get caught up in the pattern without knowing why. They are not bad people and they truly care about each other, so there must be reasons for the pattern that are not yet understood. Because their patterns are clearly hurting both of them, part of the work of treatment will be to try to understand what is compelling them and to help the couple change.

If either or both partners have proffered some explanation of their own behaviors that does not involve blaming the other, their willingness to look at their own participation in their patterns can be credited (Bader and Pearson 1988). It is important, however, to use their own words subsequently, because any change in wording may seem less palatable to them. Similarly, if the clinician conceptualizes partners' differences in style, preference, or personality, words must be found that each partner finds acceptable. In the Ruth and Len case, Ruth did not mind being seen as "careful" in her approach to work tasks but did not like the first descriptor the clinician suggested, which was "cautious." Apparently the latter connoted to her more possibility of being seen as weak. Commenting on both partners' or the couple's strengths during such discussions may serve to interrupt splitting and projective identification without evoking bad-self feelings. The partners' tendencies to see each other or the relationship as all good or all bad at different times can also be noted (Siegel 1992).

The empathic component of the interventions used in the first interview and beyond is crucial because it provides what both mates have presumably not received in childhood, that is, caring attention to their underlying needs instead of rejection for them (Slipp 1995).

The clinician keeping structure in the sessions also conveys that their anger and neediness can be contained, rather than colluding in the belief that these affect states are so dangerous they must be denied and projected. Such structure further suggests that the clinician has good boundaries and will not become overwhelmed by the partners' feelings or needs. Finally, the clinician's strength and understanding foster some hope that he or she will be able to help. Of course, a clinician working with such couples is still walking something of a tightrope. Each partner may feel some disappointment and anger that the clinician is not taking his or her side. But at some level, the partners sense that if either wins their endless battle, both will lose, and the relationship will also be untenable.

The clinician must at some point convey that both mates will have to take responsibility for trying to change their patterned behaviors, but that doing so will be hard. Not only is such a statement realistic, it tends to disengage partners from their probable fears that if they cannot change fast enough, the clinician will respond by blaming or abandoning them. It may also reassure them that change will not happen so quickly as to take away needed defenses before they are ready and leave them vulnerable. On this basis, they may be able to contract for the work of treatment to proceed.

In spite of clinicians' careful efforts, some classic narcissistically vulnerable partners may feel that needing treatment at all indicates failure; the very possibility may therefore imply narcissistic injury (Siegel 1992). If so, reassurance that coming in shows courage and strength may help. Some partners may handle their fears about entering treatment by denigrating it or doubting a clinician's competence. It is important for the clinician to empathize with, and if necessary empathically interpret, the underlying fears (Seider 1995). For example, partners might be told, "I can imagine that looking more closely at these patterns that have become so painful for both of you is frightening. You know what you now have together, and to some degree you always know what to expect. While coming here raises the possibility of things getting better, it also may feel like either of you could get hurt or things between you could get worse." Or, in a more direct interpretation of one partner's resistance, "I think it's understandable that you're questioning coming here. You may be afraid that I'll take your husband's side, since I'm a man too, and that he'll gain even more power in your arguments. I want you to know I'll try hard not to let that happen. I think you both deserve to get more from your relationship." As always, clinicians should encourage partners to tell them at any point about any negative reactions or concerns about the treatment (Slipp 1995). If couples have first idealized, then devalued and left prior treatment experiences, clinicians should warn them that the same pattern could repeat itself and that if so, it will be important to discuss their reactions rather than simply terminating.

During both early and ongoing sessions with classic narcissistically vulnerable couples, clinicians need to keep close track of their countertransference feelings so as not to act based on these (Solomon 1997). For one thing, they must be comfortable enough with anger not to totally stifle the partners' expressions of it, yet not be so intimidated or overwhelmed that they let such expressions run rampant (Goldstein 1997). The anger must be understood as serving defensive functions the partners will not immediately be able to see and modify. In the interim, a clinician must be willing to take charge and remain empathic without resenting doing so. To some degree he or she becomes a container for their rampant affects, allowing partners some respite (Solomon 1997). Some clinicians fear evoking a couple's wrath toward them if they interrupt to take control of the session or if they do not phrase something in just the right way. Such partners do occasionally turn their anger on a clinician, though more often for what they perceive as putting them down or taking sides than for maintaining structure. Clinicians must be willing to explain and perhaps modify what they are doing without feeling unduly guilty, angry, or defensive. They must realize they can never totally satisfy such couples' needs or avoid missteps, but can probably provide a "good enough" therapeutic relationship to be helpful, just as "good enough" parenting is.

Another countertransference feeling is often that of being overwhelmed or turned off by the classic narcissistically vulnerable couple's primitive neediness (Solomon 1997). One does not usually see adults being so self-centered, unempathic toward those close to them, and vindictive when their needs are not met. Or a clinician may become confused by such couples' fluctuating need and affect states, or by the sudden appearance of their strengths. Any similarity between partners' narcissistically vulnerable dynamics and those extant in clinicians themselves, their families of origin, or their current intimate relationships can arouse understandable anxiety. These couples tend to stir up any of the clinician's not fully resolved intrapsychic conflicts by the very fact that their needs are so compelling and their defenses against them so provocative. At some point in the treatment, clinicians may also find themselves guilty for having needs of their own rather than being all-giving in response to the partners' neediness (Lachkar 1992). Or they may feel exhausted and angry because they have given too much (Solomon 1997).

Self-awareness is the first step toward preventing a destructive response to countertransference. Clinicians who find that their own issues have been stirred up can discuss these with a trusted colleague, consultant, or therapist. To deal with normal annoyance or frustration with classic narcissistically vulnerable pairs, it can be helpful to remind oneself that the partners have good reasons for acting as they do. Hearing in detail about their childhood experiences, which may not happen until somewhat later in the treatment, can usually promote clinicians' genuine feelings of empathy. But even earlier, clinicians must believe that such reasons exist. It is sometimes reassuring for clinicians to recognize that classic narcissistically vulnerable partners' strengths are real, even though their anger and neediness may be somewhat primitive. Their defenses usually work for them and they are not likely to fall apart. A clinician may also try to connect with partners' likable qualities, not the least of which may be their loyalty, liveliness, and repeated if largely unsuccessful efforts to get what they need from each other.

Finally, as Slipp (1995) points out, self-examination in a particular instance may suggest that a clinician is having a countertransference reaction not because the clinician's own similar issues have been evoked, but in response to a partner's projection onto the clinician of an unwanted affect or need. This awareness may be used to understand partners better and sometimes may be shared with the couple. Slipp gives the example of a clinician who used awareness of suddenly feeling helpless to empathize with a narcissistically vulnerable partner's feelings of helplessness as a child.

Work on Communication and Beginning Insight

Part of the reason ongoing treatment of classic narcissistically vulnerable couples is so complex is that so many important goals are being worked on more or less simultaneously. The first focus of middle-phase sessions may be on communication, problem solving, and beginning levels of insight (Bader and Pearson 1988, Siegel 1992, Slipp 1995). However, it is also crucial to maintain a strong therapeutic alliance as a context in which the work of treatment can take place.

On a reality level, partners must continue to experience the clinician as a benign caretaking figure who can keep structure in the sessions and remain empathic to both most of the time. Explicit empathy and nonblame may need to be conveyed more often and for a longer time than with most couples, perhaps with comments such as, "You're both hurting," "This is no one's fault," or "You must have had reasons, because I know you're not a bad person." By devoting equal attention to both partners and not leaving one sitting with no attention for long, the clinician also allays some of partners' abandonment fears. Careful preparation for breaks in the treatment process due to vacations or other schedule changes can further enhance partners' trust. The hope is that with increased trust in the safety of the therapeutic environment, partners can gradually take the risk of becoming more aware of and able to reveal their own needs and feelings, rather than always having to project or otherwise defend against them.

When partners express realistic or transference-based negative feelings toward a clinician, listening to their concerns and responding nondefensively helps to counteract possible splitting in the clinician–partner relationship. It conveys that clinicians prefer talking out rather than acting out, because the former, even if it is angry talk, can lead to understanding and resolution (Lachkar 1992, Slipp 1995). Partners' acting out their anger or fears by threatening to leave treatment prematurely must always be explored calmly.

While classic narcissistically vulnerable partners' expressions of apparently reality-based positive feelings toward clinicians should be accepted graciously, clinicians must also be alert to the possibility that they are being idealized. For example, at times partners may bestow extravagant and unwarranted praise. Great praise is especially suspect when clinicians may have done something a partner probably did not like and when it is accompanied by increased, possibly displaced, anger toward the mate. When such idealizing occurs, clinicians should gently question it, perhaps explaining that protecting them from bad feelings is not necessary and that these are important to share. If needed, the partners' fears of expressing any negative feelings may be explored or interpreted. The pair can be reminded of their tendencies to see relationships as all positive or all bad (Siegel 1992). If either negative transference or idealizing persists, deeper interpretations of the defensive functions being served and possible underlying fears may be needed.

Most classic narcissistically vulnerable couples agree to work on their communication to try to prevent the blaming escalations that happen so often between them. They usually show most of the communication problems common to other couples, such as topic jumping or trying to talk each other out of feelings, as well. Early work on communication and problem-solving skills therefore resembles such work with other couples, but again with significant modifications. For one thing, it will usually be necessary to give more explicit attention to preventing, insofar as possible, couples' hostile escalations at home (Bader and Pearson 1988, Seider 1995). Bader and Pearson often ask partners to negotiate agreements about what behaviors are acceptable and unacceptable during their inevitable arguments. For example, the mates may decide to agree on no hitting or pushing, no threats to leave the relationship, and no leaving an argument without saying when they will return. However, partners may be encouraged to take time-outs when anger is running too high to make constructive discussion possible. They can also be told to bring difficult problems to treatment rather than trying to solve them at home.

As they do with other couples, clinicians can ask a classic narcissistically vulnerable pair to identify issues they wish to discuss in sessions. The partners will have encountered many true differences they have been unable to resolve. However, much of the focus must usually be on underlying themes and communication skills, because such couples often report a never-ending series of self-generated problems and crises (Bader and Pearson 1988). The mates can be prohibited from rehashing prior arguments unless the intent is to resolve the problems addressed there or learn new ways to communicate. Even so, the clinician may need to remind them frequently to focus on making changes for the future, not to cast blame about the past. Siegel (1992) notes that these couples often deny or gloss over problems when they are in a period of idealizing each other, but become overwhelmed and cannot stick with problem solving on their own when they are devaluing each other. Pointing out such tendencies as counterproductive, and perhaps expressing confidence in their ability to proceed differently, may help such couples gradually learn and integrate at least some new ways of talking to each other.

Highly important, of course, is that clinicians try to prevent accusatory statements and help both partners state their needs or preferences in areas being discussed. It can be necessary to say again and again things like, "I know you're upset. Try not to accuse him, but tell us what you're thinking or feeling. What do you need in this situation, or what's making you feel so bad?" And mates must be given explicit assistance to listen. A clinician might say, "I know this must stir up feelings in you. I'll want to hear your thoughts and feelings in a minute too. I really want to understand what's going on for both of you." Bader and Pearson (1988) ask partners to try hard to keep their thinking engaged when listening to their mates, even if doing so means asking for a break to walk around the room and take deep breaths to get their feeling reactions under control. It can be acknowledged that it is hard to see another person's point of view when one's own intense feelings are aroused (Siegel 1992).

For a longer time than is usual with most couples, clinicians may encourage the partners to talk through them (Seider 1995). That is, one partner can tell his or her version of a problem, with the clinician asking questions and rephrasing the content to show empathic understanding. The other mate can be asked if he or she has understood or has questions. Then the second partner can express his or her point of view, followed by the clinician's similar response. Proceeding in this way serves several functions. The clinician can model empathy, nonblame, and other listening skills. Each partner can experience being soothed and given to. Volatility is slowed down and escalations of anger can be prevented much of the time.

The thinking of narcissistically vulnerable partners is likely to be riddled with distorted cognitions, especially selective attention based on negative expectancies and inaccurate attributions, as when one mate thinks the other is being critical even when he or she is not. Again, the possibility of misconceptions must be examined empathically. The clinician may say something like, "I know you've experienced a lot of criticism with each other. But sometimes couples begin to assume that everything that *might* be meant as a criticism *is* meant that way. How about checking it out?" The clinician can then model doing so, as in, "Jack, were you feeling critical toward Jennifer when you said that?"

During such discussions, clinicians may try to strengthen partners' realistic self-esteem and individual boundaries. They may comment on good qualities, strengths, steps forward, or apparent positive motivations and efforts even if behaviors remain problematic. Care must be taken, however, not to overly reinforce those qualities partners may present mainly to impress or please others (Lachkar 1992), such as a more narcissistic partner's grandiosity or a more borderline partner's denial of his or her own needs. Individual boundaries can be strengthened by saying such things as, "You have different needs at times, like all couples do," or "Len likes to move forward quickly while Ruth is more careful, and that's fine. You're a good match because you're different." In other words, the clinician consistently conveys that being different is acceptable and that each partner is uniquely worthwhile. These messages counteract both mates' probable childhood learning that they were acceptable only if they were what parents wanted them to be rather than wholly themselves. Many classic narcissistically vulnerable partners describe parental families in which only one child at a time could be "special" or worthy of a parent's love. If they were not "in," with all the dangers of merger and control this implied, they would be "out," or emotionally abandoned. The clinician's message must be a healthier one: that both can be valued without being exploited or giving up their autonomy.

Of course, most classic narcissistically vulnerable partners desperately need help to learn how to handle many of their needs and feelings more constructively. The process can begin by exploring those that are conscious and for which the partners can readily accept help. Still, exploring coping with needs or feelings is likely not to flow smoothly because partners will be extremely fearful of revealing themselves and changing, partly due to justifiable fears that their mates will use what they say against them and partly due to deeper transference concerns. Too, one mate may interrupt exploration of the other's underlying feelings or fears out of his or her own anxiety. Clinicians must be alert to the fears of both and be able to respond with empathy, but also with a conviction that feelings can be handled differently and fears can be understood and overcome. Let us illustrate some of these points by returning to the case of Ruth and Len.

Ruth was trying to explain her anxiety about money since their business was not doing very well and their savings were getting depleted. While she was not conveying any direct blame of Len, he became defensive and said he was tired of hearing about this. Her feelings were irrational since business had begun to pick up a little. Besides, he would support her by digging ditches if he had to. The clinician stopped him and said, "Len, you've been doing a good job of listening to Ruth until just now. I wonder if what she's saying makes you kind of anxious about the business too. That would be understandable, since there are no guarantees no matter how hard each of you is working. Or did you feel Ruth was blaming you?" Len said he might be a little anxious but Ruth was driving him crazy with her constant worrying. Ruth cut in angrily that she had a right to worry, because Len was losing sales by mouthing off to potential customers.

The clinician stopped them and said, "Wait, let's try to understand what's happening here. You're both feeling anxious and frustrated with the business. That's understandable. I'm trying to find some way you can help each other with this but when you escalate, you both get hurt. Ruth, when you feel Len is criticizing you, we've talked about trying to clarify, because sometimes he isn't. Here he was criticizing when he said your feelings were irrational. But you know, another choice is to say, 'I don't like that,' or 'That makes me mad' without criticizing back. Ruth started crying and said she couldn't do that. The clinician asked if doing so felt too scary for some reason. Ruth said yes, it made her feel too weak and vulnerable.

This interview segment shows how interventions to help with communication skills and with partners' coping with needs and feelings go hand in hand in work with classic narcissistically vulnerable couples. Repeated attention must usually be given both to developing new ways of coping and to partners' fears of revealing themselves and changing. For example, it may surprise a clinician to realize that in spite of anger flying everywhere, most such partners are not aware of, let alone adept at, simple assertiveness skills. Part of Ruth's and Len's business problems turned out to be that Len was accepting impossible demands from customers because he did not know how to say no without lashing out. When Ruth and Len finally learned to make simple requests of each other, tell each other when they did not want to do something, and negotiate solutions without getting into a shouting match, their daily lives became considerably less stressful. As another example, partners may be helped to realize that they are prone to feel low self-esteem because of childhood experiences, but that they can be more careful not to trigger it in each other and can learn positive self-talk such as, "I'm an okay person even if I'm not perfect," to reassure themselves.

In all work with these couples, there is typically a "two steps forward, one (or even two) steps back" progression. Gradually the couple will begin to pick up some communication skills and use them in their daily lives. They may sometimes be able to stop the pattern of criticism and escalation at home, but these efforts will not be consistently successful. They can be helped to use self-talk such as, "I don't have to respond to a criticism with a criticism," or "If I feel like criticizing, let me think what I'm really feeling." The clinician must continue to be empathic to their disappointments when change does not come quickly or when they regress (Bader and Pearson 1988). Often, perhaps because of splitting, the partners cannot hold onto the memory of having made some progress and feel totally defeated when things go less well. The clinician can remind them of gains and conceptualize that disappointing times, too, can be expected and understood. The clinician can show optimism about further gains if doing so is realistic.

Deeper Insight Work

Successful work with classic narcissistically vulnerable couples tends to become increasingly insight-oriented over time as partners try more consistently to understand their defenses and mutual fears, especially fears of intimacy. With clinicians' help in "tracking and interpreting the couple's interlocking defensive operations," partners may be able to "work together to understand . . . how these contribute to relationship difficulties" (Seider 1995, p. 375). For example, it is highly likely that partners are dealing with a variety of underlying feelings by their pattern of criticizing each other. These can include anger at each other, specific relationship fears, and feelings of anxiety or low self-esteem having nothing to do with the couple. It can be a revelation to them that the escalation pattern has been an all-purpose means for releasing, and often for projecting, unwanted or unacceptable feelings. The clinician must at the same time empathically establish that no one is to blame, the feelings and needs are understandable, and the partners can make choices to handle these in some other way. Bader and Pearson (1988) suggest that a clinician can help partners prepare themselves emotionally to receive any insights that might be upsetting, such as by warning that what the clinician is about to talk about may be anxiety producing and asking if the partners are ready to hear it.

Many pairs can gradually be helped to get in touch with their likely fears of being engulfed, controlled, or abandoned if they let themselves be vulnerable. These issues must be validated as not making them bad or inadequate, since many people struggle with intimacy fears that have been influenced by their childhood experiences (Slipp 1995). The connection to family-of-origin experiences is at first an intellectual one. Len could fairly quickly realize that he often felt criticized or controlled by Ruth even when she did not intend these things, since his mother was critical and controlling. Again, the nature of transference must be explained and connections to both partners' childhoods made, lest one partner use new insights against the other. Partners must also be explicitly warned not to use painful material learned in treatment against each other either in sessions or at home (Siegel 1992). If there are such attacks, the clinician must focus quickly on what underlying fears or feelings have been stirred up in the attacking mate. As partners gain awareness of their fears and these become less intense, they may become better able to use new communication and relationship skills. For example, in helping with assertiveness, a clinician might say, "You didn't have any good way of fighting back when you didn't like something as a kid, because your [mother/father] was so powerful. But now the person you love isn't out to control you and isn't any more powerful than you. You're not little anymore, and you do have the power to influence [him/her]."

Eventually the insights can become more emotional ones. As partners allow themselves to show some vulnerability and both the clinician and their mates respond differently than they fear, they may become increasingly able to bring childhood learning about needs and feelings to the surface. Ruth and Len eventually recognized that in both their families, if you showed weakness, you were sure to be "ground under." It was therefore no wonder each had to attack the other when feeling vulnerable due to any strong need, feeling, or fear. This understanding helped them see their similarities, feel increased empathy for each other, and have less need to attack to avoid the dangers of closeness. Being able to recognize when they were getting anxious about anything, or when the other might be, also allowed them to cope better by saying they needed some space or would like to move into an exploration mode rather than attacking and again destroying each other's trust.

The pathway to emotional insights may be through dreams, symbolic communication, or direct discussion of relevant childhood events, as with healthier couples. Likely to emerge then in more detail and with more affect attached, as we will see in a case below, are both partners' fears that the other will not meet their needs or will abandon or try to control them. Both are likely to feel that their own needs are bad and make them vulnerable (Lachkar 1992). Being vulnerable, showing needs or fears, or not being perfect are seen as bad and dangerous. A mate whose functioning is more at the level of a borderline disorder may even reveal a fear of fragmentation.

> Gloria and Mark, a fairly healthy classic narcissistically vulnerable couple, were not explosively angry in sessions but constantly picked at each other. Each complained that the other never listened. At first, each solely blamed the other. Gloria reported Mark looking away from her sometimes when she tried to tell him about her day's events. Mark, who tended to talk rather obsessively, told of becoming furious when Gloria could no longer listen and impatiently cut him off. In early sessions, they learned some better ways of responding to each other's needs, such as Gloria telling Mark when she was getting near the end of her ability to listen. Still, their strong feelings in regard to this issue persisted. Both could see a connection to their childhoods, but this intellectual insight was only a little helpful. Gloria realized she had always felt she had to be the strong one, listening to her constantly complaining mother. Mark knew he had tried to get attention from his very busy parents by talking at length whenever he could.
>
> A breakthrough in deeper understanding came later. In one session, Gloria started crying when Mark wasn't perfectly attentive and said, "You're never there for me." Mark began reasonably to point out that he was but the clinician intervened softly with, "Let's just stick with the feelings. What else is coming to mind for you, Gloria? What scene are you seeing—just let your imagination go."

> Gloria said no one was ever there for her as a kid. Everyone was always paying attention to her mother and her sister, also a sniveler. And she blurted out to Mark, "You sound like them. You want all the attention for yourself and I can't have any." The clinician held up her hand to stop Mark, who was about to speak, and asked, "When Mark does give you some attention, what happens?" Gloria began crying again and said, "I want it so badly but I know it won't last. Then I get mad at him for making me start to believe he really cares about me." The clinician added, "So in a way it helps you not get your hopes up too far if you think Mark is going to let you down before he even does." Gloria said after a pause, "I guess so. But do I always have to be disappointed?" The clinician said these needs and fears came from some very painful childhood times, but maybe now the two could find out how they could be healed.

For most classic narcissistically vulnerable partners, the wounds from childhood are deep and the fears intense. Therefore, both may take substantial time in treatment to resolve. Often necessary or extremely helpful is partners having had or concurrently being in individual treatment. A clinician may make a referral if it seems warranted, but should not usually be the one to see partners, because in this type of couple feelings of envy, jealousy, and competitiveness would be likely (Goldstein 1997, Seider 1995). Often complete resolution is not possible in couple work, but partners' needs and fears become less intense and compelling as they are understood, and as the mates begin to cooperate more in handling them.

Finally, it is clearly the clinician's soothing words, empathy, and connectedness with partners that also allow change to happen for classic narcissistically vulnerable couples. The clinician is different from the feared parental transference figure. Some amount of corrective reparenting occurs. The clinician has accepted partners' realistic expressions of pleasure or negative feelings in the treatment relationship but questioned and interpreted splitting, whether shown by idealization or devaluation. Gradually, through more self-awareness and awareness of transference distortions toward both the clinician and the mate, partners' tendencies to resort to splitting and difficulties maintaining object constancy may be somewhat overcome. Their abilities to handle needs and feelings, as well as other communication and problem-solving skills, may have been enhanced. These changes, along with the clinician's conveying that both partners are worthwhile human beings and that their needs and feelings do not make them bad, strengthen their self-acceptance. The more the two can understand, accept, and integrate all the aspects of themselves in spite of imperfections, the less their need to split off unacceptable parts of the self and project these onto each other. This change, along with greater empathy toward the mate and less fear of abandonment, means that each partner can "begin to accept the emerging self of the other" (Bader and Pearson 1988, p. 96). And so the Gordian knot of dysfunctional dynamics is untangled to whatever extent the particular couple is able.

OTHER NARCISSISTICALLY VULNERABLE COUPLE TYPES

Obviously, an individual showing borderline or narcissistic functioning and dynamics may form a couple relationship with a variety of partners. For example, at times a clinician may see a pair in which both mates seem narcissistic or both seem borderline. But neither of these combinations tends to stay together for long. Unless they are receiving considerable approbation from others, two narcissistic partners readily become disenchanted because neither is interested in feeding the other's grandiosity for long. Two borderline disordered mates cannot provide sufficient structure for each other. They tend to show dynamics similar to those of the classic narcissistically vulnerable pair but in more extreme form. Often they break up quickly, although there may be a series of unsuccessful reunions.

More stable and more often seen clinically is the borderline-schizoid couple. Here one mate tends to show schizoid features, such as rigidity and emotional aloofness, and to control interaction by hostility or withdrawal. Object relations theorists assume that schizoid functioning reflects an underlying terror of emotions and emotional connection because of merger fears (Siegel 1992). Yet to be totally unattached may also seem unbearable (Seider 1995). The schizoid mate may be drawn to a borderline partner's apparent willingness to carry the pair's need and affect states, while the borderline partner sees the other's rigidity as able to contain his or her inner chaos and prevent merger. McCormack (1989) suggests that couple treatment with such pairs begin by helping both mates build autonomy through the ability to understand and convey their own needs, followed by insight work on the relationship itself. The latter relies heavily on clinicians' provision of a holding environment in the treatment, interpretation of individual and couple dynamics, and tolerance for slow progress with frequent periods of regression.

In two narcissistically vulnerable couple types I have identified (Nelsen 1995), a more narcissistic or borderline partner forms a long-term relationship with a healthier mate who is overgiving or codependent. Such couples are common. Let us see how their dynamics and treatment needs differ from those of the classic narcissistically vulnerable pair.

Narcissistic-Overgiving Couples

In the narcissistic-overgiving couple, one partner shows all the characteristics and individual dynamics of narcissism described earlier, although full criteria for a personality disorder diagnosis may or may not be met. This partner, who is more often male (*DSM-IV* 1994), may be a good financial provider and attractive, intelligent, or charismatic. Much of his or her time may be spent working, with involvement in repeated superficial affairs or considerable substance use also not unusual. At home the narcissistic partner is likely to be domineering and demanding, with little empathy for others' needs. While his or her ability to give emotionally in the couple relationship has probably never been great, it has usually decreased over time. This mate is likely to be an exciting but unreliable parent, coming into the children's lives with wonderful gifts or extravagant shows of affection but often being physically or emotionally unavailable.

Overgiving mates are so called because they usually end up giving much more than their narcissistic partners to the couple relationship and family. Overgiving partners almost always feel that they are less attractive and competent although the perception may not be accurate. They may show low-level symptoms of anxiety or depression, with these perhaps becoming more noticeable over time. In childhood, such partners tend to have experienced parental loss, deprivation of attention, or excessive criticism, leading to deep-seated struggles with neediness and self-esteem. Still, also usually learned in childhood was that parent figures would meet some of their needs if they were "good," gave a lot, did not ask for too much in return, and suppressed anger.

The overgiving mate's underlying needs and fears of loss or rejection, while not quite so intense as those of the more narcissistic partner, have nonetheless compelled his or her entry into and long-term participation in a dysfunctional love relationship. Both narcissistic and overgiving mates long to depend on someone who will validate them. But both fear being hurt or abandoned if they do not live up to what their childhood experiences lead them to assume are others' expectations of them. Both have a great deal of underlying anger. However, the two handle these similar underlying issues differently and synergistically. When they met, the narcissistic partner probably found the other would give a lot, including unquestioning adulation, without asking much in return. The overgiving partner gained self-esteem through being loved by someone so highly attractive or successful. He or she also perceived the narcissistic partner to be like a strong parent who would be a protector and never leave, while the narcissistic partner somehow sensed that the overgiving one needed the relationship too much to abandon it.

Yet neither of the two would expect real closeness, since having it would make them too vulnerable. They could form an unconscious pact to meet many affiliative needs elsewhere, through involvement with jobs or children and, for the narcissistic mate, possibly through affairs and substances. Each could project unacceptable parts of the self onto the other, where these would probably be accepted. That is, the narcissistic mate could overtly "carry" the pair's anger, sexuality, and need for admiration. The overgiving one could "carry" their dependency, anxiety, depression, and low self-esteem. In this stable manner, the relationship could persist for years.

When such a couple seeks treatment, this synergy has usually broken down. Often some crisis brings them in. Their children may be showing serious problems. The narcissistic partner may have been engaging in psychological or physical abuse. This partner may have been discovered having an affair, his or her substance use may have gone out of control, or the overgiving mate may have turned to one of these diversions after years of emotional deprivation. Children growing up and leaving home can also heighten an overgiving partner's emotional dissatisfaction. Sometimes the narcissistic mate is seeking to end the relationship, having found someone more attractive to bolster his or her self-esteem. More often, after an overgiving mate has been unhappy long enough and has perhaps sought individual treatment, this partner's long-smoldering anger may have begun to emerge. He or she may then threaten a breakup if the relationship does not improve. The narcissistic mate may not really be very interested in changing and may be threatened by the idea of treatment, but may consent to come in because of abandonment fears.

The nature of the precipitant to treatment will influence the clinician's immediate response. When children are having serious problems, sessions may start with the whole family. Violence or a partner's heavy substance use most often requires referral to a specialized program. When one partner has been having an affair or the two have separated, crisis work of the sort to be described in Chapter 9 is initially in order. Whether or not the contact begins in one of these ways, ongoing conjoint treatment may be indicated sooner or later if the couple wants to stay together and try to improve their relationship.

The narcissistic-overgiving couple does not usually argue endlessly, but the narcissistic partner may try to control their interaction both in sessions and at home. Sometimes this partner denigrates the idea of couple treatment or the clinician's expertise. If not too frightened of being abandoned, he or she may blame the mate for the couple's problems. Some narcissistic partners attempt to align with clinicians by acknowledging having done something wrong in the couple relationship, perhaps making a plausible excuse. When an overgiving mate is seriously threatening a breakup, the narcissistic partner may be more conciliatory or repentant in a rigid, limited way.

> Martin and Janice came into treatment when Janice, after enduring verbal abuse and emotional deprivation in a marriage of fourteen years, was threatening divorce. Both were in their fifties. There had been no physical abuse and Martin's drinking, while heavy, seemed to be under control. Martin, a highly successful businessman with a roguish charm, had been married twice before. He and his first wife had fought endlessly. Their relationship finally terminated when she made a bonfire and burned all his clothing one night when he was out. His second wife was very giving, but alcoholic and seriously depressed. After her second suicide attempt, Martin had left her. He considered Janice the emotionally healthiest of his three wives and now, in middle age, he did not want to

lose her. He admitted he should not say the kinds of things he did to her and promised to change. Janice described the relationship as hanging by a thread, as she had already seen a lawyer. Her individual therapist was in favor of ending it. Nonetheless, she was cautiously ready to give Martin a trial period to see if he could change. Even if he did, she was not sure she could ever trust him again.

With narcissistic-overgiving couples, clinicians must again establish structure in the treatment while consistently conveying empathy. As with other couples, they must attempt to reframe the pair's problems such that neither feels blamed but both see the possibility of change. Neither partner can be allowed to dominate. Offering balanced empathy is tricky, however, because empathy expressed to the overgiving mate may seem to cast blame on the narcissistic one and the reverse may make the overgiving mate feel the other is getting off too lightly. The solution can be to credit the narcissistic mate with apparent strengths—such as being a good provider—and interpret these as showing caring, while at the same time expressing understanding that he or she ended up dominating or hurting the partner for reasons not yet understood.

In exploring Janice and Martin's backgrounds, the clinician learned that Janice had come from a stable family. Her mother was not very giving, however, and her beloved father had died suddenly when she was a teenager. Shortly thereafter, Janice had been hurt in a devastating car accident that put her several years behind in school. She had to have a number of surgeries and was left with extensive scarring and a noticeable limp. Considering herself something of a "plain Jane," she had dated very little, although she had once been engaged. She and Martin met through work, and she was immediately attracted to him in spite of a friend's warning that he was "wild." She made a concerted effort to attract his attention at the time his second marriage was breaking up. He found her at first a sympathetic shoulder to cry on, then decided precipitously to propose. He had several brief affairs early in their marriage but had been faithful since. Martin was more reluctant to talk about his history but did say that his mother was a brilliant lawyer who doted on him and used him as a weapon in her fights with his father, a well-meaning but very constricted man.

Usually it is wise to reframe such couples' problems based on what can be learned of their individual and relationship histories. For example, Janice and Martin's clinician ended up suggesting that Janice had gone into the relationship with high hopes, perhaps not realizing how much wariness Martin had about closeness due to his earlier failed marriages. When Martin disappointed her with his affairs and withdrawal, she had tried to reach out to him but could not find a way that worked. Martin, meanwhile, kept Janice at a distance by verbal put-downs and involved himself more and more in his job. The reasons for his behaviors were not yet clear, but the eventual pattern meant that neither was very happy. Treatment was then framed as a place to see whether both would be able to learn how to re-engage in a more mutually satisfying way. Both could accept this conceptualization as a starting point.

It is often helpful to suggest, in early interviews with narcissistic-overgiving pairs, that the partners have gotten out of balance and perhaps out of touch with each other's real needs because of the distance that has grown up between them. The upset they are now experiencing can be an opportunity to find new ways to relate. Immediate changes can be negotiated in their ways of talking to each other or solving day-to-day problems, but deeper changes in emotional closeness will take awhile. Such a framework is realistic. But it also assuages fears by giving the partners, who are almost surely not ready to attempt any real closeness, permission not to change quickly. In our case example, Janice did not really want closeness at the outset because she had so much anger and mistrust of Martin. Her history also gave her reason to fear disaster and abandonment by a man. A month or so into treatment, Martin revealed that his mother had engaged him in an incestuous relationship during many years of his childhood. Although he denied that this experience was harmful to him, it seemed clear that Martin avoided closeness because of fears that if anyone had more control in a relationship than he did, he would be exploited.

Clinicians may have varied but often strong emotional reactions to such pairs. They may be seduced by the narcissistic partner's charm or turned off by his or her attempts to dominate, or both at different times. This partner's selfishness, lack of empathy, or disowning of responsibility for problems may also evoke anger, some of it perhaps tapping into similar issues in clinicians' personal relationships (Solomon 1997). Clinicians may want to cheer on an overgiving mate's expressions of pent-up anger or may try to become the rescuer. The overgiving mate may sometimes seem boring or frustratingly acquiescent. Self-awareness or consultation with other professionals may again be useful in sorting out a clinician's idiosyncratic responses from those that may illuminate the couple's underlying dynamics. Also helpful to keep in mind is that no matter what the partners manifest, both have good reasons for being the way they are and, at some level, both are hurting. This possibility does not mean, of course, that the clinician should permit one partner to continue to hurt the other emotionally or physically.

Ongoing treatment of narcissistic-overgiving pairs, as with classic narcissistically vulnerable couples, combines some reparenting by the clinician, work on communication and problem solving, and insight work to try to help both partners handle needs and feelings less dysfunctionally. Connections can be made to childhood experiences to help them understand reasons for their behavior and why it seems so hard to change. For example, both will usually have trouble learning to assert their needs constructively. The overgiving mate may be afraid of asking for too much and is likely to show anger by withholding and occasional nastiness. The narcissistic partner has probably never experienced an egalitarian relationship and sees the only options as being either one-up or one-down. He or she is likely, during problem solving or discussions of handling needs and feelings, to alternate between making demands and being overly acquiescent. For both partners, learning that they can negotiate but still say no at some point is often an important new lesson.

A significant intervention when the narcissistic partner has shown some minimal empathic ability may be to help him or her understand the hurt the other has endured and be able to offer an apology, if taking such a vulnerable position is possible (Bader and Pearson 1988). The overgiving partner must also be given support to assume responsibility for sharing the likely feelings of hurt and anger.

Martin and Janice worked for a couple of months on Martin's eliminating his verbal abuse and cutting down on his other controlling behaviors. Alternative ways of stating needs and feelings and problem solving about day-to-day issues helped both to communicate somewhat more constructively. Both made some intellectual connections to childhood reasons for their fears of trusting each other, and Janice was validated in having reason to mistrust the changes Martin was making because of their history together. They were enduring an uneasy truce, but no real closeness had occurred and Janice was still very withdrawn and wary. The clinician suggested that it might take a long time for more positive feelings to return, if they ever would. Martin meanwhile was given support for successfully suppressing most of his prior negative behaviors. Eventually the clinician suggested that when they felt ready, it would be important for Janice to tell Martin what it felt like to suffer all those years. The purpose would not be to blame Martin, though he had to take responsibility for what he had done. It was to try to help him understand the hurt and for her to feel understood.

Both partners were reluctant, and Janice was constricted in recounting her experiences and feelings, although her individual therapist was now also in support of her doing so. Martin repeatedly had to be encouraged to try to understand rather than becoming defensive. The clinician often offered reassurance to help both stick with the process. In a breakthrough session, Janice reported a dream in which she was asleep and some men were going to attack her. Martin was with her and it was unclear whether he would be killed as well. She found she could not cry out, and awoke in a panic. The clinician suggested that the dream might be about the process they were trying to go through together. Janice needed to "cry out" about what had happened to her during the years when Martin treated her badly, but maybe she was afraid of his anger if she did. Or she could be afraid of her own anger or of being vulnerable again. In subsequent discussion Janice began to talk about her hurt and angry feelings in a more meaningful way, and Martin made heroic if incomplete efforts to understand. Interestingly, after this session Martin began to re-experience some of his own vulnerable feelings in regard to his sexual abuse. He now agreed he needed more help with this experience and went into individual treatment. The couple also continued to be seen together.

The most positive outcome likely for a narcissistic-overgiving pair comes from significant change in the narcissistic partner, which often requires individual work. Still, in the conjoint treatment, interpretations can focus on the childhood roots of each partner's learning, and especially on their similar or complementary issues. For example, a clinician in another case might suggest, "It sounds like you were both expected to give a lot to your families as kids. In a way you, John, had to be on stage showing off your talents and learned you'd get applause and material things in return. So you keep looking for these and not expecting much else. And you, Mary, knew that if you were dutiful no one would bother you, but they wouldn't give much to you either. I think underneath you're both angry about that. You both want more real affection and validation, but you're pretty scared of getting shot down if you ask for it." Progressing into deeper insights, the same couple might be able to recognize their similar fears of rejection or abandonment if they do not give enough, and of being controlled or "used up" if they do. Both may need to mourn past losses, including the loss of a happy, unencumbered childhood and the loss of hope that their mates can give them all of what they never got then. Having experienced this sadness and anger as cushioned by empathy from the clinician and, if possible, each other, they may be able to work toward greater real closeness in their relationship.

Even if a narcissistic-overgiving couple cannot or does not wish to undertake deeper insights, they can often use treatment to arrive at a more realistic understanding of each other's needs and better ability to negotiate these. The overgiving partner may become more assertive and the narcissistic one able to give up some control, leading to a better if not totally equal balance. The synergy that keeps such couples together may then be more gratifying for each.

Borderline-Codependent Couples

In early sessions with some couples, one partner may seem fairly normal while the other shows evidence of borderline functioning. This partner may show affective volatility in the couple relationship, with anger, anxiety, or depression arising suddenly and sometimes for no apparent reason. He or she is usually very reactive to real or perceived criticism but freely doles it out. Being unreasonably jealous of the mate's other relationships is common. Less apparent but still almost always present are strong reactions to real or threatened abandonment. Sometimes these characteristics are fairly blatant or pervasive, warranting a clinical diagnosis, while in other cases they are more muted or intermittent. Often this partner functions well or adequately outside the couple relationship, although impulsivity and difficult interactions with others may mar relationships with children, at work, or with friends.

Whenever the borderline disordered partner in such a couple is physically stronger or the other mate seems frightened or acquiescent, the clinician should interview them separately to explore for battering. Even a relationship in which a borderline partner holds greater power by means of threats or one-sided psychological abuse may not be appropriate for conjoint treatment. However, in many situations the healthier mate does not seem powerless but has assumed a sort of parental or caretaker role. Because borderline personality disorder apparently occurs more often in women (*DSM-IV* 1994), and men who might warrant this diagnosis are more likely to be batterers or substance abusers, the borderline partner seen in couple treatment with a caretaker mate is frequently female.

The healthier partner, here called codependent, differs from the overgiving one described earlier in having more self-esteem and less willingness to continue giving without getting much in return. Usually this mate's functioning is good at work, in friendships, and as a parent. He or she has often put up with the vagaries of the borderline partner's functioning for some time and has tried to be understanding and helpful, perhaps going to great lengths to try to adjust to the other's needs. In one pair I know, the codependent husband had tried repeatedly to help his somewhat borderline wife deal with her need for reassurance by trying to memorize statements that she had said might be soothing to her. But no matter what he said, or with how much genuine empathy, she would find that his words were not quite what she needed. By the time these couples seek treatment, the codependent partner may have become impatient and angry that such ministrations have not been more appreciated. The pair may be arguing a fair amount. Both may be chafing at what has become an unbalanced relationship, with the codependent mate complaining of always having to be the one to take responsibility and the borderline mate complaining of being treated like a child.

The codependent partner's history will contain clues as to what propels him or her into such a relationship. There was often a major early loss, usually with the partner, as a child or adolescent, stepping in to pick up significant responsibilities for continued family functioning. Or perhaps a parent or sibling required a great deal of care because of alcoholism or health problems and the partner was instrumental in providing it. During these early years, he or she was left with some sense of competence but also with fears of being overwhelmed by family chaos. Anger, neediness, and sometimes other feelings had to be repressed. A mechanism that worked well was to cope by becoming the caretaker and identifying with the person taken care of, thereby vicariously experiencing that projected dependency needs could be met. Nevertheless, later intimacy would evoke the fear that loss or chaos might at any time be imminent.

The codependent partner initially finds the borderline mate appealing because he or she looks like someone who can be rescued. There is the chance again to meet projected dependency needs vicariously while also hoping that the mate will give enough to make up for some earlier deprivation, especially because the codependent partner will perform well in preventing chaos. The borderline partner's freedom with emotions may also provide some vicarious emotional release. Sensing the borderline mate's neediness and abandonment fears, the codependent partner is reassured that he or she will never be abandoned. And the borderline mate seems willing at first to be the carrier, through projective identification, of the other's most feared needs and feelings, including not only dependency but also anger and anxiety.

The borderline partner may at first believe that he or she has finally found the "good other" who will give endlessly without making real demands for closeness. Of course this illusion quickly fades, both because the borderline partner begins to experience merger fears and because the codependent mate cannot possibly live up to such expectations. The borderline partner then finds the other all bad and tries to make him or her the angry one, often succeeding in eliciting anger by criticizing and otherwise being provocative. The relationship may persist as long as the codependent partner, fearing chaos or abandonment, keeps trying to fulfill the borderline mate's expectations of perfect parenting. However, eventually the two are likely to seek help or break up.

In early and continuing sessions with such couples, the clinician must again provide structure and empathy for the treatment to proceed. The difficulty will usually be in controlling the borderline partner's attacks with sufficient empathy so as not to be perceived as taking sides. Clinicians' countertransference will usually be to like the codependent mate better, since he or she presents the couple's problems in a more nonblaming and even mutual way. This partner will usually bond easily with the clinician, partly with relief at relinquishing the parental role the clinician is assuming. Clinicians may need to remind themselves that borderline partners always have valid reasons for being so angry and that they are deeply afraid a clinician will not understand. Often the presenting problems can be conceptualized as something like, "The two of you have gotten into fighting that is painful for both," or "I do understand that this situation where Pat feels like he is carrying too much responsibility and Betty feels like she's being seen as irresponsible is uncomfortable for both of you." Occasionally an individual session or two with each mate will help the borderline one bond better with the clinician. It is usually helpful if the borderline partner is in individual treatment with another clinician. Antidepressant medication may also decrease this mate's volatility.

Again, as treatment progresses, there is usually work on communication and problem solving, as well as at least superficial insight into the influence of childhood experiences. An important early component of work with these couples is often to facilitate understanding and discussion of how the two can cooperate to handle particularly sensitive areas for each.

> Sheila and Joe, both lawyers in their early thirties, had been fighting a lot ever since they became engaged. They had now been married over a year and the problems continued. Sheila said she had fallen for Joe because he always seemed so calm and happy, at least early in their relationship. During their courtship he could always make her feel loved, but now his protestations that he loved her did not make her feel secure. She saw him as unreliable because he would get home late unexpectedly and seemed more invested in co-workers and his job than in her. Even in the initial session, Sheila had trouble letting Joe tell his side of the story and interrupted frequently, attacking him whenever he implied that their problems were mutual or that Sheila might not be totally in the right. The clinician repeatedly tried neutral reframing and offered a number of empathic comments to Sheila, but her reactivity and extreme sensitivity to blame persisted.
>
> Joe admitted he was concerned about what he saw as Sheila's

extreme emotionality. He had attributed it to the stresses of planning for their large wedding, especially since Sheila and her mother had often been at odds during this time and Sheila's whole family would then get involved, mostly to take the mother's side. He had tried to protect Sheila in these situations but it seemed he could never do it to her satisfaction. He assumed and hoped she would calm down after the wedding but she still seemed highly reactive to everything he did, jealous of his relationships with co-workers, and furious when he got home even a few minutes later than expected.

During a few sessions spent mainly gathering more information about the partners' backgrounds, their current interactions at home, and environmental stressors, the clinician tried hard to point out the strengths of both mates and to empathize with the fact that, so far, their marriage was not going as they wished. She acknowledged that Sheila's family seemed to place a lot of pressure on Sheila and that Joe felt bad that he could not protect her from it. She suggested that all new marriages involve some disappointments and readjustments and that they seemed to be going through these. As the sessions proceeded, Joe seemed to be relating easily to the clinician and Sheila began gradually to become somewhat more calm. The clinician suggested they take one issue at a time. What was the most pressing concern for each?

Sheila identified hers as Joe getting home later than expected. Joe could not understand why this was an issue since he was already calling several times a day to tell her his schedule and he always called if he thought he would be delayed more than half an hour. The clinician suggested they all try to understand Sheila's concern rather than put it down and Joe immediately apologized. Sheila could then admit she did not know why but she always got panicky when Joe was late, even a little bit. The clinician suggested that everyone is just more sensitive about some issues than others and there are usually good reasons, which they might look at at some point. She bet Joe would have some of these too. Before she could continue, Joe volunteered that he had always been sensitive to people not liking him or to feeling he was letting them down. The clinician said, "Maybe that's why it's been hard for you to hear why Sheila has trouble with you being even a little late, but let's work on this issue of Sheila's for now." The pair then began to discuss remedies, such as Joe's calling from his cellular phone to tell her when he'd be late at all or leaving it on so Sheila could call him if she got scared.

In this case, the clinician knew from hearing about Sheila's history and more recent stories of what went on with her family that she had good reason for her fears of being abandoned. Her mother would typically freeze her out whenever Sheila would not do what she wanted. Although Sheila would put up a fight, she could never win because the mother would play her siblings off against her, showing them the attention Sheila so desperately desired. Introducing the idea of this connection too soon, however, might frighten Sheila into thinking the clinician was putting her down by making it seem she had a more pathological background and family than Joe did. Keeping a balance between the two partners in this type of couple is extremely important, and the clinician here chose to do so rather than attempt to induce insight for Sheila at this early point. It is always a matter of clinical judgment which path will be more acceptable and helpful to a couple at a given time, but clinicians must be especially sensitive in making these choices when a partner shows borderline functioning. They must also be prepared to offer remediation when, inevitably, they sometimes misjudge.

A shift in couple dynamics such that borderline-codependent partners can begin to move out of too extreme parent and child roles must usually be accomplished on a step-by-step basis. The first step is for the clinician to help a pair identify such a pattern, if they have not already, using neutral words, such as "Jim assuming too much responsibility" or a partner's own words, such as "Ann seeing Jim always taking responsibility for things and so deciding she may as well do what she wants." The couple may be helped to see that their pattern has become more and more extreme over time, if this conceptualization is valid, and may be told each will have to assume responsibility for changing his or her part. Often it is helpful to look at the underlying feelings of the partners that compel their behavior and to help them find other means of handling these.

Peter and Gary, a gay male couple in their forties, frequently argued because Gary considered himself more responsible than Peter and would often tell him what to do or not to do. Peter felt Gary was treating him like a child. However, Peter did tend to mouth off inappropriately to friends and on his job. In treatment, Gary readily admitted that when he thought Peter was going to get into trouble or embarrass him, he would step in to try to control the situation. Peter pointed out that Gary was micromanaging their lives so much it was driving him crazy and making him furious, resulting in frequent angry outbursts. Gary would then become more officious and talk about "Peter's problem with anger" until Peter succeeded in making him just as nastily angry.

The first step in problem solving was to verify that these interactions were highly unpleasant for both. The second was to try to understand what each experienced and thought at these times. With exploration, Gary admitted that he got anxious about what Peter might say or do, especially in front of their friends. The clinician was able to make a connection to Gary's childhood, where his father, a bullying man with sudden mood swings, would tyrannize his family and frequently lose jobs. Once Gary had owned that his reactions were not 100 percent rational, Peter admitted that, besides anger, he always felt demeaned by Gary's interference. He knew from his own therapy that he had a tendency to feel low self-esteem, and Gary's actions made him think Gary saw him as a stupid fool. The clinician affirmed the insights both had shown and asked Gary if he did think Peter was stupid or foolish. Gary said no, Peter was very intelligent but sometimes didn't act like it. Peter was furious that Gary had again put him down.

Over a period of several sessions, the clinician constantly affirmed that both had a right to their feelings of anxiety or anger. But both needed to develop ways of handling them that wouldn't be so upsetting to the other and that would take them out of the parent–child mode. She suggested they discuss what would make Gary less anxious and how he could handle his anxiety differently. Gary eventually identified that his anxiety was highest in regard to Peter's perhaps losing his job or upsetting certain mutual friends when he mouthed off. In discussion, he realized Peter was unlikely to lose his job since his boss had apparently enjoyed arguing with him for years. Peter volunteered that he could be more careful about mouthing off to specific friends if Gary would say before they got together that he was anxious about this possibility, rather than saying something like, "Now be careful what you say to . . ." Gary agreed to do this. They then continued discussion about what

Peter could do when he did get mad at friends and felt like mouthing off.

Once childhood issues have been brought up with a borderline-codependent couple, it is quite helpful if both can be identified as reacting to them, as with Peter and Gary. In the first place, this interpretation will be at least partially valid. Also, having been removed somewhat from the "sick" role, the borderline partner may be more able to acknowledge and discuss his or her own part in the interaction. It can be important for the clinician to try to maintain this sense of balance even though the borderline partner is likely to be responding to his or her childhood conflicts in a more extreme way. The healthier mate will usually not object because he or she is also benefiting from insights gained and, to a degree, from the clinician's secure reparenting. Occasionally there is too much of a shift, with the codependent mate beginning to see himself or herself as quite flawed and more at fault for the pair's problems. Obviously, clinicians must work to prevent or correct this form of imbalance as well.

While all the strategies identified earlier to work on communication, problem solving, and insight may be helpful with these couples, there are often limits to how much insight focus the borderline mate can manage without the other partner's greater capacities creating too much imbalance in the treatment. The healthier and more psychologically minded the borderline partner is and the more similar the two mates' issues, the less potential there is for a problematic skew. The borderline partner being in individual treatment may also help. In a number of cases, however, conjoint treatment may terminate when the two reach a better accommodation without a great deal of closeness. Or the codependent mate, perhaps based on individual work of his or her own, may eventually consider leaving the relationship because it cannot change enough. Another possibility is that the pair will continue in couple treatment indefinitely or return periodically, perhaps because the codependent partner finds it easier to step out of the parental role when the clinician is available to assume it.

CHAPTER

9

Modifications for Special Circumstances

Sometimes clinicians using this book's integrative approach to couple treatment must tailor their interventions to help couples cope with crises or other special circumstances. This chapter reviews three commonly encountered possibilities: recently discovered affairs, separations or breakups, and partners showing mild to moderate depressive or anxiety symptoms. Often these situations are known from the outset of couple work, but sometimes they surface or develop later. In each instance, clinicians must understand what issues arise for partners and how treatment can best be conducted to facilitate positive outcomes.

AFFAIRS

The revelation that one partner has been recently involved in an affair places most couples in crisis (Karpel 1994, Pittman and Pittman Wagers 1995). Both mates usually are terribly upset, with feelings running very high. Both may feel they do not know how to cope. Usually the aggrieved partner does not know whether to try to work out a reconciliation or end the relationship. At best the couple bond is likely to be in extreme jeopardy (Charny and Parnass 1995). A wise couple seeks treatment at such a time. They should be seen as quickly as possible. To be of help, clinicians need to understand what the issues are for most couples—and for this couple—in coping with an affair. They must then carry out a form of crisis treatment that helps the couple move through several necessary coping tasks (Karpel 1994). If this work is successful and the pair wants to stay together, more standard couple treatment may follow.

Issues in Dealing with an Affair

Either sexual infidelity or a significant emotional involvement that does not involve sex but is hidden from the mate can constitute an affair. As discussed in Chapter 3, a partner may have an affair for any of a number of reasons. He or she may be struggling with individual issues, such as feelings about aging or deep-seated intimacy fears. The latter are especially likely if there has been a series of affairs. Some affairs reflect problems in the couple relationship, ranging from fairly simple communication deficits that left a partner angry or lonely to both mates' deeper difficulties with closeness. At times an affair seems unconsciously designed to precipitate a crisis in the couple relationship when it is discovered. Other influences may include peers who condoned or even encouraged an affair, ready availability of an affair partner, substance use, or the like. Usually a number of these factors are operating in combination. Assumed in the discussion that follows is that the affair has been given up and that substance abuse is not a continuing influence requiring specialized treatment.

The exact nature of an affair and the manner in which it was revealed usually affect partners' reactions. In general, one brief sexual liaison is marginally less hurtful than several or a long-term affair that involved much more than sex. However, men and women both tend to believe that sexual infidelity is a more grievous sin for women, while emotional involvement outside the primary relationship is more grievous for men (Glass and Wright 1992). An affair with someone the aggrieved mate knows or who will have continued contact with the transgressor, perhaps at work, is especially difficult. A partner who confesses an affair voluntarily may seem a little less a betrayer than one who is discovered (Karpel 1994). However, the timing of a confession or discovery may add to the pain (Westfall 1995). Out of guilt, the partner having an affair may confess it when the mate has just been especially loving. A discovery may be messy, as when the mate or children stumble on a sexual scene in progress.

Related factors also include what had been happening between the couple while the affair was going on and how the affair ended. Frequently the mate had sensed something was wrong for a while. Yet inquiries, anger, crying, or suggestions of counseling presumably fell on deaf ears. Meanwhile the partner having the affair was lying about where he or she was at given times, whom he or she was with, the reasons for unusual telephone charges, and so on. Many partners report that almost as hard to deal with as the affair itself is the betrayal of trust represented by their mate's frequent lies to cover it up (Pittman and Pittman Wagers 1995, Westfall 1995). The mate's behavior often changed in other ways as well. He or she was probably much more withdrawn and irritable. Sometimes, out of guilt, this partner even became verbally abusive for the first time in the relationship. Often he or she continued the couple's sexual relationship, if only so as not to arouse suspicion. The aggrieved mate may therefore later have to worry about sexually transmitted diseases, including HIV and AIDS (Karpel 1994, Pittman and Pittman Wagers 1995).

Finally, many affairs do not end smoothly. Often a mate who has ended the sexual aspect of an affair is ambivalent about giving up total contact, perhaps because of guilt toward the affair partner or uncertainty as to whether the primary relationship will last. There may be grief at the potential loss of the affair partner (Westfall 1995). The latter may also remain in active pursuit by calling, sending notes or gifts, making threats, or even turning up on the doorstep. Any of these occurrences, or the partner who had the affair showing any ambivalence about ending it, very much compound the aggrieved mate's pain. While struggling to understand what happened and to decide what to do, this mate may be horrified to learn that full termination of the affair is still uncertain.

In response to such vicissitudes, both partners may experience a variety of fluctuating feelings, many dealt with dysfunctionally. Most common for the aggrieved mate are, of course, extreme anger, hurt, and a complete loss of trust (Charny and Parnass 1995, Pittman and Pittman Wagers 1995). There is often a sense of humiliation at not having realized what was going on, especially if other friends or relatives knew (Westfall 1995). It is not unusual for this partner to feel guilt or low self-esteem, thinking that somehow the affair would not have happened if he or she had been a better mate. Sometimes the initial response is numb disbelief. Some aggrieved partners are troubled by intrusive thoughts or even images of the mate together with the person with whom he or she had the affair, reawakening the hurt anew (Karpel 1994).

The aggrieved partner's most constructive way of coping with these feelings or experiences may be to talk about them with a supportive friend, relative, or clinician. However, revealing the situation to a friend or relative risks turning this person against the mate who had the affair, which can be a problem in a later reconciliation. Angry feelings may be dysfunctionally acted out by taking vengeance in some way, perhaps having an affair to "pay the mate back" or precipitously ending the couple relationship (Pittman and Pittman Wagers 1995, Westfall 1995). Denial of any feelings, perhaps along with superficial forgiveness, is also not a good way to cope, because the feelings can resurface later or stay buried to prevent closeness in the long term. By the time the couple comes for treatment, aggrieved partners' feelings of anger and hurt may have been supplanted by grief and perhaps even hopelessness (Westfall 1995). The grief comes not only in response to the affair itself, but also to the perception that the couple relationship can never again be what the aggrieved partner thought it was or hoped it could be.

Meanwhile the partner who had the affair is usually struggling primarily with guilt. However, he or she will often have a number of secondary reactions as well. There may be sadness at the damage done to the aggrieved mate and to the relationship. There may be anxiety that the couple relationship may end (Karpel 1994). If the aggrieved mate has been unforgiving for what seems to the other like a long time, or if he or she has acted out in revenge, there may be considerable anger. Any of these feelings may again be dealt with dysfunctionally. Unable to tolerate the guilt or sadness, this partner may become defensive and blame the aggrieved mate for the affair (Glass and Wright 1992). Sometimes a partner who has had an affair becomes self-abasing, depressed, or even suicidal (Karpel 1994). A common defense is to deny the seriousness of what happened or the validity of the aggrieved mate's feelings. Most helpful in the long term is for the partner who had the affair to deal with guilt by trying to understand why the affair happened and how to ease the aggrieved mate's pain. Listening to the aggrieved mate's feelings and expressing empathy and true remorse are most likely to aid the latter's healing. However, not many partners who have had affairs can respond in these ways without help. What is often not recognized is that the errant partner also needs support. But asking for and finding it may be more problematic because this mate is the guilty party. Finally, this mate too may eventually feel hopeless if the situation remains largely unchanged.

Gender and ethnicity can affect both partners' reactions to affairs. In general, society is somewhat more tolerant of men's affairs and, in some ethnic groups, men's straying is seen as almost expectable (Boyd-Franklin 1989, Garcia-Preto 1996b, McGoldrick et al. 1989). Men's guilt may be less if they feel an affair was primarily sexual and not a serious threat to a couple relationship (Glass and Wright 1992). I have heard men say such things as, "The affair had nothing to do with my marriage," and "I still love my wife, why does she doubt that?" Yet women are virtually always hurt and angry when an affair is revealed. They tend to assume there has been an emotional involvement as well as a sexual one, since women more often consider the former a reason for affairs (Glass and Wright 1992). Women are likely to experience more self-doubt than men in response to a partner's affair (Buunk 1995). If men's affairs are somewhat tolerated in their ethnic group, women may feel that they have no right to protest very much. But they may still rebel, for example, by being too nervous or ill for sexual relations thereafter (Garcia-Preto 1996b).

Partners of both genders almost always view women's affairs as a worse offense than men's (Veroff et al. 1995). Women who have affairs may feel guiltier and more ashamed than men. They are more likely to react with a great deal of self-blame and to have more difficulty justifying their actions to themselves. When a female partner has an affair, a man may feel more enraged, humiliated, or both, than in the opposite circumstance. A woman is more likely to be in physical danger from an aggrieved male partner. In some ethnic groups, including those in which men's affairs are somewhat tolerated, a woman having an affair may well end the couple relationship.

More often than with heterosexual pairs, partners in a committed same-sex relationship may decide that it need not be monogamous (Okun 1996, Schiemann and Smith 1996, Slater 1994). If so, a partner who is not having outside sexual contact may still feel jealous and hurt when the other does, but may fail to express these feelings because of their agreement (Schiemann and Smith 1996). For gay or bisexual men who are HIV-negative, concerns about HIV transmission can arise no matter how careful the nonmonogamous partners are (Brown 1995b). If same-sex partners have agreed to exclusivity, breaching it may cause reactions similar to those of a heterosexual pair. Problems can also result when one partner assumes the two are being exclusive while the other does not. And there are gray areas if the same-sex pair has an agreement that they can have sexual liaisons with others but not become romantically involved. The definition of sexual contact in a relationship may not be totally clear, but romantic involvement is even more difficult to define and may happen unbidden. Partners in same-sex relationships who are upset because of an affair may feel even more confusion than a heterosexual pair about what they should feel or do about it.

Initial Sessions

If a couple presents for treatment soon after an affair has been revealed, clinicians' tasks in early interviews still include gathering information for assessment, forming a therapeutic alliance with both partners, reframing what has happened, and contracting for continued work. However, they must also move quickly to focus on helping the couple stabilize and deal constructively with their situation (Karpel 1994).

> Julie and Tom, both in their mid-thirties, came in after a telephone call in which Julie revealed that Tom had had an affair with a woman where he worked. Julie was not sure what she wanted to do but felt they ought to have counseling. She did not want to end their marriage precipitously because of their child, aged 3 months. Tom definitely wanted to try to repair the relationship. They both arrived at the session looking pale and anxious. The clinician began by saying she knew they were coming in at a terribly difficult time for both, and that it must have been very hard to do so. She did want to understand what had happened, but maybe it would be easier for them to tell her a little about themselves first. In response to questions, they related that Tom was a high school teacher while Julie was a nurse. They had been married five years and had adopted their baby after tests revealed Julie could not have a child. Julie became tearful when she mentioned the fertility problem and the baby.

Typically in the situation of a recently discovered affair, it is helpful if a clinician immediately recognizes that both partners are suffering. The one who had the affair is likely to feel ashamed and very anxious about the possibility of the clinician being judgmental. Clinicians need to be aware of their own attitudes and try neither to condone nor condemn the affair. The aggrieved mate may be experiencing any of the feelings described earlier and want support for them. Sometimes this partner is ambivalent about continuing the couple relationship but does not want the clinician to take sides. Sometimes he or she does want the clinician to castigate the mate, and the clinician must tread carefully to find a middle ground.

> After learning briefly about the early marriage and managing to note some positives from that time, the clinician gently asked if Julie and Tom were able to talk about what happened with the affair. Tom said the woman was another teacher. As he seemed about to tell what had attracted him to her, the clinician intervened and suggested focusing mainly on what had been going on between Tom and Julie or in Tom's head at that time. Tom said he was having some job stresses and they were encountering the fertility problems. He felt like they couldn't talk about either very well. Julie burst out, "If you're trying to blame me for what happened, guess again! Just when I was going through all those awful tests, you were off having your little dalliance." The clinician hastily said she was not trying to ask Tom to justify having the affair. Whatever had been going on for him or between them, having an affair was not a good way to deal with it. She also understood that Julie had every right to feel devastated and angry. She then asked more about the fertility problems and what was happening for Julie during this time.

Clearly the clinician is trying to balance several different goals here. She has some need to gather information about the affair, if at all possible without inflaming the situation more. She needs to reframe what happened in ways both partners can accept and that can lead to a workable definition of the problems. For most couples, a viable reframing is that the person who had the affair had reasons, but that dealing with them in this way has turned out to be destructive and painful for both. Such a conceptualization places responsibility for the affair with the one who had it without being morally judgmental (Karpel 1994). It also contains a seed of hope for the future in that if the reasons can be understood, perhaps they can be remediated and the same thing need not happen again (Pittman and Pittman Wagers 1995). Of course, there is a long way to go before any such outcome is likely. As a third immediate goal, the clinician must try to form an alliance with both mates, usually by not taking sides but recognizing the distress of both.

> Julie stated that when they couldn't seem to get pregnant, they both began going for tests. Tom proved to be okay but she had some problems. Some of the tests were painful and their whole sex life became humiliating and difficult. Tom seemed to withdraw emotionally and she assumed it was because of all they were going through. But she now knew the affair had started then. The clinician responded simply that this must have been a very difficult time. Tom said, "Julie, I did feel for you but I didn't know what to do. Then once I got involved with Jan I just couldn't face you. I know I was a total jerk." Julie began crying and the clinician responded softly, "It really hurts, I know." After a few minutes she said gently to both, "It's natural to be struggling with so many difficult feelings now. Julie is probably confused and angry and hurt and Tom is guilty and neither of you knows what to do. I hope coming here can help you begin to sort out what happened and where you want to go from here." After a pause she added, "I'm also wondering whether you both have the support of any friends or family. That's something people need and yet it's a good idea not to talk to too many people about what's going on." (The interview continues.)

The clinician seeing a couple just after an affair is revealed must make many judgments about what can and cannot be accomplished in the initial interview. Often there can be less assessment information than usual gathered about the partners as individuals and their relationship history. The exception is that serious depressive symptoms in either partner must be explored to rule out suicidal risk (Karpel 1994). No very complete data may be gleaned about how the affair happened or even its aftermath. The partners are too full of feelings and must be helped with them, both to build a therapeutic alliance and to forestall immediate action based on the feelings, such as a premature decision to break up. Even when one or both partners do not seem to be experiencing many feelings, clinicians can suggest that feelings in response to the affair are undoubtedly there and will surface at some point.

Both partners will also need emotional support, and clinicians must try to ascertain whether there is anywhere else besides in the couple sessions they can get it, as the clinician with Julie and Tom does. Obtaining such support is more difficult in the aftermath of an affair than in some other crises because, as noted earlier, friends and relatives are very likely to take sides and may be an obstacle to reconciliation later if they know what happened. The ideal party to give support is usually another clinician if either mate is in individual treatment or wants to initiate it. In any case it is likely that by the time of the first couple session, one or both will have told someone about the affair. The clinician can ascertain whether this experience has been supportive or can encourage both mates to find one or two supportive listeners not likely to take sides. If it is not too late, the latter should be people neither will be too uncomfortable facing later. Another possible course of action is for partners to seek support from others who will be told only that the couple is having problems, without the full reasons being disclosed.

Sometimes a pressing issue during an initial interview is that the aggrieved partner has been feeling compelled to ask for detailed descriptions of what went on during the affair. While he or she has some right to know, too much information can arouse overwhelming pain and anger. Westfall (1995) suggests clinicians ask couples not to engage in such discussions except in treatment sessions, where the aggrieved mate can be helped to understand why he or she is asking and to decide how much is really useful to know.

If either mate's feelings are too much for the partners to handle in joint sessions even with the clinician's help, or if either seems to be in excessive pain without sufficient outside support, the clinician may see the two for some adjunct individual sessions during the peak of the crisis (Karpel 1994). Other reasons for individual work, of course, might be that one partner is having trouble fully letting go of the affair, or that either wants help to consider leaving the couple relationship. In these latter instances, the clinician working with the couple should usually not be the one to see the partners individually. If children are aware of the affair or are reacting to their parents' tension, some discussion of what to tell them or even some family sessions may be indicated (Westfall 1995).

Several other tasks remain before the end of the first interview. The clinician should try to summarize what has been said and point out any strengths in the couple relationship. The pain the pair is experiencing can again be acknowledged. The clinician must ascertain whether the couple is willing to proceed. Sometimes the contract will simply be to form some further impression of the situation during a second session and then arrive at a plan. At other times, the work of further treatment can be outlined, as will be discussed below. Finally, the clinician should explore whether the couple needs any help figuring out how to manage until their next session. For example, they may be trying to decide whether to separate temporarily or how to handle a family event coming up in the interim period. A couple who wishes it may be seen for the second session within the next few days.

Subsequent Treatment

In most cases, clinicians can glean enough sense of a couple and their situation by the end of a first or second interview to have some ideas themselves why the affair may have happened. They may also be able to judge preliminarily whether there is much hope for resolving it successfully and preventing a recurrence. Most hopeful is a situation in which affairs have not been chronic, the partner who had the affair seems genuinely remorseful, the relationship has noticeable strengths, and both partners wish to see if it can be saved. While clinicians' judgment is not infallible, any optimism they can justifiably share is usually helpful to the couple.

> In the second interview with Julie and Tom, Julie discussed more of her anger and hurt because Tom not only had the affair, but lied about it when she questioned him. She also felt like such a fool because two friends of theirs knew about it when she didn't. The clinician continued to say this was a very painful time and eventually added that she knew Julie's feelings must be hard for Tom to hear. Tom began to cry at one point and said he couldn't believe he'd caused Julie so much pain. When the clinician acknowledged his crying, Julie said, "You're giving him support when he's the one who did something wrong!" The clinician replied, "I want

to give you both support because you're both suffering now, although I know you're probably suffering more." Tom asked Julie if she thought she would ever be able to forgive him. She said she didn't know. The clinician added that she might not know for quite a while. Meanwhile, they needed to think about how they wanted to proceed. She herself thought it was a hopeful sign that although they were both hurting, they were able to come to the sessions together and talk about what had happened. Of course, there were no guarantees. Julie said she was not ready to make any decision now. Tom asked what they were supposed to do.

In any crisis, people tend to feel frightened of the feelings they are facing, overwhelmed, and confused about what they need to do to cope (Karpel 1994). The crisis following the discovery of an affair is no different, and it can be very helpful for the clinician to outline and assist with coping tasks, as Julie and Tom's clinician now does.

In response to Tom's question, the clinician suggested that they see the treatment as a place to accomplish several things. First, they were both struggling with a lot of feelings in response to what had happened and most likely could use some continued help to sort out and deal with them. Julie and Tom both nodded. The clinician went on to say that, very naturally, they didn't know yet how all this would affect their relationship in the long term. It couldn't help but have a significant effect, but that didn't necessarily mean they could never have a good relationship again. It was too early to tell, but eventually the treatment might be able to help them figure this out. Tom broke in saying, "Julie, please stay with me. I don't want a divorce." Julie said she was confused and didn't know what she wanted.

The clinician stated that part of figuring out where they would end up involved dealing with their feelings, especially Julie's, but another part for most couples was to try eventually to figure out why the affair happened. This was not to blame anyone but to understand so they could feel confident it wouldn't happen again. Tom interrupted that he would never do such a thing again. The clinician said, "I'm sure you mean that. But it's not good anyway to have things going on between you or within either of you that will tend to drive you away from each other. Like not being able to talk about problems, as you mentioned last time." Julie said,

"It's so painful to talk about what happened, I don't know if I can." The clinician reassured her that these discussions could proceed at the couple's own pace and wouldn't happen all at once.

After some further talk about these topics, the clinician suggested that the first thing to work on might be deciding on a modus operandi for their relationship during this interim time. For example, who should be told about what happened, how they can manage in the house together, and so on. Julie said they are sleeping in separate rooms. The clinician said this brings up another issue that needs to be addressed, painful as it is. If Tom did not use condoms during the affair, she would suggest they not have intercourse without condoms until he can be tested for all sexually transmitted diseases. Some of these might not show up for at least six months. Tom quietly said, "Oh my God," followed by, "But Jan isn't promiscuous." Julie asserted, "No way" at the same time the clinician added, "You have to be totally sure for everyone's sake."

Over the course of treatment following revelation of an affair, the tasks outlined by Julie and Tom's clinician may be interspersed in every interview. To summarize, these include dealing with both partners' feelings, working out an interim way of functioning together, figuring out why the affair happened, and eventually deciding where the relationship should go. If the pair decides to try to save the relationship, they can then work on communication or other problems that may have contributed to the affair. Early sessions usually focus more on dealing with feelings and working out how the couple will manage their life together while their relationship remains in limbo (Westfall 1995). Clinicians will probably need to explore both mates' feelings and offer a great deal of support and normalizing, including warning that different feelings may alternate in fairly rapid succession. Another strong possibility is that a clinician will have to try to interrupt the mates' dealing with feelings in ways that could be destructive or dysfunctional. For example, the two might get into a repeated blaming-placating cycle that acts out but does not resolve their anger and guilt. Or the two may collude in denial of feelings that almost surely are there. Eventually, the partners may be able to hear each other's feelings, the most constructive response. It is especially important that the mate who had the affair be able to convey having heard and understood the other's hurt and anger.

Partners' efforts to decide how to conduct themselves during the interim period before resolution is reached can also arouse emotional issues. One of the most difficult is what to tell children who are old enough to notice their parents' upset, the extended family, and friends who are often anxiously wondering what is going on. The couple may disagree and may need to have some problem-solving discussion to decide. It may be necessary to let the aggrieved mate have somewhat more say in these situations since the affair has usually left him or her feeling so powerless in the relationship. However, the clinician can judiciously question any potential decisions that may lead to trouble later. Routine differences between the mates on how to handle money, their children, housekeeping chores, and so on will often cause even more aggravation during this time. One benefit is that the couple can be taught some communication and problem-solving skills in the course of making at least temporary decisions, unless feelings are running so high that little constructive discussion is possible.

The task of figuring out why the affair happened usually begins to take a more prominent focus after three or four sessions (Westfall 1995). Sometimes it is still too painful then and must be delayed even longer, tackled very slowly, or partially accomplished in individual interviews. In couple sessions, clinicians again must keep a careful balance in exploring reasons. They must help the couple identify how their possible difficulties with communication or unresolved problem areas may have contributed but also get to any individual issues on the part of the mate who had the affair, all without stirring up further anger and blame. In the case of Julie and Tom, the pair eventually acknowledged that they had been unable to talk about their fertility problem and give each other support, while the clinician suggested that doing so is often very hard for couples. Tom "owned" that it had always been hard for him to talk about problems, especially when they involved feelings, and that he had been guiltier of withdrawing from discussion of the fertility problem than Julie had. The clinician could then express some conviction that their communication and Tom's ability to hang in and talk about feelings were areas that could be worked on in treatment and very likely improved. Julie volunteered that she did not know what to do when Tom withdraws and that she probably becomes more demanding.

It is fairly typical, as with Julie and Tom, that discussion of why an affair may have happened leads to an examination of couple and individual problems that need attention if the relationship is to improve. The partners can usually then be given the option to recontract to work on the couple issues, such as the need for better communication and problem solving. In some instances the partner who had the affair will also need individual treatment to resolve issues that may otherwise prevent a healthy couple relationship. Feelings about the affair and decisions on how to handle repercussions also continue to need intermittent attention in the couple sessions. For example, any happening that reminds the aggrieved mate of the affair, such as a song that played on the radio the night he or she learned about it, may continue to trigger a flood of painful feelings and memories (Westfall 1995). When additional trauma went on along with an affair, such as a lengthy period of verbal abuse toward the aggrieved mate, he or she may need individual treatment, and healing between the couple may take much longer or never fully happen.

One outcome of successful treatment of an affair is usually that the aggrieved partner experiences some amount of trust returning (Westfall 1995). It is based on feeling that the mate is truly remorseful and, of equal importance, that the mate or the couple's functioning has changed such that the mate would not deal with problems in this manner again. The aggrieved mate will never forget or even perhaps fully forgive what happened, but the feelings about the affair may gradually recede and be replaced by a belief that things have meaningfully changed. Also of some help can be a promise that if the partner who had the affair ever feels the inclination again, he or she will "blow the whistle" by bringing up the problems that might be leading to it. In this way the couple could deal with them, or at least the other mate could be forewarned. The outcome in cases where one partner has had an affair is varied. Sometimes the relationship cannot be repaired, but with a clinician's help the couple can part constructively.

SEPARATIONS AND BREAKUPS

When a recently separated couple presents for treatment or two partners move to separate domiciles during the course of treatment, the pair is again usually in crisis. However, initiating a separation can represent a constructive effort to cope with severe relationship problems while these are worked on in treatment (Kovacs 1994). Even after months of being separated, some couples ask for help to try to reconcile. Finally, some partners at some point in treatment initiate not just a separation but a permanent dissolution of the relationship. Excluded from consideration below are situations in which there is violence or the threat of violence, substance abuse, or stalking. However, clinicians should be aware that all of these become more likely when one partner initiates a separation or breakup the other does not want.

Issues in Dealing with Separations and Decisions to Break Up

A separation virtually always signifies a severe rift in the couple relationship, even if partners have not made a clear decision to break up. The rift has sometimes been caused by one salient event, perhaps discovery of a recent affair or a secret from one partner's past, such as a past affair or past trouble with the law. More often it results when couple interaction has been so painful—whether due to intense arguing, verbal abuse, severe differences about handling children, or something else—that at least one mate cannot stand for it to go on. Another possibility is that partners have become very discouraged about problems in their relationship whether or not their day-to-day lives together have been terribly disruptive. In most separations, at least one partner is not sure he or she wants to stay in the relationship but may not have made a clear decision.

A host of factors influence how partners respond to a separation in which reconciliation may still be possible. Key among these are the perceived reasons for it, whether only one partner wanted it, how the idea was initiated, and how the separation is carried out. If the main reason for the separation is one partner having done something the mate perceives as a serious affront, including having hidden a dishonorable secret, the mate is usually very angry and hurt. As with affairs, there is a double blow. Besides whatever was the original transgression, the lying or secrecy about it destroys the crucial relationship quality of trust. The mate who kept the secret may feel guilty, or defensively angry that the partner is "making too much" out of something that may have happened a long time ago.

When a relationship has been characterized by painful interaction, partners may be holding considerable anger toward each other. It is very likely each perceives the other as more to blame. They may have gotten to the point of frequently saying mean, hurtful things to each other. There may have been one-sided verbal abuse. One or both may have threatened to leave the relationship, perhaps in an ugly way, such as by vowing to hurt the other financially. At times couples who separate are mainly exhausted from trying and perhaps nearly out of hope that they will be able to overcome serious relationship problems. Indeed, coming for couple treatment may represent their last hope.

If only one partner wants a separation, as is often the case, the other usually feels threatened and anxious. He or she may respond by meek acquiescence, pleading, or other efforts to evoke guilt. There may be considerable anger and attempts to bully the mate. Sometimes these reactions forestall or end a separation but leave the partners still far apart emotionally. Some separations are initiated after considerable discussion, but many are not. Especially difficult for one mate is the other's insisting on a separation or actually leaving precipitously without being willing to talk about other options. Also likely to be suffering are partners who do not want a separation but believe that they have nonetheless caused one, or those who fear that the mates who initiate separating are not sharing their true reasons or intentions.

Separations can be carried out in a variety of ways. While a decision to abstain from sexual relations or move to separate bedrooms can be considered a separation, these instances do not create the full range of issues that a move from a common domicile does. The latter requires, first and foremost, finding a place for the partner who leaves. Occasionally a partner will not reveal where he or she is going, usually to stay with someone of whom the mate disapproves. More often this partner stays with a known friend or extended family member, who must be told at least that the couple relationship is in serious trouble. Moving to a hotel or motel and eating out are expensive, but renting a new place to live signifies more permanence. In any of these circumstances, it will still be necessary to tell a few people about the separation or keep up an elaborate telephone charade. Of course, children must also be given some explanation.

During the separation, a host of new emotional and pragmatic issues can arise. While partners will have some respite from what may have become their painful interaction, both may find themselves facing new anxieties about what people will think, how they will manage financially or emotionally, and whether the relationship may end. They may or may not have others to turn to for needed emotional support. A partner who did not want the separation may feel sadness or even serious depression, with some danger of suicide. As with affairs, it is highly likely that some of these emotions will be handled dysfunctionally. A partner who feels ambivalent or guilty about having initiated the separation may vacillate between righteous anger at the other for protesting and passive acquiescence to the other's demands, perhaps eventuating in the two getting reinvolved sexually. Partners used to having their mates meet most of their needs are especially likely to push for reconnection or give in to it, often leading to confusion for the other mate (Kovacs 1994). The two may even openly get back together and separate again several times, adding embarrassment about what others may think to the difficult emotions they must already manage.

There are also many practical issues to resolve at a time when the two are rarely adept at constructive problem solving. These include making decisions about what to tell other people, how to manage finances, child-care and visitation arrangements, and circumstances under which the two will spend time together (Kovacs 1994). Sometimes an additional issue is whether the two will date others during the separation period. Often a concern of married partners is whether the other might be meeting with a lawyer while reconciliation is uncertain. Indeed, such matters as who left whom and how money and child custody are handled during a separation may influence the terms of a possible later divorce (Walsh et al. 1995).

Finally, couples who want to see if their relationship can be repaired also have to try to address whatever problems caused the separation and eventually decide whether they can be resolved. They may seek treatment to do so.

The longer any separation has gone on, the more likely the original emotional upset and practical issues will have been dealt with, whether well or poorly. When they have been, the couple is no longer in crisis. However, remediation of the problems that caused the separation and the ultimate fate of the relationship may still be uncertain. I have dealt with a number of couples who have been separated for many months, or even divorced, when they came for treatment because they were not ready to give up on their relationship. They still had some hope it could be repaired, or at least wanted to give it every chance. In one case, the two had seen each other only a few times in six months when they met for dinner and the theater to use their season theater tickets. Amazingly, they did end up successfully rejuvenating their marriage.

Whether after a period of separation or not, some partners sooner or later move toward breaking up. If they do so while being seen in couple treatment, one or both may simply say they have made up their minds, ask for help in individual or conjoint sessions to make a decision, or display behavior that implies increasing disengagement. In the latter instance, as noted in Chapter 3, clinicians may try in conjoint sessions to open honest discussion of where both partners stand or may offer them individual time as a prelude to doing so. Such sessions may help partners sort through the inevitable confused and conflicted feelings that contemplating a breakup brings forth and enable them eventually to make the best choice (Walsh et al. 1995). One partner's serious ambivalence or clear decision to break up will usually cause great upset for the other unless the other is feeling the same way. Both mates will have to deal with all the issues separating couples face as well as their emotional reactions to the ensuing final loss of the relationship. For couples with children, and for all partners with financial entanglements, the need to settle custody or money issues may constitute further complex and often daunting tasks.

Let us consider how treatment may proceed when partners separate with some apparent hope of reconciling before reviewing clinicians' appropriate responses when this hope has died.

Treating Couples Dealing with a Separation or Breakup

In initial contacts with separating or recently separated couples who still want to work on their relationship, clinicians must again do a fast assessment of what is going on and try to form an alliance with both mates. They must work to define the separation constructively (Kovacs 1994) and be prepared to focus quickly on how the couple can cope. The latter tasks are also necessary if a separation with no clear intent to break up occurs later in a case. Partners who initiate treatment after being separated for a while can usually benefit from more standard beginning interviews and couple work, except that an explicit goal will almost always be to determine the future of their relationship.

Carol called for an initial appointment with the information that she and her husband Jim had separated the week before, when she became totally disgusted waiting for him to make up his mind about whether he wanted to work on the marriage. Carol had initiated the separation, which Jim did not want, and he had agreed to come for counseling with the hope that she would take him back. Jim was staying with his sister and her husband. The couple's children, boys aged 3 and 6, were scared and upset.

At the first appointment, the clinician said that she knew from Carol that they had recently separated. She wanted to hear more from both of them about what had happened, but asked for a little basic information first. This inquiry revealed that Jim was a musician and Carol taught school. Both were 35. They had met a few years after college and had been married eight years. The clinician said she knew this might be painful to talk about, but she needed to ask what had led to the separation. Carol burst out angrily that Jim had been having doubts about whether he wanted to be in the marriage for at least the last six months. She felt they could solve their problems if each would try a little harder, and she would like to do so. The clinician turned to Jim and asked his perception of the situation. Jim replied, "Well, I have to own up to being the bad guy. I'm just not sure whether we can work this thing out."

The clinician inquired about how each saw their problems and learned that they had many differences. Carol liked to talk things over whereas Jim did not. He felt bullied and nagged, while Carol felt he was immature, bordering on irresponsible, and always wanted things his way rather than being able to compromise. The clinician asked and learned that they had had no couple treatment before. She then noted that in spite of these problems, Carol had said she wanted to work on the marriage, Jim had not wanted to move out, and they had come in together. This would seem to indicate that there were some positives or something holding them together—was this valid? Carol became tearful and said she still loved Jim. Jim said he was not sure where he stood. He was worried about the kids, and he knew Carol had many positive qualities. In many ways, she was good for him because he did tend to let stuff go and she was always on top of things.

The clinician asked if Jim was saying he wasn't sure the problems between them could be solved, but he also wasn't sure they couldn't. He said he guessed that was about where he stood. The clinician asked if he felt it would be useful to talk with someone individually about his uncertainty and he said no, he was talking quite a lot with his sister and her husband, who were on the side of giving counseling a chance. The clinician asked, "Jim, do you want to give it a chance?" He thought a minute and said, "Yeah, I guess I do, at least for now." Jim denied any specific concerns about coming to treatment when the clinician inquired. When she asked what possibly constructive purpose each saw the separation as serving for them, Carol quickly said she really wanted to use it to make a decision about whether to continue the marriage or end it. She did not want to stay in limbo any longer. Jim replied that he still didn't think being separated was necessary, but he had to agree it was making him think more about what they should do. The clinician added that being separated did sometimes help people think more clearly and gain energy to work on relationship issues.

She next wondered how the two of them were handling the separation emotionally. Were they managing okay? Did they have some support? Both said they were okay. She noted that there are some practical matters to be solved when two people are living apart—such as financial arrangements, visitation with the kids—and she wondered if they might need immediate help with any of these. Carol said Jim has agreed to keep paying his share of their expenses but she does wonder what they should do about his seeing the kids and what they should tell them. (The interview continues.)

In doing a quick assessment of separating or recently separated couples, clinicians must always be concerned about whether either partner is having significant emotional distress warranting extra individual or conjoint sessions, a referral, or even a suicide evaluation. Normal emotional reactions can be elicited and validated. Another immediate issue, of course, is whether both partners want to work to see if their relationship can be repaired, still something of an unresolved question with Jim. Carol and Jim's clinician might push the possibility of individual sessions harder to explore Jim's feelings if he proved uninvested in the couple work; it is conceivable he might be having an affair. Insofar as possible, it can be useful to reframe both a separation and a couple's problems constructively and point out positives. If there is time, pressing practical issues can be addressed, as with Carol and Jim. A special concern is helping the couple decide what to tell their children, perhaps warranting a family interview (Kovacs 1994). At the end of an initial couple session, a clinician should summarize what has been discussed, outline a possible way to proceed, and ask if the couple is willing. Usually, the goals of further treatment can be defined as coping with emotions and practical matters ensuing from the separation, defining what would have to change for the relationship to be repaired, and working to see if positive changes can indeed be achieved.

In their second session, both Carol and Jim seemed reluctant to begin. The clinician wondered gently if something had happened that they were having a hard time talking about. Carol blushed and said, "This is really embarrassing, but I let Jim stay over two nights last week." She explained that she had felt somewhat more hopeful about the marriage after the initial appointment, had been lonely, and the kids were pestering her for Jim to come home. The clinician reassured her that she need not feel embarrassed, as these things can happen when people are feeling vulnerable. Carol said it really wasn't a good idea though. She felt worse later and the kids were upset when he left again. The clinician suggested that it's hard to handle your emotions when everything is up in the air and she wondered how both were faring. Carol said she has been talking a lot to one of her friends. Jim persisted that he was okay but he really doesn't understand why they have to be separated while they work on the marriage. Carol said, "Well, you weren't working on it while we were together, and when you were over those two nights you tried to persuade me not to come back to counseling."

Now it was Jim's turn to look embarrassed, and the clinician said she knew this was hard for both of them. She would like to hear about Jim's feelings about coming in. Had he been upset or concerned about something that had happened in the initial session? Jim shrugged, saying, "No, but I guess it's easier for me just to drift than to deal with this whole thing." The clinician asked if they wanted to discuss reconsidering whether to move back in together and Carol said no, she was even more resolved now that they have to do this apart. She did wonder under what circumstances she and Jim should see each other besides when he came to pick up the kids. The clinician suggested they might want to spend some structured time together and they could discuss the possibility here. But probably their most important task was to start defining the problems in the relationship more clearly and beginning to work on seeing if they could be resolved. (The interview continues.)

Again, as with affairs, clinicians must be prepared to help separated couples with a variety of emotions and decisions, such as the issue Carol and Jim raised about how much and what kind of contact the two should have. Two further decisions eventually needed in the case of Carol and Jim were whether they should date others and whether each should see lawyers about the possibility of divorce. Although Jim claimed he had not been having an affair, he thought after a month of separation that he wanted to date other women "just to see what it would be like and whether it would help me make a decision." Jim had seemed reasonably invested in the couple sessions and had shown some ability to compromise with Carol on decisions regarding money and the children. But his preference was always to make the decisions himself or "just let them happen" rather than have to talk about them. Carol was at first devastated by the idea of Jim dating others, then decided that she would too. Obviously, such a development does not bode well for a couple reconciling, although it sometimes does not preclude this. As soon as Jim started dating, his participation in the couple sessions became perfunctory and Carol moved to initiate divorce.

One issue clinicians may need to face while a married couple is separated is the possibility that one or both partners are seeing lawyers. Doing so is a natural precaution but tends to move them further away from each other emotionally. An attempt at honest, nonjudgmental discussion in sessions may help partners sort out the pros and cons, perhaps to arrive at an agreement that they will see attorneys only to gain information and protect their rights. Still, either doing so may make the other justifiably anxious. Clinicians should be familiar with relevant laws in their locality but not give legal advice (Walsh et al. 1995). They should not discourage separating or separated couples from seeking legal consultation, and should encourage one partner to do so if the other will or already has.

In optimal situations, couples may begin to repair significant relationship problems during a separation and perhaps also learn that each can be competent and self-reliant individually (Kovacs 1994). A task at some point then will be helping them decide when to move back in together. Clinicians may encourage couples in which women are gaining more equitable power during a separation not to reunite too quickly (Brooks 1991). For any couple, doing so is usually appropriate when some problems have been worked out and there is some certainty they will stay together. However, financial considerations or partners' emotional needs may press them to make the move sooner. If needed and feasible, the clinician can help a pair decide on interim arrangements, such as perhaps staying in separate bedrooms for a while. Once a pair moves back together, there will be another period of readjustment, perhaps exposing some difficulties not evident when they were living apart. In addition, there may be feelings about whatever has happened during the separation period, such as one partner dating without the other's knowledge or mistreating the other financially. In any case, couple treatment should continue after a couple reunites.

Whenever one or both partners in a couple relationship reach a clear decision to break up, whether suddenly or after lengthy effort and discussion with the mate, clinicians should offer to help both deal with a series of tasks. One can be to review the reasons for the decision and begin to create a "divorce story" that may ease their transition out of the relationship (Walsh et al. 1995). Clinicians can encourage both mates to salvage feelings of self-worth by validating whatever efforts they have made to reconcile and trying to help them reframe the end of the relationship as no one's fault. An example might be, "Neither of you really had a very good idea of how to communicate effectively when you got together and, unfortunately, the problems this caused seem to have gone on for long enough that Bill's feelings of love could not survive." Or if one partner did have a larger role, as perhaps when one had an affair, the clinician may say this partner was dealing with difficult issues in ways that ended up making the continuance of the relationship impossible. Couples themselves may create plausible reasons for a breakup, such as, "We grew apart," or "We were too different," and clinicians should usually support these if they allow both partners to feel less guilty, inadequate, or angry.

Another major task, of course, is to help both mates deal with their feelings (Walsh et al. 1995). Doing so may prevent their behaving in ways destructive to each other or their children and, eventually, help them mourn the loss of the relationship and move on. Mates may be warned that they will have a variety of fluctuating feelings and that they will probably do and say things they are sorry for later if they do not work to manage these feelings constructively. Other necessary tasks are to cope with the myriad arrangements and decisions needed to proceed.

Couples can be encouraged to continue conjoint sessions with the express purpose of accomplishing all these tasks to work out an amicable dissolution of the relationship. Counseling in regard to divorce or breakup of a long-term relationship, especially when there are children involved, is beyond the scope of our discussion here. A good review may be found in Walsh and colleagues (1995). Individual sessions with one or both partners may also be indicated, although the couple clinician cannot realistically offer long-term help to both. An issue may then be who gets to continue seeing the clinician and who must terminate. Often the partner who has initiated the breakup is willing to let the other continue out of guilt.

PARTNERS' MILD TO MODERATE DEPRESSION OR ANXIETY

Studies suggest that up to half of all women whose marriages are conflicted are clinically depressed (Sayers et al. 1993). The prevalence of anxiety disorders in the general population during a one-year period is approximately 12 percent (Maxmen and Ward 1995). Given these data, it is not surprising that, in couple treatment, one or occasionally both partners may turn out to suffer from depression or anxiety. Sometimes a clear enough symptom picture exists to warrant a clinical diagnosis, but with no dangerous risks of the type identified in Chapter 3. At other times, some anxiety or depression is evident but it is mild enough and understandable enough, given the partners' interaction or circumstances, that a diagnosis is probably not warranted. The couple may still be having trouble dealing with these affects, however.

Discussion below considers cases in which a partner's depression or anxiety is chronic or has arisen in the course of the couple's usual interaction, rather than those in which serious rifts in the relationship, perhaps stemming from an affair or battering, have been the cause. It also assumes that the partner's symptoms are not severe enough to warrant any emergency response.

Assessing Partners' Symptoms

When partners in couple treatment show mild to moderate anxiety or depression that is not being treated, clinicians must perform enough assessment to determine whether further evaluation, either with them or someone else, is warranted. Yet, if possible, they may try not to focus so much attention on these symptoms that their alliance with both partners or the framing of the couple's problems as mutual are called into question (Sayers et al. 1993). One way to proceed is to ask about the presence of anxiety or depression in both mates when the issue arises. Another is to examine more closely the situations in which one of these affects occurs, especially within the couple interaction (Craske and Zoellner 1995, Sayers et al. 1993). These were the tactics used in the case of Linda and Jake.

> Linda and Jake were a working-class couple in their middle twenties, due to get married in six months. Linda had pressed Jake into trying couple treatment because of their frequent arguments and he had agreed to come for at least four to six sessions. In their second interview, Jake complained that Linda was crying a lot and he felt she was doing it to manipulate him. The clinician asked both to tell more about the crying and when it happened. They agreed it usually followed one of their arguments. Linda related that she cried because Jake would say such mean things to her and she had begun to wonder if their whole married life was going to be like this. She denied doing it to manipulate him, saying that she always tried to keep herself from crying. The clinician asked if Jake also felt sad after their arguments and he said he did not. However, when the clinician pressed as to what he did feel, he said he usually felt guilty about losing his temper, then mad at Linda for making him feel that way. The clinician said that clearly their arguments were taking a toll on both. She wondered if Linda was feeling sad or depressed at other times or if her sadness was affecting her in other ways, like keeping her from doing things she needed to do. Linda said no to both questions, but added that she did hope they could

find a way to stop the arguing. The clinician suggested they begin to work on this, if they both felt ready to do so.

When a partner's mild anxiety or depression seems reactive enough to couple problems that it may remit if the latter improve, clinicians may decide to try initially to work on these problems and see what happens. They must still monitor the anxiety or depression, however. If Linda and Jake keep arguing in spite of treatment interventions, their clinician can ask both whether the arguments are still getting them down and specifically inquire about Linda's crying. Another tactic is to work first on the component of a problem to which the symptoms may be most reactive. In the case of Linda and Jake, it is appropriate anyway to focus on the pair's communication during arguments and, as part of this, to try to stop Jake from saying mean things.

Another way to deal with one partner's mild anxiety or depression that is apparently reactive to couple problems, but also perhaps a characteristic personal way of responding, is to normalize it by saying that this partner seems to show his or her distress in this particular way. The groundwork is then laid to ask or suggest how the other responds to stressful situations. Linda and Jake's clinician might suggest that perhaps when Jake felt guilty or angry he said mean things to Linda as a way of dealing with these uncomfortable feelings. A benefit of this way of conceptualizing troubling affects and behaviors is that both partners may be helped to notice, whenever they are feeling or acting in their characteristic ways, that perhaps something has happened between them that they need to handle more constructively. It could be suggested that Linda tell Jake she does not deserve to be put down when she finds herself feeling like crying and that Jake tell Linda he needs to take a break from arguing when he feels like putting her down. Of course, one hopes that work to improve the couple's communication might eventually prevent so much arguing.

At times a partner's anxiety or depression does seem to require further evaluation to see whether a diagnosis is warranted or additional help of some kind is needed. Possible choices are then to suggest the partner make a separate appointment with the clinician or someone else, conduct an evaluation in the couple session, or even proceed to identify the disorder and review treatment options such as medication. Factors to be weighed in making these decisions include the partner's probable diagnosis, the clinician's estimate of how both partners might respond to discussing the condition together, and the wishes of the symptomatic partner.

Sometimes both partners are quite aware of one mate's symptoms and seem clearly able to discuss them without taking a blaming or guilt-ridden stance. For example, a depressive affect may be seen as just "who she is" or "something he's suffered with for years." Yet the partners may not know that such difficulties as having trouble concentrating are part of the depressive symptomatology and may not realize some of the effective treatments for depression that are now available. In such an instance, the clinician may ask a partner showing symptoms whether he or she would be comfortable taking a little time in the couple session to evaluate them further and perhaps discuss treatment possibilities. An individual session for this purpose should be offered as an alternative if the partner prefers it. When a couple's ability to talk constructively about one mate's symptoms seems questionable, a clinician who felt these warranted further evaluation might set up separate appointments with each partner for the stated purpose of learning more about them as individuals. This would have been the likely next step with Linda and Jake, had Linda's depression persisted or been more severe.

In cases where a partner's symptoms may signal posttraumatic stress disorder, or when one mate has apparently hidden or downplayed symptoms, the clinician should usually opt to see the partners individually for further evaluation. For example, a partner may have been reluctant to reveal the presence or frequency of flashbacks, depressive symptoms, phobias, or compulsions. In individual sessions, the clinician may be able to support the symptomatic partner in eventually revealing more to the mate or may learn from the mate that he or she already knows but has been unsure how to broach the topic. Likely to require especially sensitive handling in a symptomatic partner's individual sessions are earlier experiences of rape or childhood sexual abuse, whether or not these have led to posttraumatic stress disorder. Men and women who have been sexually abused or assaulted are typically extremely ashamed about what happened to them (Levine 1996, Rose 1991). They may need considerable support even to reveal to the clinician that the abuse or assault occurred (Talmadge and Wallace 1991). While a few prefer their partners to be present when they first discuss such experiences, many do not. They may not even have told their mates, or at least not told any details. They may be fearful that their mates will find them sullied and reject them. In individual sessions, a clinician can render support, give information to show that the survivor is not alone, and normalize his or her feelings (Levine 1996). Then the issue of when, how, and even in some instances whether to tell the mate can be addressed. A probable need for the survivor's individual or group treatment can also be discussed (Johnson 1989).

Sometimes a partner showing clear symptoms of anxiety or depression does not wish to have them further evaluated, even in a separate session with the clinician or someone else. The clinician must then decide whether to push the issue or to let the partner's preference stand. Reasons for denial of symptoms or their possible seriousness can include fears of what the symptoms imply, of being labeled, or of the treatment that might be recommended. For example, men suffering from posttraumatic stress disorder due to combat experiences may be reluctant to undergo further evaluation because they fear being asked to talk about the experiences again or being labeled as a "nut case." One way for clinicians to push further evaluation is to express concern that the partner is suffering when perhaps medication or some other treatment might help. A clinician may also inquire supportively into what is making the partner reluctant or suggest some possible reasons for the reluctance. Both mates' possible responses to such probes must be weighed against the possible benefits of the partner's getting treatment and the dangers of not doing so. Perhaps both partners need to be discouraged from seeing the symptoms as a weakness or sign of serious disturbance, a matter to be discussed below. Perhaps the nonsymptomatic mate can be encouraged to support the idea of the other seeking further evaluation.

Conceptualizing Symptoms or Disorders Constructively

When one partner suffers from a diagnosable depressive or anxiety disorder and is willing to discuss it in couple treatment, helping both mates understand more about symptoms, causes, and treatment as well as what influences symptom fluctuations can be useful. However, care must be taken to avoid arousing undue fear about the meaning of a label or creating a dysfunctional "sick" role (Karpel 1994). Decisions about how much information to share with a couple must be made on a case-by-case basis.

The first decision is what to call the disorder. Frequently best is to simply refer to the symptoms as the couple does, as in "Mary's periods of depression" or "Bob's feelings of panic." Or the clinician may seek to give the condition a little more definition by saying something like, "You know, many people suffer from depression of this kind and they often have trouble sleeping, too. Do you experience that?" Slightly more descriptive terms could be something like "Mary's depressive condition" or "Bob's panic attacks." At times, use of the actual diagnostic label will help a partner feel that he or she is experiencing something known and definable, but some labels are more user-friendly than others. *Dysthymia* is a confusing term to most people, while calling a partner's collection of symptoms *posttraumatic stress disorder* may give them legitimacy and make them seem less frightening, as long as the label is further explained.

Deciding how to proceed can be based on how a clinician *thinks* particular partners may react to a label, or how they *do* react as one partner's symptoms are more clearly defined or related to a known condition. Whether or not the clinician mentions an actual diagnosis, an appropriate next step is to ask both partners if they have questions about the condition. If needed, the clinician can offer a brief, simple explanation or ask the partner with symptoms whether he or she wants to explain. For example, a clinician's description of posttraumatic stress disorder caused by military service might be that it indicates a group of responses many people have when they have lived through combat experiences. Both partners must be helped not to see a set of symptoms or a condition as indicating weakness, that the person is crazy, or that the condition is more severe than it really is. However, if warranted, they can be told how to recognize an exacerbation and what to do if one occurs.

Sociocultural factors, especially ethnicity and social class, can be a major influence on how psychiatric symptoms are viewed and reported (McGoldrick and Giordano 1996). For example, in the June and Roger case discussed below, June's Irish background may have made her more reticent in complaining about her depression to her husband (McGoldrick 1996). Another strong influence can be partners' personal experiences with someone who has had a mental disorder or even the particular disorder in question. However, these experiences may lead to more fears and misunderstandings rather than fewer.

Clinicians can inquire whether either partner has known anyone with a condition such as the current one. Finally, exposure to media or other sources of information may be helpful or confusing to mates in a given instance. Several excerpts from an interview with June and Roger illustrate how such discussions may progress.

> After a few sessions of couple treatment focusing on intimacy problems, June, an Irish American woman aged 48, saw a doctor to be evaluated for depression and came back with the information that she suffered from dysthymic disorder. The psychiatrist had told her this was the name for a moderate-range depressive condition. The clinician asked how both partners felt about receiving this information and it turned out June had not told Roger until now. She herself felt some relief at the psychiatrist having said many people suffer from such depressive symptoms and that medication and some individual work would probably help.
>
> Roger said anxiously that he did not want his wife taking tranquilizers and that she wasn't crazy. Efforts to clarify the nature of the medication the doctor had suggested and that the diagnosis did not mean June was crazy were met with Roger's continued protestations. Finally the clinician said that what June had been told seemed to be scaring Roger and she wondered if he could say why. He burst out, "I don't want June to kill herself." It turned out he had recently watched a TV special on depression and suicide. In further discussion, June clarified that she wasn't thinking along these lines at all. In fact she felt less depressed now than before she had seen the doctor. The clinician suggested that feeling suicidal was unlikely with this mild a condition, but it was not a bad idea for June to promise she would tell Roger or her doctor if she ever did feel that way. June readily promised this. The two then asked to discuss more about the condition and what its treatment might mean for them. (The case continues below.)

Clinicians can explain most symptoms as reflecting a vulnerability to feeling states or experiences, such as panic attacks or flashbacks, that the person cannot help. It can be pointed out that the partner is still who he or she is, that the symptoms or condition are just a small part of his or her entire persona. Clinicians can comment on both partners' strengths and mention that both undoubtedly have areas of vulnerability, since everyone does. Areas the partner without symptoms needs to work on can be noted to balance a focus on the other's symptoms (Weeks and Treat 1992).

A couple's initial questions about what one partner's disorder is are often followed by others about its causes, prognosis, and treatment. While the clinician can suggest that the symptomatic partner ask some questions of the other helping professional he or she is probably seeing, further discussion in the couple sessions is usually appropriate as well. Clinicians should be knowledgeable enough to discuss biological factors, earlier traumas, or childhood history as possible influences. Usually it is best for such explanations to be fairly general at the start. Too detailed a discussion of biological influences may be confusing or raise partners' concerns about whether their children may have inherited a vulnerability to the disorder. Partners whose childhoods have been difficult may not wish to say too much about this influence to their mates, especially if there is a continuing relationship with the parental family.

The clinician should secure both partners' permission to talk periodically with the other helping professional (Sayers et al. 1993), as noted in Chapter 4. It can be explained that the clinician will not share information learned in this way with the couple without the permission of the partner in other treatment, and that the main purpose of the contacts will be to make sure the two treatments are coordinated. Another issue sooner or later may be how much the nonsymptomatic mate is entitled to know about the other treatment experience. A reasonable expectation is usually that he or she be told how the treatment is going, whether it seems helpful, and whether anything new, such as a trial on a new medication, is happening. Especially if there is to be a major change, such as an increased frequency of sessions or a termination, the mate deserves to know. Otherwise, clinicians may help draw an appropriate boundary around partners' other treatment by affirming that it is not appropriate for them to have to tell their mates many details.

Planning Management of the Symptoms or Disorder

When one partner has an anxiety or depressive disorder, clinicians can ask whether the couple would like to focus on ways to understand and manage it as part of the work of couple treatment. If so, at some point it can be useful to discuss who can be responsible for what in dealing with the disorder (Nelsen 1994). The symptomatic partner cannot help having it, but can take responsibility for optimal management. One of this partner's clear responsibilities is to seek appropriate treatment. Another is to handle symptoms so as to decrease their negative impact whenever doing so is not too difficult. For example, someone who is chronically anxious can learn not to talk constantly about the anxiety. On the other hand, a nonsymptomatic partner can provide support and try to control any dysfunctional responses of his or her own. What is relevant for both partners to discuss and understand is how anxiety or depressive symptoms are and are not influenced by the couple's interaction and in turn influence it (Chauncey 1994, Craske and Zoellner 1995, Sayers et al. 1993). The two can then usually be helped to work out better ways to handle possible precipitants, the symptoms themselves, and consequences of the symptoms, including feelings aroused in each. Let us see how the clinician begins to help June and Roger with these tasks later in the same session.

June said she had always had some problems with depression and low self-esteem but they'd gotten a little worse lately. Roger immediately said he'd noticed this and asked if the change had anything to do with him. June didn't think so, but that it probably had more to do with the impending departure of their youngest daughter, Jamie, for college. Roger replied that June shouldn't be upset by this as it was a positive thing; they were both very proud of their daughter's good grades and academic potential. June frowned and replied, "Yes, of course you're right."

The clinician interrupted to say it might not be so helpful for Roger to try to reassure June in this way. She added that he might be feeling he really didn't know what to do to help with the depression, or even if there was anything he could do. Roger replied, "That's for sure!" The clinician suggested that June would be working with her doctor on issues such as her feelings about their daughter leaving, and might or might not need help from Roger on these. But it could also be useful for them both to understand whether there was anything in their interaction that wasn't helpful to the depression and, if so, what they could each do to change it. They could possibly work in the couple sessions on this, as well as on other issues they'd identified. Roger said he would really like to know better what to do because he feels guilty when June gets depressed. But then when he says something to try to help, she often seems to withdraw further. The clinician asked if June, too, would be willing to work on how they could each cope better with their interaction around the depression, as part of the focus here. June said it was okay with her as long as this didn't keep them from working on other things that needed attention.

The choice of whether to focus first on the consequences of a partner's symptoms and their handling or on possible precipitants to symptoms in the couple interaction is largely determined by which issue seems more pressing and relevant at a particular time. One task in the former instance is usually for the clinician to ask about and, if needed, normalize both mates' salient feelings. The clinician working with Roger and June might have expressed understanding of Roger's having felt guilty when he did not know how to help June. As noted in Chapter 3, guilt, frustration, anxiety, and anger are common feelings in the mate of a partner with a depressive or anxiety disorder (Beach et al. 1994, Craske and Zoellner 1995, Tessler 1995). Symptomatic partners more often feel guilt for the burden and trouble they are causing, but they may also be angry when they believe their mates are giving insufficient support or responding unhelpfully. Often both partners' guilt and possible underlying anger make it more difficult for them to have constructive discussions of how to handle the symptoms.

Clinicians need to use judgment in deciding when to elicit partners' feelings in response to their own or their mates' symptoms, even if they can normalize and validate them. Guilt and anxiety are usually the feelings partners can most readily admit, while expressing anger is often difficult (Beach et al. 1994, Chauncey 1994, Halgin and Lovejoy 1991). Anger may also dissipate when both partners understand better what they can do to help the situation. With Roger and June, the clinician probably believed that delving into June's possible anger at Roger for cutting off her feelings about their daughter would not be useful at this time. June might not even be aware of any anger and, if she were, might be too guilty to express it. More importantly, given help, Roger could probably learn to react more constructively to June's expressing her feelings, reducing her future anger or frustration. Clinicians can always elicit partners' anger later if it is still problematic. Sometimes encouraging both partners to direct anger toward the disorder itself is useful, if they understand the mate cannot help having it.

While the partner with an anxiety or depressive disorder presumably will be receiving specialized treatment for it, the other mate may need more help with his or her feelings and concerns than can readily be given in joint appointments. Such partners may also need encouragement and support to devise better means of self-care (Koerner et al. 1994). One or a few individual sessions with the clinician may provide an opportunity to address these matters, if the symptomatic partner does not mind. A brief summary of discussions there can be brought back to the couple work. As one example, the partner of a sexual abuse survivor may have many pressing feelings about the abuse having occurred, the perpetrator if it is someone he or she knows, and the impact on the couple's sex life (Chauncey 1994, Levine 1996). This partner may wonder about his or her own sexual adequacy. He or she may be anxious listening to the abuse survivor discuss details of the trauma yet not want to cut the survivor off. Some of these matters may best be discussed individually or in survivors' partners' groups (Chauncey 1994).

Often routine help with communication and problem solving can reduce partners' stress and therefore indirectly have a beneficial effect on anxiety or depressive symptoms (Gotlib and Beach 1995). However, factors more specifically affecting these can be worked on as well. If such factors are intertwined with other problems a couple is reporting, the work can be undertaken without overfocusing on the partner with symptoms. The clinician with June and Roger now finds an opportunity to discuss aspects of couple interaction that may be affecting June's depression, one of which is probably Roger's squelching of her feelings.

> The clinician suggested that June's depression might be somewhat related to one of the issues they had come in about: the feeling that they were withdrawing from each other rather than solving problems together. She commented that both had seemed pretty unhappy about this. Roger volunteered, "I felt like you withdrew from me a few minutes ago, when I said we should be proud of Jamie." The clinician asked if June felt this was true. June said, "Well, maybe a little." The clinician suggested they focus on this

interaction as an example of what may sometimes happen between them. She added that she thought each of them might be reacting to feelings they weren't sure how to talk about together. She then asked Roger if he could get in touch with what he felt when June said she was upset thinking about Jamie leaving for college. Roger thought a moment and said, "I couldn't understand it. It wasn't what I expected at all." The clinician persisted with, "Well, given that, what were you *feeling* when June said it? I mean, you've been saying what you thought, but not what you felt." Roger looked perplexed. The clinician responded, "I know it's hard" and, after a pause, "Since you didn't expect June to be upset, were you maybe feeling sort of anxious that you didn't know what to say?" Roger readily agreed. The clinician added, "We'll try to help you with that in a minute. But first, June, can you get in touch with what you felt when Roger said you shouldn't feel upset?" June said hesitantly, "I guess I felt cut off." The clinician expressed that she thought both wanted to be more connected but needed to be able to talk about their feelings and listen to each other's feelings to be able to do so.

Later in this case, it became evident that June's depression had increased not only because of her daughter's leaving, but also due to her feelings that Roger was not very available to her and fears that he would not ever be. Work on their communication and intimacy did ultimately help her depression, as did a brief period of individual treatment with a psychiatrist and continued use of antidepressant medication. It was also necessary for Roger to learn that when June was depressed, he did not need to take responsibility for getting her out of it. But he might be helpful just by listening and giving support. June was asked to let Roger know, whenever she was depressed, whether he could help in some way or not. They also worked out that June would take responsibility at such times to do some of what her doctor had said could be helpful to her, such as trying to engage in positive self-talk.

When one partner suffers from an anxiety disorder, a direct focus on symptom precipitants in couple interaction and on how the mate can most helpfully respond may also be useful (Craske and Zoellner 1995). For example, someone with an agoraphobic mate can be helped to understand that offering too much attention and sympathy may actually reinforce agoraphobic behavior. Preliminary research suggests that partners' interaction can influence obsessive-compulsive symptoms and that couple treatment adjunct to individual treatment may help with these. In posttraumatic stress disorder due to a woman's childhood sexual abuse, the survivor may have flashbacks stimulated by the couple's normal sexual behavior that happens to resemble the original abuse situation (Levine 1996, Tessler 1995). The couple may need help to realize this and avoid sex in the afternoon, for example, if that is when the original abuse occurred. Or the survivor might need to be given control of when and how sexual intimacy occurs until such time as she has dealt in her own treatment with her fears of again feeling powerless.

In all work on better management of one mate's symptoms or disorder, clinicians must stay sensitive to both partners' feelings as well as their own. Being aware of someone's depression, anxiety, or events that caused posttraumatic stress disorder tends to stir up reciprocal sadness or anxiety. Clinicians must not steer away from such content or become overintellectual or insensitive out of their own discomfort. They must, however, be prepared to shift gears depending on partners' fluctuating responses. Either mate's strong feelings or painful memories that emerge in sessions may be handled in a variety of ways. Sometimes they can simply be recognized and support given. Clinicians may offer to slow down a discussion to reduce anxiety. Both partners can be allowed the option of changing the subject to handle their feelings, with the discussion to be picked up later or in a symptomatic partner's other treatment.

Some partners may also react more dysfunctionally to discussions of their mates' depressive or anxiety symptoms, as when one partner puts the other down, withdraws significantly, or even wants to terminate the couple treatment. Clinicians can sometimes help partners showing such responses by gently inquiring into their feelings or fears. Sometimes, for the partner who does not have symptoms, the discussion has evoked issues similar to the ones being talked about. Partners who themselves have had periods of depression, fought against low self-esteem or feelings of inadequacy, or been distressed by a parent's depression may react strongly to their mates' depressive symptoms. A man who has experienced sexual humiliation as a child at the hands of an older peer may become verbally attacking when his partner tries to talk about sexual abuse experiences. When a partner's responses seem extreme and unlikely to change in couple sessions, a clinician may suggest separate interviews to see if the more private atmosphere there allows more effective exploration.

All of a couple's work on better coping with one partner's depressive or anxiety symptoms does not take place at once or in an orderly sequence. This issue between them, like any other, will usually be picked up and worked on at times when it is especially salient. Progress on other couple problems can sometimes ameliorate one partner's symptoms. By the same token, the couple's increased cooperation in dealing with symptoms usually leads to greater overall satisfaction with their relationship, even if the symptoms do not abate. Occasionally, there are adverse reactions to a positive change. One or both mates may feel less secure if they have moved out of dysfunctional coping patterns such as arguing about symptoms, engaging in mutual withdrawal, enduring a push-pull pattern of some sort, or enacting a victim–rescuer mode. Some theorists suggest that the partner who is not symptomatic may have chosen the other out of a need to be the healthy one or the caretaker (Craske and Zoellner 1995). Partners' anxious or negative reactions to apparently positive changes in this arena, as in any other, are grist for discussion to achieve understanding and better coping.

CHAPTER

10

Progress and Termination

The longer couple cases go on, the more they begin to differ from each other. There are success stories. Some partners learn new communication and problem-solving skills, gain useful insights, or at least resolve some troublesome disagreements within a few months. Others take longer to benefit, usually because their problems are more complex, but still eventually make good progress. Couples who attempt more insight work, those who need to overcome a major disruption such as an affair, and narcissistically vulnerable couples are among those who usually need a longer period of treatment.

Then there are cases in which couples' progress is more limited. Some must leave treatment before they have achieved optimal goals because of circumstances beyond their control, such as a lack of funding. Some choose to end the work together although clinicians think it should continue. Still others keep coming but seem stuck, unable to move forward after a certain point but perhaps also unable to leave without the clinician's help. Finally, treatment sometimes stops because one or both partners wish to end their relationship.

Clinicians using this book's integrative approach will try to facilitate couples' constructive termination in all such cases. The present chapter examines how they may do so.

TERMINATION IN SUCCESSFUL CASES

Couples themselves must usually be the ones to decide when their goals for treatment have been reached and when they will terminate, but clinicians should have input into these decisions. Clearly, successful outcomes can be defined in a variety of ways and may take a shorter or longer time to achieve. In any instance, however, several specific tasks must be achieved during termination to give couples the best chance to sustain their gains.

Successful Short-Term Cases

Some couples who need help primarily with communication and problem-solving skills may pick these up quickly and benefit from a fairly short period of treatment. In managed care or limited-income cases, this time may be as short as six to ten sessions, but optimally it is usually several months of weekly appointments followed by several more at less frequent intervals. Such couples are usually well motivated, with poor communication habits that are not too ingrained. As they learn better skills within the first month or two of treatment, the partners may be surprised at how much more easily than before many of their day-to-day problems and disagreements are resolved. Usually once the two learn to listen to each other rather than rushing to their own solutions, they find out so much more about what the real issues are in a given situation that better mutual solutions can be worked out fairly readily.

As they begin to feel more confident of their skills, such couples may be comfortable with sessions every other week. This interval gives them a chance to do most problem solving on their own but still use the clinician for fine-tuning, recurrent skill problems, or particularly tough issues. For example, remaining sessions may be devoted to work on a few bad communication habits that have some tendency to recur, such as partners having more trouble listening when they are upset. Or a couple may wish to address issues that are more complex or emotion-laden, such as when to have a child.

In other cases, couples ask to focus in relatively short-term work on one or a few major problem areas they have not been able to resolve together. They may either not need, or not have much interest in learning, many better communication and problem-solving skills. While a clinician may certainly raise the possibility of broadening these couples' goals, the partners have the right to make the final decision. They may leave feeling satisfied with treatment after a few months, having simply come to better and more mutual agreements on how to discipline their children, handle meddlesome in-laws, or solve two or three problems of this sort.

Even some couples who need to develop insights into the way they handle needs or feelings or to resolve more complex problems can sometimes do so in short-term work. In one case known to me, a well functioning lesbian couple spent six sessions listening to each other's reasons for fighting about one partner's former lover, who was still her close friend. Once each understood the other's feelings and the childhood issues these had evoked, the two could work out some simple strategies for coping differently. The problem more or less disappeared and the couple terminated soon after.

Constructive termination in successful short-term cases is almost always relatively easy to achieve. While making the decision may take several sessions, termination itself often takes only one. Couples may say at a given point that they would like to consider ending. Or a clinician may raise the possibility when partners seem to have achieved their goals, have little to say during sessions, or be using them to talk about things they could apparently resolve on their own (Siegel 1992). Sometimes termination is set at the start of treatment because of managed care or other service constraints. In all these instances, clinicians must still take primary responsibility to try to ensure that the process is completed constructively.

Their first task is to judge a couple's readiness. Criteria are usually that the couple has achieved the goals they wanted help with or made as much progress as they can, and that both the couple and the clinician believe they will be able to sustain their gains (Mack 1989). Evaluating goal achievement may be relatively simple. The couple can be asked, the clinician will have an opinion based on his or her own observations, and the partners may complete any assessment tools that have been introduced earlier as a means of monitoring progress. The only difficult judgment may be to determine whether further progress can be made on a goal or not. Barring financial or other external limitations, the partners must usually be the ones to decide how long they wish to try (Scharff 1995). However, clinicians may offer an opinion, perhaps based on an understanding that no couple relationship is perfect and realistic standards must apply (Karpel 1994). Sometimes it is helpful to point out that the pair might wish to enjoy the gains they have made, with the idea that they could always return for another period of treatment if they wished to at some later time.

Evaluating whether a couple will probably be able to sustain their gains may be done in several ways. Clinicians will usually have some sense of how real any positive changes seem to be. The couple may be more or less confident. Clinicians can ask partners whether they are satisfied enough with their current interaction that they think hidden problems will not jump out to bite them. For example, a clinician might say, "Are you both pretty sure that enough of your needs are being met in the way you're now handling . . .?" or "Is either of you having any nagging feelings that you don't really like the way something's going in your relationship, so you're going to feel dissatisfied later if you're no longer coming in?" To assist such evaluation, a useful tool is often for the pair to decrease the frequency of sessions and see how they handle things (Christensen et al. 1995). They may be seen every other week for awhile, then monthly for a time or two. Some elect instead to take a break of a month or so and then have an evaluation session in which to decide about termination.

Clinicians must try to ensure that couples do not decide to persist in treatment mainly because they are afraid of not being able to hold onto their gains alone. One intervention that may reduce this fear is for the clinician to express confidence in their abilities, if it seems appropriate to do so. Another that is usually extremely helpful is to let the pair know, as soon as the possibility of terminating is under discussion, that the clinician would see them again if they felt the need at any time (Scharff and Scharff 1991). Far from encouraging undue dependence on the clinician and treatment, such a policy tends to help couples terminate more easily because they feel they have a safety net. Some do return, usually because there has been a shift in their life circumstances to which they must adjust, such as a new child or job, or because they are feeling more ready to tackle a recalcitrant problem. Rarely does the decision seem to be motivated by a perception that the original decision to terminate was premature.

During the termination process, clinicians must also offer couples specific strategies for trying to make sure they hold onto their gains. The first step is to review in some detail the important changes they have made, giving them all due credit for these (Siegel 1992). Clinicians can then initiate discussion of what both partners must continue to do so as not to regress to old patterns again. They may be asked to consider how they will continue giving positive reinforcement to each other. It can be stressed that each must actively monitor his or her own behavior and the couple interaction to notice and respond quickly to any slippage. Some clinicians ask partners to say what they would be doing if they did go back to their old ways, or even try to stage a regression to enable them to recognize one as soon as it might begin and nip it in the bud (Christensen et al. 1995, Mack 1989). In one of the options mentioned above, some couples benefit from deciding to work hard to sustain their gains on their own for a month or more and then returning with the intent to terminate if they have done so. This brief hiatus may be defined as a test period. Knowing they will be seeing the clinician again tends to reinforce their conscious attention to sustaining changes, and being able to report success can increase their self-confidence.

A final termination task is to deal with couples' and clinicians' feelings about ending, not only to preserve the partners' good memories of the work together but also to allow them to move on. In successful short-term treatment, doing so is usually not difficult. All parties tend to feel positive about what has been accomplished and about each other. Partners may be told that some people find they have sadness or other feelings about terminating. Most often couples in short-term work have only a minor sense of loss. There may be occasional acting out, such as partners canceling a planned termination session, that signals the need to discuss stronger feelings if at all possible. A final session may include a brief review of the treatment, perhaps initiated by the clinician saying something like, "It seems you weren't too sure what was going to happen here when you got started, but you've really worked hard and made a lot of gains." Then the gains can again be mentioned and the couple given credit for them. The couple is likely to say that the clinician or the treatment has been helpful. A clinician may wish to introduce discussion of exactly what a couple found useful and not so useful about the process (Mack 1989), partially for his or her own ongoing self-evaluation. Cases are likely to end with all parties saying that they have enjoyed working together and wishing each other well. A clinician may never hear from a couple again, may see them for further work at a later time, or may receive holiday cards, birth announcements, or the like in the future.

Successful Long-Term Cases

Many couples who have the option to do so remain in treatment for longer than a few months. The range is obviously wide. In my experience, most couples wish to terminate within one to two years but a few, including many who are narcissistically vulnerable, come longer. Successful long-term couple cases usually involve work on communication and problem solving plus considerable attention to more complex issues such as the aftermath of an affair, partners' difficulties handling needs and feelings that are strongly influenced by childhood experiences, and intimacy problems.

In all such cases, constructive termination still involves evaluating the couple's readiness, helping them to be able to sustain gains on their own, and dealing with partners' and clinicians' feelings about ending. However, couples seen for a longer time are likely to have more fears about terminating than those who have engaged in short-term work, and to need more help with their feelings. Part of the reason is that their regular sessions and relationship with the clinician have been incorporated into their lives. Let us look at the progression and termination of a fairly typical long-term case with a successful outcome.

> Martha and Kevin, a couple in their forties with three children aged 2 to 8, had originally come in because of unresolved issues about an affair Kevin had had two years earlier. They had sought couple treatment at that time, but the clinician they went to had seen them together for only a few sessions before placing Kevin in a group, which he had continued to attend for over a year with little appreciable benefit. The couple turned out to have many strengths but also a considerable number of difficulties. Besides issues related to the affair, they had long-standing communication problems, primarily blaming by Martha and passive withdrawal by Kevin. They did not understand the implications of each other's different ethnicities very well. Kevin was Polish American, Martha of mixed Irish, Scottish, and German descent. They were both stressed out by Kevin's heavy work commitments and the responsibility of caring for three small children, especially because both tended to have trouble limiting demands by their extended families, friends, and church. There were some important childhood influences, especially on their handling of anger and intimacy needs.
>
> Emphases for many months of treatment were on resolving the couple's leftover issues related to the affair and learning better communication and problem-solving skills. The influences of their differing ethnicities were highlighted, making it easier to resolve related problems. Their different ways of handling anger were iden-

tified, and to some degree the childhood roots of these were determined. After a year of mostly weekly sessions, the couple's day-to-day lives had become less stressful and Martha had become more trusting that Kevin would not cheat on her again. But they were still not feeling fully satisfied with their relationship. The clinician began to see Kevin individually every other week to look at some childhood influences on his fears of being open and assertive, and Martha monthly, primarily to help her cut down on overextending herself. The couple came together on alternate weeks to work on increased insights into their relationship dynamics and greater intimacy.

Late in the second year of treatment, Martha and Kevin were considering termination. They had both stopped coming individually. A review of their progress found them quite confident of their ability to do day-to-day problem solving since they had been fairly good at it for a while. Martha's trust in Kevin had returned not only because of understanding further why the affair had happened, but also because she saw him being more open with her about his needs, feelings, and activities. While both still had some fears of closeness based on childhood experiences, their intimacy had considerably increased. It seemed to have gone about as far as it could at this point, partly because they still had to deal with normal midlife stresses from work and children.

Deciding to come monthly for a few more sessions and being told about the clinician's open-door policy about returning if more treatment were needed seemed to help ease the partners' fears about terminating. While they were doing well on their own, they still had some concern about sustaining their newfound level of intimacy. The clinician tried to help them find ways to reinforce gains and to watch for slippage in this area. For example, the two were encouraged to maintain a practice they had initiated of having one sacrosanct date night per week, and they agreed to use it partly to monitor how each was feeling in regard to their continuing closeness. A few other more specific fears about regression were elicited and addressed. In each of the last two sessions, the clinician and both partners expressed feelings of loss. They finally parted somewhat tearfully, wishing each other well.

Termination in successful long-term cases like that of Martha and Kevin evokes more of partners' and clinicians' ambivalence and feelings of loss than shorter-term cases usually do (Siegel 1992). Resolution of mourning requires eliciting these and any other reactions partners wish to share. Even so, termination usually evokes less intense mourning than with individual clients because the partners still have each other. Clinicians may normalize partners' feelings of loss and disclose their own to validate that the relationship with the couple has been important to them too. The ways partners have dealt with earlier losses or separations, or even how they typically deal with anxiety, may predict how they will handle feelings about termination (Scharff 1995). If partners' feelings are acted out, for example by suddenly finding some new problem to focus on in the last session or otherwise cutting off any emotional discussion, the clinician may need to explore or suggest what is going on. The nature of the treatment so far and the partners' ethnicities should be taken into account, however, in deciding how much to push for them to acknowledge feelings. For example, Asian American or British American partners may be less willing to discuss their feelings about ending (Ho 1990).

Narcissistically vulnerable couples tend to have greater difficulty with termination because of their issues with abandonment, although the difficulty may be somewhat less if the partners have healed enough to be more secure in their need-meeting with each other (Slipp 1995). Open discussion of their concerns, perhaps connecting them to childhood issues, cutting down gradually on the frequency of sessions, and an open-door policy are very important here. Clinicians may need to help such partners acknowledge not only their sadness, but also any anger they may feel even if they have agreed that the treatment should end. Reinforcement of couples' strengths and helping them deal with feelings about termination may be needed for a longer time than with other pairs. Occasionally, the decision may be made to work on and off indefinitely with a narcissistically vulnerable couple who may not be able to hold onto their gains without the clinician's help.

TERMINATION WITH FEWER GAINS

Some couple cases do not have such positive endings, although it is rare for nothing to have been accomplished if work continues beyond a session or two. Sometimes good progress has been made, but treatment must end before couples wish it because of funding restrictions, partners' changing circumstances, or clinicians' unavailability for continued work. Sometimes couples initiate termination when clinicians believe it is premature. In still other cases, termination seems necessary when couples at some point cannot apparently accomplish any more, although their gains may be limited. Finally, some couples who attempt treatment to improve their relationship still come to the point of breaking up. Termination in all these circumstances is more complicated and difficult than with more successful cases.

Premature Terminations

Premature terminations in couple cases may be caused by external circumstances more or less beyond the partners' control, or may occur when one or both decide to stop coming against the clinician's advice. Work on basic termination tasks must be modified to take either of these situations into account.

Couples usually know from the outset when managed care contracts or other funding considerations will limit the length of service. However, they may not realize until the time for ending draws near that they will feel a need for more treatment and not be able to obtain it, at least not with the same clinician in the same period of time. Other couples may have to stop coming when they experience unexpected financial reverses, job transfers, or the like. Finally, a source of disappointment and frustration for couples who feel they are benefiting from treatment is a clinician's being unable to continue for personal or job-related reasons. Even if the time-limited nature of the clinician's availability was known in advance, a couple may be upset by it.

Positives in terminations caused by external circumstances are that clinicians can still validate any gains couples have made and help them plan how to maintain them. However, a gradual reduction in session frequency to test their readiness to terminate may not be possible and the clinician may not be able to offer a future open door. Sometimes treatment can be obtained from another clinician or under another auspice if the couple wishes it. In situations where a couple's financial situation prohibits continuing but may also improve, or where they may be eligible for more service later, the ending may be defined as a perhaps temporary period for trying their wings.

Appropriate resolution of partners' feelings about terminating is still important in such circumstances to enable them to maintain their gains or transfer successfully to another clinician. Yet their feelings may be complex while there is little time to process them. Besides acknowledging the partners' likely sadness and frustration at having to end prematurely, clinicians must be sure to give them a chance to express anger. This emotion is most likely to be present when the clinician has had to initiate termination unexpectedly, perhaps due to agency cutbacks, a job change, illness, or pregnancy. If at all possible, couples deserve to be told the reason for the change. Clinicians need to have their own feelings worked out so as not to cut off partners' sadness and anger, for example, by expressing profuse apologies. Instead, they must suggest that these feelings are normal responses to the situation and that talking about them can help. In some instances partners' anger, sadness, and anxiety may be heightened because childhood experiences with deprivation or abandonment have been evoked. For couples whose ethnicity or poverty has perhaps led them to expect disappointments from professionals, validation of sadness and anger is especially important.

Premature terminations also occur when one or both partners choose to end treatment although clinicians believe the pair could probably make further progress. Most such terminations occur early and represent a continuation of initial resistances (Siegel 1992). If clinicians have tried intervention strategies to engage partners, as suggested in earlier chapters, but have been unable to change their minds, they usually do best to validate any minimal gains, wish the couple well, and say they would be glad to see them again should they ever want to return.

When treatment has gone on longer and a couple has made gains that could be expected to continue if they kept coming in, partner-initiated proposals to terminate usually represent more complex resistances. At times a clinician has made errors or not been able to deal with partners' negative transference. More often, the couple's fears of change have been aroused. One partner may also be pushing for ending because he or she does not like the changes that are occurring, fears that a dangerous secret will come out (Mack 1989), or has decided to end the couple relationship but does not want to say so yet. Clearly, clinicians' first responses in all such cases should be to try to help the couple explore what has happened or make some interpretation of it to try to forestall discontinuance. If a partner announces a termination decision on the phone and the two will not even come in to discuss it, the clinician must try to initiate discussion of the reasons then and there or, if necessary, suggest them in a letter (Siegel 1992).

If these efforts do not succeed and termination will occur, the couple may not be willing to discuss it very fully or at all. Clinicians must then struggle with their own feelings of inadequacy, frustration, or anger while trying to end the treatment as constructively as possible (Siegel 1992). If given any opportunity, they can still try to validate gains, give the pair some help with how to sustain them, and convey an open-door policy (Mack 1989). Partners can be at least minimally helped to process any feelings of loss or anger of which they are aware. It is important in this situation for a clinician to convey respect for and genuine acceptance of the couple's right to discontinue. Otherwise it is more likely that partners' guilt, anger, or anxiety will preclude their processing the termination at all.

Occasionally, partners who might be expected to make further progress as a couple propose that one stop coming and the other continue individual treatment with the clinician. Siegel (1992) warns that the couple's hidden motivations for this arrangement may be to deal with their fears of changing but also of regressing without treatment. One partner is to carry the functions of maintaining contact with the clinician and developing further self-awareness while the other carries the resistance to progressing further. Such requests should alert clinicians to explore partners' ostensible reasons and possible fears about either terminating or continuing to come in together. At the very least, couples should be warned that if only one continues, they may not both be comfortable seeing the same clinician again if needed.

Terminations When Couples Cannot Progress Further

In some cases, termination becomes necessary either because partners cannot seem to make further progress in treatment although they may desire to do so, or because they will be ending their relationship.

When partners have made some progress in treatment but seem to become stuck and unable to move further, the clinician's first choice is always to try to help with possible obstacles to change, as discussed in earlier chapters. Consultation with a more experienced clinician may also be undertaken to evaluate what has happened and to try to develop possible remedies. If there is still no change within a reasonable period, the clinician may need to rethink whether partners may have achieved all the gains of which they are capable at the time. The next step is usually to engage the couple in careful consideration of how to proceed. Of course, the partners may also initiate such a conversation before the clinician does.

Discussion may start with the clinician asking how the partners perceive the way the treatment has been going. If they too feel that not much has been happening, the clinician may validate the partners' efforts and any gains they have already made, but wonder if these are perhaps all that are possible at the time. These ideas must be presented cautiously so as not to make partners feel they have failed.

Further options may then be discussed. One is to proceed for a while longer, perhaps trying some new intervention strategy, if the couple wishes to do so. Another is to consider individual work for either or both partners, if this possibility has not yet been tried, or referral to another clinician for more couple treatment. A clinician may say in such instances that sometimes work with a new person or in a new form of treatment uncovers new possibilities for growth. A third option is for the couple to terminate, or at least take a hiatus from treatment, to see whether they might achieve further changes on their own or be able to benefit from further work with the same or a different clinician later. Some couples resist termination although nothing much is happening in treatment because they fear regressing or not having the clinician available to meet dependency needs (Mack 1989). If so, such concerns may need to be brought to light and addressed. Perhaps then the couple will be able to at least try appointments at a reduced frequency. It may also help for the clinician to convey an open-door policy if they want to try terminating but need to return later.

When partners who have made only limited gains will be terminating, clinicians must again seek to make the process a constructive one. It is still important to help the couple take credit for any positive changes and think about how they can sustain them. The most difficult part of such endings is to deal with all participants' feelings. Clinicians are likely to feel guilty or inadequate that they have let partners down or angry that the partners could not go further. If they have liked the couple, they may also feel some sadness, but often their response is more one of relief. Partners may experience any of these same feelings toward clinicians. Either partner may also blame the other for the lack of progress and may feel discouraged or even panicky about future prospects for their relationship.

Clinicians will need considerable self-awareness not to act out their own feelings and rush through termination in such cases. Especially when treatment has gone on awhile and the partners have been quite invested in it, they should be told that they are likely to have a variety of feelings about ending and that it is important to have a chance to process them. Their possible feelings of inadequacy and blame of each other can be cautiously explored, and, one hopes, corrected by the clinician's reminding them they have made gains and done the best they could. Sadness at the loss of the relationship with the clinician can be acknowledged and the clinician's own sadness shared. It is very important to tell partners that they might understandably feel some anger at the clinician for not having been able to help them more, and the clinician can express regret that the treatment did not feel fully successful.

Such couples should be given the chance to discuss any concerns they have about what may happen to their relationship after treatment terminates, but some will not wish to pursue this line of thinking. Possible reasons may be that they have decided to make do with the relationship as it is, they are hoping it will still change, or one or both are already thinking about ending it but do not want their mates to know. Some couples do want to talk about breaking up, as discussed in Chapters 3 and 9. A few even ask if a clinician thinks they should give up on the relationship. No clinician should make this decision, and the couple's right and responsibility to make it should be affirmed. However, clinicians may in some cases say that they do not see this treatment helping the couple further but do not know what might happen with a different clinician or if the partners try to change on their own. Partners who have felt the clinician did everything possible to help them, and who do not wish to begin seeing someone else, may then conclude that their relationship is not likely to improve further and that they must decide to stay or end it based on this reality.

Finally, there are cases in which partners will be terminating treatment because one or both have decided to end their relationship. They may or may not have used sessions to process this decision fully or work out an amicable parting. While this outcome may be the best one possible in a given case, especially if the pair can achieve it without rancor, it does not usually feel very positive to them at the time. Sometimes partners have entered treatment with little or no hope that their relationship could be reclaimed. Their pessimism may show almost immediately in a lack of investment in the conjoint work. Beginnings in such cases have been discussed in Chapter 3, and the decision to stop working to save the relationship may come quickly when clinicians encourage partners to be honest about where they stand. Other partners decide to end their relationship only after a lengthier period of conjoint treatment. They may have struggled with the decision and are more likely to have used some sessions to work out how to proceed amicably. Especially after such a longer period of work, the clinician may need to help the partners deal with a double loss: that of their own relationship and that of the treatment and relationship with the clinician. If one partner will continue seeing the clinician individually, termination may need to be carried out awkwardly with the other in a conjoint session or alone in at least one individual one.

Still, a clinician needs to provide some closure to the couple work. While having appointments at reduced frequency and an open-door policy are usually not appropriate, partners can still be given credit for efforts they have made during the work together and for any gains they will be able to use further as individuals. For example, a clinician might note that they have learned better communication skills or gained self-awareness that should benefit them wherever their lives lead. Partners' feelings of loss and possible guilt or anger in regard to the clinician and treatment experience may be heightened by dealing with the loss of their couple relationship, yet the latter pain may be so great that they cannot deal with any other. Clinicians must be tolerant of whatever partners can and cannot achieve in terms of resolving feelings about the treatment termination. They can still express their own liking for the partners and sadness at the way the relationship is ending, and can sincerely wish both partners well.

Just as most couples are able to leave treatment having made appreciable gains, clinicians can learn from and grow with most of the couples they see. To do so, they must be open to such learning on both intellectual and emotional levels. They can also continue to learn from colleagues, further training experiences, and, one hopes, from books such as this.

References

Ables, B. S., and Brandsma, J. M. (1977). *Therapy for Couples*. San Francisco: Jossey-Bass.

Abudabbeh, N. (1996). Arab families. In *Ethnicity and Family Therapy*, ed. M. McGoldrick, J. Giordano, and J. K. Pearce, 2nd ed., pp. 333–346. New York: Guilford.

Alexander, J. F., Holtzworth-Munroe, A., and Jameson, P. (1995). The process and outcome of marital and family therapy: research review and evaluation. In *Handbook of Psychotherapy and Behavior Change*, ed. A. E. Bergin and S. L. Garfield, 4th ed., pp. 595–630. New York: Wiley.

Almeida, R. (1996). Hindu, Christian, and Muslim families. In *Ethnicity and Family Therapy*, ed. M. McGoldrick, J. Giordano, and J. K. Pearce, 2nd ed., pp. 395–423. New York: Guilford.

Anderson, C. M., Dimidjian, S. A., and Miller, A. (1995). Redefining the past, present, and future: therapy with long-term marriages at midlife. In *Clinical Handbook of Couple Therapy*, ed. N. S. Jacobson and A. S. Gurman, pp. 247–260. New York: Guilford.

Anderson, C. M., Reiss, D. J., and Cahalane, J. F. (1986). Marital therapy with schizophrenic patients. In *Clinical Handbook of Marital Therapy*, ed. N. S. Jacobson and A. S. Gurman, pp. 537–556. New York: Guilford.

Anderson, N. H. (1991a). Cognitive theory of judgment and decision. In *Contributions to Information Integration Theory. Volume*

I: Cognition, ed. N. H. Anderson, pp. 105–142. Hillsdale, NJ: Lawrence Erlbaum.

——— (1991b). Functional memory in person cognition. In *Contributions to Information Integration Theory. Volume I: Cognition*, ed. N. H. Anderson, pp. 1–55. Hillsdale, NJ: Lawrence Erlbaum.

Aradi, N. S. (1988). Toward a conceptualization and treatment of interfaith marriages. In *Couples Therapy in a Family Context: Perspective and Retrospective*, ed. F. W. Kaslow, pp. 71–88. Rockville, MD: Aspen.

Astor, M., and Sherman, R. (1997). Resistance in couple therapy: an integration of analytic and systemic approaches. *Journal of Couples Therapy* 7:9–25.

Atwood, J. (1993). The mating game: what we know and what we don't. *Journal of Couples Therapy* 4:61–87.

Bachman, R., and Pillemer, K. A. (1992). Epidemiology and family violence involving adults. In *Assessment of Family Violence: A Clinical and Legal Sourcebook*, ed. R. T. Ammerman and M. Herson, pp. 108–120. New York: Wiley.

Bader, E., and Pearson, P. T. (1988). *In Quest of the Mythical Mate: A Developmental Approach to Diagnosis and Treatment in Couples Therapy*. New York: Brunner/Mazel.

Bakely, J. (1996). Couples therapy outcome research: a review. *Journal of Couples Therapy* 6:83–94.

Barnett, R. C., Brennan, R. T., Raudenbush, S. W., and Marshall, N. L. (1994). Gender and the relationship between marital-role quality and psychological distress. *Psychology of Women Quarterly* 18:105–127.

Basham, K. (1992). Resistance and couple therapy. *Smith College Studies in Social Work* 62:245–264.

Bateson, G. (1972). *Steps to an Ecology of Mind*. New York: Chandler.

Baucom, D. H., and Epstein, N. (1990). *Cognitive-Behavioral Marital Therapy*. New York: Brunner/Mazel.

Baucom, D. H., Epstein, N., and Rankin, L. A. (1995). Cognitive aspects of cognitive-behavioral marital therapy. In *Clinical Handbook of Couple Therapy*, ed. N. S. Jacobson and A. S. Gurman, pp. 65–90. New York: Guilford.

Beach, S. R. H., Whisman, M. A., and O'Leary, K. D. (1994). Marital therapy for depression: theoretical foundation, current status, and future directions. *Behavior Therapy* 25:345–371.

Bischoff, R. J., and Sprenkle, D. H. (1993). Dropping out of marriage and family therapy: a critical review of research. *Family Process* 32:353–368.

Blanck, G., and Blanck, R. (1994). *Ego Psychology: Theory and Practice*, 2nd ed. New York: Columbia University Press.

Blee, K. M., and Tickamyer, A. R. (1995). Racial differences in men's attitudes about women's gender roles. *Journal of Marriage and the Family* 57:21–30.

Bloom, M., Fischer, J., and Orme, J. G. (1994). *Evaluating Practice: Guidelines for the Accountable Professional*, 2nd ed. Englewood Cliffs, NJ: Prentice-Hall.

Booth, A., and Johnson, D. R. (1994). Declining health and marital quality. *Journal of Marriage and the Family* 56:218–223.

Booth, A., Johnson, D. R., Branaman, A., and Sica, A. (1995). Belief and behavior: Does religion matter in today's marriage? *Journal of Marriage and the Family* 57:661–671.

Bornstein, P. H., and Bornstein, M. T. (1993). *Marital Therapy: A Behavioral-Communications Approach*. Boston: Allyn & Bacon.

Boyd-Franklin, N. (1989). *Black Families in Therapy: A Multisystems Approach*. New York: Guilford.

Boyd-Franklin, N., and Franklin, A. J. (1998). African American couples in therapy. In *Re-Visioning Family Therapy: Race, Culture, and Gender in Clinical Practice*, ed. M. McGoldrick, pp. 268–281. New York: Guilford.

Bray, J. H., and Jouriles, E. N. (1995). Treatment of marital conflict and prevention of divorce. *Journal of Marital and Family Therapy* 21:461–473.

Brennan, J. W. (1995). A short-term psychoeducational multiple-family group for bipolar patients and their families. *Social Work* 40:737–743.

Breunlin, D. C., Schwartz, R., and MacKune-Karrer, B. M. (1992). *Metaframeworks: Transcending the Models of Family Therapy*. San Francisco: Jossey-Bass.

Bronfenbrenner, U. (1979). *The Ecology of Human Development: Experiments by Nature and Design*. Cambridge, MA: Harvard University Press.

Brooks, G. R. (1991). Traditional men in marital and family therapy. In *Feminist Approaches for Men in Family Therapy*, ed. M. Bograd, pp. 51–74. New York: Harrington Park.

Brown, L. S. (1995a). Anti-racism as an ethical norm in feminist therapy practice. In *Racism in the Lives of Women: Testimony, Theory, and Guides to Antiracist Practice,* ed. J. Adelman and G. M. Enguidanos, pp. 13–22. New York: Harrington Park.

——— (1995b). Therapy with same-sex couples: an introduction. In *Clinical Handbook of Couple Therapy*, ed. N. S. Jacobson and A. S. Gurman, pp. 274–291. New York: Guilford.

Buckley, W. (1967). *Sociology and Modern Systems Theory*. Englewood Cliffs, NJ: Prentice-Hall.

Bula, J. F. (1996). Fostering change of psychologically abusive behavior in couples. *Journal of Couples Therapy* 6:131–147.

Burman, B., and Margolin, G. (1992). Analysis of association between marital relationships and health problems: an interactional perspective. *Psychological Bulletin* 112:39–63.

Butler, G., and Booth, R. G. (1991). Developing psychological treatments for generalized anxiety disorder. In *Chronic Anxiety: Generalized Anxiety Disorder and Mixed Anxiety-Depression*, ed. R. M. Rapee and D. H. Barlow, pp. 187–209. New York: Guilford.

Buunk, B. P. (1995). Sex, self-esteem, dependency and extra dyadic sexual experience as related to jealousy responses. *Journal of Social and Personal Relationships* 12:147–153.

Canary, D. J., Emmers-Sommer, T. M., with Faulkner, S. (1997). *Sex and Gender Differences in Personal Relationships*. New York: Guilford.

Carl, D. (1990). *Counseling Same-Sex Couples*. New York: Norton.

Carlson, K. (1996). Gay and lesbian families. In *Treating the Changing Family: Handling Normative and Unusual Events*, ed. M. Harway, pp. 62–76. New York: Wiley.

Charny, I. W., and Parnass, S. (1995). The impact of extramarital relationships on the continuation of marriages. *Journal of Sex and Marital Therapy* 21:100–115.

Chauncey, S. (1994). Emotional concerns and treatment of male partners of female sexual abuse survivors. *Social Work* 39:669–676.

Chow, C. S. (1994). Too great a price: the psychological toll of assimilation. *The Family Therapy Networker* 18:31–35.

Christensen, A., Jacobson, N. S., and Babcock, J. C. (1995). Integrative behavioral couple therapy. In *Clinical Handbook of Couple Therapy*, ed. N. S. Jacobson and A. S. Gurman, pp. 31–64. New York: Guilford.

Christensen, A., and Shenk, J. L. (1991). Communication, conflict, and psychological distance in nondistressed, clinic, and divorcing couples. *Journal of Consulting and Clinical Psychology* 59:458–463.

Cobb, J., Soule, C., Quinones, H., et al. (1995). *Separation and reunion in Latino immigrant families: narratives, rituals, and metaphors in family therapy*. Paper presented at the meeting of the American Orthopsychiatric Association, Chicago, IL, April.

Collins, P. M., Kayser, K., and Platt, S. (1994). Conjoint marital therapy: a practitioner's approach to single-system evaluation. *Families in Society: The Journal of Contemporary Human Services* 75:131–141.

Conger, R. D., Elder, G. H., Lorenz, F. O., et al. (1990). Linking economic hardship to marital quality and instability. *Journal of Marriage and the Family* 52:643–656.

Cooper, M. (1996). Obsessive-compulsive disorder: effects on family members. *American Journal of Orthopsychiatry* 66:296–304.

Cowley, D. S., and Roy-Byrne, P. P. (1991). The biology of generalized anxiety disorder and chronic anxiety. In *Chronic Anxiety: Generalized Anxiety Disorder and Mixed Anxiety-Depression*, ed. R. M. Rapee and D. H. Barlow, pp. 52–75. New York: Guilford.

Craske, M. G., and Zoellner, L. A. (1995). Anxiety disorders: the role of marital therapy. In *Clinical Handbook of Couple Therapy*, ed. N. S. Jacobson and A. S. Gurman, pp. 394–410. New York: Guilford.

Crohan, S. E. (1996). Marital quality and conflict across the transition to parenthood in African American and white couples. *Journal of Marriage and the Family* 57:933–944.

Davis, L. E., and Proctor, E. K. (1989). *Race, Gender, and Class: Guidelines for Practice with Individuals, Families, and Groups*. Englewood Cliffs, NJ: Prentice-Hall.

De La Cancela, V. (1991). Working affirmatively with Puerto Rican men: professional and personal reflections. In *Feminist Approaches for Men in Family Therapy*, ed. M. Bograd, pp. 195–211. New York: Harrington Park.

Diagnostic and Statistical Manual of Mental Disorders (1994). 4th ed. Washington, DC: American Psychiatric Association.

Elder, G. H., Jr., Eccles, J. S., Ardelt, M., and Lord, S. (1995). Inner-city parents under economic pressure: perspectives on the strategies of parenting. *Journal of Marriage and the Family* 57:771–784.

Ellis, P., and Murphy, B. C. (1994). The impact of misogyny and homophobia on therapy with women. In *Women in Context: Toward a Feminist Reconstruction of Psychotherapy*, ed. M. P. Mirkin, pp. 48–73. New York: Guilford.

Erickson, B. M., and Sinkjaer Simon, J. (1996). Scandinavian families: plain and simple. In *Ethnicity and Family Therapy*, ed. M. McGoldrick, J. Giordano, and J. K. Pearce, 2nd ed., pp. 595–610. New York: Guilford.

Erkel, R. T. (1994). The mighty wedge of class. *The Family Therapy Networker* 18:45–47.

Falicov, C. J. (1995). Cross-cultural marriages. In *Clinical Handbook of Couple Therapy*, ed. N. S. Jacobson and A. S. Gurman, pp. 231–246. New York: Guilford.

——— (1996). Mexican families. In *Ethnicity and Family Therapy*, ed. M. McGoldrick, J. Giordano, and J. K. Pearce, 2nd ed., pp. 169–182. New York: Guilford.

Fawcett, J., Clark, D. C., and Busch, K. A. (1993). Assessing and treating the patient at risk for suicide. *Psychiatric Annals* 23:244–255.

Fishman, H. C. (1993). *Intensive Structural Therapy: Treating Families in their Social Context*. New York: Basic Books.

Folwarski, J., and Marganoff, P. P. (1996). Polish families. In *Ethnicity and Family Therapy*, ed. M. McGoldrick, J. Giordano, and J. K. Pearce, 2nd ed., pp. 658–672. New York: Guilford.

Ford, D. H., and Lerner, R. M. (1992). *Developmental Systems Theory: An Integrative Approach*. Newbury Park, CA: Sage.

Freud, A. (1966). *The Writings of Anna Freud, Volume II, 1936: The Ego and the Mechanisms of Defense*, rev. ed. New York: International Universities Press.

Frye, M. (1995). Oppression. In *Race, Class, and Gender in the United States: An Integrated Study,* ed. P. S. Rothenberg, 3rd ed., pp. 81–84. New York: St. Martin's.

Garcia Coll, C., Cook-Nobles, R., and Surrey, J. L. (1993). Building connection through diversity. *Work in Progress*, no. 64. Wellesley, MA: The Stone Center.

Garcia-Preto, N. (1996a). Latino families: an overview. In *Ethnicity and Family Therapy*, ed. M. McGoldrick, J. Giordano, and J. K. Pearce, 2nd ed., pp. 141–154. New York: Guilford.

——— (1996b). Puerto Rican families. In *Ethnicity and Family Therapy*, ed. M. McGoldrick, J. Giordano, and J. K. Pearce, 2nd ed., pp. 183–199. New York: Guilford.

Gerson, R., Hoffman, S., Sauls, M., and Ulrici, D. (1993). Family-of-origin frames in couples therapy. *Journal of Marital and Family Therapy* 19:341–354.

Giordano, J., and McGoldrick, M. (1996a). European families: an overview. In *Ethnicity and Family Therapy*, ed. M. McGoldrick, J. Giordano, and J. K. Pearce, 2nd ed., pp. 427–441. New York: Guilford.

——— (1996b). Italian families. In *Ethnicity and Family Therapy*, ed. M. McGoldrick, J. Giordano, and J. K. Pearce, 2nd ed., pp. 567–582. New York: Guilford.

Glass, S. P., and Wright, T. L. (1992). Justifications for extramarital relationships: the association between attitudes, behaviors, and gender. *The Journal of Sex Research* 29:361–387.

Goldstein, E. (1997). Countertransference reactions to borderline couples. In *Countertransference in Couples Therapy*, ed. M. F. Solomon and J. P. Siegel, pp. 72–86. New York: Norton.

Goldstein, W. N. (1995). The borderline patient: update on the diagnosis, theory, and treatment from a psychodynamic perspective. *American Journal of Psychotherapy* 49:317–337.

Gotlib, I. H., and Beach, S. R. H. (1995). A marital/family discord model of depression: implications for therapeutic intervention. In *Clinical Handbook of Couple Therapy*, ed. N. S. Jacobson and A. S. Gurman, pp. 411–436. New York: Guilford.

Gray-Little, B., Baucom, D. H., and Hamby, S. L. (1996). Marital power, marital adjustment, and therapy outcome. *Journal of Family Psychology* 10:292–303.

Greene, B. (1994). Diversity and difference: the issue of race in feminist therapy. In *Women in Context: Toward a Feminist Reconstruction of Psychotherapy*, ed. M. P. Mirkin, pp. 333–351. New York: Guilford.

Gregory, M. A., and Leslie, L. A. (1996). Different lenses: variations in clients' perception of family therapy by race and gender. *Journal of Marital and Family Therapy* 22:239–251.

Gurman, A. S., and Jacobson, N. S. (1995). Therapy with couples: a coming of age. In *Clinical Handbook of Couple Therapy*, ed. N. S. Jacobson and A. S. Gurman, pp. 1–6. New York: Guilford.

Gurman, A. S., Kniskern, D., and Pinsoff, W. (1986). Research on the process and outcome of marital and family therapy. In *Handbook of Psychotherapy and Behavior Change*, ed. S. L. Garfield and A. E. Bergin, 3rd ed., pp. 565–624. New York: Wiley.

Halgin, R. P., and Lovejoy, D. W. (1991). An integrative approach to treating the partner of a depressed person. *Psychotherapy* 28:251–258.

Hart, B. (1988). Beyond the "duty to warn": a therapist's "duty to protect" battered women and children. In *Feminist Perspective on Wife Abuse*, ed. K. Yllo and M. Bograd, pp. 234–238. Newbury Park, CA: Sage.

Heath, A. W., and Stanton, M. D. (1991). Family therapy. In *Clinical Textbook of Addictive Disorders*, ed. R. J. Frances and S. I. Miller, pp. 406–430. New York: Guilford.

Heiman, J. R., Epps, P. H., and Ellis, B. (1995). Treating sexual desire disorders in couples. In *Clinical Handbook of Couple Therapy*, ed. N. S. Jacobson and A. S. Gurman, pp. 471–495. New York: Guilford.

Hill, E. W. (1996). Stability and change: understanding anxiety in marital therapy from an attachment theory perspective. *Journal of Couples Therapy* 6:65–81.

Hines, P. M., and Boyd-Franklin, N. (1996). African American families. In *Ethnicity and Family Therapy*, ed. M. McGoldrick, J. Giordano, and J. K. Pearce, 2nd ed., pp. 66–84. New York: Guilford.

Ho, M. K. (1990). *Intermarried Couples in Therapy*. Springfield, IL: Charles C Thomas.

Hof, L. (1995). The elusive elixir: fostering hope in marital-relationship therapy. In *Integrative Solutions: Treating Common Problems in Couples Therapy*, ed. G. R. Weeks and L. Hof, pp. 1–20. New York: Brunner/Mazel.

Holtzworth-Munroe, A., Beak Beatty, S. B., and Anglin, K. (1995). The assessment and treatment of marital violence: an introduction for the marital therapist. In *Clinical Handbook of Couple Therapy*, ed. N. S. Jacobson and A. S. Gurman, pp. 317–339. New York: Guilford.

Hurlbert, D. F. and Apt, C. (1994). Female sexual desire, response, and behavior. *Behavior Modification* 18:488–504.

Hurtado, A. (1995). Variations, combinations, and evolutions: Latino families in the United States. In *Understanding Latino Families: Scholarship, Policy, Practice*, ed. R. E. Zambrana, pp. 40–61. Thousand Oaks, CA: Sage.

Ibrahim, F. A., and Schroeder, D. G. (1990). Cross-cultural couples counseling: a developmental, psychoeducational approach. *Journal of Comparative Family Studies* 21:193–205.

Jackson, H. L. (1995). Treatment considerations when the therapist is the minority in the patient–therapist dyad. In *Racism in the Lives of Women: Testimony, Theory, and Guides to Antiracist Practice*, ed. J. Adleman and G. M. Enguidanos, pp. 229–237. New York: Harrington Park.

Jacobson, N. S. (1992). Behavioral couple therapy: a new beginning. *Behavior Therapy* 23:493–506.

Jacobson, N. S., and Holtzworth-Munroe, A. (1986). Marital therapy: a social learning-cognitive perspective. In *Clinical Handbook of Marital Therapy*, ed. N. S. Jacobson and A. S. Gurman, pp. 29–70. New York: Guilford.

Jacobson, N. S., Schmaling, K. B., Holtzworth-Munroe, A., et al. (1989). Research-structured versus clinically flexible versions of social learning-based marital therapy. *Behavior Research and Therapy* 27:173–180.

Javed, N. J. (1995). Salience of loss and marginality: life themes of "immigrant women of color" in Canada. In *Racism in the Lives of Women: Testimony, Theory, and Guides to Antiracist Practice*, ed. J. Adleman and G. M. Enguidanos, pp. 13–22. New York: Harrington Park.

Johnson, S. M. (1989). Integrating marital and individual therapy for incest survivors: a case study. *Psychotherapy* 26:141–148.

Johnson, S. M., and Greenberg, L. S. (1995). The emotionally focused approach to problems in adult attachment. In *Clinical Handbook of Couple Therapy*, ed. N. S. Jacobson and A. S. Gurman, pp. 121–141. New York: Guilford.

Karpel, M. A. (1994). *Evaluating Couples: A Handbook for Practitioners*. New York: Norton.

Kernberg O. F. (1975). *Borderline Conditions and Pathological Narcissism*. New York: Jason Aronson.

——— (1986). Factors in the psychoanalytic treatment of narcissistic personalities. In *Essential Papers on Narcissism*, ed. A. P. Morrison, pp. 213–244. New York: New York University Press.

Kersten, K. K., and Himle, D. P. (1990). Marital intimacy: a model for clinical assessment and intervention. *Journal of Couples Therapy* 1:103–121.

Kingery-McCabe, L. G., and Campbell, F. A. (1991). Effects of addiction on the addict. In *Treating the Chemically Dependent and Their Families*, ed. D. C. Daley and M. S. Raskin, pp. 57–78. Newbury Park, CA: Sage.

Kissen, M. (1996). Projective identification: a resistance in couples. *American Journal of Psychotherapy* 50:54–65.

Kliman, J. (1994). The interweaving of gender, class and race in family therapy. In *Women in Context: Toward a Feminist Reconstruction of Psychotherapy*, ed. M. P. Mirkin, pp. 25–47. New York: Guilford.

Koch, A., and Ingram, T. (1985). The treatment of borderline personality disorder within a distressed relationship. *Journal of Marital and Family Therapy* 11:373–380.

Koerner, K., Prince, S., and Jacobson, N. S. (1994). Enhancing the treatment and prevention of depression in women: the role of integrative behavioral couple therapy. *Behavior Therapy* 25:373–390.

Koffinke, C. (1991). Family recovery issues and treatment resources. In *Treating the Chemically Dependent and Their Families*, ed. D. C. Daley and M. S. Raskin, pp. 195–216. Newbury Park, CA: Sage.

Kohut, H., and Wolf, E. S. (1986). The disorders of the self and their treatment. In *Essential Papers on Narcissism*, ed. A. P. Morrison, pp. 175–196. New York: New York University Press.

Kovacs, L. (1994). Separateness/togetherness: a paradox in relationships. *Journal of Couples Therapy* 4:83–94.

——— (1997). The power struggle stage: from polarization to empathy. *Journal of Couples Therapy* 7:27–37.

Kroll, J. (1993). *PTSD/Borderlines in Therapy: Finding the Balance*. New York: Norton.

Kupers, T. A. (1997). Dependency and counter-dependency in couples. *Journal of Couples Therapy* 7:39–47.

Kurdek, L. A. (1995). Predicting change in marital satisfaction from husbands' and wives' conflict resolution styles. *Journal of Marriage and the Family* 57:153–164.

L'Abate, L., and Bagarozzi, D. A. (1993). *Sourcebook of Marriage and*

Family Evaluation. New York: Brunner/Mazel.

Lachkar, J. (1992). *The Narcissistic/Borderline Couple: A Psychoanalytic Perspective on Marital Treatment*. New York: Brunner/Mazel.

Laird, J. (1994). Lesbian families: a cultural perspective. In *Women in Context: Toward a Feminist Reconstruction of Psychotherapy*, ed. M. P. Mirkin, pp. 118–148. New York: Guilford.

Langelier, R. (1996). French Canadian families. In *Ethnicity and Family Therapy*, ed. M. McGoldrick, J. Giordano, and J. K. Pearce, 2nd ed., pp. 477–495. New York: Guilford.

Langston, D. (1998). Tired of playing monopoly? In *Race, Gender, and Class: An Anthology*, ed. M. L. Andersen and P. H. Collins, 3rd ed., pp. 126–136. Belmont, CA: Wadsworth.

Lansky, M. R. (1981). Treatment of the narcissistically vulnerable marriage. In *Family Therapy and Major Psychopathology*, ed. M. R. Lansky, pp. 163–182. New York: Grune & Stratton.

Lee, E. (1996). Asian American families: an overview. In *Ethnicity and Family Therapy*, ed. M. McGoldrick, J. Giordano, and J. K. Pearce, 2nd ed., pp. 227–248. New York: Guilford.

Lee, J. A. B. (1994). *The Empowerment Approach to Social Work Practice*. New York: Columbia University Press.

Lehrer, E. L., and Chiswick, C. U. (1993). Religion as a determinant of marital stability. *Demography* 30:385–404.

Lerner, J. V., Baker, N., and Lerner, R. M. (1985). A person-context goodness of fit model of adjustment. In *Advances in Cognitive-Behavioral Research and Therapy*, vol. 4, ed. P. C. Kendall, pp. 111–136. San Diego, CA: Academic Press.

Leslie, D., and MacNeill, L. (1995). Double positive: lesbians and race. In *Racism in the Lives of Women: Testimony, Theory, and Guides to Antiracist Practice*, ed. J. Adleman and G. M. Enguidanos, pp. 161–169. New York: Harrington Park.

Levine, L. (1996). Adult survivors of incest. In *The Impact of Violence on the Family: Treatment Approaches for Therapists and Other Professionals*, ed. D. Busby, pp. 185–212. Boston: Allyn & Bacon.

Lewis, J., Dana, R., and Blevins, G. (1994). *Substance Abuse Counseling: An Individualized Approach*. Pacific Grove, CA: Brooks/Cole.

Links, P. S. (1992). Family environment and family psychopathology in the etiology of borderline personality disorder. In *Bor-*

derline Personality Disorder: Clinical and Empirical Perspectives, ed. J. F. Clarkin, E. Marziali, and H. Munroe-Blum, pp. 45–66. New York: Guilford.

LoPiccolo, J. (1990). Sexual dysfunction. In *International Handbook of Behavior Modification and Therapy*, ed. A. S. Bellack, M. Hersen, and A. Kadzin, 2nd ed., pp. 547–564. New York: Plenum.

Mack, R. N. (1989). Termination of therapy. In *Treating Couples: The Intersystem Model of the Marriage Council of Philadelphia*, ed. G. R. Weeks, pp. 119–141. New York: Brunner/Mazel.

Maltz, D. N., and Borker, R. A. (1982). A cultural approach to male–female miscommunication. In *Language and Social Identity*, ed. J. J. Gumperz, pp. 196–216. Cambridge: Cambridge University Press.

Mantsios, G. (1995). Class in America: myths and realities. In *Race, Class, and Gender in the United States: An Integrated Study*, ed. P. S. Rothenberg, 3rd ed., pp. 131–143. New York: St. Martin's.

Markowitz, L. M (1994). The cross-currents of multiculturalism. *The Family Therapy Networker* 18:18–27.

Marziali, E. (1992). The etiology of borderline personality disorder: developmental factors. In *Borderline Personality Disorder: Clinical and Empirical Perspectives*, ed. J. F. Clarkin, E. Marziali, and H. Munroe-Blum, pp. 27–44. New York: Guilford.

Massella, J. D. (1991). Intervention: breaking the addiction cycle. In *Treating the Chemically Dependent and Their Families*, ed. D. C. Daley and M. S. Raskin, pp. 79–99. Newbury Park, CA: Sage.

Masterson, J. F. (1981). *The Narcissistic and Borderline Disorders: An Integrated Theoretical Perspective*. New York: Brunner/Mazel.

Maxmen, J. S., and Ward, N. G. (1995). *Essential Psychopathology and Its Treatment*, 2nd ed. New York: Norton.

McCormack, C. C. (1989). The borderline/schizoid marriage: the holding environment as an essential treatment construct. *Journal of Marital and Family Therapy* 15:299–309.

McCrady, B. S., and Epstein, E. E. (1995). Marital therapy in the treatment of alcohol problems. In *Clinical Handbook of Couple Therapy*, ed. N. S. Jacobson and A. S. Gurman, pp. 369–393. New York: Guilford.

McGill, D. W., and Pearce, J. K. (1996). American families with English ancestors from the colonial era: Anglo Americans. In *Ethnicity and Family Therapy*, ed. M. McGoldrick, J. Giordano, and J. K. Pearce, 2nd ed., pp. 451–466. New York: Guilford.

McGoldrick, M. (1989). Women through the family life cycle. In *Women in Families: A Framework for Family Therapy*, ed. M. McGoldrick, C. M. Anderson, and F. Walsh, pp. 200–226. New York: Norton.

——— (1996). Irish families. In *Ethnicity and Family Therapy*, ed. M. McGoldrick, J. Giordano, and J. K. Pearce, 2nd ed., pp. 544–566. New York: Guilford.

McGoldrick, M., and Garcia-Preto, N. (1984). Ethnic intermarriage: implications for therapy. *Family Process* 23:347–364.

McGoldrick, M., Garcia-Preto, N., Hines, P. M., and Lee, E. (1989). Ethnicity and women. In *Women in Families: A Framework for Family Therapy*, ed. M. McGoldrick, C. M. Anderson, and F. Walsh, pp. 169–199. New York: Norton.

McGoldrick, M., and Giordano, J. (1996). Overview: ethnicity and family therapy. In *Ethnicity and Family Therapy*, ed. M. McGoldrick, J. Giordano, and J. K. Pearce, 2nd ed., pp. 1–27. New York: Guilford.

McIntosh, P. (1998). White privilege: unpacking the invisible knapsack. In *Re-Visioning Family Therapy: Race, Culture, and Gender in Clinical Practice*, ed. M. McGoldrick, pp. 147–152. New York: Guilford.

McKay, M. M. (1994). The link between domestic violence and child abuse: assessment and treatment considerations. *Child Welfare* 73:29–38.

Metz, M., Rosser, B. R., and Strapko, N. (1994). Differences in conflict-resolution styles among heterosexual, gay, and lesbian couples. *Journal of Sex Research* 31:293–308.

Michelson, L. K., and Marchione, K. (1991). Behavioral, cognitive, and pharmacological treatment of panic disorder with agoraphobia: critique and synthesis. *Journal of Consulting and Clinical Psychology* 59:100–114.

Miklowitz, D. J., and Goldstein, M. J. (1997). *Bipolar Disorder: A Family-Focused Treatment Approach*. New York: Guilford.

Mirkin, M. P. (1998). The impact of multiple contexts on recent immigrant families. In *Re-Visioning Family Therapy: Race, Culture, and Gender in Clinical Practice*, ed. M. McGoldrick, pp. 370–383. New York: Guilford.

Mojas, K. (1994). How love inspires hate: the relationship between childhood perception of rejection and marital conflict. *Journal of Couples Therapy* 4:97–106.

——— (1995). The balloon theory: helping couples expand their capacity for intimacy. *Journal of Couples Therapy* 5:83–89.

Neal, J. H., and Slobodnik, A. J. (1991). Reclaiming men's experience in couples therapy. In *Feminist Approaches for Men in Family Therapy*, ed. M. Bograd, pp. 101–122. New York: Harrington Park.

Nelsen, J. C. (1994). One partner impaired: implications for couple treatment. *Family Therapy* 21:185–196.

——— (1995). Varieties of narcissistically vulnerable couples: dynamics and practice implications. *Clinical Social Work Journal* 23:59–70.

Newman, K. (1998). Working poor, working hard. In *Race, Gender, and Class: An Anthology*, ed. M. L. Andersen and P. H. Collins, 3rd ed., pp. 265–269. Belmont, CA: Wadsworth.

Nichols, M. P. (1994). Therapy with bisexual women: working on the edge of emerging cultural and personal identities. In *Women in Context: Toward a Feminist Reconstruction of Psychotherapy*, ed. M. P. Mirkin, pp. 149–169. New York: Guilford.

Nichols, M. P., and Schwartz, R. C. (1995). *Family Therapy: Concepts and Methods*, 3rd ed. Boston: Allyn & Bacon.

Nichols, W. C. (1988). *Marital Therapy: An Integrative Approach*. New York: Guilford.

Nock, S. L. (1995). A comparison of marriages and cohabiting relationships. *Journal of Family Issues* 16:53–76.

O'Donohue, W., and Crouch, J. L. (1996). Marital therapy and gender-linked factors in communication. *Journal of Marital and Family Therapy* 22:87–101.

Okun, B. F. (1996). *Understanding Diverse Families: What Practitioners Need to Know*. New York: Guilford.

O'Leary, K. D., and Murphy, C. (1992). Clinical issues in the assessment of spouse abuse. In *Assessment of Family Violence: A Clinical and Legal Sourcebook*, ed. R. T. Ammerman and M. Herson, pp. 26–46. New York: Wiley.

O'Leary, K. D., and Turkewitz, H. (1978). Marital therapy from a behavioral perspective. In *Marriage and Marital Therapy: Psychoanalytic, Behavioral and Systems Theory Perspectives*, ed. T. J. Paolino and B. S. McCrady, pp. 240–297. New York: Brunner/Mazel.

Orbuch, T. L., and Custer, L. (1995). The social context of married women's work and its impact on black husbands and white husbands. *Journal of Marriage and the Family* 57:333–345.

Papero, D. V. (1995). Bowen family systems and marriage. In *Clinical Handbook of Couple Therapy*, ed. N. S. Jacobson and A. S. Gurman, pp. 11–30. New York: Guilford.

Papp, P. (1988). Couples. In *The Invisible Web: Gender Patterns in Family Relationships*, ed. M. Walters, B. Carter, P. Papp, and O. Silverstein, pp. 200–249. New York: Guilford.

Parnell, M., and Vanderkloot, J. (1994). Poor women: making a difference. In *Women in Context: Toward a Feminist Reconstruction of Psychotherapy*, ed. M. P. Mirkin, pp. 390–407. New York: Guilford.

Peplau, L. A. (1993). Lesbian and gay relationships. In *Psychological Perspectives on Lesbian and Gay Experiences*, ed. L. D. Garnets and D. C. Kimmel, pp. 395–419. New York: Columbia University Press.

Perry-Jenkins, M., and Folk, K. (1994). Class, couples, and conflict: effects of the division of labor on assessments of marriage in dual-earner families. *Journal of Marriage and the Family* 56:165–180.

Pittman, F. S., III, and Pittman Wagers, T. (1995). Crises of infidelity. In *Clinical Handbook of Couple Therapy*, ed. N. S. Jacobson and A. S. Gurman, pp. 295–316. New York: Guilford.

Powell, D. R. (1995). Including Latino fathers in parent education and support programs: development of a program model. In *Understanding Latino Families: Scholarship, Policy, Practice*, ed. R. E. Zambrana, pp. 85–106. Thousand Oaks, CA: Sage.

Prince, S. E., and Jacobson, N. S. (1995). A review and evaluation of marital and family therapies for affective disorders. *Journal of Marital and Family Therapy* 21:377–401.

Rampage, C. (1995). Gendered aspects of marital therapy. In *Clinical Handbook of Couple Therapy*, ed. N. S. Jacobson and A. S. Gurman, pp. 261–273. New York: Guilford.

Rolland, J. S. (1994). In sickness and in health: the impact of illness on couples' relationships. *Journal of Marital and Family Therapy* 20:327–347.

Root, M. P. P. (1995). Conceptualization and treatment of eating disorders in couples. In *Clinical Handbook of Couple Therapy*, ed. N. S. Jacobson and A. S. Gurman, pp. 437–457. New York: Guilford.

Rose, D. S. (1991). A model for psychodynamic psychotherapy with the rape victim. *Psychotherapy* 28:85–95.

Rosen, E. J., and Weltman, S. F. (1996). Jewish families: an overview. In *Ethnicity and Family Therapy*, ed. M. McGoldrick, J. Giordano, and J. K. Pearce, 2nd ed., pp. 611–630. New York: Guilford.

Rosenbluth, S. C., and Steil, J. M. (1995). Predictors of intimacy for women in heterosexual and homosexual couples. *Journal of Social and Personal Relationships* 12:163–175.

Roth, A., and Fonagy, P. (1996). *What Works for Whom? A Critical Review of Psychotherapy Research*. New York: Guilford.

Rubin, L. B. (1992). *Worlds of Pain: Life in the Working-Class Family*. New York: Basic Books.

——— (1994). *Families on the Fault Line*. New York: HarperCollins.

Sachs, P. R. (1995). Marital adjustment to life changes associated with aging. In *Integrative Solutions: Treating Common Problems in Couples Therapy*, ed. G. R. Weeks and L. Hof, pp. 195–214. New York: Brunner/Mazel.

Satir, V. (1983). *Conjoint Family Therapy*, 3rd ed. Palo Alto, CA: Science and Behavior Books.

Saunders, D. G. (1992). Woman battering. In *Assessment of Family Violence: A Clinical and Legal Sourcebook*, ed. R. T. Ammerman and M. Herson, pp. 208–235. New York: Wiley.

Sayers, S., Baucom, D., and Rankin, L. (1993). Marital distress. In *Handbook of Behavior Therapy in the Psychiatric Setting*, ed. A. S. Bellack and M. Hersen, pp. 575–593. New York: Plenum.

Scharff, D. E., and Scharff, J. S. (1991). *Object Relations Couple Therapy*. Northvale, NJ: Jason Aronson.

Scharff, J. S. (1995). Psychoanalytic marital therapy. In *Clinical Handbook of Couple Therapy*, ed. N. S. Jacobson and A. S. Gurman, pp. 164–193. New York: Guilford.

Schiemann, J., and Smith, W. (1996). The homosexual couple. In *Treating Couples*, ed. H. Kessler, pp. 97–136. San Francisco: Jossey-Bass.

Schwartz, R. D. (1989). When the therapist is gay: personal and clinical reflections. *Journal of Gay and Lesbian Psychotherapy* 1:41–51.

Seider, K. (1995). Couples therapy of patients with disorders of the self. In *Disorders of the Self: New Therapeutic Horizons: The Masterson Approach*, ed. J. F. Masterson and R. Klein, pp. 365–

381. New York: Brunner/Mazel.

Shadish, W. R., Ragsdale, K., and Glaser, R. R. (1995). The efficacy and effectiveness of marital and family therapy: a perspective from meta-analysis. *Journal of Marital and Family Therapy* 21:345–360.

Sheinberg, M., and Penn, P. (1991). Gender dilemmas, gender questions, and the gender mantra. *Journal of Marital and Family Therapy* 17:33–44.

Shoham, V., Rohrbaugh, M., and Patterson, J. (1995). Problem- and solution-focused couple therapies: the MRI and Milwaukee models. In *Clinical Handbook of Couple Therapy*, ed. N. S. Jacobson and A. S. Gurman, pp. 142–163. New York: Guilford.

Siegel, J. (1991). Analysis of projective identification: an object relations approach to marital treatment. *Clinical Social Work Journal* 19:71–81.

——— (1992). *Repairing Intimacy: An Object Relations Approach to Couples Therapy*. Northvale, NJ: Jason Aronson.

——— (1995). Countertransference as projective identification. *Journal of Couples Therapy* 5:61–69.

——— (1997). Applying countertransference theory to couples treatment. In *Countertransference in Couples Therapy*, ed. M. F. Solomon and J. P. Siegel, pp. 3–22. New York: Norton.

Simon, C. (1997). Psychoeducation: a contemporary approach. In *Mental Health Policy and Practice Today*, ed. T. R. Watkins and J. W. Callicutt, pp. 129–145. Thousand Oaks, CA: Sage.

Sirkin, M. I. (1994). Resisting cultural meltdown. *The Family Therapy Networker* 18:48–52.

Slater, S. (1994). Approaching and avoiding the work of the middle years: affairs in committed lesbian relationships. *Women and Therapy* 15:19–34.

Slater, S., and Mencher, J. (1991). The lesbian family life cycle: a contextual approach. *American Journal of Orthopsychiatry* 61:372–381.

Slipp, S. (1995). Object relations marital therapy of personality disorders. In *Clinical Handbook of Couple Therapy*, ed. N. S. Jacobson and A. S. Gurman, pp. 458–470. New York: Guilford.

Snyder, D. K., Wills, R. M., and Grady-Fletcher, A. (1991). Long-term effectiveness of behavioral versus insight-oriented marital therapy: a 4-year follow-up study. *Journal of Consulting and Clinical Psychology* 59:138–141.

Solomon, M. F. (1997). Countertransference and empathy in couples therapy. In *Countertransference in Couples Therapy*, ed. M. F. Solomon and J. P. Siegel, pp. 23–37. New York: Norton.

Steinfeld, G. J. (1997). The cycle of violence: an integrative clinical approach. *Journal of Couples Therapy* 7:49–81.

Steinglass, P. (1978). The conceptualization of marriage from a systems perspective. In *Marriage and Marital Therapy: Psychoanalytic, Behavioral and Systems Theory Perspectives*, ed. T. J. Paolino and B. S. McCrady, pp. 298–365. New York: Brunner/Mazel.

Stiver, I. P. (1991). The meanings of "dependency" in female–male relationships. In *Women's Growth in Connection: Writings from the Stone Center*, ed. J. V. Jordan, A. G. Kaplan, J. B. Miller, et al. pp. 143–161. New York: Guilford.

Sue, S., Zane, N., and Young, K. (1995). Research on psychotherapy with culturally diverse populations. In *Handbook of Psychotherapy and Behavior Change*, ed. S. L. Garfield and A. D. Bergin, 4th ed., pp. 783–817. New York: Wiley.

Sutton, C. T., and Broken Nose, M. A. (1996). American Indian families: an overview. In *Ethnicity and Family Therapy*, ed. M. McGoldrick, J. Giordano, and J. K. Pearce, 2nd ed., pp. 31–44. New York: Guilford.

Talmadge, L. D., and Wallace, S. C. (1991). Reclaiming sexuality in female incest survivors. *Journal of Sex and Marital Therapy* 17:163–182.

Tannen, D. (1990). *You Just Don't Understand: Women and Men in Conversation*. New York: William Morrow.

Tessler, N. S. (1995). Deconstructing the "covered bridge"—couples therapy with sexual abuse survivors and their partners. *Journal of Couples Therapy* 5:29–45.

Timmer, S. G., and Veroff, J. (1996). Family ties and marital happiness: the different marital experiences of black and white newly wed couples. *Journal of Social and Personal Relationships* 13:335–359.

Tolman, R. M. (1992). Psychological abuse of women. In *Assessment of Family Violence: A Clinical and Legal Sourcebook*, ed. R. T. Ammerman and M. Herson, pp. 291–310. New York: Wiley.

Troise, F. P. (1993). An overview of the historical and empirical antecedents in the development of the co-dependency concept. *Journal of Couples Therapy* 4:89–104.

Tsemberis, S. J., and Orfanos, S. D. (1996). Greek families. In *Ethnicity and Family Therapy*, ed. M. McGoldrick, J. Giordano, and J. K. Pearce, 2nd ed., pp. 517–529. New York: Guilford.

Turner, R. J. (1991). Affirming consciousness: the Africentric perspective. In *Child Welfare: An Africentric Perspective*, ed. J. C. Everett, S. S. Chipungee, and B. R. Leashore, pp. 36–57. New Brunswick, NJ: Macmillan.

Unger, R., and Crawford, M. (1996). *Women and Gender: A Feminist Psychology*, 2nd ed. Philadelphia: Temple University Press.

U.S. Bureau of the Census (1998). http:\\www.census.gov\

Vega, W. A. (1995). The study of Latino families. In *Understanding Latino Families: Scholarship, Policy, Practice,* ed. R. E. Zambrana, pp. 3–17. Thousand Oaks, CA: Sage.

Veroff, J., Douvan, E., and Hatchett, S. J. (1995). *Marital Instability: A Social and Behavioral Study of the Early Years*. Westport, CT: Praeger.

Veroff, J., Sutherland, L., Chadiha, L. A., and Ortega, R. M. (1993). Predicting marital quality with narrative assessments of marital experience. *Journal of Marriage and the Family* 55:326–337.

Visher, E. B., and Visher, J. S. (1996). *Therapy with Stepfamilies*. New York: Brunner/Mazel.

von Bertalanffy, L. (1968). *General System Theory: Foundations, Development, Application*. New York: George Braziller.

Wakefield, P. J., Williams, R. E., Yost, E. B., and Patterson, K. M. (1996). *Couple Therapy for Alcoholism: A Cognitive-Behavioral Treatment Manual*. New York: Guilford.

Waller, M. A., and Spiegler, M. D. (1997). A cross-cultural perspective on couple differences. *Journal of Couples Therapy* 7:83–98.

Wallerstein, J. S. (1994). The early psychological tasks of marriage: part I. *American Journal of Orthopsychiatry* 64:640–650.

——— (1996). The psychological tasks of marriage: part II. *American Journal of Orthopsychiatry* 66:217–227.

——— (1997). Transference and countertransference in clinical interventions with divorcing families. In *Countertransference in Couples Therapy*, ed. M. F. Solomon and J. P. Siegel, pp. 113–124. New York: Norton.

Walsh, F. (1989). Reconsidering gender in the marital quid pro quo. In *Women in Families: A Framework for Family Therapy*, ed. M. McGoldrick, C. Anderson, and F. Walsh, pp. 267–285. New York: Norton.

Walsh, F., Jacob, L., and Simons, V. (1995). Facilitating healthy divorce processes: therapy and mediation approaches. In *Clinical Handbook of Couple Therapy*, ed. N. S. Jacobson and A. S. Gurman, pp. 340–365. New York: Guilford.

Wasserman, E. B. (1995). Personal reflections of an Anglo therapist in Indian country. In *Racism in the Lives of Women: Testimony, Theory, and Guides to Antiracist Practice*, ed. J. Adleman and G. M. Enguidanos, pp. 23–32. New York: Harrington Park.

Watzlawick, P., Beavin, J., and Jackson, D. D. (1967). *Pragmatics of Human Communication: A Study of Interactional Patterns, Pathologies, and Paradoxes*. New York: Norton.

Watzlawick, P., Weakland, J. H., and Fisch, R. (1974). *Change: Principles of Problem Formation and Problem Resolution*. New York: Norton.

Weeks, G. R. (1995a). Commitment and intimacy. In *Integrative Solutions: Treating Common Problems in Couples Therapy*, ed. G. R. Weeks and L. Hof, pp. 55–76. New York: Brunner/Mazel.

——— (1995b). Inhibited sexual desire. In *Integrative Solutions: Treating Common Problems in Couples Therapy*, ed. G. R. Weeks and L. Hof, pp. 215–252. New York: Brunner/Mazel.

Weeks, G. R., and Hof, L. (1995). Anger and conflict: theory and practice. In *Integrative Solutions: Treating Common Problems in Couples Therapy*, ed. G. R. Weeks and L. Hof, pp. 55–76. New York: Brunner/Mazel.

Weeks, G. R., and Treat, S. (1992). *Couples in Treatment: Techniques and Approaches for Effective Practice*. New York: Brunner/Mazel.

Weiss, R. L., and Heyman, R. E. (1990). Marital distress. In *International Handbook of Behavior Modification and Therapy*, ed. A. S. Bellack, M. Hersen, and A. Kadzin, 2nd ed., pp. 475–501. New York: Plenum.

Westfall, A. (1995). Working through the extramarital trauma: an exploration of common themes. In *Integrative Solutions: Treating Common Problems in Couples Therapy*, ed. G. R. Weeks and L. Hof, pp. 148–194. New York: Brunner/Mazel.

White, R. W. (1963). *Ego and Reality in Psychoanalytic Theory: A Proposal Regarding Independent Ego Energies*. New York: International Universities Press.

Winawer, H., and Wetzel, N. A. (1996). German families. In *Ethnicity and Family Therapy*, ed. M. McGoldrick, J. Giordano, and J. K.

Pearce, 2nd ed., pp. 496–516. New York: Guilford.

Yank, G. R., Bentley, K. J., and Hargrove, D. S. (1993). The vulnerability-stress model of schizophrenia: advances in psychosocial treatment. *American Journal of Orthopsychiatry* 63:55–69.

Zavala-Martinez, I. (1988). *En La Lucha*: the economic and socioemotional struggles of Puerto Rican women. In *The Politics of Race and Gender in Therapy*, ed. L. Fulani, pp. 3–24. New York: Haworth.

Zimmerman, J. L., and Dickerson, V. C. (1993). Separating couples from restraining patterns and the relationship discourse that supports them. *Journal of Marital and Family Therapy* 19:403–413.

Zuniga, M. E. (1988). Assessment issues with Chicanas: practice implications. *Psychotherapy* 25:288–293.

Index